INEFFABILITY

D1205909

SUNY Series, Toward a Comparative Philosophy of Religions
Frank E. Reynolds and David Tracy, editors

INEFFABILITY

The Failure of Words in Philosophy and Religion

Ben-Ami Scharfstein

State University of New York Press

Published by
State University of New York Press, Albany

For information, address State University of New York Press,
State University Plaza, Albany, N.Y. 12246

Production by Marilyn P. Semerad
Marketing by Theresa A. Swierzowski

Library of Congress Cataloging-in-Publication Data

Scharfstein, Ben-Ami, 1919–
    Ineffability: the failure of words in philosophy and religion/
Ben-Ami Scharfstein.
        p.   cm.—(SUNY series, toward a comparative philosophy of
religions)
    Includes bibliographical references and index.
    ISBN 0-7914-1347-0. — ISBN 0-7914-1348-9 (pbk.)
    1. Ineffable, The.   2. Language and languages—Philosophy.
I. Title.   II. Series.
B105.I533S33   1993
121' .68—dc20   92-7544
                                                                         CIP

10 9 8 7 6 5 4 3 2 1

To Ghela again and always

Contents

Foreword

Frank E. Reynolds

Notions of the all-encompassing power of language and word have been ubiquitous in the history and philosophy of religions. So too, has been a recognition of the inability of language and word to give full expression to the realities that constitute and engage human beings and the world in which they live. These two religiously crucial intellectual options have been formulated in various times and places and in various genres associated with myth, philosophy, and poetry; they have, in various situations, been the focal point of highly sophisticated disagreements and debates; and attempts to reconcile them, both in theory and in relation to practice, have been legion. But the issues that these options raise (either separately or in juxtaposition) remain at the very heart of many contemporary reflections and disputes not only in religion, philosophy, and aesthetics, but in the social and natural sciences as well.

In the present volume, Ben-Ami Scharfstein tackles these perennial issues of language, ineffability, and their relationship in his own very distinctive and illuminating way. Adopting a boldly comparative strategy that combines empirical description and imaginative interpretation, Scharfstein presents "classic examples" of both positions. His examples range over a wide variety of cultures, including especially those of India, China, and the West. What is more, Scharfstein utilizes his carefully honed descriptions and analyses to prepare the way for the presentation of his own insights and conclusions.

Through his empirical descriptions and analyses Scharfstein skillfully constructs a very compelling argument for the pervasive power and necessity of language on the one hand, and for the coexisting importance of various kinds of ineffability on the other. In so doing he provides new grist for the mill of constructively oriented philosophers concerned to delimit, for our own contemporary purposes, the possibilities and limits of language. At the same time, he provides historians and anthropologists with the kind of sharpened sensitivities and conceptual tools that will enable them to refine their own interpretations of historically diverse approaches to the efficacy and limitations of language (and word). What is more, these same sensitivities and conceptual tools will enable historians and anthropologists to more accurately identify and interpret the very different kinds of ineffability that are valorized in particular cultural contexts and in specific cultural artifacts.

Many of the prospective readers of this book will be acquainted with the four volumes that have previously appeared in the *Toward a Comparative Philosophy of Religions Series* (two volumes of collected essays that I have edited with David Tracy under the titles *Myth and Philosophy* [1990] and *Discourse and Practice* [1992], Lee Yearley's *Mencius and Aquinas: Theories of Virtue and Conceptions of Courage* [1991] and Francis X. Clooney's *Theology After Vedanta* [1992]). With those readers especially in mind, it should be noted that the publication of Scharfstein's *Ineffability* represents a new departure in at least two significant respects.

Unlike the authors whose work is included in the earlier volumes, Scharfstein has not been involved in the succession of conferences and discussions devoted to the comparative philosophy of religions that have taken place over the past six years at the University of Chicago Divinity School. Instead, he has been involved in a remarkably similar enterprise that has been developing simultaneously—without any initial connections or mutual knowledge—in the Department of Philosophy at the University of Tel Aviv. When we in Chicago came across the first in the series of volumes being generated at the University of Tel Aviv and published in a *Philosophy and Religion Series* edited by Shlomo Biderman and Scharfstein (*Rationality in Question: On Eastern and Western Views of Rationality* [Leiden: E. J. Brill, 1989]), we were delighted by the obvious congruence with our own endeavor.* Thus we were very excited to learn that Professor Scharfstein had a book-length manuscript in process; and we are extremely pleased that he has allowed us to publish it in our *Toward a Comparative Philosophy of Religions Series*. Clearly, this first

---

* The next two books in *Philosophy and Religion Series* are also collections of essays edited by Biderman and Scharfstein published by Brill. The second volume is entitled *Interpretation in Religion*. The third volume will be *Myths and Fictions: Their Place in Philosophy and Religion, East and West*.

break beyond the circle of scholars who initiated the Chicago project has brought a welcome infusion of new insights and ideas.

The second and more specific respect in which Scharfstein's book represents a new departure can be located in his use of psychological research and insights. In the earlier volumes that have been included in the series (particularly in *Myth and Philosophy* and *Discourse and Practice*), there has been a strong emphasis on the necessity of taking seriously into account data, methods, and insights drawn from more empirically oriented disciplines in the humanities and the social sciences. The focus, however, has up to this point been almost exclusively on the assimilation of the kinds of empirical work being done in the history of religions and in anthropology. Thus Scharfstein's adroit and convincing use of research and insights drawn from the field of empirical psychology makes a major theoretical and practical contribution. It adds still another very important dimension to the contours of the new kind of comparative philosophy of religions that we are gradually beginning to discern.

Plans for the next publications in the *Toward a Comparative Philosophy of Religions Series* are already well advanced. The first draft of a manuscript by José Cabezón on the phenomenon of "scholasticism" with special reference to Buddhism in Tibet is already in hand. In addition, drafts of papers have already been written for a third volume of collected essays that will deal with the topic of *Religion and Practical Reason*.

FEBRUARY 15, 1992

Acknowledgments

I have a number of expert friends to thank: Yoav Ariel for going over my pages on Chinese thought, mainly on Lao Tzu and Chuang Tzu, with whom he has an almost personal relationship; Frits Staal for reading and suggesting changes in my account of Indian thought, especially of Bhartrihari, whom he knows as few others do and, luckily, appreciates; Eli Franco for carefully checking translations and paraphrases of Bhartrihari and Nagarjuna against the Sanskrit originals; Hilary Putnam, for a careful scrutiny of the pages on Cantor and Gödel; Shlomo Biderman for reading it all—psychology, religion, and philosophy—and for convincing me that my doubts were exaggerated; and Dan Daor for reading it all and for confirming the doubts that needed confirmation.

"It is what I contain of the unknown that makes me myself . . . Gaps are my starting point." Paul Valéry, *Monsieur Teste*

Introduction

We are the animals that use words and that complain rather often that they fail us. Thinking of the effect we should prefer but fail to make, we say, "I can't put it into words." We seem to imply that if we were able to use words well enough or if words were a more faithful medium, we could transmit our experience exactly and be appreciated for what we know ourselves to be. It seems that we all share in the dream, however latent, of perfect communication and communion, and we are unhappy whenever our attention is drawn to the dream's failure. The poets, who make such great imaginative and linguistic demands on themselves, naturally share the same dream and use their poetically heightened words to make the same complaints. And the theologians and philosophers voice their complaints—which they transmute into a convention of praise—at the ineffability of whatever ultimate they show to be beyond expression in words.

My view of ineffability takes into account all such complaints because it is my strong conviction, which I hope the reader will come to share, that the various forms of ineffability are relevant to one another. For just as there is something of our prosaic, everyday difficulties with words in the ineffable reality of philosophers and theologians, there is something unformulated and perhaps unformulable and finally mysterious in the prosaic, everyday successes and failures of words; and the musicality of music itself is echoed in the less concentrated but inescapable musicality of our speech and—I believe—of our philosophical and theological doctrines. The reason for this mutual encroachment of the known and unknown and the prosaic and poetic is the mutual inclusiveness and entanglement of worlds: each of us alone and in company is an approximately unified world in itself; and all these approximately unified worlds constitute a single, encompassing, unimaginably various world of worlds; and in all of these worlds, as in the encompassing maybe limitless world of all worlds, every distinguishable quality is related to every other in somewhat the same way as our bodily activity is related to our emotionality, to our social needs, to our logic, and to the rhythms and intonations, both individually and generically human, in which we speak and remain silent. We are all divided, subdivided, joined, ruled, and self-ruled in complex, subtly related and unrelated ways; and so it is no wonder that our problems with words are not simple to categorize or easy to grasp.

Out of the desire to understand philosophy and religion by encompassing the many forms of ineffability, I take a broad view and use the term to describe every serious failure to put into words what we should like to say or write if only we could. I show that in order to explore this failure, we must think less of ineffability in the singular and more of ineffabilities of every kind. I also show that, to be worth the name, the exploration must draw on the resources of the different fields of psychology, for which reason I begin with a psychological prelude. This prelude should be a convenient reminder because, to the best of my knowledge, the evidence from these fields has not so far been gathered with an explicit emphasis on the difficulties we undergo in putting things into words—difficulties we meet in the prosaic run of life and, more strongly, in moments of great stress. Since I argue that this evidence is relevant to the larger issues, I summarize it in what I take to be enough detail for its nature to be understood and its relevance made clear.

Like so many others, I am drawn to the borderlands where knowledge fades into ignorance and into real and imagined mysteries. I am drawn, too, to the kinds of thought of which I have had no living experience. The result is that when I reach religion and philosophy, the scope of the discussion grows wide enough to include, at least in principle, the whole of human culture. I begin with the extraordinary creative powers that have been attributed to language everywhere and go on to the idea, even the ideal, of ineffability as it has appeared in the thought of the great philosophical cultures, those of India, of China and Japan and the other countries in which Buddhism flourished, and of the West, with which I associate most Islamic thought that is explicitly philosophical.

The religious or philosophical examples I have chosen to discuss at length are important both for their cultural influence and for the power of thought they display. I give relatively long accounts of thinkers central to my exposition but less widely known than the others. As common sense dictates, I have not made what in this context would have been the fatal attempt to be complete, historically or otherwise; and so my examples, although they demonstrate a wide range of possibilities, might easily have been supplemented or replaced by others.

The final chapters draw on all the subjects that have been taken up previously, and they make the attempt to grasp what appear to me to be the deeper or more general reasons for the attitudes taken by the thinkers I discuss. I stress the words *what appear to me* because I have been objective enough in presenting the material to allow readers to judge for themselves, and because I am not under the illusion that my own judgment is in any way definitive. But although I have tried to give the evidence fairly and have deferred the explanation of my own view, in the end I confront the issues directly and solve them by my own lights. Or I argue that the issues are insoluble either philosophically or religiously because they are reflections of the difficulties that human beings must by nature face and can never really think, meditate, or act away. But I never consciously distort my descriptions to favor my own position and always leave the door open for judgments that differ from those I have made.

I count on the reader's desire to go on an intellectual adventure. My own adventure has come mostly in putting things together, in comparing views that have hardly ever been compared before, and in drawing conclusions from a perspective that is as wide as I could reasonably make it. To see how far I could go in understanding, I have made psychological interpretations of philosophical and religious views, with the result that psychologists are more likely to agree when I do so than are theologians and philosophers. My excuse is that my interest in the creations of the human spirit has to make its peace with my philosophical naturalism; but I do not seriously suppose that any intellectual or empirical discipline or attitude can rule over the others or be sufficient to explain things to the end. As I will later repeat, the assigning of a nonphilosophical or nontheological motive or reason does not imply that psychology or sociology is the superior discipline, but only that under particular intellectual circumstances the more empirical kind of explanation may prove to be more helpful or will at least add a more prosaic, matter-of-fact voice to the chorus of abstractions we will encounter here.

The information I have used comes from good sources, and I have been careful to consult the interpretations made by respected contemporary scholars. I have also asked specialists to read certain critical sections of the text. But finally, of course, this book is something that I've dreamed up and for which I alone am responsible. In writing it I have learned a great deal. I hope that my readers will share my pleasure in wrestling with the problems, tractable or not, in traveling to intellectually and perhaps emotionally strange places, and, all the while, in learning how the world can be experienced by others both quite like and quite unlike ourselves.

Chapter 1

Psychological Prelude

I am much less sure of how to open a book than how to open a door or even a conversation. Verbal openings, especially written ones, are likely to be difficult. The words flow slowly and irregularly in the beginning, and the ideas, too, are reticent, as if they are lodged in a place different from that of the words to which they have to become attached before they can be spoken or written. And when the words are still shy or we are too shy to expose them, we make excuses for their absence. Such a difficulty is not, of course, confined to openings, although any great change, especially any great happiness or sadness, opens into a different quality of life and finds us at a loss for words. Our words seem adequate only for the most ordinary experiences at their most usual intensities.

It is true that I can imagine people who will not complain (or boast) of their lack of words. I can imagine a great orator intoxicated with his eloquence or a poet or prophet in the full flight of inspiration. Yet those who show the most artful mastery of words, the poets, often complain, like old Plato, that words are inadequate to express exactly what they would like to say. Nature creates, writes Emily Dickinson, while we name; we pass, while she abides. "We conjugate Her Skill / While She creates and federates / Without a syllable."[1] And we know of the mystics, theologians, and philosophers, some of whose ghosts will emerge on these pages, who are certain that reality, whether named or denied a name, is beyond the reach of words.

How can this certainty be evaluated? In answering, I think it best to begin with a psychological prelude that explains what is known of our nonphilosophical difficulties with words, and only then to take up the difficulties in which the philosophers and theologians have been most interested. So this first chapter is on the shyness of words, their tendency to vanish when we most need them. If I were to use a few catchwords to describe the content of the chapter, I should say that it deals with the extent to which the words we use are unshared, insufficient, reluctant, suppressed, forgotten, or (by their very categories) inappropriate. In spite of the inclusiveness of these five catchwords, which give a general indication of the chapter's progress, I will not use them as its explicit headings because the matters we are dealing with are too fluid to be separated so neatly from one another.

A Summary View of the Psychological Characteristics of Ineffability

The words are coming easily now, but I think I should check their natural flow for a moment. The reason is that I intend to turn to a wide variety of sources and to give many, sometimes extensive examples, so I begin with a brief summary of the main characteristics, as I see them, of psychological ineffability. Naturally, the emphasis will be on what is most relevant for the comparative philosophy that follows; but here, too, I hope to resist a narrow view.

1. The understanding of language depends upon shared experience. The most fundamental experience we share is that of our immediate selves, by which I mean our bodies, modes of perception, emotions, and social needs. When we try to explain unshared experience, we have no choice but to fall back on what has already in fact been shared, and when we fall back on it, the process of explanation is likely to be word-consuming, time-consuming, and not very successful.

2. The meaning of spoken words is enhanced by facial expressions, gestures, shifts of the body, changes in gaze, and the personal and emotional qualities of the words' sounds—their vocal contour. The cooperation and conflict between these means of expression lends the words much of their often ambivalent subtlety.

3. Our attempts to explain ourselves in words prove to be endless. This shows that it is difficult and, beyond a certain point, impossible to say quite exactly what we feel, want, believe, and construe intellectually. Experience and research both teach us that words are not necessarily exact equivalents to underlying thought processes. Likewise, our individual thoughts do not necessarily correspond with what we think in a more complete, dense way, and conscious thoughts are certainly not the

whole of what we in some sense think. A certain degree of ineffability is therefore inescapable.

4. The silences with which speech alternates and the rhythm and kind of this alternation also convey meanings. The alternation has its personal and social styles, which, we know, make communication fuller.

5. There are also personal and social styles of self-disclosure. What is impossible to disclose to one partner or in one situation may be possible to another partner or in another situation. In this sense, too, ineffability is relative.

6. Especially sensitive listening, of the sort recommended to psychoanalysts and clinical psychologists, is likely to discover messages concealed behind the ordinary meanings of speech and to make what may have been ineffable before, possible to put into words.

7. Both self-revelation and self-concealment are at their extreme in schizophrenics, whose speech is at times an extraordinarily interesting union of the effable and ineffable. Schizophrenic speech can suggest (or even be) poetry, prophecy, revelation, or mysticism.

8. The feeling and the fact of ineffability both depend on our inability to recover our memories fully, as well as on our ability to remember unconsciously what we have consciously forgotten.

9. Our dependence on concealed memories is dramatically accentuated in cases of amnesia and aphasia, when a person's previous knowledge continues to have an effect even though it has become concealed from consciousness.

10. The ability to remember depends upon a variety of types or subtypes of memory and on the relations between them. The complex nature of memory must affect what we can and cannot put into words, whether in general or under particular circumstances.

11. The condition known as synesthesia shows to what an extent our ability to use words depends upon the relationship between perception, shared experience, and memory. Fully synesthetic experience is hard to convey in words because words can give a relatively accurate reflection of only the usual, shared kind of perception.

12. Like synesthesthia, music has an aura of ineffability, the result of its emotional, structural, and neurological differences from speech. The aura of ineffability surrounds speech itself in that its utterance is by musical means—the intrinsic music of a particular stretch of speech cannot be fully expressed in other words.

13. We get a clue to the nature of ineffability by comparing the experience of persons who see and hear normally with that of the deaf and the blind. The differences in their experience are, of course, reflected in the use and, even more, in the understanding of words. Under favorable circumstances, the lack of one kind of perception can be largely compensated for by a sensitive use of the remaining kinds. With their help, the range of the ineffable can be restricted to a surprising extent.

14. Yet the sensory difference between the blind or deaf and the others is never compensated for completely. As the result of the lack of common experience, a complex gap is created; and because what is unshared is impossible to put into words, it exerts an effect that can never quite be overcome.

If the ideas I have just summarized are plausible, ineffability has different nuances and, considered carefully, is of different kinds. Sometimes, as we will see, it is relative and sometimes perhaps absolute. Understood most generally, it is the receding limit of every attempt to express ourselves, the horizon of language, which always appears when we want to extend our field of expression, but which, horizonlike, recedes just as quickly as we move toward it.

The Understanding of Language Depends upon Shared Experience

Here, still at the beginning of our investigation, the difficulty I feel most keenly is that I do not know just what I share with the reader, yourself, in background, ideas, and interests. Even apart from our strangeness to one another, it is probably not clear in what kind of experience our mutual understanding begins. As I say this, I ask myself what allows complete strangers using the same language to assume that they understand it in much the same way. The answer is, briefly, that we are not abstract linguistic creatures—bodiless angels who communicate by means of an identical, purely logical syntax. On the contrary, our use of language presupposes and reflects the physical structure of our bodies, our emotions and appetites, the ways in which we perceive, the kinds of spaces in which we live, and the cultures we assimilate as we become human in their image and in ours.

Let me be more specific. Think first of how our language depends upon the kind of bodies we human beings have in common. It might be too distractingly playful an exercise if we imagined our bodies made differently, but we get some sense of what the result might be when our bodies malfunction. Later, we will encounter the deaf and the blind and consider how their lack affects their understanding. Even now, however, we can try to imagine the degree to which our understanding and ability to communicate would be affected by the loss of any one of our senses. To make the exercise easier, suppose we consider not our experience as such, but only our experience as reflected in the words we use.

Suppose we begin with the words that depend upon the use of our eyes. *See*, we remember, is the most usual of synonyms for *understand*. To understand, we watch, look, perceive, observe, keep an eye on, peek, spy, notice, gaze, peer, contemplate, scrutinize, and witness—I forbear to add words, but Roget has much more. And *blind*, we remember, is a usual synonym for *unable to understand* and *ignorant (of)*. If we were all to lose our ability to see and, with it, all the words meaning *see* or using vision as a metaphor in one sense or another; and if we lost all the literal and metaphorical meanings of *blind*; and if we added to these losses, as we should be forced to, all the other words literally or metaphorically related to *darkness, light*, and *color*, we should have lost not only the visual part of our vocabulary but also the corresponding part of our ability to think.

This about vision and its lack is evident enough (*evident* is from *videre, to see*). It is less evident how our experience is made possible—is lent its structure—by the sense of touch; by the sense of balance; by the (so-called proprioceptive) awareness of the position of the body resulting from the testimony of receptors in our muscles, tendons, and joints; and by the union of the testimony of all these with the testimony of sight, hearing, smell, taste, and whatever other senses there may be. And so body is or becomes mind; and so, too, we orient ourselves intellectually, in the first place in relation to our bodies, with opposites such as *near-far, left-right, front-back, toward-away from*, and all the other positional concepts. These spatial relationships—which have their many metaphorical extensions—are extended by others such as *center-periphery, part-whole, full-empty*, and *closed-open*, each of which is also extended metaphorically.[2]

Furthermore, the resistance of things to movement and the reactions of our bodies to this resistance are essential to our understanding of force; and our eyes and proprioceptors—and not they alone—are essential to our ability to understand the concept of motion either in general or in any particular direction. Briefly, if we had souls perpetually divorced from bodies we could think neither literally nor metaphorically of any of these body-related concepts, and it is difficult to imagine how we could think at all.

To begin to get an idea of the extent to which our thought depends on body-related concepts, one need only turn to an edition of *Roget's Thesaurus* organized by its original word categories and see how these categories depend, directly or indirectly, on our experience of our bodies. I do not now mean to suggest that body terms be used to renew the Kantian analysis of what makes experience possible, but only that in the absence of their bodies, human beings could have no experience, not even of the kind that is called *abstract.*

✤

Now if all this is granted, that is, if we grant that we understand one another's words because we have similar bodies and basically similar lives, there remain the misunderstandings that come from our lack of the particular shared experience that, although less basic, remains essential for the meaning the words are intended to convey. Misunderstandings that stem from the lack of shared experience are as common in the most everyday matters as in the most exalted; for a word recalls something we have experienced and can be used efficiently only if the person who uses it and the person who hears or reads it can both relate it to their experience in a similar way.

I think that this little truth is important enough to be driven home with the help of an example or two. Try using nothing more than the definition in a book in order to imagine the taste of an unknown fruit— maybe the guanabana, also known as the soursop and described as the large, dark green, slightly acid, pulpy fruit of a small West Indian tree. Or try to imagine how you might explain the taste of a fruit you know very well, for instance an orange—defined as a globose, reddish yellow, bitter or sweet, edible citrus fruit—to someone who has never tasted it. You will certainly help yourself by naming fruits with a similar taste and texture, but if the person listening to you has never tasted a citrus fruit of any kind, the explanation will be quite difficult. It would surely be an unexpected triumph if, on first tasting an orange, the person would say, "It tastes exactly as I imagined it from your words."

But whether descriptions succeed or fail, shared experience remains indispensable to them. In its absence, words remain mere sounds. When the shared experience is extensive enough, single words can replace complete sentences; and when the shared experience is both extensive and intensive, speech can become sparse and hints—not necessarily verbal—more effective; and then the sheerly abstract information the speech conveys is understood in the light of its intimately personal qualities. Such speech creates the fullest, most natural tie between people, one of idiosyncratic, emotionally colored conceptuality.

The Meaning of Spoken Words Is Refined and Extended by Nonverbal Means

It is plain that the understanding of the abstract content of words is affected by the manner in which we speak them. Because the grammar of actual speech does not conform to the 'official' kind, a person who speaks 'correctly', in complete accord with the official grammar, sounds artificial, as if adhering to the standards of writing instead of those of speech. In fact, writing and speech are rather different means of expression. What speech loses by its grammatical laxness it makes up for by its emotional immediacy, by the quality of the speaking voice, and by the face and gestures that are its accompanying instruments. In a broad sense, then, the meaning of our speech is a union of its abstract content, conversational matrix, vocal quality, and gestural expression. For the most part, we are only marginally aware of the physical ways in which we vary the abstract content of our speech; but actors learn their craft by studying these ways, because they know that speech is not only spoken but performed.[3]

As a performance, gesturally expressive speech, with its coordination of the arms, shifting of the body, and changing facial expression has the quality of a spontaneous dance. This is the more apparent when we think of such speech not as a solo performance but, at the least, a conversational duet; with many persons in the act, it becomes a whole unconsciously danced opera (or operetta). If restrictions are placed on the freedom of this danced talk, they are compensated for—the drama, such as it is, must go on. So when, for experiment's sake, speakers are told to sit with unmoving hands, they pause more and use more words that describe spatial relations; and when the speakers are restrained from making any large gestures, their imagery grows more sparse. The implication is that the very freedom to make large movements, to point out things, to use gestural depth, and to draw spatial contours, suggests the images that can be used to enhance the effect of speaking. To make up for the absence of the large gestures, the speakers make more numerous or more emphatic small ones—of the eyebrows, eyes, mouth, and fingers.[4]

Then there is the speaker's gaze, which contributes its changing focus to the performance of speech. Normally, it remains fixed for only a few seconds at a time. It is more often fixed at the ends of sentences or long clauses, when the speaker has finished saying something relatively complete and wants to be guided by the listener's reactions (other reasons for pausing will soon be mentioned). Unusually rapid blinking betrays tension, while enlarged pupils betray strong, often sexual, interest. Although we hardly need to be told so, the experimenter observes that pleasure tends to open the eyes rather wide and surround them with wrinkles, pain to close the eyes and arch the eyebrows, fear to freeze the eyes wide open, and anger to narrow them.[5]

Then there is the voice. Every kind of emotional response elicits its own purely vocal contour, and every individual has a characteristic vocal contour and quality. There are, as we easily recognize, happy, friendly voices. The rhythms of such voices are regular and the sounds they make have gentle upward variations of pitch. In contrast, hostile or angry voices are loud, harsh, and fast, and their pitch, which is often lowered, has sharp upward variations. Dominance, likewise, has its characteristic voice; submission has its voice; and so, even, does credibility.[6] And a hollow, exaggeratedly flat, unresonant voice is said to be common to repressed persons, to very retarded ones, and to those who suffer from certain brain diseases.[7]

What happens when a gesture we make, our facial expression, or our tone of voice is in conflict with the literal meaning of the words we use, when, for example, we use our voice or facial expression to reverse the literal meanings of *good* and *bad*? In reversing meanings in such ways, we of course tangle them, express our ambivalence, and, in addition, give clues to our mood and nature. Not surprisingly, a study shows that happy faces making positive statements are regarded as sincere and very positive. More surprisingly, such voices may be taken to suggest dominance and even pride. Happy faces out of which come negative statements are taken to show either great insincerity, great submissiveness, or, often, a joking quality. Angry faces that make positive statements are interpreted as insincere, bitter, and derisive, or, in a single word, sarcastic. And sad faces saying submissive things tend to make listeners sympathetic—or so the experimenter, bound to the conditions of his experiment, tells us.[8]

It appears that in talking we are able to say much more than the dictionary allows; and yet our complaints against words, if we make them, take little account of how subtly we really use them. Recall, as a simple example, the resourceful technique with which a person may say, "I just can't put it into words!"

Our Attempts to Explain Ourselves Leave a Finally Ineffable Residue

Whether or not we express ourselves clearly, we are often aware that we have to make an effort to explain ourselves or risk being misunderstood. The risk is held in check by our prior agreement on the conventions of conversation and writing.[9] But even so, explaining oneself is an always unfinished process. A serious attempt to give a full explanation would prove intolerably long, I think; but just how much it is best to explain we discover only in imperfect practice. The persons who write manuals of instruction for electronic devices have the same difficulty: they fail to give unambiguous instructions for ordinary users because, it seems, it is not clear to them just what these users know and do not know. The shared context of knowledge turns out to be inadequate, an inadequacy that makes it so hard to say exactly what we want.

Even if we explain ourselves well, if we are reflective, we gradually become aware of a certain mutual impenetrability of speaker and listener: for all kinds of reasons, we cannot grasp other persons as they themselves would like to be grasped. Attentively as we may listen, we often miss the exact point that someone is trying to make. This is not necessarily our fault. It turns out that it is extraordinarily difficult, if not impossible, to speak or write unambiguously for long, even about rather simple practical matters. Speech has the advantage over writing because of its gestural, dancing quality, and because the listener can tell us what is not clear and encourage us to continue explaining as long as need requires and patience allows. But for all of its immediate advantages, speech, too, leaves us only imperfectly understood.

As I have said, our impenetrability is mutual, and it is as difficult for others to understand us to our satisfaction as for us to understand them to theirs. The difference in context of understanding can be blamed, but we do not always really want to know what it is in our words that is unclear to others. One reason is that we often find it difficult to listen carefully to others—difficult because we are much more eager to expound ourselves than to assimilate what, if we take it seriously, might be destructive to our opinions or pride; and difficult because we prefer our own ideas to remain at the center of attention.

Another, maybe embarrassing difficulty: We may in time discover that we find it hard to explain ourselves to others because we do not know ourselves well enough. Our transparency to ourselves is too limited. When we are alert, we are relatively conscious of how we think, and we may then seem to construct our thoughts by a process over which we rule; but if we pay attention to the way in which we think, we become aware that many of our thoughts arise in us by means of inward processes we do not understand at all. For in thinking we are always drawing on abilities we have learned that we contain; but we hardly know whether in the final analysis (if there is any truly final analysis) these are fully intellectual, logical processes that are silent, that is, impenetrable to consciousness, or whether they are sublogical, subintellectual processes from which fully intellectual ones emerge, or, as is perhaps more likely, they are both kinds of processes or processes intermediate to both, processes either unstructured enough or flexible enough to fit the needs of a very adaptable organism that is, at once and by turns, emotional, musical, verbal, and mathematical. Why should we assume that these processes—which we must classify as thought and as either knowledge or the precursors of knowledge—are easily and fully translatable into words?[10]

What rules here and how does it rule? Having begun to speak, we do not consciously order the details of the activity of our organs of speech. There is not nearly enough time to choose words consciously (normally we speak two or three per second) let alone choose the sounds (about fifteen per second) we use in articulating them.[11] Nor, as native speakers, do we consciously establish the grammatical order of the words we use. Nor—except when arguing formally, as philosophers, logicians, and the like—are we conscious of the principles of reasoning we use. This is with good reason, because conscious attention paid to the principles of reasoning is just as inhibiting to the natural flow of thought as conscious attention paid to any of our other activities. To think fluently, we have to let ourselves go. Criticism easily kills the skill it is meant to further.

What rules the process of speech, and how and to what purpose does the ruling work? It is easy to ask and hard to answer why we use just the words we do rather than familiar synonyms for them. Is the choice of one synonym rather than another made because of its unique range of meaning, its sound, or its meaning and sound together? And why do the words come out organized in one allowable sequence rather than another equally allowable one? Do the alternative possibilities of words and word sequences increase the possibilities of thought by increasing the range of its possible transformations? Do the independent associations of the sounds and their irrelevance to the meaning they convey create a kind of randomization that allows us to escape mere automatism and reinvent our thought as we are expressing it? Does freedom of intellectual choice therefore depend on freedom of phonetic association or—to choose another possibility—freedom of structural association? Does the translation of thoughts into words externalize them and make it easier to change them because they have become hearable or visible structures?[12] And why do we so often have the feeling that we understand what we are saying but find it difficult to explain our meaning in words other than those we have actually used?[13] And what accounts for the whole quirkish path in which our thoughts flow, the sequences deflected as if they were flowing along a particular terrain with its rises and falls, rocks and floating debris, and channels that meander as they can and must?

It is evident that much of the seemingly wayward direction our thoughts take is the result of unconscious 'mechanisms', for consciousness appears only when we are paying attention. Consciousness, we discover, is for learning—we do something consciously in order to learn it well enough to forget how we do it. Consciousness is also for regulating—we need to make thoughts conscious in order to slow them down, expose them to view, and regulate them as we prefer. Words are so helpful for these functions not only because, being external, they are manipulable, but because, like the expressions that contain them, their ranges of meaning are broad and vague enough to invite change.[14]

Our usual ignorance of *how* we think is accompanied by a partial ignorance of *what* we think. We are partially ignorant because, thinking with our whole person and experience, we generate ideas from a substratum that is opaque to consciousness and resists transmutation into concepts. It is true that part of our more abstract thinking may be done in snatches of inner speech, but external speech is not ordinarily generated from preceding speech of any kind. Each of us experiences the appearance of abstract thought from nothing we know that resembles it. We find the same sort of disparity in accounts given by writers, scientists, and even philosophers.[15] Einstein testifies that words seem not to play any role in the mechanism of his scientific invention, the elements of which are "certain signs" and "more or less clear images" that he is able to reproduce and combine. Only at a later, secondary stage, he says, is it necessary to search laboriously for "conventional words or other signs."[16] A young dyslexic mathematician, who can speak easily but has great difficulty in reading and writing, reports that from an early age he found many things were easier to think about without language. Like his father, he says, he creates and manipulates visual images, especially when he is trying to make or to understand an intricate mechanism. In mathematics he never feels he understands something unless he finds a way of visualizing it, although this visualization is not usually a substitute for the mathematical symbols. Sometimes the 'thought' is by way of muscular sensation. He explains:

> If I am trying to remember a complicated knot when no rope is available, I usually imagine the finger movements involved and the feel of the knot being tied without picturing it in my mind or moving my hands at all. Knots are examples of things that are extremely hard to describe and remember in words, and people who attempt to do so usually forget them very quickly and are poor at spotting similarities between complicated knots.[17]

This mathematician, whose difficulties in reading and writing do not extend to mathematical symbolism, reports that he can usually assimilate a mathematics book by "reading the equations and occasionally looking for key words in the text." He adds that much of his mathematics "is done completely without words of any kind . . . Thought is not necessarily hindered by reading and writing difficulties, but the availability of things to think about is."[18]

Speaking in a rather similar vein, Wittgenstein says that there are really

> cases in which the sense of what a person wants to say is much clearer in his mind than he can express in words. (This happens to me very often.) It is as if one saw a dream-picture distinctly, but could not describe it in such a way that someone else, too, could see it.[19]

These are persuasive testimonies to the frequent disjunction between thought and words, and to the view I have adopted, that external speech is not always generated from earlier speech but from its unknown substratum. This evidence makes it easier to grasp why we do not know exactly—cannot explain exactly—what we mean. I am not referring to the changes that occur in our views. If we consider only a period during which the basic lines of our thought remain the same, we discover that, even so, we are incapable of saying with enough clarity and detail exactly what our views are. The more time we take to explain, the more unclear or at least idiosyncratic the explanation is likely to become.

We begin to explain ourselves and in the process draw our thought out of ourselves much as magicians pull long strips of gauze out of their mouths. Drawing thought out so, we slowly explain ourselves not only to others but also to ourselves, the explanation beginning with an opinion, elicited more or less spontaneously, which we then elaborate, possibly in defense. What we are going to draw out of ourselves, even in the immediate future, we cannot predict; and now and then we find that what emerges is genuinely surprising. Even when conveying the 'same' meanings, spontaneous 'sayings'—the way the words actually emerge each time we utter or write them—vary in structure, imagery, and verbal detail, although, as I admit, we all repeat characteristic opinions and tell the same old jokes.

Needless to say, I do not know why the process of eliciting our views from ourselves takes so long or why, in effect, it never ends. The only general reason I can propose is that we are internally so complex and personal an environment for the creation of thoughts that the internal 'attitudes' and 'positions' cannot be stated quickly and cannot be fully stated at all; and, furthermore, that personal conditions change their nuances quickly and often, and with each change elicit an at least subtly different verbal response from ourselves and a correspondingly changed response from the listener, so that the whole flow of ostensibly similar thoughts may take a distinctly different path each time.

As we know, the process of eliciting views from anyone follows a fairly fixed pattern of statement and response: After I have finished explaining myself, clearly or not, my interlocutor is apt to respond by paraphrasing what I have said or by indicating in some other way what he takes my meaning to be. He shows that he has made my meaning his own by translating it into his individual language. If the discussion goes on, I am likely to answer that, no, that was not exactly what I had meant; and the process of statement and response and corrective counterstatement and counterresponse continues, dialectically, as some of us say; but it is never really ended, and in its course I not only explain myself further but learn details of my meaning I am not aware of until they are elicited by what I take to be misunderstanding. For that reason, much of my grasp of my own position is developed by means of my responses to the misunderstanding of others.

Yet in a way I know what I have not yet consciously learned about my position. I mean that I never fail to sense the alien quality in another person's paraphrase or extension of my position, a position I am able to enlarge on as soon as I have heard from the other person what it appears to him to be, that is, what he has wrongly taken it to be. Knowing that, like my immune system, I can sense any alien intrusion, I remain confident that I can go on describing my still unexpressed position, as confident as if it were an object I was looking at directly and describing to someone in another room. I am in firm possession of views that I have never yet expressed in detail and, in this sense, contain but do not consciously quite know. This kind of knowing what one does not yet exactly know never changes.

❧◉❧

What I have described of my conversation with myself and others is characteristic not only of informal interchanges between individuals but also of the larger 'conversations' that make up the history of culture. To show this I cite a persuasive comment on the development of science:

> Science is a conversation with nature, but it is also a conversation with other scientists. Not until scientists publish their views and discover the reaction of other scientists can they possibly appreciate what they have actually said. No matter how much one might write and rewrite one's work in anticipation of public responses, it is impossible to avoid all possible misunderstandings, and not all such misunderstandings are plainly 'misunderstandings'. Frequently scientists do not know what they intended to say until they discover what it is that other scientists have taken them to be saying. Scientists show great facility in retrospective meaning-change.[20]

The Meanings of Speech Are Also Conveyed by Its Alternations with Silence

Silence is obviously necessary to speech because words or phrases are distinguishable by the brief intervals of silence that separate them. When spontaneous, speech is produced in spurts that last on the average about two seconds and consist of about five words. These spurts seem to reflect the rhythm in which consciousness focuses on successive units of words-to-be. Hesitations between the units show us where difficulties arise, where, for instance, one is changing direction or searching one's memory.[21]

But silence is also used to convey meanings that are awkward to put into words. Affected by the awkwardness, a person turns his face away and stops talking, or closes his eyes as his voice trails into a whisper and disappears. It is because we speak that we learn to convey messages by silence and that silence is needed for the sequential eloquence of words. I give the example of the silences that characterized the "inspired confusion" of the French sociologist and anthropologist Marcel Mauss (1872–1950). As one of his students recalls, "His discourse was all articulations and elasticity. Most of his sentences came up empty, but it was an emptiness that invited you to build. That's why I said the most characteristic things were his silences."[22]

In Western culture, silence is easily interpreted as reserve or rudeness and sometimes arouses suspicion—who knows what criticisms are being made or plots hatched in the silent person's mind?[23] It is evident, however, that there are individuals and cultures that do not feel that silence creates an anxious void that ought to be filled with speech, or that one must speak because silence is boring or because one needs to dominate the situation. Among Native Americans, relative silence is interpreted as control, cooperation, and attentiveness to others. Navajos, even when speaking in English, pause longer than non-Navajos are able to tolerate; but the Navajos pause out of inbred politeness, to allow the listener time to digest what has been said and to reflect on an answer.[24] The verbally very different Igbo of Nigeria cultivate oratory, salt their speech with proverbs, and are in general highly verbal and extroverted. The silence they practice for ritual purposes is therefore eloquent by its difference. So, too, is the custom by which they sit in silence when they visit a bereaved person, for they feel that words would only intensify the grief of the mourner. By their silence they also show that they dare to appear before the hovering spirit of the dead person, as they would not if they were in any way responsible for the death.[25]

In accord with their acute social consciousness, the Japanese practice what they call "wordless communication" (*haragei*) because they feel that speech at a particular moment is out of place or likely to lose the essence of what one wants to say. The shared silence implies an intimacy like that of people who are close enough to one another to need only the merest hint in order to hear not so much the spoken words as their overtones. The deliberate refusal of the Japanese to speak assumes this sensitivity to overtones, for silence is interpreted as conveying more than words can. In Japan, we are told, psychotherapists are far more economical with words than are their Western counterparts and expect their patients to understand what, from a Western standpoint, is merely hinted. Because the Japanese are trained from early childhood to be sensitive to the feelings of others, the more emotionally important the message, the less likely it is, even if put into words, to be more than hinted at.[26]

Franz Kafka celebrates the force of silence in his miniature parable-like story, *The Silence of the Sirens*. He imagines that Ulysses put wax in his ears so as not to hear the Sirens' songs, but that Ulysses did not understand that they have "a still more fatal weapon than their song, namely their silence." It was impossible, the text says, to escape from their silence; yet Ulysses triumphed over them because he mistook their silence for singing he could not hear.[27]

Kafka is the philosophical storyteller, but the outright philosopher Maurice Merleau-Ponty not only praises silence but regards philosophy as a way of joining silence with speech. "We should be sensitive to the thread of silence from which the tissue of speech is woven," he writes. "Philosophy is the reconversion of silence and speech into one another."[28] These remarks need interpretation but, by Merleau-Ponty's own criterion, they are telling enough to deserve not to be interpreted at the moment; but his idea hints at others yet to be expressed.

Self-Disclosure and Therefore Ineffability May Be Relative to One's Partner and Situation

We recognize that silence, like speech, can both conceal and reveal the self. As it happens, self-disclosure has been a field of psychological research for some time.[29] In contrast to early expectations (but in keeping with experience in other psychological research), self-disclosure has shown itself to be such a complicated matter that it has left us with more questions than answers.[30] As usual, human beings evade a simply formulaic understanding.

Because I have relied and will continue to rely on psychological observations and research, I should like to take a moment to explain how this well-confirmed observation—that human beings evade formulaic understanding—affects my reliance on the research. It has become clear that all scientific data, theories, and research remain perpetually in question. Practical experience joins philosophy in showing that literally nothing in empirical science, however professionally hallowed, can be beyond question. Yet with the exception of physiological psychology, the subject matter of psychology is such that doubt is and should be more general and immediate. Unlike at least some experiments in physics, psychological experiments of any interest can always be immediately faulted. The objects of the experiments—human beings—are so plastic that the experimenters cannot be fully successful in narrowing the possibilities so as to make their conclusions unambiguous.

Even in physics, the inability to repeat the initial conditions of an earlier experiment with complete exactness argues that fully exact repetitions are only an ideal. In psychology, the differences between experimenters, between the experimenters' human subjects, and between the situations of different experiments are such that the difficulties in repeating experiments and in narrowing down the number of immediately plausible explanations are indefinitely greater than in, say, chemistry. There is of course a great, sometimes very great, difference between a competent and an incompetent experiment in psychology; but even the most competent could have been more careful and therefore more convincing than it in fact turns out to be—the possibilities for more care in planning, execution, and interpretation are practically infinite; and once the experiment has been carried out, a practiced critic can always suggest an improvement.

For us, the upshot is that whatever I report as the result of psychological observations or experiments should be regarded as suggestive rather than final; and while I may not use terms implying doubt, the doubt is always there. It stands to reason that none of what I am saying should be interpreted as scorn for psychological experiment but only as a reminder of how intrinsically difficult it is in psychology to arrive at conclusions that are even relatively firm. Even so, the experiments have tended to rule out certain possibilities and strengthen others, and have done a great deal to deepen our ability to understand human thought and behavior. When the occasion arises to illuminate philosophical problems by psychological means, it will not be because I assume that psychology, unlike philosophy, is immune to doubt, but because it is able to cast a different, more empirical kind of illumination on a problem that philosophy has not solved convincingly enough.

Now back to self-disclosure. Psychologists have measured this act in terms of two dimensions, the one of breadth—which refers to the range of the matters disclosed—and the other of depth—which refers to the degree of intimacy that is reached. These two dimensions are assumed to go together more often than not. The intensity of the emotion involved has been considered a separate dimension. So has the time, that is, the slowness or quickness with which the disclosure is made, the hesitations or silences with which it is interspersed, and the length of time spent on it—a longer time spent in self-disclosure implies an intensified feeling of intimacy. Psychologists have also identified a dimension of flexibility, the ease with which self-disclosure responds to changed circumstances.[31]

It is natural for one's style of disclosure to adapt itself to different events and partners. Perhaps surprisingly, an open conversational style is not necessarily revealing—one wears a confession as a lifelike mask. That is why, in estimating self-disclosure, authenticity should be taken into consideration. So, too, should the degree of risk that one is willing to take in revealing oneself.[32]

The critical need that prompts self-disclosure, no matter to whom, is surely the need for emotional closeness. Persons who grow up in close, helpful intimacy with their parents anticipate that intimacy will be achieved and disclose themselves unselfconsciously. Unlike them, persons who have suffered from neglect in their childhood or have been painfully cut off from their parents, whether by death or otherwise, regard themselves less favorably, anticipate rejection, and, in fact, are rejected more often. Such persons are apt to go through life afflicted by the feeling that no one wants or is able to understand them. A pathological extreme of self-disapproval and fear of disapproval is a genuine fear of intimacy.[33]

One person's disclosure naturally stimulates that of another. The intimacy that arises between adolescents and adults continues or revives the initial intimacy between infant and parents. Having found someone to be intimate with, the person who confesses hopes for sympathy and an equivalent to pardon even though what is confessed is shameful. For most of us, confession of any depth comes hard, and though it sometimes takes place in the excited crowd typical of certain religious or quasi-religious confessions of sin, it is more usually confined to a pair, its two members free of social pressure, matching confession against confession, and taking pleasure in their undivided attention to one another's concerns.[34]

Anyone under heavy emotional pressure either confides in a trusted companion—who may well be under the same kind of pressure—or becomes deeply lonely. But the person who discloses much pain or unhappiness is trapped in a dilemma because the expression of unhappiness annoys those who have to listen to much of it. As we probably know from our own experience and as impersonal evidence shows, people who complain of their suffering inspire dislike.[35] Almost everybody therefore learns to conceal some degree of pain, or to show it in ways that disturb others as little as possible. Egotistical persons exploit those who listen to them by helping themselves at the expense of their listeners' comfort. Less egotistical persons learn to moderate their disclosures.[36]

There are interesting differences in self-disclosure between men and women. The usual view, which is that men are more inhibited than women, is too simple. One study maintains that the most open, deep disclosure is between pairs of women and the least between pairs of men, that paired men and women are intermediate between the two extremes, and that both women and men disclose more to a woman than to a man. Men are said to be more direct, especially when they are expressing their need for power, while women more often influence men's decisions indirectly. But both sexes withhold personal information that might put them under the power of those who learn their secrets.[37]

Marriage can either increase or decrease the depth and frequency with which one reveals oneself. As those who are married discover, it probably does both, in the selective manner that fits the marriage. Styles of self-disclosure in marriage have been given a simple classification. One style is the conservative or traditional. Married persons who live by this style emphasize their positive feelings and limit the kinds of subjects they talk about even in the deepest of confidence. Their morality, implicit and explicit, reduces their expectations of one another and perhaps the friction between them, just as it sets the bounds to what they allow themselves to reveal to one another. Untraditional marriages, those in which the terms of marriage are less clear and must be learned or negotiated as time goes on, allow freer expression of negative feelings and greater open dissension. This relative freedom of disclosure may make the marriage more interesting and lend it a more varied intimacy, the result of more open emotional sharing and the seesaw of emotions that go with quarreling and making up. But there are also untraditional marriages that reject intimacy, the partners remaining lone wolves, emotionally separate and carefully guarded in their relations with one another.[38]

Especially Sensitive Listening May Allow the Previously Ineffable to Be Put into Words

The difficulties related to self-disclosure bring us to the threshold of psychiatry, psychoanalysis, and clinical psychology, the professions in which the greatest care is taken to listen to what a person says and, in saying, reveals even involuntarily. In Freudian psychoanalysis, the analyst is supposed to remain as neutral as possible and allow the patient's speech to retain as many of its uncontaminated nuances as possible. The therapist of whatever kind (except the behavioral) believes that the patient's speech expresses more than can be consciously grasped or even intuited, yet hopes to hear enough to be able in the end to strengthen the patient's self-understanding. In principle, the therapist wants to be the self-abnegating listener, one who understands that the patient is struggling to find words to explain, is trying to overcome the shame of self-revelation in the most unflattering of lights, and is afraid that the weakness revealed will become the talk of others. Therapists who themselves become patients also have to struggle for words for the same reasons.[39]

The therapist's own psychological reactions may stand in the way of the analysis. It is all too easy for the therapist to become insecure, especially if the patient is acute enough to invert the relationship by discovering the therapist's weaknesses; and sometimes the therapist in effect silences the patient by talking in an unintelligible jargon or putting words into the patient's mouth.[40] The patient is eager to reveal but cannot avoid hiding as well, so that the therapist has to listen beyond the words to the manner in which they are said, to the form they take as a whole, to the emotion invested in them, to the similes and metaphors used, and to the hesitations, silences, and apparent irrelevancies.

It is because all this is far too much to attend to at once that the therapist's peripheral consciousness and literary sensitivity must be enlisted. For instance, the patient' grammar, such as the use of passive rather than active forms, may be significant; or the patient may use abstract words rather than more immediate, natural ones; and the metaphors that come up both reveal and conceal. Memories recalled speak for themselves and, as well, for the relationship between patient and

therapist. To fathom as deeply as possible, the therapist has to call on
emotion, fantasy, and internal dialogue until the feeling comes—correctly or mistakenly—that the flow of words is now understood.

The assumption is always made that the words of the patient *must* be
revealing, if not in their abstract content then in the manner of their saying
and their associations.[41] Except for con men and other mythomaniacs, total
lying seems impossible—and the con man, the practiced, supreme liar,
eventually wants to have his lies become known so that he can take
pleasure in the others' recognition of the artistry of his deceptions.

Therapy encounters significant silences, such as mean *I have
thoughts but can't tell them to you*, or *I don't want to tell you what I am
thinking*, or *My mind is a blank*. In one instance, a therapist reports, a
patient sat silently, thumb in mouth, staring at the floor, and now and
then letting out an irritated remark or curse. The therapist answered
silence with silence, at times for as long as half an hour. Although these
sessions went on for over a year, the patient kept coming back. Eventually she confessed that during her silent period she had improved a good
deal. As became clear, her silence had been an attempt to return to an
'archaic' relationship in which she had been dominated and made to feel
miserable, a relationship in which it seemed wrong to her to speak, so
that she would fall silent, holding out, as in the archaic past, against
attack. Her silence turned out to be communication more telling than any
verbal one.[42]

In another case, an analyst and her patient discovered that the
patients's black silence during entire months expressed the need to live
out, "without retaliation, his primary hatred of a genuinely powerful
mother." He had lost her emotionally to his only brother, born when he
was eleven years old, but he had been required by her to love and revere
her unstintingly.[43]

The analyst (N. E. C. Coltart) who reported this case said to her
audience of analysts:

> Some people *suffer* more from the unthinkable than others, and for
> these we have to do all in our power to help towards the therapeutic
> transformation, to bring thoughts to the unthinkable and words to
> the inexpressible. Gradually the rough beast may, within the framework of the analytic relationship, slouch towards being born, and
> the new creature emerging from the birth is the increasing happiness
> and peace of mind of the patient . . . But there is always a mystery at
> the heart of every person, and therefore in our job as analysts.[44]

A patient may also be silent by drowning the analyst in words that
say nothing because the talking, even crying voice is empty of emotion.
Or the patient may break off a sequence of ideas in the middle and

switch ideas again and again, so that nothing stable is communicated, not even the underlying cohesiveness of free association. Narcissistic patients, an analyst says, may react in this way because they perceive themselves to be walled off, enclosed in a cocoon. "In this cocoon they maintain the illusion that they can nourish themselves and need nothing from others—that they are in fact omnipotently self sufficient." Such patients refuse to communicate in order to maintain the illusion that they are self-sufficient. This illusion is nourished by their fear that the person to whom they show genuine emotion will have gained the means to dominate them. The illusion may be a revival of the very early tie in which child and adult communicate without words.[45]

Silence in therapy can have quite opposite functions. The silence of the therapist can be understood as benevolent or contemptuous, as implying, on the one hand, the possibility of being loved, or, on the other, the indifference that, like a parent's, implies lovelessness. The silence of the patient can be understood, for example, as the repetition of the mother's refusal to speak—a refusal that long ago provoked the child's punitive anger and the mother's answering threat. A parent's continued silence verges on emotional abandonment, while the even implied command to be quiet gives the child the order to vanish, and by metaphorical extension, the order to stop existing. Yet silences between analyst and patient, like those between any two persons, can be moments of communion for which words are too gross.[46]

Everything I have said about self-disclosure and therapeutic listening strikes me as relevant to the philosophical problems of ineffability we will soon encounter. Success in communicating with God depends, the believer believes, on the occasion, the subject to be communicated, the nature of the believer, and the nature of God—a selectivity like that we find in the self-disclosure of one human being to another. For the therapist, the patient represents the hidden meaning that has to be brought to light and put into words, while for the patient, the therapist is able, like a god, to draw out into understanding what was earlier impossible to feel consciously, see clearly, say aloud, or say at all.

Schizophrenic Speech Is an Extraordinary Union of the Effable and Ineffable

The therapist's problems with language lead on to a brief consideration of the language of psychotics or, more narrowly, schizophrenics. To keep what I say in perspective, it should be understood that we know of no embracing disease called *schizophrenia*. Schizophrenia is, rather, an enigmatic group of disorders distinguished only vaguely from disorders that are given other names. Although it would be too difficult at present to abandon schizophrenia as a diagnostic category, for all we know, the category bears as little relation to the cause or causes of the disorders it names as would a common medical name for all the diseases that are accompanied by fever. The brain's dopamine network appears disturbed, but no general cure is known and none of the theories proposed for schizophrenia explain all of the manifestations given the name.[47]

If this is so, it is not surprising that there is no uniform kind of language that one can attribute to schizophrenics. Some of them speak in a normal enough way.[48] Their diagnosis is based primarily on the bizarreness of their beliefs and the degree to which these beliefs undermine their ability to understand themselves and others. The content of their speech naturally reflects their condition. As I have noted earlier, their speech is often 'flat', emotionless. Occasionally its grammar breaks down, contains strange new coinages, becomes strangely diffuse, or turns into gibberish; and there is always an undertone of suffering.

Schizophrenic speech can be understood only if it is given the same imaginative attention we give to the more obscure poets. At times the schizophrenics attribute the strange things they say to someone or something that inhabits their speech and compels it to take its odd course. Then they feel that they are not responsible for what comes out of their mouths, speech and body having become separated, or the real person having become separated from the person who speaks out.

Let me give an example. A certain elderly schizophrenic, who referred to herself as "we," once stated that she was repeating what had been said to her by many young gentlemen, since there were people all over space and put into the body, some with neither soul nor reason and needing help. When she was asked how she could help these people, her answer was, "Because one can't speak, so I can't. . . ." She also claimed that they had a tape that spoke. "When you are speaking now?" she was asked, to which she answered, "Yes, that's a tape too. And it's an old skin, I don't know. . . ."[49]

Schizophrenia can pose a challenge to philosophy and, even more so, to theology.[50] The kind of schizophrenic I have dwelt on speaks a language unintelligible without exegesis. The more paranoidal schizophrenics construct whole symbolic systems and, like prophets and gurus, speak in the name of some compelling reality only they recognize clearly. What they say and how they say it are symbolic of their state of being. It is true that what we consider to be only symbols the schizophrenic takes to be real, but a poet, too, may easily fall into a mood in which the image used seems less a symbol than a reality. The schizophrenic's near symbols are a sign of disability, but they can carry more than a suggestion of the power for which we praise the creative individuals on whom human culture depends. The unreason of psychosis, whether it is the freeing of what is most primitive in us or the construction of a new but false world, is not far from what is called *sublimation*, to which we attribute the mysterious power of creativity.[51]

The Feeling and the Power of the Ineffable Also Depend on Hidden Memories

So far, our discussion has centered on the insufficiency of words to convey just what we intend, on our reluctance to express in words what we would rather leave unspoken, and on our actual suppression, even from ourselves, of matters too painful to reveal. In one way or another, all these difficulties involve memory. Memory is also relevant because the feeling of ineffability is at times the effect on us of something remembered but hidden from consciousness and therefore impossible to put into words.

The hiding begins early. Our ability to recall events begins at about the age of ten months, but almost no one consciously remembers anything that happened before, roughly, three and a half. Freud believes that this childhood amnesia is the result of the repression of everything having to do with childhood sexuality. The argument is that this amnesia is needed for the transformation of the helpless but hedonistic infant into a disciplined adult.[52] But adulthood does not confer on us a memory as good as we should like. Even the most memorable events in our adult lives are too hard to remember exactly. The bare facts may be recorded well enough, but exact quality of every event in each of our lives is unrepeatable. This uniqueness eludes the categories in which the memory is in part retained and in which it must be expressed when reported.

What the adult finds difficult, the young child finds impossible. Its experiences are too unstandardized to fit into the still unlearned linguistic categories with the help of which the adult remembers.[53] On similar grounds, it has been argued that the young child lacks a crucial form of memory by which events are recorded, or that memories are recorded in the nervous system in a different way and become unavailable. If so, the child's forgetting resembles one of the forms of adult amnesia.[54] For our immediate purposes, it is enough that Freudian and non-Freudian explanations relate the feeling of ineffability to the disparity between very early experience and later experience, which words fit.

The memories we do retain return to us involuntarily, no doubt because of some association. In an account of her involuntary memories, a Russian novelist who studied in Berlin during the 1920s tells us that she would get sudden brief, inexplicable sensations of homesickness, of "something precious in the past, reassuring by its mere existence," related, she thinks, to the mere glimpse she had caught of the aspect of a street, a color, a face.

Sometimes, however, the associations were more clear to her:

> As I reached the gateway on to the Unter-den-Linden, I halted. I looked up, and saw a small white cloud slightly to my right: at once I was transported home, to the street in which we lived, on just such a summer afternoon, but with a sky unmistakably stretching over my native town.[55]

Such memories were so precious to the writer that they sustained her and gave her courage to live while an utterly insecure émigré. There were involuntary memories that "had the glory and freshness of a dream, but others were nightmares" that she tried to shake off. Sometimes she was aware of "how the mind inserted a lie, without interfering with the physical details of the picture: ingenious rationalizations were put in the place of suppressed moments."[56] She concluded that the memories of all whole events (and some fragmentary ones), which bring back emotions that give the feeling of living in the past, are probably associated with a lost disturbance, but that

> we all carry innumerable other floating fragment-memories—of faces, names, numbers—which are easily distinguishable from the kind of 'precious fragments' I have been considering by the fact that they carry no strong emotions, do not give the feeling of living in the past, and never come back involuntarily.[57]

Such fragments of memory may be compared with the kind left by a thought so brief or so crowded out of consciousness that all that remains is the consciousness of having thought of something or having intended to say something. A speaker may try to recover the memory, hesitate, and give up and begin another train of thought. "The experience slips by so quickly that few of us have been able to pay attention to it . . . any more than any of us have had a good look at a hummingbird feeding."[58]

The Inability to Forget Makes the Use of Words More Vague and More Difficult

The Russian novelist I have cited had become sensitized to the different kinds of memory in which she relived her past, and she took refuge in the return of emotion-filled events. Unlike her and most other persons, there is an occasional unfortunate who can forget only with the greatest difficulty. In his well-known book *The Mind of a Mnemonist*, A. R. Luria tells of one such person, whose memory, to Luria's astonishment, had no distinct limits in capacity or time. Even though tested without warning as long as fifteen or sixteen years after memorizing long lists of words, he remembered them perfectly, forward and backward; and he remembered every detail of the occasions on which he first memorized the lists, including the suit Luria was wearing and the expression on Luria's face.[59]

In view of what has been said above about childhood amnesia, it should be added that the mnemonist had an extraordinary ability to recall his early childhood. Luria's explanation is that the mnemonist's memory had remained childishly primitive, lacking the usual psychological apparatus for shaping memories into words, and kept summoning up images, some of which, the mnemonist contended, went back to the time when he was not yet a year old.[60]

Even such a receptive memory had its imperfections. The mnemonist saw faces as changing patterns of light and shade and complained that they were too unstable to remember easily. His grasp of the texts he heard or read was not good because when a passage was read fairly rapidly, its images would collide with one another and turn into in a blurred chaos; and even when the passage was read more slowly, images irrelevant to its meaning continued to appear.[61]

As can be imagined, figurative writing and, above all, poetry were the most difficult texts of all because their images aroused personal associations and conflicting images; and the associations led him back involuntarily to his childhood. Although he was able in a practical sense to master what he had to, he could not escape his struggle with superfluous images and sensations. His grasp of reality was unstable, and "he gave himself up to dreaming and 'seeing' far more than to functioning in life."[62] The mnemonist simply could not forget enough or control his memories well enough; the mere progression of abstract ideas or of the events of a story threatened to escape into ineffability.

The example of the mnemonist raises the possibility that human beings keep a perfect internal record of everything that happens to them. This possibility was supported by a memorable set of observations made by the neurosurgeon Wilder Penfield and his associates. While operating on a patient's brain, Penfield experimentally stimulated its surface. The result was sometimes a detailed memory-like 'flashback'. Penfield was sure that an old memory, the stream of a former consciousness, had been revived. His view is now often regarded skeptically because it is assumed that what had been stimulated was a feeling of pastness, a fragmentary evocation of a remote time, in fact reconstructed out of present thoughts and ideas.[63]

One conclusion that fits the revised view of Penfield's experiments is that the realistic quality of both true and false memories results from the stimulation of an area of the brain, the limbic structures, that gives the 'remembered' experience its temporal and emotional quality. When this area of the brain fails, the result is automatism, confusion, and amnesia. If the limbic structures really color everything either perceived or remembered with emotion, and if the emotion is a precondition for perceiving and remembering, then everything we remember *must* have its emotional coloration, however slight. This necessity would be in keeping with Freud's belief that everything is remembered in its emotional setting because otherwise there would be no reason to recall it. Why remember anything to which we were totally indifferent?[64]

Clinical experience seems to strengthen the view that every memory is marked by a particular emotion, the recurrence of which makes the memory return more easily. Experiment shows that depressed persons recall unpleasant memories more easily, quickly, or in greater detail than pleasant ones; but when their mood improves, the opposite occurs.[65] Therefore different persons remembering the same event are apt to call up different memories of it, not only because their experience was in itself different, but also because they were in a different mood at the time they recalled it.

For us, the main lesson taught by the dependence of memory on emotion is that a memory we can recover and put into words in one mood may in another be irrecoverable and, in this sense, ineffable.

The Relations between Memory and Ineffability Are Dramatically Accentuated in Amnesia and Aphasia

Amnesia, the loss of much of one's memory, can be created artificially by hypnosis. The hypnotist suggests that on awakening from the hypnotic trance, the subject will be unable to recall anything until a certain cue word is pronounced. A person who nevertheless recalls what happened during the trance does so with difficulty, even though what is recalled happened only a few minutes earlier. Such forgetting has sometimes been minimized on the grounds that it is not a true forgetting but only an attempt to comply with the hypnotist's suggestion. This opinion seems too extreme; posthypnotic amnesia seems not unlike some other forms of forgetting. What is especially relevant here is, again, that the person who 'forgets' what happened to him knows something but may not be able to recover it at will.[66]

Memories that vanish from consciousness for psychological or organic reasons can be remembered unconsciously. The most dramatic instances of psychological repression are those of shell shock, now more often called battle fatigue, combat neurosis, or, in more general terms, posttraumatic stress disorder. Its symptoms include a feeling of self-estrangement, connected, the soldier feels, with some wartime event he cannot recall until—thanks, maybe, to a drug or hypnosis—he is overwhelmed by the force of the now remembered details and breaks out emotionally.[67] The soldier suffers until his memory is reinstated in his consciousness and he becomes more consciously whole again.

Sometimes the whole past is suddenly forgotten. The reason may be organic, but if it is psychological, the person is likely to be fleeing from pain (to be in this state of *fugue* is to flee, as the latin *fugere* suggests). With memory gone, the person vanishes from himself—personal identity lies more in memories than fingerprints—and must be renewed. Even if the ability to remember returns, the victim of amnesia may know of the past only that it has been forgotten, along with personal identity. A new identity must be assumed and new skills learned. But sometimes all of the past except for the time of the fugue itself is regained.[68]

As usual, what lies on the surface is misleading. Studies with words suggest that what amnesiacs forget they in a sense remember. Given their still good short-term memory, they can learn pairs of words. They soon forget the words, yet one of each pair is likely to be remembered if the other is mentioned. And though lacking a long-term memory, amnesiacs may gain a complex new skill—one of them, who began each session by claiming that he had never worked a computer before, learned to program the computer.[69]

Such an ability to remember in action what has been forgotten in consciousness leads to the conclusion that the tie between memory and consciousness is breakable. The amnesiac who remembers habits and learns new ones makes it evident not only that memories can become unconscious but that memories can be acquired unconsciously.[70]

Like an amnesiac, a person with a so-called split brain may seem to be of two different minds. As experiments show, the right half of the brain, apparently languageless, can direct the hand it governs (the left) to do many things on demand, for example, to point to pictures that represent spoken words such as *house* or *table*. An experimenter says, "There is a certain eerie quality in watching a hand draw or point to places when the left brain of the patient does not in fact know under what command the left motor system is responding."[71] The impression of two minds arises when the 'dumb' hand—the one that responds to the unconscious, right side of the brain—tries to carry out a command that the left, conscious side tries to stop.

The phenomena involved are complex and not well understood, but study of split brains may show that language is less important to the process of thinking than we usually suppose. The reason is this: The two halves of the brain are interdependent, as are brain's component systems essential to our 'intelligent' responses. It is therefore not difficult to assume that the language system compiles information given to it by other brain systems. As a compiler, the language system may be separate from the systems that carry out mathematical and even inferential reasoning. To the extent that it really is separate, language is not the source of intelligence but the reporter that describes what other, 'intelligent' systems have concluded.[72] As a researcher says, "It is unconceivable that all knowledge about the world be recast, and subsequently manipulated, in the form of sentences or sentence-like structures."[73]

The distinction between the linguistic and the mathematical is borne out by reports such as that of the dyslexic mathematician I cited earlier. An even more striking case is that of a scientist who suffered a severe head injury and lost much of his ability to use language. Yet (as put in the tester's technical language) "although unable to perform better than a 4- or 5-year-old child on verbal tests of comprehension, and with severe jargon dysphasia, he performed normally or above average on non-verbal tests, viz. Advanced Progressive Matrices, short-term memory, long-term maze learning, and visual 'closure'."[74]

Memory and, with it, the ability to speak and think seem strangely and unequally divided and subdivided. We discover this most clearly in the study of brain injuries. A bilingual person with a brain injury may lose only one language or part of it. What is recovered first, if anything, is probably the language in which mental sums or other routine thinking were done in the past.[75] In some cases (of *Wernicke's aphasia*), the person whose brain has been injured speaks with the usual modulations of the voice but makes little sense and is unable to make sense of the speech of others, yet the modulations must have a kind of sense of their own. In other cases (of *Broca's aphasia*), the person's speech is stammering and telegraphic but basically understandable. The motor coordination needed for speech is defective, and the right arm or leg may be weakened as well. Here we see the simultaneity of movement, structure, and meaning: the ability to move the speech organs, move the limbs, control the structure of speech, and understand structurally complicated speech are all weakened together.[76]

Persons suffering from this aphasia may lose, in particular, the ability to read, to write, to identify verbally what they see, or in a more restricted way, some class of what they see; but even if unable to identify verbally, they may still be able to identify by gesture or sound. The inability to recognize faces is a puzzlingly specialized kind of forgetting. It is often (not always) accompanied by the inability to distinguish between individual instances of a certain type, of cars, for instance, or of birds. Other specialized forms of forgetting are suffered by persons who can read, write, and speak but are unable to recognize spoken words (this is *pure word deafness*); or who are unable to recognize objects by their shape and size; and so on. At least one case of aphasia has been recorded in which the affected person would say the opposite of what he obviously meant, such as "Get rid of the shoe!" when he wanted his shoe put on, or "Please leave me!" followed immediately by "I don't want to be alone."[77]

Two conclusions are especially important for the understanding of ineffability. The first is that apparently unrelated abilities may be affected together—speech, for example, and the ability to move the right hand—because, it appears, they share the same neural circuits.[78] Speaking is a series of movements designed to produce sounds that represent, translate, carry, or externalize thoughts—choose whatever verb seems most plausible.

The second, so far inexplicable conclusion is that what we take to be a single mental ability is, in fact, divisible: Persons who cannot recognize familiar faces may be able to identify facial expressions, and vice versa; and those who cannot recognize a word they see may be able to recognize its letters one by one and the whole word by its spelling. As I have said in describing amnesia, the difficulties in remembering may be those of conscious memory. Someone who has become unable in the usual sense to recognize the faces of familiar persons may show by changes in the electrical conductivity of the skin that the faces are, after all, familiar.[79]

Many instances of brain injury show the decomposition of the varieties of memory and thought. They also strengthen the evidence I have already cited for the separability of consciousness from words and of words from the ability to think. When I say this I cannot help remembering Luria's book, *The Man with a Shattered World*. The hero whose perseverance the book celebrates is sublieutenant Zasetsky, a soldier in the Russian army whose brain was penetrated by a German bullet on March 2, 1943. The bullet very nearly erased his brain's ability to make impressions cohere, but it left intact the part or set of circuits needed for effective planning.

At first Zasetsky could not recognize who he was or what he could know or do. To himself he seemed a newborn creature that looked, listened, observed, repeated, but had no mind of its own. He had forgotten places, people, and ideas, had forgotten how to wave his hand in order to call someone or say goodby, and had forgotten how to kiss. Sometimes he even forgot where the parts of his body were. His sight was never of wholes. When he looked at a spoon, he saw only the left tip; and when he looked down, he sometimes could not see his hands and feet.

What could so shattered a man do with his language and thought? He writes that he is always in a kind of fog, his memory is a blank with hazy visions suddenly appearing and disappearing. What he does remember, he says, is broken into disconnected bits, so that he reacts abnormally to every word and idea.[80]

It took unbelievable persistence for Zasetsky to connect his thoughts with the words in which he wanted to record them. He notes that he has lost track of even such common words as *table, sun, wind,* and *sky,* and that when he does recover them, he has lost track of their meanings. Sometimes, he reports, it takes him an entire day to think of and become able to say a word for something he has seen. Or he hears a word but cannot visualize or remember what it means:

> Every word I hear seems vaguely familiar (after all, I once learned enough to get through three years at a polytechnic institute). As far as my memory's concerned, I know a particular word exists, except that it has lost meaning . . . This means that if I hear the word 'table' I can't figure out what it is right away, what it is related to. I just have a feeling that the word is somewhat familiar, but that's all.[81]

Memory Is Complex and Has Complex Effects on What We Can and Cannot Put into Words

It is clear that there are many kinds of remembering and forgetting. I have no desire to list all those that have been assumed by researchers. However, I have already mentioned conscious or explicit memory and unconscious or implicit memory, and short-term and long-term memory. To these there may be added: episodic memory—that of events; semantic memory—that of linguistic meanings; procedural memory—that of modes of action, of the way things are done; and declarative memory— that of conscious inspection, of knowing *that* something is so, that the sky is blue, for instance, or that one is writing a book.[82]

Memory gives us the ability to recognize something and the separable ability to retrieve its trace; and we have separate memories and intensities of memory for each of the senses, and separate abilities of memory for location in space, in time, and so on. The list can be made quite long, though it is not very helpful until it is analyzed in the light of the relevant evidence. A critical question is always the extent to which the loss of any of these abilities affects understanding; and understanding, too, must be understood as a complex of abilities with a unity that is as dramatic as it is neurologically ill-understood.[83]

When we attempt to analyze and explain what these abilities may be and how they are related to one another, there is a natural conflict between the many particular losses that can be listed and the desire to explain them all by means of a failure as general as possible. Solutions turn out to depend upon functions whose interrelationships are not really understood. I'm sorry that the words *not understood* recur; but although they do not do justice to some research, they are true enough.

Practical observation of the decomposition of the mind results in a more intricate (and less clear) grasp of what understanding may be. How, for instance, is language related to the different abilities that can be subtracted from it? We see that our experience is integrated into certain patterns the loss of which is the loss of self. At times even body and mind lose their usually clear, maybe only apparent, distinction from one another; and in the absence of this fundamental distinction, many of the distinctions that words embody become less clear.[84]

These are abstractions, but I follow them with a concrete instance and a direct challenge. Decide what can and cannot be said of the understanding of the unfortunate young man whose brain tumor left him with "the bizarre deficit of being able to voice only random numbers. Seeing him grimace," says the doctor who describes him,

> I would ask, "What's wrong? Is something hurting?" I hoped he would respond by pointing to the site of his pain. But instead he pursed his lips and a look of intense concentration overcame his face. After a minute or two he attempted speech, but "four" or "ten" or "three" was all that would come out. And then he would cry.[85]

The Relationship between Perception, Shared Experience, and Memory Makes Synesthetic Experience Hard to Express

I go on to the relation between language and the sensory excess called *synesthesia*, in which one modality of sensation, for example sound, is accompanied by another, usually color, so that the person who enjoys or suffers the synesthesia hears colors or, to put it the opposite way, sees sounds.

All children are synesthetic at birth. We know this because, as the electrical activity of their brains shows, the effect of light spreads to the nonvisual areas. To judge by this evidence, a newborn child not only sees sights but hears, smells, and twitches them (responds to light by moving its muscles). By adult standards, the inner experience of the infant must be undifferentiated and kaleidoscopic.[86] Even actions and sensations may not be distinguished—a six-week-old that seems to be imitating when it sticks its tongue out is only responding automatically—it will stick its tongue out if someone swings a ball toward its mouth.[87] At the age of one month, the investigator imagines, the infant who feels something knobby in his mouth "sees knobbiness, and hears and tastes and smells knobbiness; and when he sees something knobby, he feels knobbiness, and also hears and tastes and smells it."[88]

The attempt to describe the infant's totally knobby perception shows that synesthetic experience can be described only in glaringly inadequate words. Among adults, very few are synesthetes—their number has been estimated to be about one in five hundred thousand persons.[89] Drug experiences, epilepsy, and temporal lobe disease may have synesthetic effects. An investigator reports, for example, that about an hour after he took LSD, he could see sound waves passing before his eyes when he clapped his hands; and when two people clapped at different sound frequencies, he saw two differently-sized sets of waves that seemed to collide. His sense of time was also quite distorted; a quarter note strummed on a guitar seemed to linger for a month. He says, "Boundaries between self and nonself evaporate, giving rise to a serene sense of being one with the universe."[90] To explain, he makes the educated guess that an area of the brain (the locus coeruleus) "lumps all types of sensory messages—from sights, sounds, tactile pressures, smells, tastes, into a generalized excitation system" and "causes the drug user to feel that sensations are crossing the boundaries between different modalities."[91]

We find a remnant of synesthesia in our ability to compare the intensity of a sound with that of a light, or in the reinforcement of visual acuity by a sound, smell, pinprick, or pressure. The equivalence of the senses, which we all recognize, was demonstrated on one rare occasion when an adult whose lifelong blindness was overcome by a corneal graft was almost immediately able to recognize everything he already knew by touch (although shadows confused him).[92]

The remarkable memory of Luria's mnemonist was attributed in part to the childish synesthesia he retained. In an experiment, a tone pitched at a certain level (30 cycles per second) made the mnemonist see a strip of color like old, tarnished silver that changed into a glistening silvery object. A much higher tone (pitched at 2,000 cycles) looked to him like fireworks tinged with a pinkish red and, rather like a briny pickle, rough and unpleasant to the touch . . . "You could hurt your hand on this."[93] (Another synesthete in whom musical sounds evoked colors and tastes used to speak of "a mouthful of music" and, after the sounds had ended, of "digesting" the music.[94])

When the experiments with the mnemonist were repeated, the same stimuli caused the same reactions; and every sound caused an experience of light, color, taste, and touch. To him, vowels were simple figures and consonants were splashes, each with its distinct form. An *a*, for example, was long and white. Among numbers, *one* was firm, complete, and pointed; *two* was flatter, rectangular, and whitish gray; and so on. Voices, too, had their distinctive appearances. When he met anybody, the mnemonist would be struck first by the color of the person's voice, the color fading because it interfered with understanding; and if another voice broke into the conversation, blurs crept into the sounds and interfered with their clarity. In the mnemonist's memory, a ringing bell would call up the image of a small round, rolling object that felt rough like a rope, was white, and brought a salty taste to his mouth. Each kind of perception ran indescribably into that of another—I say *indescribably* because the words, clear as they are, convey nothing we can clearly grasp.[95]

Contrary to what we might suppose, synesthetic perceptions are as convincing to the synesthete as our 'normal' ones are to us. The colors or colored shapes that accompany the hearing of music are seen just as clearly as the music is heard, and the same sounds always call up the same colors. But each synesthete has his own perceptual matching. A violin, which sounded chrome yellow to one synesthete, sounded pale blue to another; and the same sound that the one person saw as red lines was seen by the other as green spheres.[96]

The ability of synesthesia to go beyond verbal categories is exhibited in many kinds of correspondence: those of certain traditional systems of music, of mystical symbolism, and of visionary poetry and painting. Chinese music correlates its five basic scale tones with colors; and the Hindu musical modes, the ragas, are taken to correspond with colors.[97] In poetry, to take an almost random example, Baudelaire's *Correspondences* reflects, all at once, his experiences with hashish, his reactions to the doctrines of Swedenborg and others, and suggestions of an intensity of sensual experience so great that it rises above itself into 'infinity'.[98] Kandinsky is a painter particularly sensitive to color-music correspondences—in Moscow, on hearing a performance of Wagner's *Lohengrin*, he had fantastic visions of color and lines.[99]

The most openly synesthetic of contemporary composers is Olivier Messiaen. He says, "When I hear music, and also when I read a score, I see internally, with the mind's eye, colors that move with the music . . . A certain complex of colors corresponds to each complex of sounds, to each chord, to be more exact," the color becoming paler when the chord is transposed to a higher pitch, and darker when transposed to a low one.[100] To Messiaen, "colored music" brings us closer to the reality of God, who is beyond words, thoughts, and concepts. On resurrection, he says, when we will come to know God, "this knowledge will be a perpetual dazzlement, an eternal music of colors, an eternal color of musics."[101]

Music Is Neurologically Distinct from Speech and Largely but Incompletely Ineffable

Music needs no synesthetic accompaniment to express much that escapes speech. The neurological evidence on the relation between the two defies simple generalizations. However, put cautiously—with the help of words like *majority* and *mostly*—it is possible to say that in the majority of right-handed persons emotional, musical, and spatial abilities are concentrated mostly in the right side of the brain, while motor skills, logico-mathematical ability, speech, and consciousness are mostly concentrated on the left side.

The neurological defect called amusia (the musical parallel to aphasia) suggests that what we think of as musical ability is really a complex of abilities. The inability to recognize melody is different from that to recognize rhythm, and both are different from the inability to recognize pitch; and all of these are different from the inability to analyze chords, read musical notes, reproduce melodies, or transcribe music.[102]

There is some confirmation of the left-right speech-music distinction in the puzzling instances of idiots savants, now more humanely considered to be instances of the savant syndrome. During the past hundred years, there have been fewer than a hundred reported examples of the highest level of such ability. Common to them all has been a very low I.Q, an extremely vivid visual or auditory memory, and an extraordinary aptitude, most often for numerical calculation or music.[103]

I give the astonishing example of John. He is blind, his right arm and hand are spastic and paralyzed, he is epileptic, and he is intellectually so retarded that he can hardly be tested. But although he does not understand even the concepts of big and small, he sings and he plays the piano with his left hand. When playing, he attends closely to the varying dynamics of different kinds of music. His repertoire includes Broadway musicals, jazz, classical music, opera, and popular music; he can sing and play for as long as eight hours without repeating a tune. His ability to improvise, imitate, transpose from key to key, change style, and embellish, make it appear that he has either learned in some unknown way or that he has innate access to the rules of music.[104] Researchers describe his skill as comparable to that of normally intelligent musicians. "It seems that intense practice, together with an intact neurological substrate for coding a musical symbol system, are sufficient to explain J.L.'s performance."[105]

A study of five musical 'savants' shows that they have genuine ability to invent as well as to reproduce music by culturally familiar rules, and they play and compose without consciously knowing how. The researchers generalize that every person has a separate musical intelligence, which is enough by itself for improvisation and creation; but they add that creativity is limited by one's general level of intelligence.[106] An unproved but not implausible explanation of the 'savants'' musicality is that injury to an ability or area of the brain—more usually or severely the right side—can lead to the compensatory development of another ability or area.[107]

Whatever truth there is in this speculation, there are instances, such as that of Maurice Ravel, that do not easily fit into the initial right-left distinction. His stroke, on the left side of the brain, affected his speech; and although he was still able to recognize melodies and notice any error in performance, it was hard for him to identify notes and impossible to write down music or play the piano.[108] Other cases show other complications of the right-left stereotype.

It is not surprising, therefore, that a more careful look at the stereotype shows how unlikely it is that musical abilities are all located on the right side. For timbres, the right is dominant; for pure tones, no side is dominant; for complex tones, the right is dominant, in direct proportion to the number of overtones. Pitch, it seems, is grasped and stored differently from other dimensions of sound—as shown by the neuromagnetometer, it is organized in the temporal lobe in the form of a tonal map not unlike a piano keyboard. Melody and sensitivity to rhythm seem to lodge in both hemispheres.[109] And in musicians, especially those who use visual imagery often, the left hemisphere is more involved than that of laymen; but even the musicians' analysis of chords takes place on the right side.[110]

I do not know enough about the relation between words and music to be categorical about any but the simplest things. In some ways, words are much more definite, in others, music. But the voice, the vehicle of speech, is also the first complex musical instrument we hear and the first we learn to use. It remains the musical instrument–percussive instruments excepted—in relation to which all the others are innately measured. The instinctive musicality with which it composes words is indispensable to human relations. It also causes all music to carry intimations of speech and makes it impossible for us to divide ourselves into purely musical and purely verbal creatures. Stravinsky says that he cannot begin to take an interest in music "except insofar as it emanates from the integral man . . . armed with the resources of his senses, his psychological faculties, and his intellectual equipment." He adds, I think exaggeratedly, that music "is nothing other than a phenomenon of speculation" dealing with the elements of sound and time.[111]

It follows that although music, words, and thought can be separated for special purposes, when experience is wanted whole, they join like lovers who have been separated for too long. Writing, too, though abstracted from the voice, retains a tie to music even in its organization. As Milan Kundera remarks, novels have a musical structure:

> The chapters are measures. These measures may be short or long or quite variable in length. Which brings me to the issue of tempo. Each of the parts in my novels could carry a musical indication: *moderato, presto, adagio,* and so on . . . To compose a novel is to set emotional spaces side by side—and that, to me, is the writer's subtlest craft.[112]

The Deaf, to Whom Sound Is Unknown and Ineffable, Can Learn to Restrict the Range of Its Ineffability

Synesthesia expresses the failure of sensory perception to divide clearly into its various modes. Idiots savants show how far abilities can develop to compensate for the absence of other abilities. Words and music are separated in the idiots savants and in amusia, but they interact both as wholes and as complex combinations of abilities, some shared, some not. Looked at closely, all of these are examples that show how complex the relationship is between what we lack, have, achieve, and know.

Consider the blind and the deaf. They lack what others regard as an irreplaceable medium for knowing the world. Their lack has been supposed to reduce their understanding. Even if they learn to compensate, their experience of the world is different from a heard and seen one, and its translation into the experience of the hearing and sighted is incomplete. Further, the heard, seen image of the world causes misunderstandings when translated into that of the deaf and blind.[113]

To those born deaf or blind, their condition is normal, and they are likely at first to think that it is the hearing or seeing persons who are abnormal. If brought up by parents or with other children having the same disability, deaf or blind children begin by reacting with surprise at the oddity of the people who hear or see, as they are told. Deaf children who live together and communicate in sign language wonder what is wrong with adults who, instead of making the usual gestures, face one another and keep moving their lips. And a deaf child immersed in the life of his deaf family may suppose that his hearing neighbors are unable to communicate. As the member of such a family, a deaf child uses *deaf* to mean *us* or *friends who behave as expected*. A man who had grown up in a deaf, signing family recalled that until the age of six he had never suspected that he was different from his parents and siblings and was able to hear.[114]

In Europe, an active interest in deafness goes back to at least the eighteenth century.[115] The origin of language was then a favorite philosophical subject, as was the possible identity between speech and language and language and thought. Denis Diderot, whose works include a remarkable 'letter' on the blind and an equally remarkable one on the deaf, writes that a society consisting of five persons, each having only one of the five senses, would be amusing because each of the persons would have a worldview based on the sense he possessed and would look on his four companions as senseless.[116] According to Diderot,

> If a man who possessed the gift of sight for only one or two days were to find himself among a people who were blind, he would either have to make up his mind to remain silent or else resign himself to be taken for a madman. Every day he would reveal some new mystery to them, a mystery that would be such only to them and that the skeptics would congratulate themselves on not believing.[117]

Speaking critically and, no doubt, satirically, Diderot put into the mouth of the blind scientist Saunderson the argument that to be convinced of the existence of God he would have to touch him. Diderot also reported that when he asked a blind man if he would be glad to have eyes, the blind man answered that if not for curiosity, he, the blind man, would prefer to have long arms because he supposed that what he learned by the use of his hands was more instructive than what other people learned by the use of their eyes. Diderot added that to a philosopher blind from birth, the mold of thought would be his sensations of touch, so deep thinking would tire his fingers as much as it tires our heads.[118]

Because deaf children learn to speak slowly and hesitantly, and because speech is assumed to be necessary for clear thought, it is easy to conclude that deaf children have a slow intellectual development. Not knowing any language well, deaf children can be "trapped in the non-symbolic world of all other non-human animals?" and live in "a partial, ragged, fragmented, and gapped skeleton of a world?"[119] The fact is that deaf children are often backward in grasping symbols and may have difficulty even during adolescence with ordinary abstract concepts—*positive* and *negative* are cited as instances. "The concept-world of deaf students is global, restricted, and often presented in polar types. It lacks fine, precise pictures/signs/ideograms with which to partition reality, especially as such realities are experienced in industrialized, urbanized, pluralistic, technological society."[120]

Often, the deaf child discovers the nature of symbolism by merely imitating at first and then by slowly coming to understand that language can symbolize everything.[121] The prolonged *Ahh!* of the revelation that an image can be a symbol is an enormous reward to the teacher who makes the revelation possible. Such a breakthrough, a teacher says, makes "the hair stand up on your neck."[122] In her famous account, the blind and deaf Helen Keller recalls how as a child she would stand between two persons who were talking, would touch their lips, and would then move her own lips and gesticulate frantically but uselessly. When she was nearing seven years of age, on the most important day of her life, in her estimate, she managed to realize that the word *w-a-t-e-r* spelled out in her hand "meant the wonderful cool something that was flowing over my hand. That living word awakened my soul, gave it light, hope, joy, set it free!" She dropped the mug in her hand and stood as if transfixed. Highly excited, "she learned the name of every object she touched, so that in a few hours she had added thirty new words to her vocabulary." Within two weeks, a wild creature was changed into a gentle child.[123]

Recalling the lessons she gave a deaf, prelingual man of twenty-seven, a teacher writes that when he came to grasp the meaning of numbers, he underwent an intellectual explosion. Another climax came after thousands of repetitions of sign-words, especially the sign for *cat*. Suddenly! the man knows—the sign now carries a meaning. The teacher remembers, as if in the present, how the man, his face opening with excitement, slowly and then hungrily sucks in everything, the door, the bulletin board, the chairs, the students, as if he has never seen them before. "He has entered the universe of humanity, he has discovered the communion of minds. He now knows that he and a cat and the table have names."[124]

❧❀❧

Most deaf children are born to families that hear, so they usually learn to speak, read, and sign not at home but in special classes and schools. These children learn to communicate by means of lip reading (a quite difficult skill) and speech (often not very intelligible), by finger spelling, by gestural translation of the ordinary spoken language, and by an independent gestural language such as the American Sign Language. These means can be combined—finger spelling is used to clarify something, for instance a name, for which the gestural language is insufficient. (The finger spelling of names resembles the way in which Chinese and Japanese write a character in the air to distinguish it from a homonym.) It often happens, not for linguistic reasons alone, that the conversations of the deaf in their own, hearing families are limited and that they feel freer and happier with the other deaf.[125] It has been established that when the deaf talk with the deaf, sign language is their most nuanced and efficient means.

The American Sign Language is one of a group of true though gestural languages. As such, it has its individual character, resembling now one natural language and now another. The forms of its signs often bear some resemblance to the forms of the things to which they refer, but analysis has shown that the signs are genuine grammatical units put together into grammatical structures. While the vocabulary of the language is relatively small, it can be enlarged, as in German and Chinese, by combining existing words to make new ones. Unlike all spoken languages (but like Egyptian hieroglyphics and Chinese characters) more than one meaning unit can be presented simultaneously—one by each hand—for example *little/boy.*[126]

To understand the capacity of the American Sign Language, one must grasp not only the number and morphology of its hand gestures, but its more or less standardized use of other parts of the body. Hand signs change their meaning in relation to five points on the face, one point for the neck and one for the trunk. The head moves as part of certain signs; the shoulders and elbows may move alone; the cheeks and mouth sign—for *balloon* the cheeks are puffed out; and the eyes and eyebrows and the mouth are used. There is also, of course, facial expression.[127] As Diderot saw, a whole true language can be gestured rather than spoken; and if a language of gestures has deficiencies in comparison with a spoken one, the gestural language may well have the resources to overcome them.

Because of the difference in syntactic structure between the American Sign Language (Sign for short) and English, Sign fits the reading and writing of English with some awkwardness. But deaf children may either supplement Sign or replace it with an internal code using finger motions like those of finger spelling, or using visual imagery—Helen Keller and her teacher remembered "in their fingers."[128]

Surprising as it may seem, a signed language has advantages over a spoken one. Deaf children of deaf, signing parents learn language in a sequence like that of hearing children—repetitive 'babbling' of significant hand-shapes followed by more complex babbling and then 'babbled' sentence-like structures. But since manual dexterity develops earlier in an infant than control over articulation, signing should have an initial advantage over speaking.[129] It is surely reasonable to suppose that a practiced signer has a more diversified and subtle control over the expression of everything related to space, shape, or motion. Imagine how much more expressively and accurately a signer can describe the gestural aspect of any human encounter, whether an ordinary conversation, an argument, a fight, a parade, or a dance. For Sign is not, as might be supposed, a mere succession of one gestured word after another, but is modulated like speech and music; and because it cuts back and forth between times and distances, it may be experienced like a movie that does the same.[130]

The performance of a poem created by a deaf poet for a deaf audience gives the poem the quality that we associate with dancing, except that the motions are those of a dance made of exact word meanings. Recalling one such poem, an 'auditor', which is to say, a spectator, writes, "The lingering feeling one has long after watching the poem performed is the arrangement of sensation: the harmony and softness in the lines, the chaotic, dissonant elements, and their contrast with the harmonious conclusion."[131]

Surprisingly, there has been what is described as a successful translation into Sign of Lewis Carroll's *Jabberwocky*. The art of the translation is said to lie in the way the poet, Eric Malzkuhn, "mirrors Carroll's word creations with equally fantastic sign creations. Just as Carroll formed words from parts of other words—'slithy', for example, from 'slimy' and 'lithe', Malzkuhn recombined parts of ordinary signs." For the sequence *gyre and gimble*, the poet used "part of a sign for flat surface, but combined with odd movement, suggesting an irregular and spooky wave." The poet says he translated *Jabberwocky* in accord with the way it felt; but he was clearly making use of the word-forming system or morphology of the signed language in order to create new words.[132]

Such exceptional accomplishments show what is possible in a signed performance before an audience able to appreciate its subtleties. Yet accomplishments like these do not lessen the distrust that many of the deaf have for those who hear, whose superiority they both feel and deny. Reacting like reluctant self-disclosers of other kinds, they sometimes refuse hearing people information about themselves because the knowledge might increase the hearing person's natural power over them.[133]

What can the deaf make of the sounds they never hear? Their interest in sound is not a matter of curiosity alone: If only out of a concern for their social life, they are obliged to learn how to control sounds that hearing people find unpleasant, to modulate their voices, and to laugh like 'normal' people.[134] "The trick for Deaf people [*Deaf* meaning *the deaf who live in a signing culture*] is to figure out the complicated meanings attached to various sounds. Deaf people develop good theories about these sounds, but at other times the meanings of sound are much too elusive."[135]

What expedients can the deaf use to learn about sound? They can gain direct clues to loudness, especially of the low frequencies, from the vibration of the sounds, so that the deaf learn in practice how sound resonates and carries.[136] A profoundly deaf person may perceive (though never hear) a piano chord by placing her hand on the piano, or may recognize a highly amplified voice. From the standpoint of hearing persons, this sensitivity to vibration may become extraordinarily acute.[137]

The Blind Can Learn to Restrict the Ineffability of Visual Experience

Different as the blind are from the deaf, they, too, start life with a lack that affects their language and thought.[138] A careful observer has noted how relatively little a blind infant of five months old reaches out. Some blind babies have 'blind hands', used to bring things to the mouth, not to explore objects or stretch out toward the world. A blind baby may therefore fail to create a firm psychological bridge between its body and the external world and live for a long time "in a world of magic, where people and things manifest themselves by emerging from a void and returning to a void."[139]

Because blind children have no visual stimulation, it has been concluded that their language must be fragmented and distorted. Perhaps the blind child's early synesthesia makes things easier than they might otherwise have been—as might be guessed, blindness promotes synesthesia.[140] For the more fortunate or able blind child, the delay or confusion in which language may begin does not hinder the course of its growth. The reason is that the child's life gives it clues that make up for enough of the missing visual information. The structure itself of the language helps to make a more subtle understanding of the language possible: language helps itself to grow.[141]

The blind learn to use what sensory clues they have with an attentiveness that astonishes others. Helen Keller could recall particular persons by the grasp of their fingers and the characteristic tightening of their handshakes.[142] Diderot says he knows a certain blind man of Puiseaux who judges the closeness of a fire by the intensity of its heat,

> the fullness of a vessel by the sound of the liquid he pours into it, and the nearness of bodies by the movements of the air against his face. He is so sensitive to the least changes in atmosphere that he can tell a street from a dead end. He has a marvelous ability for judging the weights of solid bodies and the capacity of vessels . . . He can also judge duration of time much more accurately than we, by the succession of his actions and thoughts.[143]

John Hull, who became blind relatively late in life learned to use the sound of a voice to reveal the speaker. In his words:

> With the people I know very well, I find that all of the emotion which would normally be expressed in the face is there in the voice: the tiredness, the anxiety, the suppressed excitement and so on. My impressions based on the voice seem to be just as accurate as those of sighted people.[144]

Granted, then, that a blind person can learn a great deal for which we think vision essential, is there anything in language or understanding that the blind person necessarily misses? What of all the phenomena and words that depend directly on light? What does a blind person make of the distinction between *to look* and *to see*, or of color names, or of such verbs as *to notice* and *to dazzle*?

Let me begin my answer by quoting what Diderot reported of the mathematician Nicholas Saunderson, who lost his sight before he was a year old:

> Saunderson professed mathematics at the University of Cambridge with astonishing success. He gave lessons in optics; he lectured on the nature of light and of colors; he explained the theory of vision; he dealt with the effects of lenses, of the phenomena of the rainbow, and of many other things relative to sight and its organ.[145]

Although he was said to see with his skin, Saunderson had no alternative but to grasp light as a scientist and learn and teach optics by means of mathematical abstractions. Yet such abstractions are not all that a blind person can draw on; our direct experience of light is colored by many associations. *Red* is associated with *red-hot, fiery red*, and *blood red*; and we redden with shame and anger. We say *white as snow, white as chalk*, and *white as milk*; and we associate whiteness with purity and cleanliness, and much else. And to be colorless means to us to be faded, pallid, dull, and much else.

Although the blind person lacks the basic sensations that unite a certain tangle of associations with a particular color and with colors in general, he learns each of the associations and intuits or codes its unity and connection with color in general. In one sense, this unity he creates is quite without color; in another, it is practically the color itself, maybe closer to the seeing man's experience of color than the scientist's of a particle he knows only by means of the combination of elaborate theories and elaborate instruments.

The result is that a blind child of six can use visual words like *see* and *look* in ways normal to children of her age. Thinking of a direction in which she is facing, a particular blind girl of six says "I am looking out the window." She holds up a bag of beads and says, "Look what I have!" She can understand that her mother looks, in the sense of explores visually, and listens, in the sense of trying actively to hear—and understand this even though she herself cannot see, that is, cannot apprehend anything by sight. If she wants to know if you are seeing something, she asks *See?* and not *Look?* because she distinguishes between the passivity of seeing and the activity of looking; and for the same reason, she uses the imperative *Look!* rather than *See!*[146]

Asked to define and distinguish these two terms, a blind adult says that to see is "to use your eyes to perceive something to get an image of it to know it's there. You look with your eyes, and how you see is how you interpret it." Continuing to define visual words, he says that to notice is "to see something that comes into your view. But not only to see but to perceive it and understand it. You could sit on this rocking chair and not notice the color of it at all. Might have to be looking at something specifically to notice it." Challenged to define the word *dazzle*, the blind man says that it means "to brighten, to make it so bright that you can't see for a second, something sudden . . . like turning on a bright light in a dark room. But also isn't it more like shimmering glowing? Like you think of it with jewels."[147]

Blind children of twelve learn from hearing to distinguish the names of the warm from the cold colors. The little girl mentioned above learned ten different color names, which, like other quite young children, she used freely and incorrectly. At about the age of four, an age when children can match color words with colors, she understood her blindness well enough to ask for help in answering color questions.[148] (I insert the parenthetical observation that Ved Mehta, the blind Indian writer, is able to get along so well by himself that the woman he loved thought he could feel the difference between red and blue. At first Mehta lied and said, "Sometimes," but then, throwing himself on her compassion, he told the truth and said "There's no way I can tell colors."[149])

Despite what she could not know, the girl, to whom I return, learned what kinds of things had what characteristic colors or had no color at all. She knew that dogs are sometimes gold or brown but never blue. And she came to know that abstractions could be thought about only "in your head," and that color was irrelevant to the nature of abstractions. [150]

I think that my point has been made in enough detail, and so I refrain (reluctantly) from quoting the astonishingly accurate characterizations made by persons doubly disabled, both blind and deaf, of such visual terms as *stare*, *dazzle*, and *glare*.[151] My general point, which I have been making throughout this chapter on psychology, is that ineffability appears in many experiences and has many forms and modalities, and that it keeps varying, with the result that much that at one time or in one way appears opaque to words, at another time or in another way appears translucent and even quite transparent.

As the Deaf and Blind Show, Unshareable Experience Is Both Socially Isolating and Ineffable

The example of the deaf and the blind teaches us to what an extent the abilities of human beings can neutralize a gross void in their experience, and to what an extent they can learn and put into words what seems completely beyond them. It is true that the void we have been thinking of, the absence of the sensory modality of sight or hearing, cannot simply be filled, and that the void is bridged, as far as possible, by the fallible means of associations and abstractions. Yet the bridge is to some extent also sensory because it is also created by the sharpening of the remaining senses to a point—of vibratory 'hearing' or of facial 'vision'—hardly possible to those who hear and see.[152] There are other, to us still mysterious, abilities to perceive vaguely, without the usual sensory awareness and sometimes without even the sensory apparatus we consider essential. One example is 'blindtouch', the ability to locate a touch on one's skin although one is unaware of being touched. Another example is 'blindsight', the better-than-average guessing of the presence of something that brain injury prevents one from seeing in the normal sense.[153]

Yet the blind and the deaf are jealous of the others. As a perceptive blind man says, "Blindness is a little world, authentic and integrated of itself, and yet surrounded by and held within a greater world. How shall the little understand the big without jealousy, and how shall the big understand the little without pity?"[154] For although the blind and the deaf can overcome so much of their lack, if they have never seen or heard, they find us, the seeing and hearing, to be in some way beyond their understanding, just as we find that they are beyond ours—to which I add that the blind as a group and the deaf as a group are also to a degree unknowable to one another; and that persons who are both blind and deaf, though fortunately few in number, are also to a degree unknowable to those who suffer from blindness or deafness alone. For that matter, the South African poet and novelist David Wright, who became deaf at the age of seven, says that he is unable to imagine the condition of those who were born deaf.[155] Each group is isolated from the others by its lack, is both isolated from and joined with them by its sharpened use of its remaining perceptual abilities, and is joined with them by its common humanity and its ability to understand (or almost understand) and explain (or almost explain) what it is that isolates and what it is that joins it.

I wonder to what extent the relation of the deaf and the blind to the world they perceive with sharpened senses but without, in deafness, ever exactly hearing it or, in blindness, ever exactly seeing it, resembles the relation of philosophers and theologians to the metaphysical reality they believe they perceive vaguely and try to perceive better by sharpening their sensitivities, although disbarred, most of them believe, from ever perceiving it exactly.

Chapter 2

The Exaltation of Words

A small fantasy to set us on our now philosophical and religious way: Suppose that we were as technologically advanced as we are pictured in science fiction, and that we wanted to build something that would demonstrate the workings of all known kinds of communication—an all-communicator. In a similar exercise, meant to demonstrate the sensory origin of human speech and consciousness, Condillac imagined a marble statue constructed inside like a human being, with senses that were opened up for use one after another. In the exercise I propose, we imagine not a statue but a superlative computer that inhabits and informs a superlative humanoid robot.

Even before we endow our robot with any power of expression, we know that it cannot be static either in relation to itself or its surroundings. I am referring to its nature as a physical object, construed by physics to be an enormous multitude of particles mutually attracted and repulsed by means of the subparticles they exchange. Of course, our imagination falls short of representing this quantal face of the world; but when we represent it as we can, in the abstractions of science, it turns out to be much stranger than even Alice's looking-glass world, because it is ruled not by inversion-minded queens but by an extraordinarily complex, dematerialized pushing and pulling, as if Plotinus's universe of qualitative tensions had become an even less imaginable one of exactly quantifiable, probabilified, paradoxical, tension-like existences, all of them in immediate local and nonlocal communication. No quantum is a particle unto itself.

Having realized the physical contiguity of our robot with the universe, we give the robot the first of its overt powers of communication, which is to change posture as living creatures do in order to convey a message. And so the robot is empowered to imitate schematically or merely symbolize *every* actual communicative posture: the arched back of a frightened cat, the penguin's crouch against a rival for territory, the courting display of a spider, the dragonfly's courtship flight, the dance of the honeybee returned from foraging, the chimpanzee's or human's hand raised in anger or stretched out in greeting or consolation.

This is only the beginning, for the robot is flexible enough to make a schematic imitation of all kinds of communicative touching, by mouth, nose, arms, or skin. It is an everyway toucher. Furthermore, it can release or symbolize the release of every kind of communicative odor, whether that of a lion marking its territory, of an ant marking its path with chemical data, of a moth attracting a mate, or of a snake leaving a trail. And it can make communicative electrical displays like those of electric fish.

As a soundmaking or symbolizing electronic device, the robot we are imagining is also able to repeat or represent all signal-sounds: the sounds humans can and cannot hear made by whales, elephants, and bats; and the sounds that insects, spiders, crustaceans, and fish make by tapping, bending, clicking, rasping, or scraping. It can also imitate or otherwise represent the drumming of birds on trees, of rabbits on the ground, and of gorillas on their chests; and all the kinds of squeaking, barking, howling, roaring, screaming, and calling, and lastly—for human beings the most pleasant of sounds—all the kinds of singing, mostly those of birds and humans.

In imitating, schematizing, or symbolizing all these kinds of communication, our robot would recreate for us the enormously varied communicative environments in which we and other living things are found. For the living world reverberates with signals: it shapes itself, touches itself, releases electrical impulses and smells, and postures, dances, buzzes, roars, and sings, to such an extent that no living thing can be quite isolated. Everything alive on our planet communicates directly or indirectly with everything else alive and binds the living world into a whole beyond detailed comprehension. So by the force of our imagination, our robot has become a set of simulacra of the world of living things as an enormous complex of signals that, like this world itself, forms a coherent-'chaotic' whole.

If we wanted to inform the intelligent beings of another planet about the communication of living things on earth, it would be enough to present them with the robot, in which they would find it all miraculously condensed. But we should also want the robot to convey our own especially human kind of communication, the kind that is the most successful in separating itself from its immediate environment and that transmits messages in extraordinarily flexible translations and abstractions. I mean, of course, human speech and the writing that records, simplifies, and complicates it.

I hope that we are able to grant our robot a sufficient memory because, to be as informative as possible, it not only has to record or simulate all human languages throughout their history, but also, for each language, the way it develops from human childhood to senescence.

Childhood to senescence. The words remind us that it is time to abandon the incredible robot and think of the quite real but equally incredible child. I use the word *incredible* not only to characterize the verbal abilities of a child as compared with every other living thing, but also to mark our difficulty in understanding the child's accomplishment. The painstaking recording and analysis of the early speech of children has not given us much insight into the functions of the brain that children need in order to learn language and other forms of symbolization.[1]

It is remarkable to see little children search the world with their pointing fingers and endlessly repeated *what?* and *who?*. This children's search is made possible by the discovery, maybe the greatest in their lives, that everything has a name.[2] Once the discovery is made, every child tries tirelessly to compile its own dictionary with which to communicate its interests and desires.

Apart from names, the two most useful words children learn are *yes* and *no* (and their equivalents), which make self-assertion much easier and mark each child out more definitely as a particular being. Children also learn to think and to define themselves by talking to themselves, at first aloud and then inwardly. Their egocentric or inward speech, which they seem to begin by conversing with themselves in the same way as with others, serves to designate them as separate persons. By using it, each of them is doubled and learns to conduct conversations in which, both a speaker and a listener, it responds to itself.

Altogether, children learn to regard and refer to themselves as detached beings; to refer to absent persons and things; to coordinate objects, actions, and ideas; and to become generally more objective creatures. As such, they are able to see themselves with the borrowed eyes of others and remember and anticipate with greater detachment. By then in their lives they can remember and refer to a whole world of things that they can break, play with, and reassemble in verbal, symbolic form. The words in which they name and play with the world connect them with the community for which the language spoken is the currency of self-expression and social solidarity.[3]

I have been speaking only of words, but children also grow familiar with other forms of symbolization. They learn to draw and transform the marks they so willingly make on paper into fixed shapes, and the shapes into recognizable though symbolically simplified persons and objects; and they learn to manipulate and make shapes having three dimensions. They learn numbers and the rules by which they are used; learn pictures, diagrams, and maps; learn, by listening and singing, the relationships between musical sounds; and learn to read and write. Sometimes, too, they learn to play a musical instrument and to read music. And they learn to refer to all of these other symbolic forms in the encompassing language, that of words.

The move I want to make from the individual child to all mankind is not difficult: Just as the greatest discovery in the child's life is the realization that every object has a name, so the greatest invention in the life of mankind is the ability to give names, or, more broadly, to use language. In the absence of the invention, how could mankind have become truly human? Think of the enormous new power that language confers. Once it has been invented, records can be kept; traditions can become richer and more exact; and laws can be promulgated and directions and commands given, not only for people close at hand, but also for those far away in space and time. Given language, government can be set up on a large scale; history can be consciously invented and studied; every form of literature can be composed; education has a medium that is economical, exact, and flexible; and thought can become disengaged from the immediate situations that arouses it. Writing serves to magnify all these possibilities and powers. From this generalization, India must be excepted in part, for it shows how detailed and extensive a tradition can grow in the absence of writing and how the holiness of language is confined to its spoken form. In principle, the expression of Indian religiousness has been by means of voice alone, so that traditional India has had nothing that can literally be called a scripture.[4]

A Brief Recapitulation and Prospect

Now that homage has been paid to the importance of language, we are ready to go on to ineffability in philosophy and religion. The preliminary discussion on the psychological reasons for ineffability will be drawn on mainly in the final chapters of the book. The present chapter, on the exaltation of language, makes the following points:

1. Every culture appears to have recognized and even exalted the power of words. Such exaltation is exemplified here by the great Mesopotamian epic of creation, as well as by views held in ancient Egypt, Israel, Greece, and China.

2. Belief in the formative power of the word has been widespread among the so-called primitive or tribal cultures and has been a

basis for their ritual practice. The examples given here are the tribe of the Dogon, in Africa; a number of South American tribes; and, lastly, the Navajo, whose doctrine has an astonishingly philosophical cast.

3. The power of the word has been exalted in the most complex metaphysical detail in India, where Speech was early celebrated as an omnipotent goddess, and Syllable, Name, and Formulation were granted cosmic roles.

4. In India, certain verbal formulas, mantras, became the basis of a metaphysics in which reality was identified with the creative power out of which audible speech emerges. A Kabbalistic parallel to such metaphysics is described.

5. In keeping with such metaphysics, Indian grammarian-philosophers created a unique system in which 'words' and the ineffable Word from which they issued were taken to be reality as such. This philosophy of grammar, whose chief exponent was the fifth-century Bhartrihari, is of much more than antiquarian interest because it develops the view that reality as such is constructed of meanings.

6. This Indian philosophy of grammar has partial Eastern and Western analogues, the Western ones ranging from the mysticism of Jakob Böhme to the 'criticism' of Immanuel Kant and the contemporary hermeneutical philosophy of Hans-Georg Gadamer, who builds on the idea that it is our language in which the world presents itself.

The Word Is Empowered in Ancient Mesopotamia

We discover that the word has been exalted everywhere. Every culture of which we know (more modestly, of which the writer knows) has recognized the power of the word, whether that of the ruler, of God or the gods, or of the inspired prophet, legislator, or poet. Conceived as a power in itself, the word has been assumed to precede God or the gods and, like scientific laws, to explain the universe and to sustain or comprise it metaphysically.

The power of the word is exhibited in the mythology of the earliest civilizations, whose cuneiform or hieroglyphic texts preserve human thought as it was when writing was still a specialized, numinous art. Take, for example, the great Mesopotamian epic of creation. Names, spells, and commands are so powerful in the epic that its creators, whoever they were, must really have thought that it was only with the help of potent words that the world could have been set into order.[5]

Rather than reduce the epic to a brief abstraction, I will reflect
something of its narrative Mesopotamian form. I see no reason why such
a myth should be treated with less attention than a more overtly philosophical belief. Why always rob beliefs of the color by which they are
known to those who hold them?

According to the epic, when the world was nothing but a watery
chaos, when neither heaven nor earth had yet been named, when no
gods had yet appeared, no names had yet been pronounced, and no
destinies had yet been decreed, two gods were born of the mingling of
the fresh waters and the salt waters—the fresh waters being the primal
father-god, and the salt waters, the primal mother-goddess. When the
two gods came into being and their names were pronounced, the creation of the ordered world began. More gods were born; and when these
new gods would meet, they were noisy and annoying to their elders. The
primal mother remained indulgent, but the primal father, unable to rest
by day or sleep by night, threatened to disperse the new gods and
abolish their ways. The primal mother was furious at this threat, but the
father-god refused to relent.

Told of their danger, the younger generation of gods consulted the
ingenious Ea, who recited the words of a pure, superb spell that drenched
the father-god with sleep; and then Ea took the father's crown and radi-
ant mantle, killed him, and established his house above him. Since then
the sweet waters have remained underground, subdued.

Ea and his wife now gave birth to Marduk, a hero so perfect that
"his godhead was doubled" by four enormous ears and four all-piercing
eyes, limbs fashioned with an incomprehensible ingenuity, and lips that
blazed fire. This formidable child, given the four winds to play with,
made a flood wave that stirred up the ocean, the primal mother, who
heaved restlessly and endlessly. Unable to rest, the gods close to her—
those who could not put up with the new ways—persuaded her that
even though she had not avenged the death of her lover, the god of the
sweet waters, her belly was being stirred up on purpose and they all
were being maliciously prevented from sleeping; and so they urged her,
for her sake and for theirs, to go to war. The mother-goddess agreed, and
to ready herself for the coming god war, she gave birth to giant, sharp-
toothed snakes whose bodies were cloaked with fearful rays and filled
with venom instead of blood. Continuing with her creation of a terrible
host, she gave orders "so powerful they could not be disobeyed."[6] Then
she cast a spell that made her new lover Kingu supreme in the gods'
assembly, set him on a throne, and gave him the Tablet of Decrees that
embodies the supreme powers of the universe, saying, "Your utterance
shall never be altered! Your word shall be law!"[7]

I pause with the story for a moment in order to explain what is meant here by *decree*, for which *destiny* is often preferred. The word translates the Akkadian *simtu*, which refers to something—an attribute, power, property, or heritage—that is assigned by someone to someone else. A *simtu* acts as a 'determinant' of what a person or thing has or is. When *simtu* refers to the good and bad fortune allotted a person— fortune including the nature and sequence of the events in his life—it is equivalent to *destiny* or *fate* and is often so translated. A scholar suggests that it amalgamates the meanings of the Greek concepts of *moira* (fate) and *physis* (origin, nature, natural form).[8]

To continue with the story, messengers were sent to the mother-goddess to get her to change her mind, but they failed. The gods she planned to attack sat in silent, tight-lipped consternation until one of them suggested asking Marduk to champion them. Marduk agreed, but on condition that the council of gods transfer their power to him so that his utterance, not theirs, would fix fate and the decree of his lips be irrevocable.[9]

The threatened gods met in assembly and were told of the impending war. Filling themselves with grain, good wine, and sweet beer, their mood changed and, now carefree and merry, they agreed to Marduk's terms. They proclaimed that his destiny was without equal and his word supreme, that they thereby gave him "sovereignty over all of the whole universe." But needing proof that he had actually come into possession of this power, they set up a constellation in their midst and said to him, "Speak and let the constellation vanish! Speak to it again and let the constellation reappear!" Marduk spoke "and at his word the constellation vanished. He spoke to it again and the constellation was recreated." Seeing the power of his utterance, the gods rejoiced and proclaimed him king.[10]

A terrifying battle ensued. Toward its end, Marduk wrested the Tablet of Decrees from the enemy general, clasped it to his breast and, turning back to the mother-goddess, he killed her. Then he split her monstrous body, putting half of it up to roof the sky, drew a bolt across the sky, set a guard to hold it, and arranged the goddess's waters to make it impossible for them to escape.[11] And then—such is the happy end-ing—he ordered the world into a true cosmos: He set up constellations; divided the year; arranged wind, rain, and clouds from the spittle of the dead mother-goddess; opened the Tigris and Euphrates rivers from her eyes; and so on. He also created mankind, from the enemy general's blood, to serve the gods and release them from menial work, for they were meant to be the administrators of heaven and earth and not builders or providers of sustenance. The cosmos was now as it should be and is.

Another great threat to order is recalled in the Sumerian myth that tells how the metaphysical norms of the universe were stolen from one god and city and transferred to another, whose preeminence they ensured. Norm here is the translation of the Sumerian term *me*, other senses of which are *name, law, dynamic force, modus operandi, nature, essence, standard, regulation,* and *duty*. The term reminds me of the Chinese *li* in one of its many uses—even of *tao* in a restrictive sense—and of the Indian *dharma*. A *me* sets the nature of an entity or phenomenon and keeps it operating stably. It is a principle of cosmic and social categorization, rather randomly chosen by our standards and rather more like a thing's essence than the decree by which the thing is established (I find it hard to distinguish between the Mesopotamian notions of *decree* and *norm*). The holy *mes* of the myth are, it seems, the attributes of civilization, derived from the gods.[12]

In the myth, the keeper of the norms is Enki, the god of intellectual resourcefulness (wisdom and cunning combined), whose request to his mother resulted in the parthenogenetic birth of man.[13] The lord of wisdom and guardian of all the norms, the great, pure, *me's*, it is he who organized the world by setting its waters in their place, instituting agriculture, building stalls and sheepfolds, fixing boundaries, establishing the occupations of the city-states, and appointing the gods who ruled over the places and functions he had established.[14]

The young, beautiful, willful Inanna, patroness of harlots and alehouses, goddess of rain, war, and the morning and evening star was dissatisfied with the powers that Enki had given her.[15] The myth tells us that on a fateful visit to Enki, the two drank a great deal of beer together, until Enki, with inebriated generosity, offered Inanna the norms that established high priesthood, godship, and kingship. Inanna took all three. Enki then offered her the ability to enter and leave the underworld, the various arts of lovemaking, the power of the penis, the art of prostitution (ordinary and cultic separately), and many others.

The giving and taking went on until Inanna had all ninety-four norms, which she acknowledged one by one. The powers included those necessary for her cult; and heroism, power, dissimulation, straightforwardness, kindness, and fear; and the various crafts and occupations. The norms particularly relevant to language were: truth, deceit, the art of forthright speech, the art of slanderous speech, the art of ornamental speech, the art of song, the art of lamentation, the perceptive ear, the power of attention, the giving of heart-soothing judgments, and the making of decisions. It is hard to know what to make of this list of norms; but it seems that they were formulas, structures of order, perhaps analogous to Plato's Ideas or to our natural laws, except that they could be applied, like human decrees, by literal commands.

In the myth, Inanna stowed the norms into the Boat of Heaven and made off. When Enki sobered up and realized that he had given away all his norms, he tried six times, once with the help of fifty *lahama* sea monsters, to recover them, but failed each time. After the Boat of Heaven docked at Innana's city Uruk, the norms were unloaded and presented to its inhabitants, whose pride was great and whose profit was thereafter assured.

The Word Is Empowered in Ancient Egypt, Israel, Greece, and China

In Egypt, too, it was believed that the name of a thing or person was its equivalent. To know a person's name—his true, secret name—was to gain power over him. The gods had a different name for each different power or function. Properly chanted formulas were believed to create order and dissipate it, and kill and restore to life. In the so-called Theology of Memphis, probably of the third millennium B.C., the god Ptah conceived the elements of the world in his mind—his heart as the Egyptians called it—and brought them into being by his spoken command.[16]

Echoes of the word conceived as a cosmic power are found in the Bible, of course. Creation is described there as proceeding by means of God's repeated commands and by his naming of Day, Night, Heaven, and Earth. In Genesis it is man who gives each living creature its name, in this way, we may suppose, formalizing man's dominion over the creatures the nature and status of which he fixes by naming them. The godly act of naming followed by the human act can be taken to imply that names embody the reality attributable to language.[17]

Elsewhere in the Bible there are passages such as those in which God's word is said to be like fire and like a hammer that breaks the rock into pieces, or said to go forth from God's mouth and accomplish that which he purposes.[18]

It should be no surprise to find that there were similar views in Greece, the neighbor to both Mesopotamia and Egypt. The Athenian philosopher Socrates became convinced that it was impossible to act in a consistently ethical way without understanding the true formulaic definitions of ethical principles. And then, we know, his pupil Plato hypostatized such definitions and came to believe that they were the Ideas, the indwelling principles, realities, or essences of everything, souls excepted, that had true existence.

In the *Cratylus*, Plato plays with the Mesopotamian and Egyptian (and Amerindian, Chinese, and Indian) notion that every object has a name that by nature represents it. Speaking in the guise of Socrates, Plato raises the possibility that a name can be a true vocal imitation of the nature of the named object, the elements of the sound of the one corresponding with the elements of the reality of the other. Cratylus goes so far as to declare that "he who knows names knows also the things which are expressed by them" (*Cratylus*, 435). But a difficulty arises. Plato declares that names lose their usefulness if wrongly assigned, so that we must be able to distinguish beforehand between the essences to which the names are applied. To make the distinction, says Plato, we have to learn how to know essences directly "through themselves and each other," a problem that he sets aside in this dialogue as too difficult.[19]

Both Hebraic and Greek conceptions were united in the famous New Testament text that says "In the beginning was the Word, and the Word was with God, and the Word was God. He was in the beginning with God; all things were made through him, and without him was not anything made that was made" (John 1:1–3).

Although we may not be surprised to discover similar attitudes toward the word in neighboring cultures, what are we to say if we find them in a tribal culture in Africa or America? We may argue that the African tribal culture was influenced by the Egyptian or even by the anthropologists who reported its views, and that the Native Americans are our contemporaries and necessarily influenced by the culture that surrounds them. What then are we to say if we discover similar attitudes, highly developed, in ancient India? Even if we were to believe that all the similar attitudes—so different in detail and cultural context—were diffused from the same source, the thoroughness with which they were developed in individual ways is evidence enough that it is natural to human beings to recognize, celebrate, embroider on, and make mythology and theology out of the power of words. Because our ability to understand and manipulate the world rests largely, as the myths imply, on our ability use words, the myths we retell here are symbolically true, and the conviction of the Mesopotamians, Egyptians, and others that the world cannot be understood in the absence of verbal symbolism is, I should say, literally true.

The Chinese, too, had a deeply instilled reverence for words, especially of their old texts. Their reverence extended to the unchanging characters in which the texts were written; to the calligraphy and the literary style in which, they thought, a person bared his character; and to the breath of cosmic vitality that entered into a particular writer's literary rhythm or calligraphic style. All these transmitted the Way or Tao, the disposition, ability, and character that, in human life, unified both family and empire.

Except for the playful or mystical Taoists and the nirvana-oriented Buddhists, the Chinese assigned a unique social and administrative role to language. To the Confucians in particular, language had to be used with moral precision. This meant that semantic duplicity, which confused right with wrong, must be avoided and acts must be called by their right names. It also meant that persons should be called by their proper ranks and relationships, so that all social roles would be played in accord with their true, normative model: a son would act the son's part, a father the father's, a minister the minister's, a ruler the ruler's, and so on, the players exhibiting their human worth by the quality with which they interpreted their individual roles and fitted into the predetermined social hierarchy. By this conception of ethics, simultaneously linguistic, ethical, and metaphysical, the inflections of language should always be those proper to time, place, person, and the unchanging intuitive sense of humanity. This intuitive sense rests on and gives the ability to "rectify names."[20]

To give a sense of the importance the Chinese attributed to the proper use of language, I cannot do better than quote from a famous passage attributed to Confucius and taken to be imbued with his authority:

> If names are not correct, language is not in accordance with the truth of things. If language is not in accordance with the truth of things, affairs cannot be carried on to success. When affairs cannot be carried on to success, proprieties and music will not flourish. When proprieties and music do not flourish, punishments will not be awarded. When punishments are not properly awarded, the people do not know how to move hand or foot. Therefore a superior man considers it necessary that the names he uses may be spoken appropriately, and that what he speaks may also be carried out appropriately. What the superior man requires is just that in his words there may be nothing incorrect (*Analects* 13.3.5–7).[21]

Believing as they did in uniform linguistic standards, Confucians denounced the Chinese kind of sophists, whose malignantly playful doubts, they were sure, made the social consensus so much the harder to maintain and caused language to be debased in the same way as weights and measures were debased by counterfeiters:

> To split up propositions, and to invent names without the authorization to do so, thereby throwing the correct terminology into confusion, causing the people to have doubts and delusions, and numerous persons to engage in disputations and lawsuits, must be regarded as a major crime. Its guilt should be treated as equivalent to counterfeiting the tallies used for orders and contracts, or measures or length and capacity.[22]

In Chinese eyes, language used correctly had something of the force of a ritual properly carried out.[23] Like ritual, correct language could embody the truth of things because the cosmos, language, and moral action echoed and influenced one another. It was therefore contrary to nature itself to separate names from their proper referents. As the Confucian philosopher Tung Chung-shu (ca. 179–ca. 104 B.C.) explained by way of quasi history (its manner not unlike that of eighteenth-century Europe):

> The ancient sages emitted ejaculations which mimicked (the sounds of) Heaven and Earth, and which were called appellations. When issuing orders, they uttered sounds which were called names. Thus names may be described as sounds uttered to give orders, while appellations may be described as ejaculations uttered in mimicry . . . Names and appellations are variously pronounced, but have the same origin in that all consist of sounds and ejaculations uttered to make known the meaning of Heaven. Heaven speaks not, yet it enables men to make evident its meanings. It acts not, yet it enables men to conduct themselves in accordance with the mean. Names, therefore, constitute Heaven's meaning as it has been discovered by the sages, and as such they should be deeply looked into.[24]

In the Chinese scheme of things, therefore, everyone and everything was to be set in its place with the help of well-used names, rightly named acts, and properly exercised functions. In its bureaucratic translation—all China became a theoretically model bureaucracy—this meant that everyone had to act as his proper bureaucratic category demanded. Every category was supposed to have its name, which is to say, its concept or essence. Every departure required its mental and moral integrity to be restored by a process of disambiguation or, in Chinese terms, "rectification of names." If this is not all that the passage or that Confucius himself intended, it fits later traditional China at many times and in many situations.[25]

The Word Is Empowered by Africans, South Americans, and Navajos

Earlier, when Africans were mentioned, I was thinking mainly of the Dogon, who live in the mountains of central Mali. Their system of beliefs has been investigated with admiring care, and a detailed monograph has been written on their view of language. Because I mean to use anthropology a good deal, I feel it necessary to add a warning here, like the one concerning psychology. I have, of course, used only anthropological interpretations that appear to be reliable. But the anthropologists who have made them are difficult for us to check because they deal with cultures about which we know too little. It should not be surprising if some of these anthropologists prove to have remained alien to the cultures on which they report, to have emphasized the views of unrepresentative or over-inventive informants, or to have formalized or crystallized native ideas that are personal or fluid to begin with and to have created an amalgam of native ideas with their own systematic biases. It has become apparent that Marcel Griaule's famous accounts of Dogon philosophy represent such an amalgam, his Dogon informants having elaborated and rationalized their thought in answer to his very persistent attempts to piece together a world-view that he presupposed far more elaborate, consistent, and uniform than it actually was.

However this may be, the anthropologist (of the Griaule school) who writes on Dogon views of language tells about each of her four main informants, mentions various minor ones, and produces actual texts. She reports that the Dogon believe that each individual creates speech within himself. As the Dogon explain, the elements that compose language exist within the body in a diffuse state, especially in the form of water. When a person speaks, the water of thought, which is internal speech, begins to swirl in ways that accord with the nature of the speech (false, calm, angry, or windy), and the water-thought, warmed by the heart, comes out in the form of spoken vapor. The words spoken imply an auditor, a listening ear, in the absence of which no message could even take form.[26]

Put briefly, (I am afraid to repeat in detail what may be misleadingly systematic) the Dogon's metaphysics requires a network of communicative relations the key to which is the power of "the ancient word." It is the key because words are taken to end in the objects and acts that result from them. "The object is the word—speech—because, considered technically, it is a manifestation of the person. The act is the materialization of the word, its final outcome."[27]

In accord with this conception, it was by means of God's literally fecundating word that the world was created. In the world so created, everything, every particle of matter, every blade of grass, every fly is an encoded message directed at human beings and reflecting the language that humans as such already contain. For the Dogon, (no doubt thinking in collaboration with the French anthropologist who reports this) the world is therefore like a book whose message must be decoded; and they are naturally concerned to interpret this "speech of the world" that everything speaks. Parallel to the world, language itself is "a vast field of 'signs' in which are grouped islands of distinctively structured words, attracted to one another, like iron filings by a magnet, by the influence of the principles on which the Dogon vision of the world is established."[28]

To the Dogon, to utter the exact name of a being or object is equivalent to exhibiting it symbolically or, better, "giving it life" by bringing the water of the word to its 'grain'. There is not room here to explain all the consequences of this belief, which are the mythical, social, amorous, and artistic powers ascribed to language. But the belief makes the sage into a personage of the most practical importance, since he is the master of a power, perfected during a long human apprenticeship, that can affect everything. The sage, "he who knows the word," has the power to infuse vitality into the human body, into forged implements, into cultivated crops, and into much else. And so it is by means of its parallelism with the world that language, "the most refined product of human intelligence, constitutes something like a résumé, a synthesis of the principal techniques by which man is able to establish and maintain his rule over nature."[29]

To shift from Africa to the Americas, among the Indians of both South and North America, sounds in general and names in particular can have great metaphysical power—I use the present tense even though much of the testimony relates to the past. In some South American tribes, it is believed that language is rooted in the images that appear in the primordial world. These images are involved in human existence because a person is inherently an image-soul, the essential nature of which is shared by dream, thought, speech, and creativity of every sort. That is why for the Campa tribe the discovery of the meaning of one's spiritual existence makes visible the links between the different levels of reality. Often, the act of creation is believed to be carried out by means of the creator's dream or song, for in the same way as a dream-soul is associated with the faculty of human speech and song, so a thought-image or word-image in the creator's mind is associated with the utterance of creative speech.[30]

In South America, it can be said, a human's essence is a pattern of sound. The pattern is literally visible: One's essence or name is to one's being as one's being is to one's face; and so, viewed rightly by the right person, one's face is visible as the projection of the sonic structure disclosed by one's name. A name is nothing less than a force of existence. In the view of one tribe, the Kari'na,

> a name, like game meat, is a basic form of nourishment, one's first taste of transitive but sustained worldly existence. Unlike the consumable meat the father will bring home to feed the child later in its life, the name becomes constant food for thought because the 'voice', one's name, has the power to call significant beings to it throughout the person's lifetime.[31]

Because every species is constituted by its unique sound, when a father names and thereby imposes a certain species of sound-shape on his child, the father kills the other possibilities for forming his child's personality. For "*saka* (voice) is, at root, a sacred sound that attracts and captures spirits. It is for this reason that it forms the basis of wisdom"—it is, in essence, the deep, unmanifested self. To receive a name, capture a sound, call other modes of being within range, know by name, and give voice to others is to mold one's entire being to the shape of one's sound.[32]

The role played by sound in the process of the world's creation is spelled out a little in the following words:

> The sung texts of creation scenarios frequently consist of no more than "I am [the name of the supernatural being], I am, I am." The very fact that the being makes an audible sound reveals its presence. The very sound of the name in song performs the function of a revelation of the nature of the being. It also calls into being a new disposition of spiritual existence, that of the hearer.[33]

Yet the sounds, the words, that human beings form have their negative functions. Much of human speech may be seen as borrowed from the sounds made by other, sacred beings. Among the Kari'na, it is known that the power of human words can be guarded only as long as the true meaning of the sounds is respected. During speech, the Kar'ina say, the human mouth is like the serpent's mouth, its fangs both wisdom and magic power.[34]

The philosophically most interesting description I know of tribal views of speech is that of the Navajo Indians. By "philosophically interesting" I mean clear, consistent, systematic, and consciously subtle. Before their particular beliefs are described, it should be recalled that North American Indians—like Mesopotamians, Egyptians, Hebrews, Greeks, Chinese, and the South Americans just described—used their songs, which were often spells or prayers, to control the world. But the Americans sought individual inspiration and, in addition to tribal songs, had personal songs that exerted the force of spells or prayers. A man who possessed many songs was thought rich, and a man who recited them exactly was likely to be thought wise.[35]

As for the Navajos, in their account of creation, the first, Holy People became aware of things with the help of symbols, which they organized by the power of thought. They used these symbols in prayer and song to organize the inner forms of things and instruct them where and how to carry out their functions. This process is more understandable when one knows that according to the Navajo

the director and controller of all animation is the mind. All movements, events, and conditions are ultimately controlled by the thought
of one or more beings. Although entities without the capacity to
think have the ability to move, their movements are caused and
controlled by some being who has the power to think. The world
view resulting from these metaphysical presuppositions is an all-
pervasive determinism in which all matter and energy, events and
conditions are ultimately controlled by the thought and will of intelligent or thinking beings.[36]

Believing that the world is thought and sung into existence, the
Navajo finds it easy to go on and believe that the world is classified and
controlled by language because words, like thoughts, have creative power.
In Navajo mythology, "things came into being or happened as people
thought or talked about them."[37] The creative power of the words is their
influence on the inner forms of everything that exists. For earth, sky, sun,
moon, rain, water, lightning, and thunder, each has a form, "an animate
being that lies within." Such "in-lying ones" resemble human beings in
their nature and appearance, and, like humans, are individuals. It was
First Man, First Woman, and others who thought into being the inner
forms of all the important phenomena of nature. These inner forms can
hear and see what goes on in ritual. The inner forms of human beings
are the 'wind souls' thanks to which they have foresight and are able to
speak.[38]

> This world is an arena in which the inner forms of the Holy People
> and the inner forms of the earth surface people interact. This is
> manifested in the movements and interactions of their outer forms.
> Since the movements of outer forms are representative of the thoughts
> and intents of inner forms, these actions and interactions are sym-
> bolic in nature. The world is, therefore, a stage of symbolic action.[39]

In the Navajo view, thought and speech cannot be separated, for
speech is no more than the outer form of thought, which it extends and
reinforces. "This reinforcement reaches its peak after four repetitions,
and therefore a request made four times cannot be easily denied." Ritual
comprises the ways in which speech imposes the form of thought on
whatever needs to be created or restored.[40]

In the Navajo metaphysical order, knowledge always comes first.
The essential reality or inner form of thought—knowledge—is listed as a
primordial element of the universe. And as knowledge is the inner form
of thought, thought is the inner form or reality of speech. Therefore, the
hierarchy of reality is: knowledge, thought, speech, inner forms, and
natural phenomena of all kinds, that is, all processes and beings.[41]

In contrast to Buddhists and others who will be discussed, the Navajo do not assume that language falsifies reality. The idea that it might do so

> goes directly contrary to the Navajo scheme of things. This world, they believe, was transformed from knowledge, organized in thought, patterned in language, and realized in speech (symbolic action). The symbol was not created as a means of representing reality; on the contrary, reality was created or transformed as a manifestation of symbolic form. *In the Navajo view of the world, language is not a mirror of reality; reality is a mirror of language.*[42]

Much of this seems to me astonishingly close to the thought of India we now encounter. It is close not in any literal sense, but in fundamental tendencies. It is interesting that there is also a similar choice of the air (a choice also made by the Chinese) as a principle of both force and understanding. Like the Indians and Chinese, the Navajo believe that air is the fundamental power of motion in the world and, at least like the Indians, that it is the final source of knowledge of every kind. By controlling air, say the Navajo, human beings share in its omnipotence and omniscience; and they control air by speaking, that is, by putting highly refined air into controlled, patterned motion.

> Thus the speech act is the ultimate act of knowledge and power, and by speaking properly and appropriately one can control and compel the behavior and power of the gods. This is the ontological and rational basis of the compulsive power of speech.[43]

Considering the geographical and cultural distance between the Navajo and the inhabitants of ancient India, it is curious to find such a general affinity between their forms of thought, for in India, too, thinking was considered the internal form of speech, which became external when the energy of the breath that constituted it was increased.

Ancient India Empowers the Word

The Vedic hymns and the older Upanishads, which together constitute the most ancient literature of India, are dated respectively (and uncertainly) from the fifteenth to the tenth centuries B.C., and from the eighth to the sixth centuries B.C. We have to keep in mind that this literature does not reflect a single, consistent point of view. Although it came to have scriptural authority and to be studied and memorized, forwards and backwards, with the most jealous care, a religiously or philosophically plausible unity was something that only resourceful theologians or philosophers could confer on it.

Take as an example the relationship between the various deities that appear in the Vedic hymns. A particular deity is often extolled without limit, as if it were in utterly successful competition with every other deity. Considering all the hymns, it might seem that every great deity was greater than every other, a situation that does not fit the common laws of logic anywhere. For this reason it is hard to assess the importance of the praise so fulsomely bestowed on herself by the goddess Speech (or Language, or Holy Utterance [Vac]) when she proclaims that she is first among all those worthy of sacrifice because it is she who accompanies and inspires the greatest gods. In this hymn (*Rigveda* 10.125), Speech, who is both the formulaic speech used in sacrifice and speech as a cosmic principle, reveals that the gods divided her so that she dwells in many places and enters into many forms. "Whom I love," the goddess says, "I make powerful; I make him a carrier of Formulas, a seer, a sage." She says that she comes from within the waters and extends herself through all the worlds; and she adds, climactically, that she blows forth like the wind, taking all creatures to herself, and has grown beyond the sky and beyond this earth, so great has she become.[44] Often she is equivalent to the Holy Utterance or Holy Knowledge called Brahman, which was later to be identified in Hinduism with the inward principle of reality as such.

Another traditionally important hymn (*Rigveda* 10.71) is on the origins of language and on access to the power of language.[45] Therefore *Speech*, as I consistently translate the Sanskrit *Vac*, applies to language in general but also, more restrictively, to the magically powerful language of ritual. In the hymn, we first hear of the invention of language by the most ancient, superhuman seers. The hymn says that, moved by love, they established "the first beginning of Speech" by assigning names and so revealing the "best and purest good" hidden within themselves. Put in our less imaginative style, the seers made their deepest and most precious secret available to others and invented language by associating specific meanings, primarily those embodied in names, with specific sounds. This process is intelligible only if we regard meanings as essences the power of which can be transferred to the sounds assigned to be their names.

The hymn continues, making references that are sometimes only vaguely understandable—my paraphrase is interpretive. We are told of later poet-seers, human beings as compared with those referred to in the beginning. These poet-seers are bound together in a fellowship whose members are expected to show loyalty to one another, but they compete *against* one another as participants, it seems, in sacrificial rituals. The hymn says that when the seers made Speech with their thought, sifting it through a sieve like grain, it became possible for the later poet-seers to recognize their fellowship by the sign of beauty that marked their Speech. Is this an allusion to beauty in the ordinary sense or to the 'beauty' of refrains that were the trademarks of the guild? From our standpoint, there is a curious identity between what we now think of as poetry and as ritual magic. But why should prayers not be improvised or composed anew for each new ritual occasion? Ritual appears to have been a key to everything; and in the hymn we read that it was with its help that the poets followed the traces of language, which they found within their predecessors and, having uncovered language, shared it among many others.

The hymn goes on to distinguish between persons with and without insight. Some persons see and hear but can neither see nor hear Speech. For she, a goddess, reveals herself only to some, just as a loving, well-adorned wife reveals her body to her husband alone. Then the hymn says that a poet who shows himself to be rigid is not encouraged to participate in the contests, because the Speech he has heard has neither fruit nor flower. His rigidity excludes him from the fellowship of inspiration.

In these last verses, we are given to understand that Speech is the collective concern of those whose profession it is to create poetry for ritual, that is, to capture the formulaic intensity of the *brahman* and the power it gives to those who intuit and chant it. According to the hymn, any member who abandons a comrade in knowledge has no share in Speech; and even if he hears, he hears in vain, since he does not know the path of meritorious action. This (as we may interpret it) means that in the same way as Speech depends on knowledge, meritorious (perhaps ritually meritorious) action depends on Speech.

The hymn goes on to say that some poets have unequal flashes of insight; and some are like shallow ponds and some like deep ones, good for bathing in. When the Brahmans' intuitions are shaped in their hearts and they sacrifice together as comrades, the less knowing ones drop behind, while others get ahead because of their power to extol. Those who are unworthy Brahmans use Speech badly without understanding. But all rejoice in their comrade who returns from the contest famous and victorious. He saves them from error (is this ritual error?) and bestows food upon them. It is he who shows himself to be a worthy contender.

We see that the poets-seers of this hymn need the good will of their fellows and that they believe that nothing powerful can be known or chanted to good effect without inspiration. The creative power that shows itself in verbal inspiration is felt to be of the same kind that creates and governs everything else, and the need for inspiration is a theme that repeats itself as often in the hymns as it does in the Romantic poetry of Europe.

We feel the Vedic poet's hunger for inspiration in the words that speak of his miraculous 'thinking' and of the light in his heart that makes him "glitter in verses" and "shine" for the god he is praising. There are, the poet knows, a hundred barriers between his mind and its object, and he must get around them all. The thread he weaves must extend from his heart to the sky. He asks Heat to warm him within, and asks Fire to clarify the poem as it clarifies the soma drink with its flame-filter, for what he learns is secret and must be kept so from the uninitiated. Even if he finds inspiration, the poet must yoke words together, he says, to make a poem; and he polishes and ornaments it like a prized horse. Once the poem is done, it gives the inexhaustible "milk of the sky." Or, in an erotic rather than nourishing image, the poem is a beauty going to her rendezvous. The poem trembles as it searches for its love, the god Indra.[46]

Because the Vedic hymns are sacred and powerful, anything that constitutes them is apt to be thought powerful in its own right. Apart from Speech herself, such powers are Syllable and Brahman (in the sense of Formulation). To the Vedic poet, Syllable is a power because everything spoken or chanted can be reduced to it, because it is the least thing that can be pronounced, and because, significantly, it has a homonym meaning *imperishable*. One finds Syllable, the beginning element, at the cosmic beginning of time. After it is found, it guides us to the whole complex hymn. Syllable is the measure of Speech, which consists of so many Syllables in a particular order; and in its measuring and measured way, Syllable upholds the cosmic order. Formulation, which is sometimes indistinguishable from Speech, is speech formed properly, according to the rules of sacred poetics. By the laws of linguistic cosmology, Formulation can be regarded as the material out of which heaven and earth are formed.[47]

The whole Vedic poem—and, later, the whole Upanishad—is regarded as a representative fraction of the world and shares the power of its wholeness. It is born with the world and is of its substance; it is not only the truth of all bodily existence but the bodily—that is, sonic—existence of the truth. To become effective for a particular purpose, it has to be recited with meticulously correctness, in accord with prescribed ritual.[48]

Given such possibility of gaining such power, the ancient Indians, like modern scientists, attempted to learn what its origin and nature might be and how it might be captured and used. We can briefly follow the beginnings of a relevant attempt in the Upanishads, the hypotheses of which are at once psychophysical and cosmological. One of the more influential hypotheses is that the Self, both in the human and cosmic senses, has three basic constituents, which are Mind, Speech, and Breath. According to this hypothesis, it is the Mind with which one essentially sees, hears, desires, imagines, and so on. And whatever is known is a form of Speech, because Speech, like Mind, is intelligibility. Speech is, to be sure, every kind of sound and culminates in human Speech. Breath, however, is unknown, so everything unknown is a form of the unknowingness that is Breath. Everything that at all exists is classified according to these three great components of reality. For example, the father is equivalent to Mind, the mother to Speech, and the child to Breath—therefore the father thinks, the mother talks, and the child exists. On the cosmic level, Speech is this terrestrial world on which men live; Mind is the atmospheric world; and Breath is the celestial world. The three powers and realms are all alike, all infinite. Whoever worships them as finite or infinite wins, respectively, a finite or an infinite world (*Brihad-aranyaka Upanishad* 1.5.3–13).[49]

The Indians (and Kabbalists) Invent a Cosmos Derived from Speech which Is Itself Derived from an Ineffable Source

The idea of the analysis of formulaic words into elements led to something resembling a mystical chemistry of formulas or mantras.[50] Mantras were and are often still regarded as having great power to harm and help; but what interests us here is the metaphysical reality they embody, for they are presumed to be beyond mundane language and to draw on, penetrate to, or even *be* the sacred or metaphysical source of language. This source, though embodied in words, is inexpressibly above them and—most obviously in Tantrism—densifies them into the unimaginable unity of the source of all.[51]

Significantly, many Vedic mantras are musical chants with musically structured rhythms. It is said that in some cases "the sounds, with their themes and variations, inversions, interpolations, and counterpoint" create a structural parallel with Bach's oratorios.[52] The most sacred of mantras is the syllable *om*, used, for instance, in Vedic ritual at the beginning of a hymn. In one Upanishad it is taken to bring and therefore to be equivalent to success. Since the *o* is a contracted diphthong, *om* is decomposed into *a+u+m* and equated with everything triple, for example: fire, air, and sun; male, female, and neuter; and past, present, and future. A fourth possibility is added when the three letters are considered in relation to the whole word of which they are composed. The word as a whole is then equivalent to the state of transcendence. For example, the three letters are the three states of the self, namely, waking, dreaming, and deep sleep, while the word as a whole is the unitary state that includes and transcends all three.[53]

Such speculation led to complete systems of phonic metaphysics in which the cosmos evolves from pure phonic energy, the inaudible, transcendent level of speech out of which audible speech emerges.[54] In a Kashmiri variant of this metaphysics, the supreme god or reality, Shiva, is identical with language at its supreme level, which is consciousness in its supreme, wholly luminous density. Out of this perfectly dense reality the successively lower, thinner, weaker levels of reality are emitted. The evolutionary series of emissions is described as follows:

> The sounding forth or uttering of reality or emitting or vomiting of reality takes place as part of the agency of the power of Shiva. The process occurs on four levels corresponding to the four levels of speech: the supreme level, the first 'vision' of what is to come, the intermediate stage, and the fully embodied stage of everyday speech. In this way, language, like reality, runs the full gamut from the level of supreme nonmanifestation, where we speak more aptly of a silence that abounds in possibilities, down to the fragmented, divided, and conventional level of everyday expressions.[55]

The idea that a mantra concentrates energy in a form that can be used by those privy to the secret obviously resembles the idea held elsewhere that the recitation of divine names or the like can lead one closer to the divine. In Islam, this is characteristic of the Sufis in particular; and it is akin to the belief held by Moslems and Jews (especially by the Kabbalists) that each letter and name of the sacred text concentrates in itself ineffable meaning and energy.[56] Such faith in a written text and its letters is significantly different from the Indian faith in spoken syllables as recalled by their virtuosos of memory.

The most imposing and systematic Kabbalistic attempt to develop this faith was that of Abraham Abulafia, who lived in Spain during the thirteenth century. To Abulafia, language—the Hebrew language, primarily, chosen by God for its perfection—constituted a universe superior to the natural one. He wrote:

> All languages are included within the language that underlies them all, i.e., the Holy Language, expressed through 22 letters and five ways of pronunciation . . . for there is no speech or writ but this and there are no other letters, for they are holy and this is the sanctified language.[57]

According to Abulafia, in the end of days, when all the differences between languages will end, they will be absorbed into Hebrew, their Mother. The structure of Hebrew is such, he says, that it is far more effective than philosophical study in teaching us the nature of reality, including the laws of nature. The reason is that "the letters are the real forms of all phenomena that exist, for they were created by means of the Divine use of the letters."

Each letter is in itself a divine name, intelligible as such when it has been freed from its ordinary, pedagogically helpful verbal ties. These names reach their full density and efficacy only when they are isolated and recombined creatively; and whoever dissolves the Biblical text into its constituent letters and infuses them with new meanings is transformed into a prophet, one who transcends nature and conquers it. By breaking language into its elementary constituents, he returns to the superlative state of mind in which God revealed His truths; for God's creative consciousness precedes and underlies the intelligibility of words. God's prelinguistic potency can therefore be found in letters, not words or sentences.[58]

Before we turn to more clearly philosophical aspects of Hindu thought, it should be said that most of this thought, like most Western philosophy until recently, was also theological. This is true even though Indian religious thought may accept the truth of the sacred text as such, without reference to any divine promulgator. In any case, the common orthodox position defending the sacredness of the scriptural words was shared by many of the 'schools' of Hindu thought—specifically, the 'schools' of Mimamsa, Vedanta, Samkhya-Yoga, Kashmir Shaivism (a philosophical form of Tantrism), and the School of Grammar, to be taken up soon.

According to the orthodox position, alluded to earlier, language is not a derived, secondary phenomenon at all, but primary and transcendental. With respect to the sacred texts, the sound, the meaning, and the relation between sound and meaning is eternal and (some hold) uncreated, in the same sense as the Greek atomists take atoms and the laws by which they function to be eternal and uncreated. Plato's theory of Ideas is also analogous in this respect. One Indian philosopher of the Mimamsa persuasion says that considering how great the differences are in accent, dialect, and the like, we can explain how human beings communicate only if we assume that words are eternal and unchanging in their meanings.[59]

Such an interest in sacred texts remained characteristic of India. The nature of language, sacred and secular, became a basic subject in a number of Indian philosophical systems (Grammar, Mimamsa, Nyaya, and, to a lesser extent, Buddhism and Vedanta).[60] Indian philosophers and grammarians learned to argue, much like those of today, that the meanings of words are best understood from their everyday uses. They also had a clear understanding of the difference in level between saying something and commenting on what had been said, that is, between the level of the object language and the metalanguage. A good example of the Indian awareness of linguistic levels is the distinction drawn between the rules for language and the rules for using these rules.[61]

Bhartrihari Develops a Metaphysics in which Language Is the Reality of the World But Is Projected from an Ineffable Source

At this point, I should like to explore the enormous respect of Indian thinkers for words and their allied conviction that words culminate in a reality that is beyond verbal expression. I think that I can do this best by concentrating on Bhartrihari, the most important thinker of the School of Grammar, who made his philosophy of language into an embracing metaphysics.[62] He remains intrinsically interesting, and because he is relatively unknown in the West, I want to give a careful description of the relevant aspects of his thought.

Bhartrihari lived about A.D. 450–510. His chief work, *On Sentence and Word (Vakyapadiya)*, consists, Indian style, of some two thousand succinct verses with a commentary traditionally, though doubtfully, supposed to be by Bhartrihari himself. Whether written by Bhartrihari or not, the commentary is often as obscure as the main text, sometimes because of its involved sentences and sometimes because of its extreme terseness.[63] There are also three later commentaries. Because my aims are general, I will not point out the differences in point of view between the text and its several commentaries, and sometimes I include their interpretations without noting the fact.

There would be no point here in more than mentioning the purely dogmatic characteristics of Bhartrihari's thought, that is, his conviction that the Vedas are revealed truth, inseparable from the Sanskrit, the sacred primal language, in which they are embodied; that the whole, true knowledge is concentrated in a single word, the mantra om, "the creator of the worlds"; and so on. Bhartrihari is simply a believer, though by his own grammarian's standards. He says, "Even if the doctrinal schools disappeared, people would not turn away from the religious law issuing from revelation and tradition" (*revelation* translates the Sanskrit *heard*, applied to directly authoritative texts; *tradition*, in contrast, applies to texts whose authority is indirect because dependent upon memory) (*Vakyapadīya* 1.133).

What remains philosophically interesting in Bhartrihari is a group of interrelated ideas on the nature and importance of words, or, more broadly, language:

1. The 'word', used in the sense of *language*, has an inward meaning and an outward expression.

2. To be meaningful, the 'word' cannot be the isolated, unrelated word but only the sentence.

3. The sentence is grasped as a whole, by means of intuition. Only then can its words be grasped individually.

4. All thought and therefore all knowledge are inseparable from 'words'.

5. The world is essentially the same as the language by which it is known, because it is nothing other than a structure of meanings as grasped in words or, rather, sentences or thoughts.

6. The structural relations between words are established by grammar. These relations are, essentially, the relations between the different levels of reality. Grammar, therefore, is the basic science.

7. The process by which our transient, material world was evolved from the fixed, spiritual reality must have begun in and followed the process by which language was evolved.

8. Even though the world is nothing other than a structure of meanings, latent and expressed, its indwelling principle is utterly beyond words.

To go through these points one by one, in the same order, we may begin by distinguishing between the outward form and the inward sense of the word, that is, of language. The outward form is, of course, the sound, the word (its quotes now omitted) as audible. Among the phoneticians of India there were various speculations on the cause of the audible word. Some believed that the audible word is only the movement of the air set into motion by the speaker's effort, and others that a word is made of the atoms set into motion and collected, like a cloud, by the effort of articulation. Still others, more concerned with the transition

between thought and sound, believed that a spoken word is the transformation of the subtle form in which, to begin with, it is identical with the
inner intention, that is, with the knower. Then, when the knower is
'ripened' by bodily heat and enters "the air called breath," the word is
uttered. In this way, air, now 'colored' by the qualities of the mind,
becomes mind's substratum (1.107–14).

Bhartrihari recalls both the teachers who contended that understanding is different from words and those who contended that they only
appear different because seen from different points of view. Bhartrihari
explains his own position by means of an analogy: The fire latent in
sticks kindles other, visible fires when the sticks are rubbed together and
makes itself and other things visible at the same time. Just so, he says, the
word inherent in the mind, a unity containing seeds of differentiation,
causes the audibly differentiated words to manifest themselves. That is,
the inner word completes its germination and then, impelled by the
speech organs, manifests itself in differentiated successive sounds and
makes both itself and other things known (1.45–46).

As the commentator explains, there is a relation of identity between
the word and the meaning on which it is 'superimposed'. Before the
word is uttered, it is visualized by the mind and then seems to change its
form to the pronounceable one that it projects on the meaning. Put
otherwise, the mind searches for a pronounceable form of the word (like
a computer searching its memory, we might say) and relates it to what
the speaker intends it to signify. The pure inner meaning, the word in
itself, is fixed and timeless, but it shows itself as a succession of sounds.
This differentiation of sounds is the property of the sounds and does not
affect the word's unity, which is that of its meaning (1.47).

In Bhartrihari's image, the relation between the word in itself and
the sound in which it is expressed is like that between the moon and the
water that reflects it, the reflection being immobile in itself but perceived
as if joined to the water and moving with its waves. So, too, the word in
itself takes on the properties of the sound that externalizes its meaning
and, like the sound, appears to move, whether quickly, moderately, or
slowly (1.49).

To use another Bhartriharian image, the word, or knowledge, or
meaning in itself that is awakened by the speaker's desire to say something is like the yolk in a peahen's egg, which shows its many potential
colors when the bird's emergence from the egg turns the yolk's uniformity into a rich diversity (1.51). In still another image, when a painter
wants to paint something made up of parts, he first scans it gradually as a
sequence of parts; then he has a unitary vision of the whole picture; and
then, though he grasps it as a whole, he paints it, as he must, part by

part. Analogously, the speaker who wants to convey a thought first thinks of the fitting word, which he isolates, as it were, from all the words around it, then speaks it in a sequence of sounds. The listener hears the sounds in the same sequence but then grasps the form of the word, suppresses the sounds' sequentiality, and grasps the word or meaning itself (1.52).[64] Word and thought belong together like the two sides of a coin and are separable only by means of abstraction.[65] As in the analogy of fire, the word is always both revealer and revealed, for it has two powers that are really one: the meaning embodied in the form and the form in which the meaning reveals itself (1.55).

So far, the word has been used with caution, at first in quotation marks to indicate that it can be taken in the sense of *language*. This is because Bhartrihari contends that single words are not really the basic units of meaning. The unspoken word in itself, the latent word, the *sphota* as it is called, is in fact a whole thought and is therefore equivalent to a sentence, the least linguistic form that is complete. The opponents of Bhartrihari (such as the Mimamsa) claim that each word has its separate meaning, which it retains within a sentence; but words or (as some Mimamsa say) word meanings become mutually dependent in a sentence and convey a meaning the words do not have when taken separately. Put more technically, the separate words are universals the joining of which restricts and particularizes them.[66]

Bhartrihari disagrees and begins with the whole sentence. Nothing less, he insists, has an independent meaning. There are, he acknowledges, practical ways of establishing individual word meanings. A sentence can in fact be analyzed into components with artificial, secondary meanings. This can be done, he says, because a sentence is primarily an expression of some action or process, so that in analyzing it we first isolate its main word—its main verb—to which we assign the particular meaning it has in that particular sentence. In saying this, Bhartrihari is taking a position in the old argument between, on the one side, the grammarians and the adherents of Mimamsa, and, on the other, the logicians, the adherents of Nyaya. The argument is over the primacy of verbs, whether even nouns (or nominal stems) are derived from verbs (or verbal roots)—many Sanskrit sentences, especially those in the 'nominal style', are without verbs. Of course, Bhartrihari is on the side of the grammarians and verbs.[67]

And so, according to Bhartrihari, all words that are not verbs are accessory and are assigned derivative meanings in order to help clarify the action or process.[68] But words by themselves are indefinite, appear in many different forms, and have no fixed meaning, in the absence of which they are not only unclear but useless. Only words used together have fixed meanings; and the smallest clear, fixed meaning is that conveyed by a sentence. It is true, Bhartrihari acknowledges, that even before a sentence is finished, one grasps a vague meaning, not yet fit for communication; and as the later words appear, the first, vague meaning is abandoned or refined, up to the moment when the sentence ends and its full meaning can be grasped: the speaking out of the meaning and its grasping is itself a process of clarification.[69]

Bhartrihari acknowledges that single words can in fact be compressed sentences, clear enough in the context of their use. But the simple addition of individual words each with its supposed separate meaning, or the analysis of sentences into such words, must fail. The sentence is hardly more separate from its words than its words are from the sounds (more accurately, the phonemes) that make them up. Bhartrihari says, "Just as there are no parts in phonemes, there are no phonemes in the word. Nor do words have any existence separate from the sentence" (1.73). A picture may well have an overall color even though it contains colors not those of the picture as a whole. Likewise, although one may experience the flavor of each of the ingredients of a drink, the drink will have its own unique flavor.[70] The same is true of words in relation to sentences.

The meaning of the word in itself, conveyed by the spoken sentence, is grasped by intuition, not analysis. Intuition cannot dispense with reasoning or with context, which makes meanings more exact. This nonanalytic, intuitive ability to adapt is already present in newborn children; and the truth is that all life shares in intuition, *pratibha*, which has the connotation of light or shining forth:

> It is something which arises spontaneously in all beings. It is like the power of intoxication which some substances develop when they become mature, without anything special being done to them. It is due to this *pratibha* that birds and animals engage in their natural activities, without any prompting or instruction. It is because of this that birds build their nests when the time comes and the cuckoo sings in spring.[71]

Intuition comes from within. It is the voice of conscience; it is reliable; and its authority is accepted by everyone. With more immediate relevance to our subject, intuition is the ability to understand a sentence. This intuitive understanding comes in a flash, sometimes even before the sentence has been finished. (Agreeing on the speed, Noam Chomsky says that the mind makes an unconscious, virtually instantaneous 'computation' of a sentence's meaning.[72]) Although we cannot define the flash of understanding to ourselves and certainly not to others, we can see that it applies to the sentence as a whole and is manifested by the meanings of the individual words. The indefinability of the intuition does not cause any doubt of its presence and effect.[73]

Bhartrihari goes on to say that intuition has many causes and examples, of which I omit the purely religious or miraculous, such as the special insight of saints and the special power granted by a god. Intuition is essential to ordinary life and is manifested in familiar ways, for example in the instinctive ability of experts to distinguish genuine from false coins or precious stones. Being indefinable, their ability to assess cannot be communicated to others. It is certainly no inference; if it were it would have an inference's ordinary grounds.[74]

It should by now be apparent that all thought and all knowledge are inseparable from words:

> All knowledge of what is to be done in this world depends upon the word . . . There is no cognition in the world in which the word does not figure. All knowledge is, as it were, intertwined with the word . . . If this eternal identity of knowledge and the word were to disappear, knowledge would cease to be knowledge; it is this identity which makes identification possible . . . It is this that is the basis of all the sciences, crafts and arts. Thanks to it, whatever is produced can be classified . . . The consciousness of all living beings is of the nature of the word; it exists within and without. (1.121, 124, 125, 126)

Some explanation is in order. The ability to identify and to remember is inseparable from words because it is inseparable from cognition, which is inseparable from words. This is the more true when technical distinctions have to be made in a vocabulary invented for the purpose (1.119, commentary). Even something that in some sense exists "is as good as nonexistent as long as it does not come within the range of verbal usage" (1.121, comm.). Even fantasies and imaginary objects and logical impossibilities are endowed with what measure of reality they have when they are brought to mind by words. And even children understand what they do because they have understanding in some vague sense, the result of "the residual traces of words from their former births" (ibid.)—an ability that we, along with Chomsky, might consider to be of genetic origin.

Explaining his position, Bhartrihari says that when we first see something, it is possible that we do not grasp its particular qualities and have no word or words by which to identify or recall it. Knowledge, as we experience, can be indeterminate. For example, when "one walks quickly and treads on grass and clods of earth," what knowledge we have of them is an indeterminate, unverbalized awareness or sensation of the grass and clods of earth, the meaning or 'word-seed' of which is only

latent, only ready to sprout.[75] Such a sensation has little if any effect as
long as we are unable to give it a verbal form, without which the sensation remains too indefinite to grasp. What has not been identified by
thought is to that extent unknown and near to unknowable, and, surely,
incommunicable and unremembered. And because without words nothing can be grasped, nothing has any graspable form, and nothing is
intelligible, when there is no language, there is no latent word, no spiritual activity, no science, no art, no craft, no communication, no consciousness, no memory, and no self (1.123–25, comm.).

Obviously, then, the consciousness and self-consciousness of all
beings has the nature of the word (1.126). Similarly, the reasoning based
on human intelligence (not written tradition) is by the power of words
(1.137). Knowing all this, we can dare to say that the world is indistinguishable from the words by which it is known. And if we take one more
metaphysical step, the nature of which will be discussed, we can decide
with Bhartrihari that the world is nothing other than a structure of meanings as fixed in language, its external aspect the visible or hearable form
of its latent, unspoken form or meaning. So "the power that controls this
universe is based on words . . . As has been said, 'It is the word that sees
the object; it is the word that reveals the object that was lying hidden
[within itself]; it is on the word that this multiple world rests . . .' " (118
and comm.).

Therefore, adventurously but reasonably, we conclude that the
world is made of words, that words are made of latent words or meanings, and that meanings are made of consciousness. Consider an
analogy: All objects made of gold have gold in them, which for this
reason can be regarded as their substance, their original material, and, in
this sense, their origin and cause. So with the Brahman, the Word of
words:

> All its manifestations, though they appear to be distinct from one
> another, are in the nature of the word, because in all of them, the
> original material persists. Because in our cognitions we identify ob-
> jects with their words and our cognitions are intertwined with words,
> they are essentially of the nature of the word. (1.1., comm.)

The understanding of language in this encompassing metaphysical
sense teaches us that latent or implicit speech is the permanent possibility of cognition and cognition is the permanent possibility of the existence of the world we know.

This becomes very evident if we examine the way in which we
know anything at all. Take an undramatic but representative example.
When we know, that is, cognize a jar and say "This is a jar," the word *jar*

in the sentence is identified both with the cognition and the jar that is the content of the cognition; and because the reality of the cognition and its object, the jar, is their indwelling universal, it makes sense to say that the word (or sentence) is the same as the jar; so that it is the jar that is derived from the word, and not the opposite.[76] Jars of clay come from verbal *jars*. The word conveys its form to the object, which it pervades and dyes with a particular meaning; and the meaning of the object is its power to function in a particular way—the meaning of a pot is its power to carry water.[77] Every object, to be itself and not another, must be determined by its verbal form, so that everything in the world consists of the outward appearances of inward forms.[78] Words make the world. Or, put more carefully, words make up the ideal structure of the world, and, reciprocally, the world is this structure's imperfect mirror.

For all these reasons, the basic science is grammar, which establishes the structural relations between words and is high in the hierarchy of reality:

> The expression of what one wants to say (the principle of the use of things) depends upon words and the truth concerning words cannot be understood except through grammar . . . It is the door to salvation, the remedy for all the impurities of speech, the purifier of all the sciences, and shines in every branch of knowledge . . . Just as the universals of all things depend upon the form of their words for their communication, so is this science (of Grammar) the basis for all the other sciences . . . This is the first step in the ladder leading to liberation; this is the straight royal road for all those who desire salvation. (1.13–16)

To explain and supplement this claim, all the sciences depend upon the correct, grammatical formation of language, so grammar is their universal basis. Corrupted forms of language do not have a fixed meaning and are the cause of sin (1.15). "It is the word, language, that is the sole teacher" (1.137, comm.). The very ability to conduct a reasonable discussion depends on the immutable power of words to convey a meaning based on their primary sense and contexts, indicative signs, syntactic constructions, and other grammatical considerations (1.137, comm.).

Assuming that the world and language always go together, to discover how the world evolved, we turn to grammar and see how language evolved. In the beginning, we are aware, there was, as there is and will always be, the Word. The Word, which is Brahman,

> is endowed with all powers, which are neither identical with nor different from it; and it has two aspects, that of unity and that of [apparent] diversity . . . It is, in all states, unaffected by beginning

and end, even though the manifestations appear in worldly transaction in a temporal and spatial sequence. (1.1)

There is a riddle here, of a kind that will become familiar. The powers of the Word are indefinable because, being many, they lack its unity; but although words produce opposite effects, they cannot be opposed to one another because they all exist simultaneously in the same one Word or Brahman that constitutes them without remainder or difference. The riddle is that words can have no existence apart from this one Word, and their paradoxically separate-non-separate existence-non-existence is a differentiation into forms that are unreal as dreams are unreal (1.4).

Grammar leads us to the Word as the metaphysical principle of the world, and leads us, therefore, to salvation (1.142).[79] The technique of salvation does not concern us, except in that it is an ascent toward the Word that reverses the direction of the world's evolution. Whoever aspires to grammatical salvation learns to see the constant Word without distinction. Such seeing requires intuition in its fullest sense, free of all the differences of which the Word is the source (1.142, 1.5). To get to the Word in itself, one must learn to suppress sequential thinking. As has been hinted, this requires perseverance in the use of grammatically correct forms.[80] Take note how the unrelaxed punctiliousness of the grammarian's distinctions leads to the terminal bliss of indistinction![81]

I must still explain that Bhartrihari regards time as the metaphysical principle of activity.[82] The world, he thinks, is projected mainly by time, a supreme power of the Word, identical with it except in that it appears to separate itself as the regulator of the Word's transformations. Time is the creative power of the Word (1.1). It is causality and plays with objects as if they were toys (chap. 3, pt. 2: 9.62, 9.72).[83] As the god of all sequences, it determines the sequences of action of the lesser powers that emerge from their latency in the Word (ibid., 9.46). It also projects (or appears to project) the temporal succession of phenomena, which change like a turning waterwheel whose revolutions are the seasons of the year (chap. 3. pt. 2: 9.14).

The world-projecting power of time acts by infusing its life-giving force into the causes of the various phenomena. It controls these causes much as puppeteers control their puppets: "Time has been called the wire-puller of the world Machine. It regulates the universe through prevention and permission" (3.2: 9.4). In another simile, time regulates the world as fowlers control the flight of the small birds used as bait for larger ones, by tying their feet to a string that allows them a short radius of flight or hopping.

The world-projecting power of time (*kalashakti*) prevents chaos. It does so by governing the grammatical tenses and the phenomenal appearances of past, present, and future; and by governing the phases of the creation, preservation, and dissolution of the phenomenal world. Bhartrihari says, "Time is the very soul of the universe. Hence it is identified with activity itself" (3.2: 9.12). He compares the power of time to the current of a stream that carries and returns things to its banks. But though it appears in changing forms—now spring and green-leaved trees and now winter and bare trees—it never changes in itself (1.3).[84]

There is no need to go into the details of the world's evolution. It is enough to recognize that it is the Word's projection, in accord with which it develops. Yet though the universe is nothing other than a structure of the meanings of words, latent and expressed, the Word itself, their initiating cause and indwelling principle, is utterly beyond words. Why so? The Word, we remember, is described as free of all temporal and spatial characteristics and beyond all differentiation and relation (1.1). It is also identified as Brahman, an indescribable self-luminous and illuminating unity that is, through and through, pure consciousness. The highest of universals, the Word is the meaning of all meanings, which are its illusory transformations.[85] The unity of the Word is said not to be contradicted by its powers' diversity, an illusion, the explanation goes, prompted by the special power of illusion making. Yet the Word, though a superlative unity, differentiates or appears to differentiate itself into subject, object, and experience.[86]

The brief answer to our question "Why so?" is simply, though inscrutably, that the Word is beyond any consciousness but its own, and beyond any words, which depend upon all the characteristics—the samenesses and differences and other relations—that the Word does not and cannot have except in a kind of unimaginable, matrixlike unity that has the potentiality of all diversities but is in no way itself diverse.

There Are Western Analogues to Bhartrihari's View That Individual Words Are Not the Units of Meaning and that the World Is a Structure of Meanings

This answer leaves intact the more fundamental question, why the Word or why any supreme metaphysical principle should be assumed to be a unity by nature inexpressible in words. The question will be dealt with seriously; but first I should like to comment on two ideas in Bhartrihari's philosophy that seem especially interesting, that individual words are not the basic units of meaning and that the world as a whole is a structure of meanings.

Both ideas affect the manner in which ineffability is conceived. The first leads us to repeat the question already asked by Indian disputants, how words, which lack meaning, acquire it when they are put together?—a question related to the psychological one, how nonlinguistic processes become linguistic ones. The second idea implies kinship or even identity of language and world, so that a conclusion applying to the one is likely, even certain, to apply to the other. If it does apply, then the problem of ineffability becomes one of the adequacy of language to explain itself either in part—by translating itself or reflecting on its nature—or as a whole complex structure, something Bhartrihari attempts in his philosophy but denies can be done completely.

The idea that individual words are not the basic units of meaning has an initial plausibility because the sense of words is so dependent on their context; but if we include in their context much more than the immediately adjacent words, the dependency of the words is stretched out to vaguely great lengths. Herder observes that the words of every language are organized as a systematic whole, each drawing its meaning from the others, so that the utterance of a single word presupposes the whole of the language as a semantic and grammatical structure.[87] Herder may be implying a more ordered unity than actually exists, but, even so, supports the predisposition to deny that there are truly isolated words. If he is right, it follows that it is impossible to state the full meaning of even a single sentence in a limited number of words; and it follows that it is impossible to make a fully accurate translation of even the most matter-of-fact statement from one language into another.

This issue is not one that can be dealt with briefly or simply, and I propose to do no more with it than report that Bhartrihari's position has had eminent recent advocates, including the French philologist Michel Bréal (1835–1915), the anthropologist Bronislaw Malinowski, the logician-philosopher Gottlob Frege, the psychologist A. R. Luria, and the philosopher W. V. Quine. Their ideas have a past I do not mention, and their emphases are different; but my point is only their very general Bhartriharian tendency.*

Bréal, the first of those I have just mentioned, says, "It is not the word that forms a distinct entity for our mind: it is the idea . . . Once made part of a locution, the word loses its individuality and becomes disengaged from any outside influence.[88] Frege holds that one should never "look for the meaning of a word in isolation, but only in the

---

*Fodor and Lepore's *Holism*, which was published too late for me to make use of it here, deals with 'meaning holism' (as against 'semantic atomism' and 'semantic nihilism') from the standpoints of six contemporary philosophers, W. V. O. Quine, Donald Davidson, David Lewis, D. C. Dennett, Ned Block, and Paul Churchland. The authors' conclusions are agnostic: "There are, it would seem, lots of possibilities . . . Contrary to widely received philosophical opinion, there are, as far as we can tell, practically *no* closed options in semantics; the arguments that were reputed to close them are, in our view, comprehensively flawed" (pp. 206–7).

context of a sentence."[89] Malinowski says, similarly, that "isolated words are in fact only linguistic figments, the products of an advanced linguistic analysis." Luria's opinion is that "simply naming something without formulating a thought or idea is quite artificial, whereas the expression of a complete thought or the formulation of an idea is the basic unit of communication."[90] And Quine says that contextual definition has resulted in a semantic revolution that has taught us that the sentence, not the word, is the primary vehicle of meaning. Not unlike Bhartrihari, Quine holds that

> we learn some words in isolation, in effect as one-word sentences; we learn further words in context, by learning various short sentences that contain them; and we understand further sentences by construction from the words thus learned . . . The meanings of words are abstractions from the truth conditions of sentences that contain them.[91]

The idea that the world as a whole is a structure of meanings depends on the far-reaching assumption that knower and knowing are somehow identical with what is known. This assumption will be discussed before long. For the rest there is little to say because any serious grappling with the idea of the world as a structure of meanings would soon turn into an analysis of philosophical idealism both Eastern and Western.[92]

Perhaps, if we look at the comparison quite generally, we may find a partial Western parallel to Bhartrihari in the mystic Jakob Böhme (1575–1624), to whom language is essentially internal and immaterial.[93] The Word, Böhme says, is in itself free of time and motion, for it is the verbal command that exists undifferentiated in God and is mirrored in the human soul. "Through the agency of human articulation," writes an expositor, "each word of every object becomes a temporal subject causing its own series of verbal actions within three dimensions." What has been created has evolved from the Word. Böhme's esteem for speech leads him to declare that its organ, the mouth, emits divinity itself, because "the mouth is the point in the universe through which divinity moves into manifestation as well as the position within the vocal mechanism where the idea becomes speech."[94]

Gadamer, to Whom Language Is the Original Unity Of 'I' and World, Grants Language a Bhartriharian Supremacy

It is possible to imagine a contemporary defence of Bhartrihari along Kantian or Hegelian lines. A Kantian Bhartriharism would argue that everything we know exists by virtue of the implicit structures of language, the empirical forms of which are derived from the internal language we know as thought. A Hegelian Bhartriharism would stress that Hegel, having transformed Kant's world of phenomena into "the self-presentation of the noumenal world," builds a great conceptual hierarchy based, like Bhartrihari's, on the unity of thought and being.[95]

Of all well-known contemporary philosophers, it is Hans-Georg Gadamer who is closest to Bhartrihari and most obviously earns his place in this chapter on the metaphysical exaltation of words. He earns it for two reasons: his emphasis on the metaphysical or, better, existential priority of language, and his endlessly optimistic assurance that human beings can learn to come closer to one another by the mainly linguistic means of the "fusion of horizons."

Gadamer has something unknowingly in common with Bhartrihari, and knowingly, I suppose, with the Neoplatonists I will speak of later. He begins with Heidegger's conviction that understanding is the mode of human existence and language is the medium of human understanding. Along with Heidegger, he believes in a single historical consciousness, in which vague understanding precedes any attempt to make understanding exact or full. According to Gadamer, we learn to understand ourselves from within our own matrix.[96] This learning is natural, he says, because, to begin with, there is no basic gap between the human being—the subject of knowledge—and the world in which the human being lives—the object of knowledge. Nor is there such a gap between one's conceptual scheme and the world that one conceives. The understanding that is achieved is genuine, and the relativists are simply wrong to argue that we have no common standards of judgment.

Language, says Gadamer, is inescapable. Every complaint against it, every feeling of its inadequacy, is necessarily expressed in language. "Hence language always forestalls any objection to its jurisdiction. Its universality keeps pace with the universality of reason." Fortunately, understanding is equal to any attempt to interpret anything in any way, so that language, in which understanding is formed, transcends any possible bounds.[97] For this reason, human beings seriously concerned with understanding one another are in principle always able to create some fusion of their respective worlds.

Unlike the Indians, who prefer oral over written tradition, Gadamer extols writing. He stresses that language realizes itself fully only when writing extends it beyond the time in which it was first used, and that it allows all traditions to coexist and all persons to have access to everything that has ever been written.[98] However, writing involves a certain distance or alienation from oneself. The variety of languages also creates a problem: The particular language within which we live seems to us to be the most natural and fitting possible, even in the names it assigns different objects.[99] But every language is able to say everything it wants to, and the unity of language with thought enables us to compare the various forms of this unity and discover that it has been preserved in the midst of all its variety. Language transcends its individual peculiarities because understanding, interpretation, and language are not simply objects of thought but comprise whatever can possibly be such an object.[100]

Now come passages reminiscent of Bhartrihari. Gadamer speaks of "the inwardness of the word, which constitutes the inward unity of thought and speech," and he continues:

> In language the world presents itself. The experience of the world in language is 'absolute'. It transcends all the relativities of the positing of being, because it embraces all being-in-itself, in whatever relationships (relativities) it appears. The linguistic quality of our experience of the world is prior, as contrasted with everything that is recognized and addressed as being. The fundamental relation of language and world does not, then, mean that world becomes the object of language. Rather, the object of language and of statements is already enclosed within the world horizon of language.[101]

Unlike Bhartrihari, Gadamer does not believe that "the world that appears in language and is constituted by it" is objective in the sense that the natural sciences understand objectivity. Likeness reappears, however, in Gadamer's contention that we have no access to a world outside of what we get in any and every language. "There is in every language a direct relationship to the infinite extent of what exists," and therefore "whoever has language 'has' the world."[102]

The likeness between Gadamer and Bhartrihari persists in Gadamer's belief that language as meaning or understanding encompasses everything. Gadamer writes sentence after sentence that could, rhetoric apart, be attributed to Bhartrihari:

> Every word breaks forth as if from a center and is related to a whole, through which alone it is a word. Every word causes the whole of the language to which it belongs to resonate and the whole of the view of the world which lies behind it to appear. Thus every word, in its momentariness, carries with it the unsaid, to which it is related by responding and indicating ... All human speaking is finite in such a way that there is within it an infinity of meaning to be elaborated and interpreted.[103]

No doubt there is a world of difference between Gadamer and Bhartrihari; and it is not surprising that Gadamer, willing fuser of horizons though he is, has had difficulty in fusing his own with those of Eastern thinkers.[104] After all, Bhartrihari's is so ancient and so Indian a philosophy: Everything is Brahman the Supreme Self, who is Language, the 'Word' from which everything emanates, including every human as inner 'word', self, or language; and as the undifferentiated differentiates, the self within becomes the mundane ego-sense, and the world within becomes the external, spoken word.[105] Is Gadamer at all like this? The answer is an emphatic *no* followed by a soft but firm *yes* that relates Gadamer to what he calls "the Greek logos-philosophy" and to medieval thought. As Gadamer reveals, he is taken by the Neoplatonic idea of an emanation that does not lessen the source from which it emanates—he prefers this doctrine in the clearly atemporal form given it by Nicholas of Cusa. Gadamer is also taken by the metaphor of "the light of the mind" made visible by making other things visible; and so on.[106]

My point, however, is not the soft *yes* but the focusing of all reality in language as self and self as language. This, I assume, is a metaphysical likeness related to a psychological likeness between the two exalters of language. The decisive similarity—the supremacy granted language— comes clear when Gadamer summarizes, "Our inquiry has been guided by the basic idea that language is a central point where 'I' and the world meet or, rather, manifest their original unity."[107]

Chapter 3

The Devaluation of Words

We have now witnessed the exaltation of words in mythical, moral, grammatical, and hermeneutical guises. We have seen it in Marduk, whose words revoke and reinstate a constellation; in the Confucians, who insist that human welfare rests on the meticulous use of right names; in the Americans, to whom all things are thought or talked into existence; and in the goddess Speech, who transforms those she loves into seers armed with her Formulas. And we have seen how, in Bhartrihari, the exaltation becomes a grammatical architectonic, and in Gadamer, an infinitely pliable reconciliation of standpoints. But not everyone is prepared to love, honor, and obey words; and in stark contrast with the exalters, there have always been the thinkers I propose to call *word-devaluers*. These include the skeptics of India, China and Japan, and Europe. They preach philosophical modesty, but some of them take an immodest pleasure in their dialectic—perhaps because, being sophists and having no game of their own, their game is to discourage the games that others play. Maybe Gorgias, whose arguments I will review, is a sophist of this kind.

The doubts of the skeptics are most pertinently aimed at the grand dogmatic systems: the traditional Indian ones with their substances and rules for establishing the truth; the Chinese, with their moralizing, ceremonious filiality; and the Greeks, with their Ideas and their God (Platonic, Aristotelian, Neoplatonic, or Stoic) that became the philosophical armature of European thought. The devaluation suffered by the systems is that, of course, of their basic concepts and the concepts' vehicle, language.

Beyond the mere skeptics, there are the religious thinkers who devalue words because, they believe, words miss the profound objects of faith. Devaluers of this believing kind include the Taoists; the Buddhists of India, China, and Japan; and, in Europe, many philosophers and all or almost all theologians. In Europe, as elsewhere, there are also the

simply mystical, who devalue everything mundane; and there are the
philosophical individualists whose doctrines of ineffability I discuss in
the present chapter.

A Summary of the Views of Word-Devaluing Philosophers

1. Among ancient Greek thinkers, Gorgias is notable for his sharp-
   etched argument that nothing exists; that even if something
   existed, words could not capture it; and that even if they could
   capture it, they would be unable to transmit what they had
   captured.

2. Buddhist philosophers argue that words are inherently misleading. Among these philosophers, Nagarjuna is the most inci-
   sive and uncompromising devaluer of words. His technique is
   to demonstrate, by any logical means his opponents propose,
   that they contradict themselves; and his conclusion is that language as such is self-contradictory and, by its own standards,
   self-destructive. Whether Nagarjuna implies something 'positive' is unclear and hardly to be clarified, he says, by talking
   about it; but one need not doubt the sincerity of the religiousness he proclaims. Even now, his thought can be given an
   acceptable, not to say fashionable, interpretation.

3. In order to escape the bonds of conceptuality, the Buddhists
   propose a hierarchical series of meditations by means of which
   one is supposed to be able to rise beyond words and into the
   ineffable state of 'emptiness'.

4. In ancient China, perhaps the most famous source for the devaluation of words is the book called *Lao Tzu*. This book makes
   a repeated though inconsistent attack on the ability of words to
   capture (to 'name') the Tao in the sense of reality in itself.
   Because the Tao is the creatively diverse and diversifying mother
   of everything, she is beyond words, for every description of
   her is too limiting.

5. In the poetic, irreverent book named *Chuang Tzu*, words are
   convicted of being too fixed, too logical, too subject to the
   polarities of *this* and *that*, *yes* and *no*, and *good* and *bad*, to be
   adequate to reality. But though nature is more varied and in-

constant than words, they, too, have their relative place in the inconstant scheme of things.

6. The Ch'an (Zen) Buddhists, whose Buddhism is strongly tempered by Lao Tzu and Chuang Tzu, are often radically opposed to the notion that words can be truthful. They invent techniques by which the contradictions implicit in the use of concepts drive the meditator beyond all conceptualizing.

7. In Europe, Søren Kierkegaard, obsessed with the transformative beauty of language, sees language as the revealer and destroyer of truth. He takes comfort in parody, in the ineffability of the individual, and in the truth, which he recognizes by its self-contradictory nature and the pain it causes him

8. Arthur Schopenhauer argues that we need words because of their practical usefulness, but that, unlike art—most especially music—they have no hold on reality in itself, which is the bodiless will that projects the world. The valuation of music over words is adopted by Nietzsche and by German composers including Wagner, Mahler, and Schoenberg.

9. Beginning as a follower of Schopenhauer, Friedrich Nietzsche attacks words, along with logic and science, for obscuring the real differences in the world. He claims that the axioms of logic, which depend on the false assumption that things can be identical, imprison us in a pseudo-reality of our own invention.

10. Ludwig Wittgenstein, another philosopher influenced by Schopenhauer, believes that words can convey only the abstractions of the logical world they constitute. At least during the earlier part of his philosophical career, he argues that language is the limit beyond which lie the values of ethics, aesthetics, and religion, to which it can give no direct access.

11. Not unlike the early Wittgenstein, Heidegger rejects the logic and mere practicality of words and searches for the primordial unity he believes to be preserved in poetic language. Heidegger is compared and contrasted in this respect with the writers Antonin Artaud, Samuel Beckett, and Paul Celan.

12. The last devaluer to appear here is Jacques Derrida, who agrees with much of Nietzsche's and Heidegger's attack on words or concepts. But Derrida adopts a less openly heroic attitude than they and searches among words, with only intimations of suc-

cess, for stray hints of the ineffably 'real' that words exhibit in the very concealment they impose on it. Derrida himself gives the examples, apart from Nietzsche, of Freud, Valéry, and Artaud.

Of the Greek Sophists, Gorgias Is the Most Incisive Devaluer of Words

Greek sophists, who teach the arts of persuasion, argue that argument can establish only relative truth; and it is easy for them to translate their pride in their rhetorical gifts into the confidence that words, so pliant to their will, can always be made to subvert one another. Among the Greek sophists, it is Gorgias who argues most drastically against the ability of words to establish the truth about the world. According to his argument, nothing is, nothing really exists. Having demonstrated this (whatever it may exactly mean) to his own satisfaction, he goes on to argue that even if anything is, man cannot know or comprehend it. In other words, not only does Gorgias flatly deny that language can grasp the truth but adds that if it were to do so, it would be impossible to transmit the truth to anyone else.

Consider the argument that Gorgias opposes to our most natural convictions: It is our eyes that determine what is visible; we do not deny the existence of visible things because we do not hear them. By analogy, if thought, like vision and hearing, were its own criterion for existence, everything we think should be known to exist simply because it is thought. But this is absurd because we think of many impossible things. Therefore the testimony of thought cannot have the veridical force of that of the senses; and we must conclude that the existent we assumed for the sake of argument is neither apprehended nor thought.*

---

*There is an analogous Buddhist argument. I give it in the words of the eighth-century Buddhist philosopher Kamalashila commenting on a polemical text written by his teacher Shantarakshita: "Between words and external things, there is no such relation as that of *sameness* or of *being produced* by virtue of which relation the words expressing such things would be regarded as true. For instance, the relation of *sameness* is not possible between them because of such reasons as their being apprehended by different sense organs; i.e. words are apprehended by a sense organ which is different from that by which things are apprehended; for instance, word is apprehended by the auditory organ, while things are apprehended by the visual and other organs" (*The Tattvasangraha of Shantaraksita, With the Commentary of Kamalashila,* trans. G. Jha, 2 vols. [Delhi; Motilal Banarsidass, reprint 1986], vol. 2, p. 753).

Finally, Gorgias argues that even if anything exists and is apprehended, it cannot be communicated. The reason is that if we assume that there are externally existing objects of vision, hearing, and the senses in general, the visible things among them are apprehended by vision, not hearing, and the audible ones by hearing, not vision. How, then, can things seen or heard be revealed to another person? After all, the means by which we believe we reveal them is *logos*, which is speech or thought; but *logos* is not the same as the existing things it is supposed to reveal. Actually, therefore, we reveal to others not external existing things but only *logos* (speech or thought), which is quite different from them; for just as visible things cannot become audible, so the assumed external things cannot become our *logos*; and because they are not *logos*, they cannot be revealed to another person.

The Truth, argues Gorgias, is that *logos* arises as the result of external things impinging on us. Encounter with a flavor causes us to think and talk about the flavor, and encounter with a color, to think and talk about the color. This shows that *logos* does not reveal the external object but, on the contrary, that the external object reveals or explains the *logos*. Whatever is visible is perceived by one organ, the eye, but *logos* (speech or thought), by another. Therefore, just as the substances do not manifest one another's different natures, the *logos* does not manifest the multiplicity of substances.

Summarily, Gorgias's argument is that each sense is the unique medium for what it alone can convey, is unlike any other sense, and is unable to convey what any other conveys. The medium of words, too, is unique and is different from that of any of the senses, which alone convey external reality; speech or thought cannot convey what the senses do. One kind of speech may be better than another, but speech is unable to convey external reality because it cannot *be* that reality—how can chalk teach us about cheese? To convey external things, words or thoughts would have to correspond with them, or be the same as they are, or, briefly, to *be* them. But this is impossible, for words or thoughts are too different from things, so what *is* cannot be thought or expressed.[1]

It appears that Gorgias agrees with the common Greek view, adopted by Aristotle as we will have occasion to recall, that to perceive or know something is to be identical with it. He may also be a predecessor of the view, later so common among romantics, that words are ordinarily distant from any direct human experience, for which they are a poor substitute.

Sextus Empiricus, who reports the views of Gorgias, has various other arguments against the truth-revealing ability of speech. Because of his encyclopedic ambitions, he also writes against the correctness of grammatical rules, against the possibility of teaching anything by means of speech, and against the possibility of proving anything by means of logic.[2]

The Buddhist Devaluation of Words Is Carried Out with the Greatest Philosophical Adroitness by Nagarjuna

In India, the devaluation of words is an integral part of much of the Buddhist tradition. From the beginning, Buddhists opposed the misunderstanding involved in the use of the word *I* to refer either to one's substantial ego or, as the Indian materialists and others would have it, to one's body. Generalizing from this attitude to ego-implying words, the Buddhists contended that we should not be led to metaphysical conclusions by common turns of speech.

If we follow a modern Buddhist interpreter, early Buddhist scriptures can be given a Wittgensteinian turn. One example is Buddha's reported criticism of the statement that the soul is extremely happy and without defect after death. Buddha takes this statement to be meaningless because those who make it cannot attach any meaning to a sort of happiness they have themselves never experienced.[3] This matter of direct experience is important to the Buddhists because, like Hume, they hold that we never experience any metaphysical ego, and so, lacking any referent, all terms or statements implying its existence are baseless.

It is true, the Buddhists concede, that Buddha made use of common turns of speech of the sort that have misleading implications for the unenlightened, but for him they had no such implications. He was using conventional language for everyday purposes and did not intend to imply either that chariots, persons, or other apparent wholes are more than temporary assemblages, or that the names given them, *chariot, person,* and so on, are more than conceptual fictions.

Here we find the origin of the Buddhist theory of different levels of truth and, maybe, of the 'linguaphobia' of Buddhist philosophers, who regard reality as nameless, indescribable, and, to the ordinary intellect, impossible to conceive.[4] According to the philosophical elaboration of this view, what really exists is a flux of evanescent, atom-like occurrences that vanish at the very moment of their appearance. These ultimate, unique, self-contained particulars are beyond verbal description. They are beyond description because they are in themselves neither related nor unrelated to one another, neither the same as nor different from one another, so that we can know of their existence by inference alone, not by perception.

In favor of the Buddhist position, we might argue that we are able to use words as generalizations or universals only because we rely on the useful but questionable assumption that the world is made of identical, similar, and different things. By imposing identity, similarity, and difference as measures of experience, and by providing names by which to call things, words or concepts encourage us to construct the world and make practical sense of it. This happens because thought and language are inseparable, as interdependent as two sticks that stand by supporting one another; and it is with the concepts constituted by them that we create the structure of the quasi-fictional, everyday world in which we appear to ourselves to exist.[5] Such is the prevailing attitude among Buddhist philosophers (although Dignaga, of the fifth century, may be an exception).[6]

The surest, most combative, most logically adroit philosophical guide to the Buddhist devaluation of words is the philosopher Nagarjuna (ca. 150–250 A.D.).[7] Nagarjuna tries, he says, to prove nothing, but only to use his opponents' principles and modes of argument to show that these lead—by the opponents' own standards of correct reasoning—to self-contradiction. All the logical possibilities open to them, he claims, prove to be self-contradictory, which is to say, meaningless, empty; and so, too, all their arguments, substances, and dreamed-up worlds are empty.

According to Nagarjuna—whose detailed refutations I omit—there is no coherent account of causation, of time, of motion, or even of Nirvana. Nothing can be shown to have an essential nature. Things cannot be conceived as either identical with one another or as different, or as either substances or attributes. In other words, every thing and every idea of every thing is empty, as space in and by itself is empty. In his *Hymn to the Inconceivable [Buddha]*, Nagarjuna writes that Reality (a word used as a makeshift indication for that which is beyond words) transcends the dualism of being and not-being and yet transcends nothing at all; because Reality is without foundation, unmanifested, inconceivable, and incomparable. To repeat Nagarjuna's comprehensive negations in his own words, he says that the Inconceivable [Buddha]

has declared that all phenomena are merely abstractions. Yes, even the abstraction through which emptiness is conceived is said to be untrue. [That which] has transcended the duality of being and nonbeing without, however, having transcended anything at all; that which is not knowledge or knowable, not existent nor non-existent, not one and not many, not both nor neither; without foundation, unmanifest, inconceivable, incomparable; that which arises not, disappears not, is not annihilated and is not permanent, *that* is [Reality]

which is like space [and] not within the range of words [or] knowledge.[8]

An ancient commentator on Nagarjuna explains that the absolute
cannot be an object of any kind of understanding and is therefore outside of the range of language, but he does make an ambivalent Buddhist
concession:

> Even though the absolute is unutterable, the absolute truth can be
> communicated to some extent by examples relying upon the rela-
> tive. But as its nature is devoid of all relative procedures it cannot
> really be spoken of . . . Thus the teaching about the absolute func-
> tions as a means while the attainment of the absolute is the goal.
> Otherwise it cannot be taught.[9]

Is it possible to argue so without using one's own, independent
logic and without in some sense trying to prove the nonsubstantiality
or emptiness of the world? Should Nagarjuna's contention that he holds
no thesis be understood as also a rejection of all philosophical positions that relate to conventional reality? Should Nagarjuna be interpreted as positing an indefinable entity that he defines, though vaguely,
by his series of negations? Nagarjuna himself appears to believe that
he has developed a mode of argument immune to refutation because
it sets all assertions against all others without, in theory, making
any assertions itself. Can he do all this and continue reasonably to
believe in a conventional empirical world that, words and all, *must*
somehow be used to help one arrive at the different, totally indescribable whatever-it-may-be? Or does he think, as he sometimes says, that
emptiness too is empty—that there is no meaning to the idea of an
ultimate reality because everything we can think is made up of concepts (as Nietzsche says and Heidegger and Derrida concur) that we
ourselves invent and cannot accurately apply to anything outside of our
conventional concerns?[10]

These are questions that not only we can ask but were asked and
answered with philosophical acuteness by the ancient Indian philosophers,
both the Buddhists and their opponents, the 'Logicians' (the Nyaya) and
others. On both sides, the argument depends considerably on what one
thinks of negation as used in logical argument. Both in India (in Shankara,
e.g.) and in the West (in varied ways, in Ibn Sina [Avicenna, A.D. 980–1037],
Francis Bacon, Spinoza, Hegel, Bergson, and others) one finds the natural enough doctrine that affirmation is by nature prior to negation because one can negate only something that either exists or possibly

exists.* Negation, it is often said, necessarily presupposes affirmation.[11] Buddhist partisans of Nagarjuna were themselves divided on such issues, some of them complaining that others were too preoccupied with negative argument.[12] A contemporary partisan of a more positive interpretation of Nagarjuna says, with understandably less than complete clarity:

> The world is originally established as the clouded occlusion of worldly convention and functions through its own worldly and conventional reason, which in itself is opposed to ultimate meaning . . . In religious awareness, worldly convention itself is completely negated in ultimate meaning, and by that same ultimate meaning worldly convention is resurrected from its hopelessness to live once more within ultimate meaning.[13]

One of the difficulties involved for the Buddhist philosophers is that the whole discussion—including their basic distinction between relative and absolute and their demonstration that the truth must be empty—is conducted in conventional, relative language, and, by their own standards, should make no true sense or true (refutable) nonsense. It is not the weakness of words that makes them impossible to apply to a transcendent reality, to 'emptiness'; to these Buddhists, words cannot refer because there are no determinate entities for them to refer to. "What is, and the emptiness thereof, will simply not submit to the language of determinateness."[14]

However, the very clarity of this explanation must be inadequate because it is given in words that Nagarjuna himself dooms to inadequacy of a sort that words are by nature not fit to state. The usual Buddhist response is that words may hint what they cannot quite state, but hints are not usually difficult to expand, and what is devalued, and devalued mercilessly, is the coherence and adequacy of language as such. Any compromise in this devaluation puts the devaluation at risk. As a modern interpreter says, "Everything that comes to be in language, including all worldly conventional negations, are not in fact negations at all. The true working of negation is found in silence."[15] But this interpreter's kind of 'resounding' silence is, typically, only a small hole in a great cloud of words explaining the significance of emptiness. Of commentators there

---

*But in referring to ultimates such as 'emptiness', the Indians often practice bi-negation, by which is meant that something is said neither to be nor not-be. An explanation of this usage is that "the bi-negation is positioned at a linguistic junction between the ultimate and conventional truths or realities. It is applied to conventions but describes their emptiness and is as close as one can get linguistically to emptiness. It is more adequate than other devices because it does not ascribe properties of qualities to emptiness and so does not phenomenalise emptiness" (P. Fenner, *The Ontology of the Middle Way*, p. 39).

is no end, even though there has not been and cannot be any final description of what neither is, nor is not, nor both is and is not.[16]

A further difficulty, parallel to that experienced by some late medieval philosophers, is that if Nagarjuna is interpreted as accepting the minimal, antirealistic position that tempts many of our exact contemporaries, his view seems incompatible with unquestioning religious faith. But this is an incompatibility of which there is no evident sign in Nagarjuna or his great Buddhist successors, although Dignaga goes so far as to say that sacred ('scriptural') tradition is as fallible as any other form of verbal communication.[17]

These difficulties need not remain unanswered. A contemporary admirer of Nagarjuna sketches a response that, with historical adjustments, might have been given by a sophisticated ancient Nagarjunian. The response has the advantage of accepting everyday language without any special reservation. A reservation arises only when language is used with logical or Platonic pretensions in order to arrive at an unconditional statement of the truth:

> The pragmatic demands which shape ordinary language require an underlying framework sufficiently flexible that the resulting instrument is adaptable to all the uses to which language may be put. When we seek to systematize the framework through the application of purely logical criteria, we necessarily do violence to our common-sense ontology. No metaphysical theory can be fully adequate to the nature of the world.[18]

The Buddhists Seek Enlightenment Despite Words but with Their Help

Attainment of the Buddhist goal of emptiness is considered to be a difficult task. The modes of thought that have to be combated are so entrenched that persistent effort is needed to overcome them; and slowly graduated states of meditation are essential to this effort. These states of meditation were conceived by the early systematizers of Buddhism in two different series, which were in time joined. One of these series, with which I will not deal, is aimed at total insight (*vispassana*) into the emptiness, impermanence, and painfulness of everything that exists—including the states of the other series, that of meditative concentration (*jhana*), the aim of which is total serenity. By what looks like a compromise between advocates of different methods, 'cessation', the goal of both series, is said to require the union of total insight with total serenity.[19]

What concerns us here is the nature of meditative concentration, not the exact progress of its states. This style of concentration, which resembles classical yoga, requires consciousness to be fixed on a series of objects that decrease in their materiality or definiteness until, with consciousness fixed on 'nothing', there is neither sensation nor thought. To begin the series of meditations, the turmoil of discursive thought is eased and the mind made tranquil, after which the mind is fixed on an object as featureless as possible, for example, a disk very evenly covered with dawn-colored clay of the sort found in the Ganges River.[20] With eyes open neither too little nor too much, one stares at the color and simultaneously thinks its name or concept—such as *earth, earth*—repeated many times, now with eyes shut, now with eyes open. When the image and name have become firm, one can sit elsewhere and develop the image until its purified, colorless, and shapeless counterpart-sign breaks out in the mind, which becomes concentrated. The initial disk and color fill consciousness in a now dematerialized form, the ordinary life-continuum is interrupted, and a stream of more profitable impulses can be experienced.[21]

The description I have given is highly abbreviated from its scholastic source. I give it only to suggest how psychophysical processes are enlisted to dematerialize and finally 'do away with' all the world's sensory, cognitive, and emotional content. The first meditation, described just above, is said to give a rapturously "uplifting happiness" with power enough "to levitate the body, make it spring up into the air."[22]

In a second, higher state of meditative concentration, the consciousness of materiality is thinned and one enters into a state devoid of "applied thought" and "sustained thought," both of which are "quieted, quietened, stilled, set at rest, set quite at rest, done away with, dried up, quite dried up, made an end of."[23] The result is again rapturous. But then, as one emerges from the second stage of meditation, happiness itself appears gross; and as happiness fades away and the third state of meditation is entered, one feels a clear-minded neutrality toward everything and, though not aimed at, the greatest possible bliss. And now, at the beginning of the fourth state of meditation, pleasure and pain of all sorts are abandoned and mindfulness is clarified by equanimity.[24]

Four states of ascending, immaterial transcendence are left. The first is one in which—going beyond perception of material shapes, sensory reactions, and perception of variety—one thinks unbounded space. Transcending this state, one thinks unbounded consciousness. Transcending this state, one thinks no-thingness, "there is not anything" and "void, void." Then, transcending this state, one thinks neither perception nor nonperception. And then, although very rarely, there is a great final leap of transcendence and all perception and feeling come to an end.[25]

By means of such a process, one is supposed to think away or transcend any and all perceptions, conceptions, and emotional states. Having also (in full scholastic theory) attained insight by the other necessary meditations as well as by the essential bodily and moral discipline, one can simply cease to be. That is, although one's body continues to retain its vital heat, all mental and bodily functions, including breathing, come to a stop for as long as a week or more because one's mind has 'perished' and one has, while still alive, entered the Unborn and Unmanifest state, which is the 'postexperiential' state of Nirvana.[26]

❦

These descriptions, from a source that reflects a probably earlier Buddhism, were accepted with different philosophical accentuations by the schools under Nagarjuna's influence. One of the issues that arose was the opposition between insight attained gradually and attained immediately. Although Buddhists believed that they had time and lives enough to work slowly toward Nirvana, personal experience, Taoist or other influences, and perhaps ordinary, un-Buddhistic impatience must have made some Buddhists anxious to arrive as close to Nirvana as quickly as possible.

One response of the more patient teachers is quite predictable: Although the goal is intuitive insight unattainable by conceptual knowledge of any kind, it is the hoped-for result of systematic guidance by experienced masters. These masters not only teach how to practice Buddhist compassion and discipline body and mind, but also subject their students to a dialectical process of the kind suggested by Nagarjuna's reasoning. To realize that something comes from nowhere, one must begin by asking where it comes from and where it is going. Intelligent thought is part of the process. Put in an image, to succeed in turning the duality of conceptual knowledge into the unity of the nonconceptual is like rubbing together two firesticks (representing conceptual duality) to produce fire (nonconceptual unity) by means of the friction between them.[27]

The Buddhist philosopher Kamalashila, who held a historic debate in Tibet (about 792 A.D.) against Indian and Tibetan advocates of sudden enlightenment, argued that nonconceptual knowledge could not be attained by the simple neglect of cognition or of attentive effort. Our thought, he said, is too obstinately moored in mental habits that lead us to believe in the existence of material and immaterial entities.[28]

For the contrary position, historically the loser in Tibet, it was easier to quote texts or invent striking images or intriguing paradoxes than to develop a consistently reasoned position. To believers in sudden enlightenment, the systematic means proposed by others seemed incompatible with the desired goal. They asked how it was possible to use the pure delusions of ordinary life to find something of a different, purer nature. How is thought-construction itself, of which we hope to free ourselves, able to discover what is beyond it? How can we talk about what we cannot talk about, a subject which, with respect to words and concepts, is literally nothing at all?

> To turn the light of the mind towards the mind's source—that is contemplating the mind. This means that one does not reflect or examine whether conceptual signs are in movement or not, whether they are pure or not, whether they are empty or not. It also means not to reflect on nonreflection. This is why the *Vimalakirti Sutra* explains: "Non-examination is enlightenment."[29]

In Tibet, the dominant position came to be the gradualist one espoused by the Gelugpas, an order of monks founded in the fourteenth century. The members of this order maintain that certain concepts furnish a method for access to the ultimate. Concepts can serve in this way, they believe, because conceptual thought and direct perception are essentially the same: both are by nature clear and knowing, and the concentration of the one and insight of the other are mutually reinforcing. Insight is gained not by leaping over a chasm between two basically different kinds of experience but by shifting from the one mode to the other.[30]

How does one transform conceptual thought into the direct perception of 'emptiness'? The answer is that one "alternates between analytic meditation and stabilizing meditation" until the point is reached where analysis does not interfere with stabilization and stabilization does not weaken analytical reasoning. Instead, each enhances the other. In this way, beginning with the correct conceptual framework, one strives to achieve "a direct, non-dualistic cognition of emptiness that is like fresh water poured into fresh water. Subject and object—the mind and the emptiness—are fused as one." [31]

Lao Tzu Devalues Words as Inadequate to Tao, the Mother of All

For China, I begin with Lao Tzu, a sage whose very existence it is possible to doubt.[32] If this oddly unbookish "historiographer in charge of the archives of Chou" is not a figment of the historiographical imagination, he may have lived, as Chinese tradition says, during the time of

Confucius, the sixth century B.C.; or he may have lived during the third century B.C., a date scholars now generally prefer.[33] If Lao Tzu did ever exist, he wrote or compiled the *Tao Te Ching* or *Classic of the Way and Its Power*, which I refer to here because of its suggestive power, its enormous influence in China, and its frequent stress on ineffability. Its romantic-sounding obscurities still continue to goad on translators and commentators.

There is more than enough evidence that a philosophically consistent explanation of the text as a whole ends by becoming forced. The inconsistencies of the text would be explained if it were only a compilation edited by someone more interested in making a poetic, religious, and social effect than in being consistent; or would be explained, in keeping with romantic attitudes, if the author were a poet-sage doubling as a political adviser, who considered self-contradiction to be a virtue allowing him access to a more than merely logical understanding. The compiler or poet-sage, whoever he may have been, believes that the power of nature can be drawn out by a deep, canny so-to-speak nonmanipulation. It may be added that this compiler or poet-sage does not feel any particular reverence for ordinary humanity. He is primarily interested in his own kind of 'over-man'.

The tao of the book's title has many meanings in Chinese but translates comfortably enough into *way*, with all the meanings of *way*. According to most commentators, the ineffability of the way in its most basic sense is expressed in the book's traditionally famous first, key sentences: "The way that can be spoken of is not the constant way. The name that can be named is not the constant name."[34] This translation is only one of two different possibilities, because the character rendered *be spoken of* can be rendered with equal or, I feel, superior plausibility by *followed* or the like. The two oldest known manuscripts—discovered in 1973 in a tomb at Ma-Wang-tui village—have a less ambiguous text for the first sentence, which translates, "The way can be spoken of (*or*, The way can be followed), but it will not be the constant way." Then comes a second, symmetrical sentence, "The name can be named, but it will not be the constant name."[35]

If we accept the conventional translation of the traditionally accepted text, we discover that the ineffable 'constant' tao, which, for good measure, is declared unnameable, is nevertheless often given a name, such as *mother, ancestor, storehouse, uncarved block, great form*, and, of course, *tao* itself.[36] The constant, primal tao is also often described, as, for example, *unchanging, everlasting, inexhaustible, independent*, and *natural*.[37] The tao is also given many negative characterizations, such as *invisible, inaudible, vacuous*, and, above all, *non-being*. Therefore, despite what 'Lao Tzu' often says, the tao as he conceives it is not something to which words can in no sense be applied; and sometimes 'Lao Tzu' prefers to speak not of the impossibility but only of the great difficulty of assigning a name to the tao he praises with the fervor, almost, of a worshipper:

> There is a thing confusedly formed,
> Born before heaven and earth.
> Silent and void
> It stands alone and does not weary.
> It is capable of being the mother of the world.
> I know not its name
> So I style it 'the way'.
> I give it the makeshift name of 'the great'.[38]

It turns out that the Taoist worthy of the name is as hard to describe as the tao itself; and so the ancient Taoist sage can be given only a "makeshift" description, for he is "minutely subtle, mysteriously comprehending," not to say "tentative," "hesitant," "formal," and, to change metaphorical course, "Thick like the uncarved block; / Vacant like a valley; / Murky like muddy waters."[39]

I do not think that I should struggle for what Lao Tzu calls, in the translation I am using, a "makeshift explanation," meaning, as I understand it, a forced, unsatisfactory one. Still, I think that something fairly plausible can be said to explain the ineffability the text so often insists upon and the names and adjectives, positive and negative, that it nevertheless proliferates.

It appears to me that when Lao Tzu—or the group of Lao Tzu's who may have written the text—refers (or refer) to ineffability, he is (or they are) thinking of the view, discussed in the previous chapter, that the way to proper understanding requires that words be applied with the utmost care for correctness, especially as they concern human behavior. To the philosophers who held this view, it was essential that morally relevant concepts should be applied with no concessions to rulers or to the relativists who might serve the rulers' destructive purposes. Although Chinese philosophers thought of the world in terms of processes rather than fixed objects, the insistence on exact terms implied that concepts have the fixed essential meanings by which we are obliged to guide our behavior.

As has been said earlier, all this is deeply Chinese, but Lao Tzu will have none of it. He refuses to believe that nature can be neatly categorized or that anything of importance can be caught in a concept, a literally proper 'name'. In particular, Lao Tzu does not believe that such a name can fit the inaudible, invisible, all-pervading, all-determining 'some-what'. To Lao Tzu, truly fitting (truly revealing) names can never be given to the unchanging *tao*, the unchanging *way* that things basically are, the unchanging principal or law of action that modulates the chang-ing, often cyclical interactions, that all things undergo.

The reason Lao Tzu most often gives for the inability of language or logic to be adequate to the tao is that tao in its absolute sense is the mother and ancestor of everything, the mother who merits the obscure name *nonbeing* (analogous, I think, to potentiality) rather better than she does the name *being* (analogous to actuality); and yet tao is both being and nonbeing because the fluidity, diversity, and endless creativity of the source of all must depend on the interplay of both polarities. We name a particular thing in order to assign it limits in relation to other, also limited things. But how can we 'name' the unparticular, unlimited source of everything particular? For the tao in its absolute sense is taken to be all-inclusive and all-creative, as different from everything nameable as the inexhaustible source must be from the ten thousand creatures, activities, and fates that it brings to birth.

As evidence for this view of Lao Tzu's understanding of ineffability, I should like to cite the interpretation given by his earliest surviving commentator, the philosopher Han Fei Tzu, who lived during the third century B.C. Han Fei writes, "Tao is the way of everything, the form of every principle" by virtue of which every thing comes into being as just what it is. "Tao is the cause of the completion of everything," because it rules, that is, orders things.[40] Each thing has its own principle, different from that of all others, and is responsible for its separation, distinctness, transformative power, and ability to enter into orderly relationships with other things.

Tao, which gives everything its definite nature and particular trans-formative powers, is commensurate with the limited principles of all of them. Tao is therefore present everywhere, contains all qualities, and suffers no restraints.

> Near as you might suppose it to be, it travels to the four poles of the world. Far as you might suppose it to be, it always abides by the side of everybody. Dim as you might suppose it to be, its gleam is glitter-ing. Bright as you might suppose it to be, its body is obscure. By its achievement heaven and earth are formed. Thus everything in the world owes it its formation. By nature the inner reality of Tao is neither restrained nor embodied. It is either soft or weak according as the occasion is, and always in correspondence with principles . . .

Thus, people die of it, live owing to it, fail because of it, and succeed on account of it.[41]

Han Fei continues that although it is impossible to hear or see Tao—which I now capitalize as an absolute—the true sage "imagines its real features in the light of its present effect. Hence the saying, 'It is the form of the formless, the image of the imageless' . . . What is eternal has neither a changing location nor a definite principle" of its own, so it is not bound to any definite locality. "That is why it is said that it cannot be told," even though the sage, seeing its mysterious emptiness, can give it the forced name, Tao.[42]

To this explanation by Han Fei, I should like to add that, by Taoist principles, trying to name things is an effort of the same overexplicit, overambitious sort that estranges a person from his instincts and hardens him against changing as life, his own deep life, flows, turns, returns, rests, and goes on again, all in consonance with the natural forces that shift from one large but subtle equilibrium to another. According to Taoism, a serious conscious effort, for instance, to stiffen moral principles by naming them 'rightly', leads to misunderstanding and, probably, to harshness and crime. To the Taoists, to name something is to detach it egregiously from its being and nonbeing. Like a fish out of water, something named is out of nature; it can be handled easily, but it is dead.

By a Taoist chain of reasoning, conscious effort should be given up for Waywardness because

> in the pursuit of learning one knows more every day; in the pursuit of the *way* one does less every day. One loses every day until one does nothing at all, and when one does nothing at all there is nothing that is undone . . . Therefore the sage keeps to the deed that consists in taking no action and practices the teaching that uses no words.[43]

Nothing in Lao Tzu is built with the intellectual care we ascribe to philosophers. Yet his view of the relation between determinate things and tao and between the nameable and unnameable is clearly like the views of European philosophers who devalued words. Like many philosophers, Lao Tzu thinks that the reality from which everything is generated cannot be described in words but is described least inadequately in contradictories and negations. Perhaps, as I will say, Lao Tzu fell into a pattern of thought from which it is difficult for philosophers to escape—

although, if we turn out to be lucky, no need to escape from it may be needed.

Chuang Tzu Relativizes Words with Love and Inconsistency

From Lao Tzu, I go on to Chuang Tzu, the second great Taoist classic. This too is a composite work, compiled, perhaps, in the second century B.C. But its so-called "inner chapters" are plausibly attributed to the individual whose name the whole work bears, an individual who lived during the fourth century B.C. He is therefore likely to have preceded the author or compiler of the *Tao Te Ching*, whose name was linked with his many centuries later as a leader of the merely retrospective school of philosophical (Lao-Chuang) Taoism.[44]

Even if the interpreter confines himself to the inner chapters of Chuang Tzu, he faces a difficult alternative—to interpret him in the light of a long tradition, or to try to interpret him almost anew, in the light of the terse, often discontinuous text alone. The main difference is that the first alternative makes Chuang Tzu a mystical believer in the one Way, preaching Illumination, while the second alternative, according to the interpretation I have adopted (mainly from Chad Hansen), makes the 'inner' Chuang Tzu a more nearly consistent skeptic, who does not believe in but even argues against the one Way, in favor of what might be called *wayness*, an indeterminate multiplicity of ways, points of view, and discriminations. Blindness is then equivalent not to the inability to intuit the Tao but to narrowness, the refusal to see that there are no limits to experience and no real adjudicator among points of view.

Chuang Tzu is surely a complex, sharp, imaginative, poetic, and irreverent individual, whose extraordinary command over words is emphasized by his recurrent devaluation of their significance; whose love for the exuberant creativity of nature is matched by his lack of possessiveness and his nonchalance toward life and death; and whose relativism seems not to be contradicted by his praise of an unassuming but elusive naturalness. He accepts every experience as it comes from and goes nowhere or everywhere, delights in every bodily organ and function, and tries to understand what governs the order or disorder by which nature functions and the parts of the body interact; but he neither regrets nor profits from the ability or inability to find any answer to the question who, if anyone, or what, if anything, rules.

Unlike Lao Tzu, Chuang Tzu often speaks the language of reason even while controverting it, so there is a better chance of understanding what he says and why he says it. He doubts all statements, but this does not mean that he thinks the world is different from the way it appears to merely innocent vision. He accepts this innocence; he values common sense; and the artisans' easy skill is his model of the adjustment of human existence to the natural world. The reasoning he prefers is not abstractly logical, categorical, or argumentative, and is not grounded in unchanging principles. Instead, it is transparently sensitive to occasion and it 'grades' things and varies itself exactly as the occasion demands.

This reasoning is spontaneous, economical, practical, graceful, clear, and sagelike. Above all, it is an effortless participation in nature rather than an attempt to impose oneself on it. And because it has no unchanging principles or fixed logic, words cannot describe it, except fleetingly or in the guise of the paradoxical acceptance and rejection of paradoxical statements such as can be developed if one begins with Chuang Tzu's words, "Saying is not blowing breath, saying says something; the only trouble is that what it says is never fixed."[45]

Saying? Words? There is so much to say of them because what exactly we should say of them is not clear, at least not clear when put into words. If you think that words are more freighted with abstract meanings than are the chirps of baby birds, is there or is there not any distinction to prove that what you think is so? How does it happen that ways, taos—resilient, mutable, and impartial as they are—become so obscured that we are obliged to distinguish the genuine from the false? By what can words—which fix things arbitrarily—become so obscured that they are blindly put to use to affirm and deny whatever it is that they affirm and deny? How can anyone act in some determinate way if there is no way on which to go? And yet, whatever standpoint is taken, how can there be words that are simply inadmissible?

The difficulty is that ways, taos, are obscured by small accomplishments, while words are obscured by an ornate style. Therefore society is confronted with the rigid Confucian and Mohist debates on rights and wrongs, one side affirming what the other denies and denying what the other affirms, each exercising logic from its particular standpoint.[46]

What is so from one standpoint, we see, is otherwise from another. We discover that everything involves its opposite, comes from it, and is born simultaneously with it. Because everything involves its opposite, to live is simultaneously to die; for living requires constant changes that are small dyings, so something can die only if it is alive at the same time as it dies; and, likewise, to die is simultaneously to live, for dying is a condition of which only living things are capable. Likewise, to allow something implies that it is simultaneously hedged about by limitations and is therefore also restricted, which is to say, forbidden.[47]

To allow and forbid is to make distinctions, and the making of distinctions, like the evaluations that must accompany them, can only lead us astray. For instance, when we evaluate something as either perfect or flawed, our evaluation depends upon the taking of a definite, limited point of view—like the judging of all zither performances by the particular style of zither playing that one has adopted. Therefore the sage, he who makes use of clarity, disdains the glib but implausible debates that fixed standpoints encourage. Unlike him, we confuse truth with the winning of arguments and the verdicts of the necessarily prejudiced judges.[48]

To understand without limitation or prejudice, we must see that the ways—the taos—cannot simply be one Way because being one requires being more than one. If I say that heaven, earth, the innumerable things, and I are all one, I have already implied that there are two 'things' that can be enumerated, because the very act of saying—that heaven, earth, and the innumerable things are all one—is something additional to the postulated oneness. And two things and saying they are two make three, and so on.[49]

As these examples show, analysis is by nature misleading, and the effort even to distinguish one thing from another can never be quite successful. Reason shows and intuition confirms that

> to "divide" . . . is to leave something undivided: to "discriminate between alternatives" is to leave something which is neither alternative. "What?" you ask. The sage keeps it in his breast, common men argue over alternatives to show it to each other. Hence I say: "To 'discriminate between alternatives' is to fail to see something."[50]

Yet though discrimination between alternatives is misleading, and though the words we use for the discrimination are too rigid, words are also natural and inevitable; they too have their momentary plausibilities and effective approximations; and they can even express our ability to assume points of view other than our own and, in moving from position to position, to escape our limitations. And words even allow us to savor illuminating contradictions, develop poetic intuitions, and move verbally with the assurance and unselfconscious skill that show that we have found a natural way.

Briefly, every object, experience, and truth is ineffable but not completely so, because speech is natural, distinctions are needed, and the assuming of viewpoints is inevitable. Just as words can go beyond themselves in persuading us that the way and the ways are ineffable and that words are useless, so our ability to sense the degree to which they are ineffable illuminates for us the necessity and naturalness of useless talk. In this sense even useful talk is tolerable because it is really also useless.

Knowing this helps keep us from harm, Chuang Tzu implies. Is he serious or only playing the fantastic humorist (or both serious and humorous) when he speaks of the ideal perfected man, a man daimonic in the Greek sense, whose complete waywardness makes him immune to the blazing fire of the woodlands, to the freezing waters of the great rivers, and to fear of anything? "A man like this rides the clouds and mist, straddles the sun and moon, and wanders beyond the four seas. Even life and death have no effect on him, much less the rules of profit and loss!"[51] The full appreciation of the ineffability of the Taoistic ways can take us as far as such perfection (or, less astonishingly, such a metaphor for perfection).

It is reasonable to construe Chuang Tzu's position to be rather like that of the sophisticated exponent of Nagarjuna. However, unlike the Buddhist philosophers we have discussed, he is not much burdened by the seriousness of seeing through words and other illusions, and not at all by the conviction that his own existence is illusory. It is true that there are Zen monks who come close to Chuang Tzu in their irreverent insouciance; but, as monks, they are too burdened, from his standpoint, with dogmatic attitudes, minutely prescribed duties, and a fixed morality.

The Zen Buddhists Use Words to Overcome Words by Solving Verbally Insoluble Riddles

Although the abstract background of Ch'an, that is, Zen Buddhism, is clearly the thought of Nagarjuna, it is also to a great but not measurable degree that of Lao Tzu and Chuang Tzu. After a clash between advocates of sudden and gradual enlightenment, suddenness won and became characteristic of Zen.[52] So did antiverbalism, and although they publicized texts that spread their views, Zen monks sometimes made a point of attacking Buddhist texts because they, too, were texts; and on rare occasions, to drive home the pointlessness of texts, a radical might actually burn some of them. The erection of statues, the service of elders, and virtuous deeds in general, might also be declared unnecessary by such a radical. A historian of Zen ascribes the radicalism to the conjunction of the Buddhist with the Taoist:

> The mixing of Buddhist and Taoist elements resulted in a contribution to religious history that was both unique and enriching. Zen disciples burn Buddhist images and sutras, laugh in the face of inquirers or suddenly shout at them, and indulge in a thousand follies.

Though they may behave like fools and possess nothing, they feel themselves true kings in the liberating energy of enlightenment. They know no fear, for they desire nothing and have nothing to lose.[53]

Once they finished the lighthearted play that symbolized their freedom, says the historian, the monks returned to read sutras before the Buddha's image. Radical or not, Zen monks were all in search of transcendental freedom. By means of repeated exercises in transrationality—such as the 'solving' of rationally insoluble riddles—they sought to break through the inferior level of words and reason to the 'emptiness' that was (by the usual Buddhist formula) neither objective nor subjective, nor both at once, nor neither. To break through the barriers of verbalism and rationality usually required prolonged efforts. The moment of breaking though might be accompanied by speech, but the monks understood that this was speech in a void in which there was neither speaker, nor speech, nor anyone to hear the 'non-existent' speech. Naturally, to those who "remained entangled in the meshes of semantic articulation," what was uttered in such contexts sounded merely nonsensical.[54]

A believer in Zen considers the experience of emptiness to be quite indescribable. Yet attempts to describe it, both in poetry and prose, were made and continue to be made, especially in Japan. Hakuin (A.D. 1685–1768), the renewer of Rinzai Zen, wrote notable descriptions of his lesser and greater experiences of satori, descriptions that furnished a precedent for other Zen monks. We learn from them that as the negation of everything logical or determinate takes effect and meditation grows more profound, sensitivity to light, color, and sound increases. The insight or surge of emotion that may follow may be only a preliminary state.[55] A state of true enlightenment, satori, may be precipitated by the master's gaze directed at the disciple's eyes, or by the master's gesture or touch. The enlightenment that follows may be relatively weak, or may be of the very 'root of nothingness'.

As the descriptions show, the state of enlightenment is a sense beyond words of the oneness, holiness, and purity of all (including, indistinguishably, oneself) or, in alternate terminology, a sense of the identity of nothingness, the universe, and the Buddha. A disciple who broke through to enlightenment reports that familiar words he had read— "Clearly I know, the mind is mountains, rivers, and the great earth; sun, moon, and stars"—pierced his entire body like a bolt of lightning. Joy burst forth, he recalls, like the roaring of the surf, and he uttered a cry and burst out laughing. He knew that this was a true experience. "He had gotten up and was tearing at the blanket and thumping the bed with both knees when his wife and child appeared in consternation. His wife tried to hold his mouth shut with both her hands."[56]

In China it grew common by the seventeenth century to say that the true experience of poetry was like that of Zen, and the old, Taoistically tinged belief in the artist's outbreaks of creative vitality was discussed in terms borrowed from Zen. Like the literati in general, Zen monks often occupied themselves with poetry, calligraphy, and painting. The claim was even made that "outside of poetry there is no Zen, outside of Zen there is no poetry."[57] However, there were poets who held that spontaneity was valid only if it came after a long preparation or came within and because of the traditional rules of poetry.[58]

Opponents of the comparison of poetic with Ch'an experience said that the truth of Ch'an cannot be expressed in words, while the very being of poetry depends upon words. They argued that Ch'an is concerned with what is elusive and distant, while poetry is concerned with what is actual and familiar in ordinary human existence.[59] As the result of such a distinction, the Chinese monk Chiao-jan (A.D. 730?–799?) decided late in life

> to give up the writing of poetry, believing that it was not proper for a practitioner of Zen. Vowing to "speak no more words" but to devote himself entirely to meditation, he ceased his literary endeavors and ordered his disciples to take away his writing brushes and ink stone.[60]

Although there were Zen masters both in China and Japan who took fierce exception to the composition of poetry by monks, the ironic fact is that the depth of person's grasp of Zen might be measured by his facility in writing, a measure that in Japan was applied especially to writing in the Chinese language. A critic says that most of the poetry written by Zen monks was stereotyped and strove for novelty by way of ingenious variations on stock themes. Zen freedom-seeking inevitably developed its own poetic habits.[61]

In Europe, Kierkegaard Loves and Devalues Words and Seeks the Truth in Contradictions

The shift from Chuang Tzu and Zen Buddhism to Søren Kierkegaard (1813–55) is sudden, yet they all take a thematically similar attitude to language. True, he is as much an individual in his attitude to language as to anything else. He is, to begin with, the sort of person who prefers inner over outer vision. Dreams give him indescribable happiness, the obverse of his basic unhappiness. Like the Englishman's home, his sorrow is his castle or, rather, his theater, and in his mind he plays the immoral roles of a thief and a miser, and the painful one of a dying man.[62] But a mental picture is not enough for him; it has to be created in eloquent words, whose power and order fascinate him.[63] Words affect him like a lover. His susceptibility is reflected in his report that the grammatical rules he has learned for the indicative and conjunctive have caused an extraordinary change in his consciousness; and he comes to sense that everything depends on how a thing is thought, "so that thought in its absoluteness replaces an apparent reality."[64] Musing one day, he says to himself that "all of human life could well be conceived as a great discourse in which different people come to represent the different parts of speech (this might also be applicable to nations in relation to each other). How many people are merely adjectives, interjections, conjunctions, adverbs; how few are nouns, action words, etc.; how many are copulas."[65]

Words are quite real to Kierkegaard, and he loves them so much that sometimes he is able, he says, "to sit for hours enamored with the sound of words, that is, when they have the ring of pregnant thought; I have been able to sit for hours like a flutist entertaining himself with his flute."[66] He even feels he can charm the words into physical existence.

But the relation with words can grow difficult. Kierkegaard finds that, for all their creative power, words go to extremes and then become too painfully real or too painfully unreal. Both extremes are joined in the novel he imagines writing, in which one of the characters goes mad while writing it and he, the author, finishes the novel in the first person.[67] Words, he feels, can be the medium for truth and existence but also for their opposites. Language is therefore no less dangerous to man than his fleshly appetites; its false sublimities seduce him into appearing more noble than he is. If one took away man's language, his medium for misrepresentation, he would at least have to be sincere.[68]

No less evil than good, says Kierkegaard, language destroys and creates, is demonic and angelic, judges and is judged. When intoxicated with his verbal ability, he thinks it possible for words to constitute a whole individual existence; yet all told, they are disappointing, and he attacks the ideas they voice for not being what he has imagined them to be, even though to us, his readers, his words still cry, laugh, and seduce in his place, until the time comes when they more and more often confine themselves to attacking and praying.

And so this short Dane with a hurt spine comes to hate and depreciate words as much as he loves and exalts them. He prefers to take refuge in the individual, in the irrational, in what lies beyond words, and in the paradox or translogical jump that links the necessary and eternal with the unnecessary and passing. While the discovery of the paradox causes suffering, he says, surrender to it is a victory. In Kierkegaard's words, "One should not think ill of the paradox, for the paradox is the passion of thought, and the thinker without the paradox is like the lover without passion: a mediocre fellow." Revealingly, Kierkegaard adds:

> But the ultimate potentiation of every passion is always to will its own downfall, and so it is also the ultimate passion of the understanding to will the collision, although in one way or another the collision must become its downfall. This, then, is the ultimate paradox of thought: to want to discover something that thought itself cannot think.[69]

Kierkegaard writes with eloquent intimacy on the paradox of erotic love that transforms the lover beyond his own recognition; and he compares this paradox of self-surrender with the paradoxical passion of the understanding that strikes up against the unknown. This passion is for the unknown that can be named only *god*; but "it hardly occurs to the understanding to want to demonstrate that this unknown (the god) exists."[70] Such a relation to what exists is difficult because one can get from existence to reason but never the opposite. What good can it do to declare that we cannot know the unknown and, if we could, would be unable to express it? "Just saying that involves a relation" and a limit beyond which the understanding can go no further.[71] Fortunately, a limit is just the passion's torment and incentive.[72]

The paradox grows terrifying: The understanding cannot retain its own nature while accepting the answer *god*, and yet it cannot evade its paradoxical passion. In the passion of its willed downfall, understanding and paradox may achieve mutuality and the encounter, like the mutual self-surrender of erotic love, may turn out to be happy. The understanding may flaunt its virtues and denigrate the paradox, but the truth is that "everything it says about the paradox it has learned from the paradox" itself.[73]

Schopenhauer Makes an Influential Attack on Words in Favor of Art, Especially Music

The choice of Kierkegaard to represent the devaluers of words is obvious, but he is so much the self-conscious virtuoso of language that his attack on words has an undertone verging on irony. His self-refuting eloquence and his emphasis on the individual are a suitable introduction to the group of individualistic philosophers—Schopenhauer, Nietzsche, Wittgenstein, Heidegger, and Derrida—that I will use to illustrate how words have been devalued by strategies no less literary than philosophical. Judged in abstract terms, these strategies are not very original, I am afraid to say, and are rescued from their weariness only by the great talent, even genius, of the five. I assume that it is no accident that every one of this group of devaluers is able to reason sharply and write eloquently. It takes a clearly flexible mind to carry out an effective attack using words—for lack of a better weapon—to persuade us that verbal persuasion is empty.

I will react to this paradox later. For the moment, I turn to Schopenhauer, especially to his attack on words or concepts, to his glorification of music in their place, and to the variants of his attack in the thought of Nietzsche and Wittgenstein.

Schopenhauer believes that the reality within us, which he calls by the Kantian name *noumenon*, is beyond our grasp. However, he argues, we know enough to realize that although inaccessible, it is the very being of each of us; and we know and feel that this being of each of us is the same as the will that moves us both physically and spiritually. And because reality must be one and the same everywhere, everything external to us must be the manifestation of the same will that constitutes us internally. This, the internal and external reality, is the cosmic will expressed by all things, living or not, in their movements, pressures, tensions, attractions, repulsions, and transformations—in the same way as my body is the external form of my will, the universe is the external form of the cosmic force of will.[74]

This is the tenor of Schopenhauer's metaphysics of the will. His philosophy of language and art rests on the sharp contrast he draws between abstract thought and perception. He thinks that in order to live efficiently, we have to turn our attention away from the richness of perception and abstract from it what is most useful to us. To do so, we use our unique human powers of abstraction and create instruments of thought that are practical because the knowledge they yield is easy to fix, retain, and communicate.[75]

So far, so good; but although our powers of abstraction prove so useful, they are also limiting, says Schopenhauer. One reason is that only a very small number of concepts can be present in consciousness at the same time. A second reason is that abstractions, which are knowledge in its communicable form, are also knowledge at its most impoverished. By contrast, perception, which is richly simultaneous and incomparably immediate, cannot be retained or communicated because everyone is confined, as a perceiver, to a single skin and skull. Wisdom and genius, says Schopenhauer, "are rooted not in the abstract and discursive, but in the perceptive faculty." To him, perception is both the source of knowledge and its unconditional form, the only kind that can enter into man's inner nature and impart insight.[76]

If, with Schopenhauer, we grant the primacy of perception, we grant that of art and artist. The artist, who creates in response to phenomena, is led by them toward their sources, which are Ideas (in a somewhat Platonic sense). In Schopenhauer's view, Ideas participate directly in the noumenon, reality as such. Art therefore gives us the pure pleasure we experience when our consciousness is suffused with an Idea—the direct, timeless, and spaceless manifestation of the noumenon.

In Schopenhauer's eyes, life is inescapably tragic, because the very acts of will that constitute us emerge from deficiency and desire, which are by nature endless. As against our desires, our fulfillments are meager and brief, so that as long as our consciousness is dominated by our will, we can never become really happy or peaceful. Whether we pursue or flee from the objects of our desire, we remain restless and fundamentally unhappy.[77] Only when we succeed in tearing ourselves away from the will by means of art, especially poetry and, more especially, music, do we enter into a world in which nothing agitates us violently. Then, for the while, we stop being individuals and become altogether "that one eye which looks out from all knowing creatures, but which in man alone can be wholly free from serving the will."[78]

⟨◦⟩

Schopenhauer's metaphysical evaluation of music deserves a brief historic preface. His severance of art from words is typical of the European romantics. To them, as the poet Novalis expresses it, all that is seen clings to what we cannot see; all that is heard clings to what we cannot hear; all that is touched clings to what we cannot touch; and all that we think clings, perhaps, to the Unthinkable.[79] The romantic philosopher Schelling praises art in hymnal style as, so to speak, opening to the philosopher "the holy of holies, where burns in eternal and original unity, as if in a single flame, that which in nature and history is rent asunder, and in life and action, no less than in thought, must forever fly apart."[80]

The romantics, who proclaim the tie of music to imaginative literature, go further and often judge music to be superior to anything words can in any way convey. Music, says Novalis, has acoustic control of the soul; and Schumann, who feels forced to put into music everything extraordinary that happens to him, says that "music speaks the most general language, affecting the soul in a free and totally undetermined way. And yet the soul feels as though it were in its homeland."[81]

When such an attitude prevails, it is not difficult to believe that the wordlessness or purity of instrumental music enhances its power; and it becomes possible to claim, along with E. T. A. Hoffmann, that only instrumental music, unassisted by any other art, can give pure expression to the nature of music. Music alone, says Hoffmann, unlocks a world quite apart from the external, material one and makes it possible for us to surrender ourselves to the inexpressible. It is in this vein that he praises Beethoven's Fifth Symphony for scorning the help of poetry and advises composers not to try to describe definite feelings or events.

Idiosyncratic though he is, Schopenhauer fits well into this landscape of romantic European thought. He is convinced that music is the deepest and most powerful of the arts.[82] Its depth, the infinitude of its truth, is proved, he says, by the ability of everyone to understand it at once; and it has a certain infallibility in that it is governed by numerically expressible rules. Related directly to the innermost being of both world and self, he says, music is independent of the merely external world. Unlike the other arts, therefore, it is a direct copy and objectification of the cosmic reality, the will-in-itself.

Schopenhauer is happy to startle his readers by claiming that music could exist to a certain extent even if there were no physical world: The other arts speak of the shadow of the will-in-itself, but music is of its essence. Schopenhauer recognizes in music all the grades of the (idiosyncratically Platonic) Ideas in which the will objectifies itself—from the ground bass, which objectifies inorganic nature as the mass of the planet, to melody, which connects everything, from beginning to end, in a meaningful sequence. Unlike the abstractions of reason, he says, melody tells the story of the intellectually enlightened human will, the story that, copied or embodied in 'actual' life, is the series of this will's deeds. Melody, however, does more than tell the story; it penetrates into and repeats aloud this will's most secret history, every least of its agitations, every movement from a desire to a satisfaction and from the satisfaction to a fresh desire. For this reason, melody constantly deviates from but always returns to a harmonious interval, especially to its keynote, all in a language that one's faculty of reason is unable to follow.

Schopenhauer reminds us that music is a generalized kind of expression. He means that it expresses the inward nature of a will, its "extracted quintessence"—not any particular, definite instance of emotion, but only "joy, pain, sorrow, horror, gaiety, merriment, peace of mind *themselves*, to a certain extent in the abstract, their essential nature . . . without the motives for them. Nevertheless, we understand them perfectly in this extracted quintessence."[83] (Whether or not Schopenhauer was aware of the fact, this doctrine of distanced, unindividual emotions and their closeness to the mystical experience of reality as such is the most usual doctrine of Indian aesthetics.)

To Schopenhauer, we recall, the will as expressed in the individual always leads to suffering. In music, however, because the will is as if abstracted and depolarized, we get not the pain of frustrated acts of willing but the painless experience of the will as it is in its own unsuffering, indescribable being. Actually, the goal of music, he is sure, is the same as that of philosophy. Its means, however, are superior because the "exceedingly universal language" of music makes use of the homogenous material of tones in order to speak the inner being of the world, the "in-itself" or cosmic will. In comparison with music, philosophy can explain the world only by making use of very general concepts. Loving music very deeply (and hating or despising most philosophers), Schopenhauer dares to say that

> whoever has followed me and has entered into my way of thinking will not find it so very paradoxical when I say that, supposing we succeeded in giving a perfectly accurate and complete explanation of music which goes into detail, and thus a detailed repetition in concepts of what it expresses, this would also be at once a sufficient repetition and explanation of the world in concepts, or one wholly corresponding thereto, and hence the true philosophy.[84]

So music expresses everything and the word, nothing—except, if successful, explains the superiority of music. Given Schopenhauer's devaluation of words, it is natural for him to argue that music does not need the words of a song or the action of an opera, which remain foreign to the music and of secondary value to it.[85] Yet he has a kind of complaint to make even of music because it strengthens the delusion of life by creating the simulacrum of a harmony that the nature itself of life makes impossible. Music assuages our pains at the cost of supporting our delusions.

Schopenhauer's philosophy of music, with its denigration of words, was extraordinarily influential. In *The Birth of Tragedy*, Nietzsche approves of it and quotes it at length.[86] He is not, however, the complete disciple and thinks that music is not a copy of the will but gives it only symbolic expression; and he does not refer to Ideas. He is also less pessimistic philosophically and believes that art can transfigure life and, by its acts of creation, justify the desire to remain alive. Yet, he, too, assigns music a superlative function and says "Only music, placed beside the world, can give us an idea of what is meant by the justification of the world as an aesthetic phenomenon."[87] Toward the end of his sane life he still echoes Schopenhauer when he describes art as "the *redemption of*

the sufferer—as the way to states in which suffering is willed, transfig-ured, deified, where suffering is a form of great delight."[88]

Nietzsche also says, as Schopenhauer would surely have approved, "Compared with music all communication by words is shapeless; words dilute and brutalize; words depersonalize; words make the uncommon common."[89] In Nietzsche's own not quite translatable German, this apho-rism goes, "Im *Verhältniss zur Musik* is alle Mitteilung durch *Worte* von schamloser Art; das Wort verdünnt und Verdummt; das Wort entpersönlicht; das Wort macht das Ungemeine gemein."

Wagner's regard for Schopenhauer grew so extreme that he claimed (unbelievably) to be too bashful to meet him. Even after he had felt it necessary to correct some details of Schopenhauer's system, he was ready to say in homage to the philosopher that in him he found himself "fully understood and clearly expressed" by means of "an intellectual under-standing which, by revealing me to myself, at the same time reveals the whole world to me!"[90]

By about 1900, Schopenhauer's metaphysics of music, transmitted by Nietzsche and Wagner, had become the aesthetic doctrine of most German composers. Together with Wagner, the two philosophers were among Mahler's early idols. It was Schopenhauer's belief that music re-flects the universal will that justified the universal ambitions that Mahler displays in his Third Symphony.[91] Schoenberg, too, reflects Schopenhauer's philosophy. Words, he thinks, are only a secondary form of expression, while music is a direct, unmediated capture of the essence of the world. For that reason, according to Schoenberg, when a poem is set to music or linked with a program, the text is only a metaphor for the "true language" of the music.[92]

Nietzsche Attacks Language and Logic

At the outset of his career as a philosopher, Nietzsche fell dramati-cally under Schopenhauer's spell. Schopenhauer apart, the discovery that opened Nietzsche's eyes most widely was that God had died—not that God had never existed, for he had existed in human need and belief, but that, tragically, he had died. Like Kierkegaard and Schopenhauer, Nietzsche assumes that most persons prefer to live in illusion. As he puts it early in his philosophical career, for practical reasons, the intellect—at least of the less robust persons—dissimulates, so that man typically lives in de-ception, by flattery, lies, and wearing of masks.

In this negative, almost nihilistic mood, Nietzsche asks how our language, with its dissimulating concepts, comes to be formed. His an-swer is that a concept begins in a visual image that someone can designate by a particular sound. Once used for this purpose, the sound is detached from the image to which it was first related and serves as a 'metaphor' for the countless number of more or less similar images. Such a generalized use of the sounds, which turns them into concepts, is necessary to make our experience orderly and help us master it. But this 'metaphorical' extension of sounds into concepts deceives us; it seems to us that by knowing the concepts we have invented, we know the things themselves that we see and name—the trees, colors, snow, flowers—but all we really know are the empty metaphors for them.[93]

It turns out, then, that concepts, the basic material with which the scientist and philosopher works, are not derived from the essence of things. Every concept makes us fall prey to the same basic misunderstanding: Because one leaf is never exactly the same as another, and because we arrive at the concept *leaf* by discarding the differences, we think that we have somehow failed to get at the true, unindividual leaf that fits the conceptual form perfectly. Nature, however, "is acquainted with no forms and no concepts, and likewise with no species, but only with an X which remains inaccessible and indefinable for us."[94]

The truth that human beings do bring to light, says Nietzsche, is completely anthropomorphic; at bottom, the searcher for truth is trying to make the world into something that resembles himself. Concept-creation by language has been continued in later ages by science, which constructs a great beehive of cells filled with the honey of concepts. In Nietzsche's mixed metaphor, this beehive of concepts is the graveyard of perceptions. By now, truth can no longer be recognized and "everything which is knowable is illusion." As a result, our culture and everything we value in it depend upon an illusion that will shipwreck science and lead to the tragic insight that life "needs art as a protection and remedy."[95]

Nietzsche's early acceptance of much of Schopenhauer weakened or vanished in time; but from early in his career, when he set down the notes I have been quoting or paraphrasing, he continued to argue that words, that is, concepts, were by nature deceptive. In *Human, All-Too-Human* he repeats the argument and adds:

> *Logic* too depends on presuppositions with which nothing in the real world corresponds, for example on the presupposition that there are identical things, that the same thing is identical at different points of time. . . . .It is the same with *mathematics*, which would certainly not have come into existence if one had known from the beginning that there was in nature no exactly straight line, no real circle, no absolute magnitude.[96]

Zarathustra is Nietzsche's attempt to escape from language as a lie, and he plays in it with the idea of a private language that transcends the public one.[97] As the story goes, Zarathustra falls silent for a time, or speaks only to himself or to the animals that embody him—the proud airborne eagle and the clever earthborne snake. He stigmatizes all public speech as idle talk based on resentment and designed to hide our anxiety from ourselves. On returning to his cave from a voyage of discovery, he finds that his motherly, beckoning, smiling, true home is his solitude. Here, in solitude, he can pour out all his reasons and obscure feelings. "Here the words and word-shrines of all being open up before" him and "here all being wishes to become word, all becoming wishes to learn" from him how to speak.[98]

This speaking solitude excludes the world "down there," where everyone talks everything to pieces and betrays everything. Up in solitude, Nietzsche's inner world is so fully open to himself that everything that is said is said in private and, for this reason, is true—truth is the quality of the words one talks, in happy silence, to oneself; falsehood or concealment is the quality of the words one talks across the void to the stupid, the ignoble, the vicious, and "the researchers and testers" whose sagacity is a digging of graves: the lie is the mean otherness of the other, smaller persons.[99]

Zarathustra uses his new freedom of language to call things by their true names. But he hears his abyss, his ultimate depth, coming; he hails it and collapses into a silence that lasts seven days. His animals ask if some bitter new knowledge has come to him, and they engage him in conversation. "How lovely," he responds, "that there are words and sounds! Are not words and sounds rainbows and illusive bridges between things which are eternally apart?" Solipsistically, he continues, "To every soul there belongs another world; for every soul is an afterworld. Precisely between what is most similar, illusion lies most beautifully; for the smallest cleft is the hardest to bridge." Even more solipsistically, he adds,

> For me—how should there be any outside-myself? There is no outside. But all sounds make us forget this; how lovely it is that we forget. Have not names and sounds been given to things that man might think things refreshing? Speaking is a beautiful folly: with that man dances over all things.[100]

Zarathustra's animals urge him to sing, and Zarathustra himself urges his soul, to which he has now given all, to speak, to sing to him. The animals' understanding shows itself to be too limited and their faith in his ability to sing new songs to be too simply optimistic, too likely to turn the song he has invented for himself into an external, hurdy-gurdy song. They urge him to fashion himself a new lyre for his new songs and fulfill his destiny and teach the eternal recurrence; and then they fall silent.[101]

Zarathustra, who does not hear their silence, lies still, conversing with his soul. Perhaps the truth of the eternal recurrence or the overman is too hard to express externally just as it is. Perhaps externalizing the truth robs it of its precision, depth, and terrible beauty. Zarathustra tells his soul that he understands the smile of its melancholy. If his soul is not to weep, it must sing till the world listens to "the nameless one for whom only future songs will find names."

To close this part of *Zarathustra*, there comes the "bird-wisdom" that tells Zarathustra-Nietzsche to sing, not speak, because all words are "made for the grave and heavy," and are "lies to those who are light."[102] He lusts after eternity; he has not found the woman from whom he wants children—unless this woman he loves is eternity.

Later, in "The Song of Melancholy", a discouraged Nietzsche assumes the role of the Old Magician, the Adversary, who calls Zarathustra the monster he loves against his will and sings, "*This*, the suitor of truth?/ No! Only fool! Only poet!"[103]

Toward the end of his sane life, Nietzsche again stresses that the axioms of logic are not adequate to reality but only "a means and measure for us to *create* reality, the concept 'reality' for ourselves." Not only are there no identical cases, but "the character of the world in a state of becoming" is "incapable of formulation. . . . Knowledge and becoming exclude one another." We do not know any facts but only interpretations. Even the 'subject' is an interpretation, "something added and invented and projected behind what there is"; and even the assumption that behind the interpretation there is an interpreter is only an invention or hypothesis. For the inner world, with its relation of subject and object, is hidden from us and perhaps imaginary. The world "has no meaning behind it, but countless meanings."[104]

Schopenhauer had been happy to find his truths foreshadowed, though unsystematically and unscientifically, he thought, in the Upanishads and in the Buddhist scriptures; and despite the incomparable eminence he attributed to himself, he sometimes counted himself a Buddhist.[105] Unlike Schopenhauer, Nietzsche had no reason to approve of the Indian denial of the ultimate value of life on earth. While his doubts concerning the ego's existence resemble those of the Buddhists, he took his life-affirmation to be the opposite of the passivity and life-negation he attributed to Buddhism. Yet he had considerable respect for the Buddhism he knew, that of the earlier, Theravadic kind, which appeared to him, unlike Christianity, to be mild, unrancorous, lofty, and philosophically quite consistent; and he studied it with considerable interest and speculated, not unhappily, on the chance that a European Buddhism might temporarily replace a worn-out Christianity.[106] Had he been familiar with Nagarjuna or Dignaga, he would have delighted, I think, in the coincidences with his own thought. I wonder if his pride would have been hurt if he had known of the Hua-yen school of Buddhism, which flourished in China from the seventh to the tenth centuries A.D., and which taught a perspectivism much more detailed than his own and equally radical.

Wittgenstein Regards Words as Limited to Externals

Like Nietzsche, the young Wittgenstein was powerfully influenced by Schopenhauer. To be sure, there were many early influences on Wittgenstein, including scientists such as Ludwig Boltzman, under whom he was eager to study. Nonscientists who influenced his style, his views, and even his model of what a person ought to be included Karl Kraus, Otto Weininger, Nietzsche, Tolstoy, and Emerson. At times he would quote "in the name of the great Kant."[107] However, despite these influences and his later disparagement of Schopenhauer as a fundamentally shallow thinker, his early *Notebooks* and his *Tractatus* show that Schopenhauer exerted a strong, sometimes decisive influence, which he acknowledged in private (to Georg von Wright, G. M. Anscombe, Peter Geach, Rudolf Carnap, Friedrich Waismann, O. K. Bowsma, and M. C. Drury).[108]

It is strange that Wittgenstein does not mention Schopenhauer at all in his *Tractatus Logico-Philosophicus* because it is at times a running discussion with him, in agreement and disagreement; but Wittgenstein evidently preferred to appear in public as an independent thinker—in the preface to the *Tractatus* he says that he does not care whether or not his thoughts have been anticipated by others. However, the discussion with Schopenhauer so dominates parts of the *Tractatus* that a clear understanding of it is impossible unless one refers to the corresponding Schopenhauerian texts. Otherwise reading Wittgenstein is like trying to understand a conversation from only one of the two voices engaged in it.[109]

To begin with what Wittgenstein rejects in the *Tractatus*: He rejects Schopenhauer's doctrine of the thinking subject, at bottom a will, that thinks the world as representation; and he rejects Schopenhauer's doctrine of the world as the manifestation of a great, unindividuated cosmic will of which individual wills are only manifestations. Earlier, in his *Notebooks*, Wittgenstein retained more of Schopenhauer, for while he rejected the thinking subject, he did accept the subject as will. In the *Notebooks* he wrote, "If the will did not exist, neither would there be that center of the world, which we call the I. . . . "[110] But in the *Tractatus* he rejects the will as either cosmic or individual reality. He rejects both for reasons I will not repeat; but it is essential to keep in mind that Schopenhauer's argument depends on belief in the absolute regularity and necessity of physical causation, in which Wittgenstein sees only the fallible hypotheses broached by scientists.[111]

What Wittgenstein does by and large accept from Schopenhauer is all that has to do with ineffability. Schopenhauer says and Wittgenstein agrees that words can communicate only abstract knowledge. As we have said, according to Schopenhauer, intuitive knowledge, which is essential for aesthetics and ethics, is truer and deeper than abstract knowledge. Impossible to communicate in words, intuitive knowledge can, however, be shown or demonstrated. Again, Wittgenstein agrees.[112] In the *Tractatus* he writes "There are, indeed, things that cannot be put into words. They *make themselves manifest*. They are what is mystical" (6.522).

An example of what Wittgenstein means by saying that the ineffable can be manifested—even in words themselves—is given in a letter he wrote to his friend Paul Engelmann. At the time, when Wittgenstein was completing the *Tractatus*, Engelmann sent him a poem by Uhland that touched him very deeply. Wittgenstein's response was, "The poem by Uhland is really magnificent. And this is how it is: if only you do not try to utter what is unutterable, then *nothing* gets lost. But the unutterable will be—unutterably—*contained* in what has been uttered!"[113]

In a note he made many years later, Wittgenstein asks: "So how do we explain to someone what 'understanding music' means?" Wittgenstein's answer explains his distinction between the expressive power of showing and saying:

> There is a certain *expression* proper to the appreciation of music, in listening, playing, and at other times too. Sometimes gestures form part of this expression, but sometimes it will just be a matter of how a man plays, or hums, the piece, now and again of the comparisons he draws and the images with which he as it were illustrates the music. Someone who understands music will listen differently (e.g. with a different expression on his face), he will talk differently, from someone who does not.[114]

Both Schopenhauer and Wittgenstein were faced by a problem I have attributed to other thinkers: If verbal knowledge does not give access to knowledge of a kind that is really important, of what use is philosophizing such as theirs? Schopenhauer thinks that a philosopher in particular should draw on intuitive knowledge and understand that what is given by books is only a reflection, a counterfeit, of the original. He should look down on the world as if surveying it from a mountaintop.[115]

In keeping with the view native to Chuang Tzu, Bhartrihari, and the Buddhists, Schopenhauer answers that to a man who studies to gain insight, books and studies are

> merely rungs of the ladder on which he climbs to the summit of knowledge. As soon as a rung has raised him one step, he leaves it behind. On the other hand, the many who study in order to fill their memory do not use the rungs of the ladder for climbing, but take them off and load themselves with them to take away, rejoicing at the increasing weight of the burden. They remain below for ever, because they bear what should have borne them.[116]

Bhartrihari's equivalent is that "grammarians propound means for the understanding of language which, once grasped, can be thrown overboard."[117] An old Buddhist equivalent is that the raft one has improvised for crossing a dangerous stretch of water is not carried further after the crossing but discarded.[118] A Zen equivalent is the advice to take "the further leap after climbing to the top of a pole one hundred feet long."[119] Wittgenstein's now often-repeated equivalent is that his

> propositions serve as elucidations in the following way: anyone who understands me eventually recognizes them as nonsensical, when he has used them—as steps—to climb beyond them. (He must, so to speak, throw away the ladder after he has climbed up it.)
> He must transcend these propositions, and then he will see the world aright. (*Tractatus* 6.54)

Perhaps the crucial likeness between Schopenhauer and Wittgenstein is the doctrine of the limit beyond which nothing can be thought. Schopenhauer, basing himself on Kant, says that the person, the subject, knows all and is known by none and is therefore the supporter of the world and the condition for everything that appears or exists. The forms of all knowledge in time and space always presuppose the subject, the knower. "We never know it [the subject], but it is precisely that which knows wherever there is knowledge."[120] In another passage, Schopenhauer says, "That which precedes knowledge as its condition, whereby that knowledge first of all became possible, and hence its own basis, cannot be immediately grasped by knowledge, just as the eye cannot see itself."[121]

Wittgenstein does not accept the metaphor of the eye (common in Indian philosophical argument) because it requires us to assume the eye's existence inside the empirical world.[122] But he does accept the metaphor of the boundary or limit beyond which nothing can be thought. To think about our world objectively, we should have to get outside it, a place always beyond us. In other words, we cannot think fundamentally *about* language, logic, and thought because we cannot isolate and analyze them by means either linguistic, logical, or cognitive—thought cannot escape itself far enough to observe itself in its own absence.

As Wittgenstein says, "The world is my world: this is manifest in the fact that limits *of language* (of the only language I understand) mean the limits of my world" (*Tractatus* 5.62). For the world has the logical, a priori structure we ourselves give it in conformity with our logic and our language. The logic pervades the world, and the language determines the limits beyond which thought is impossible, even though we may suspect and feel what lies beyond it.[123] Wittgenstein shows this suspicion or feeling of the beyond in the same letter to Engelmann that I have quoted before:

> *Our* life is like a dream. But in our better hours we wake up just enough to realize that we are dreaming. Most of the time, though, we are fast asleep. I cannot awaken myself! I am trying hard, my dream body moves, but my real one *does not stir.* This, alas, is how it is![124]

For a time at least, Wittgenstein retained this feeling. We meet it in a note of 1931 in which he writes, "Perhaps what is inexpressible (what I find mysterious and am not able to express) is the background against which whatever I could express has meaning."[125]

I will not go into the views of the later, more flexible, more complicated Wittgenstein, though a commentator says plausibly that "the sense of the mystery of the ego, which had been concentrated at a single point, is now diffused over a wider area"—the area of the mysteriously familiar, which disappears from view just because of its familiarity. Wittgenstein's idea that language cannot represent the point from which it is understood has disappeared, the commentator says, and has been replaced by the idea of the indefinitely many though connected uses of language.[126]

I should like to conclude this account of Wittgenstein with a note, written in 1948, relevant to our general theme. By then, Wittgenstein had abandoned his earlier opinion that thinking is a kind of speaking:

> There really are cases where someone has the sense of what he wants to say much more clearly in his mind than he can express in words. (This happens to me quite often.) It is as though one had a dream image quite clearly before one's mind's eye, but could not describe to someone else so as to let him see it too. As a matter of fact, for the writer (myself) it is often as though the image stays there behind the words, so that they *seem* to describe it *to me.*[127]

The Primordial Speech of Heidegger and Others

Heidegger has an extreme, even inordinate, love for language, to which he remains faithful, but only in his own fashion. It is possible to put him among the exalters of words; and yet he finds his not unnatural place here among its devaluers because he loves only what he calls *primordial speech* and withholds his love from ordinary, utilitarian prose and ordinary prosaic logic. What he loves and praises is the poetry that unites the musical, imaginative, and logical powers of language. He loves this poetry as the mystic loves the union in which all separate things are inconceivably one. The tragic poets of ancient Greece inspire his ardent nostalgia because he is convinced that their poetic 'saying' was close to the 'divine' and let the truth 'occur' in its full 'primordiality'.

Then, long ago, says Heidegger, the ancient Greeks enjoyed the unbroken, primordial experience that can be recaptured only by returning to the oldest meanings of words. By way of returning, he ascribes unfamiliar old meanings to familiar words, turns nouns or adjectives into odd verbs, and coins neologisms. One of the Greek words to which he returns is *logos*, the usual translations of which include *saying, speech, discourse, definition, ratio*, and *reason*. In early Greek philosophy, Heidegger tells us, especially in Heraclitus, *logos* still has its deep root-sense of *collecting* or *holding together*. He explains the full original meaning as *occurrence of uncovering*, which is to say, *the occurrence of revelation*.

According to Heidegger, thought had not yet acquired its merely abstract use and was still intrinsically close to Being. As he says, the original meaning of Being (*physis* in Greek) is close to *growth, emergence*, or *becoming present*, or, in Heidegger's neologism, *presencing*. In early Greece, he explains with poetic yearning, Being was also radiance and harmony. As these meanings inform him, all that exists (*das Seiende*) opened up to the primordially speaking Greeks and disclosed its Being in its 'gatheredness'. It was then—when the Unthought sustained all thought, when thought fitted the man-Being relationship instead of willing to grasp, divide, and conceive abstractly—that the Truth shone in obscuring and revealing mysteriousness and the thinker enjoyed the unending power of the simple.[128]

To Heidegger, it is art that embodies and expresses the true fullness of early Greek experience. Because of its poetic nature, art, he believes, "breaks an open place" in our usual existence; and in this open place everything is "other than usual." What *is* then "casts itself toward us" and "everything ordinary and hitherto existing becomes an unbeing." For art, says Heidegger, which is all essentially poetry, is in the deeper sense a bringing into the open for the first time of something that *is*. Such bringing into the open creates our world, for "language, by naming beings for the first time, first brings them to word and to appearance." Our speaking is our humanness, and it is our nature (better demonstrated by some of us, I add, than others) always to be speaking:

> We speak when we are awake and we speak in our dreams. We are always speaking, even when we do not utter a single word aloud, and even when we are not particularly listening or speaking but are attending to some work or taking a rest. . . . In any case, language belongs to the closest neighborhood of man's being. We encounter language everywhere.[129]

Heidegger's repetitions of portentous words (which, mutatis mutandis, reminds me of Gertrude Stein), the neologisms he invents, and his often prolix rhythms, create a feeling to which paraphrases are inadequate. He understands this very well, for he considers that true thought and the language in which it is cast are indissoluble. He also feels that the awkwardness and incompleteness of language can testify to its genuineness:

> When does language speak itself as language? Curiously enough, when we cannot find the right word for anything that concerns us, carries us away, oppresses us or encourages us. Then we leave unspoken what we have in mind and, without rightly giving it thought, undergo moments in which language itself has distantly and fleetingly touched us with its essential being.[130]

Given his beliefs, it is no wonder that Heidegger prefers to imagine going both backward and forward in time—back to unspoiled Greek thought and forward, with the help of Kierkegaard, Nietzsche, and Hölderlin—above all Hölderlin—to the hoped-for effect of his own thought on the present he supposes so destitute of Being. When he thinks beyond the West, he imagines holding a deep conversation about language with persons of the other great traditions, who have had a presumably different primordial experience and are tenanted in a 'house of Being' that originated neither in Greek nor German, the two Western languages in which alone the authentic logos came to expression.[131]

It was in this spirit that Heidegger came to be have more than a superficial interest in Taoism and Zen Buddhism. His interest in Taoism was publicly demonstrated as early as 1930, when he tried to explain his lecture *On the Essence of the Truth* by reading aloud a passage in Martin Buber's version of Lao Tzu.[132] His interest in Zen dated back to at least 1938, when a Japanese acquaintance presented him with the first volume of Suzuki's *Essays in Zen Buddhism*, which Heidegger was eager to discuss. His interest was particularly aroused by the story of the ninth-century Zen master Lin-chi, Rinzai in Japanese. According to the story, Lin-chi asks a Zen master three times what the essence of Buddhism is and each time gets a blow in answer.

I do not know just what Heidegger learned from Zen, but the Zen tradition contends that the real teaching of Buddhism cannot be transmitted in words, but only directly from one mind—mind in the true sense—to 'another' mind. As Lin-chi's master said:

> People in the world cannot identify their own mind. They believe that what they see, or hear, or feel, or know, is mind. They are blocked by the visual, the auditory, the tactile, and the mental, so they cannot see the brilliant spirit of the original mind . . . This mind is illuminated, and pure as the Void, without form. Any thought deviates from the true source.[133]

The point of the story Heidegger was so interested in is that it is impossible to say anything true in words about the essence of Buddhism because the very idea of an 'essence' or 'cardinal question' is totally misleading. The blows are meant to teach this to Lin-chi as directly as possible, and by means of the resulting pain and confusion to inspire him to make the necessary effort to dislocate his misleading, worldly thought. Lin-chi is also helped when he realizes that in hitting him his teacher has shown him true compassion because the blows have been meant to direct him toward the truth.

To go back to Heidegger's interest in Chinese thought, in the spring of 1946, he asked a friendly Chinese scholar to collaborate on a translation of Lao Tzu. The two met regularly in Heidegger's mountain cabin. In the course of their work over the summer, the Chinese scholar found Heidegger to be modest, remarkably attentive, and remarkably committed to the penetration of the chapters they were working on. Heidegger's thinking was so thorough, the Chinese scholar reports, that they finished only eight of the eighty-one chapters. In spite of his respect for Heidegger's thoroughness, the Chinese scholar was troubled by his tendency to go beyond what was permissible in a translation. Cut short for some reason, the collaboration was never resumed.[134]

At the time Heidegger was working on the translation, his fortunes and spirits were at their lowest ebb. Because of his earlier enthusiasm for the Nazi regime, he had undergone denazification proceedings and had been forbidden to lecture in public; and he had suffered financial difficulties as well. As a result, in early 1946 he put himself under the care of the psychiatrist Victor von Gebsattel, a 'phenomenologist' no doubt sympathetic to his views; and he appealed to a former teacher, the Archbishop Gröber. Gröber reports that he told Heidegger the truth, which Heidegger tearfully accepted. It is therefore not hard to guess that his study of Lao Tzu was also a refuge from his difficulties.[135]

However that may be, Heidegger found the formulaic profundities (or pseudo-profundities) and antiverbalism of Lao Tzu enough like and unlike his own to want to grasp and translate them. It was from Lao Tzu that he learned to emphasize that a jar is not essentially its 'being' but its nothingness or emptiness. In *On the Way to Language*, lectures delivered in 1957 and 1958, Heidegger equates *tao* in its "proper nature" with *logos* in its "proper nature" and adds:

> Perhaps the mystery of mysteries of thoughtful Saying conceals itself in the word 'way', *Tao*, if only we will let these names return to what they leave unspoken, if only we are capable of this, to allow them to do so.[136]

Heidegger had distinguished Japanese students, and his influence on Japanese philosophy was greater than that of any other recent Westerner.[137] Noting that his Japanese students used his thought in order "reappropriate" their own, "he considered the dialogue between Europe and the Far East to be as necessary as it was difficult; he did not want to overlook the element of foreignness that remained in every encounter." In 1953/54, on the occasion of the visit of a Japanese professor (Shuzo Kuki), he held a long dialogue with him, which was published in 1959.[138]

Both partners to the dialogue, the Japanese and Heidegger, who names himself the Inquirer, are much concerned with what is undefined and indefinable. The Inquirer insists that the "indefinable something not only does not slip away, but displays its gathering force ever more luminously in the course of the dialogue." The Inquirer then speaks with disparagement, more than tinged, I fear, with animus, of the thirst for knowledge and greed for explanations, which never, he says, "lead to a thinking inquiry"; and he denounces curiosity as "the concealed arrogance of a self-consciousness that banks on a self-invented *ratio* and its rationality."[139]

Although Heidegger more than once professes to respect science in its own right, the unrelenting quality of his disparagement sounds strange in a contemporary. As the dialogue continues, the Japanese praises the reserve that Heidegger exhibits when asked about "the mystery of Saying." There is too much speaking *about* language, they both agree, which turns language into an object and makes its reality vanish. The interlocutors are moving, they see, in what Heidegger had earlier called a "hermeneutic circle," which is a dialogue "from language" that has been summoned "from out of language's reality." True to his reserve, however, Heidegger finds that talk of this circle is necessarily superficial and he insists (he says) on avoiding a presentation of it just as resolutely as he avoids speaking *about* language.

A true dialogue, the interlocutors now agree, which is one "*of* language, as needfully used of its very nature," has a character of its own, and contains more silence than talk. "Above all," the Inquirer says, "silence about silence. . . . " "Because," the unsilent Japanese adds, "to talk and write about silence is what produces the most obnoxious chatter." Although the dialogue continues briefly, I end it with the question asked by the Japanese, "Are we not attempting the impossible?" and with Heidegger's answer, "Indeed."[140]

Another Japanese (Tetsuaki Kotoh), writing on Heidegger and Zen, remarks that according to Zen, when one is able to let go and forget both body and mind and let things happen and simply follow along without forcing things or expending one's mind, the true self becomes one with the world. This state, in which subject and object are not yet separated, is one in which experiences remain, unjudged, just as they are.

> There the world, which has hitherto been rigidified by linguistic segmentation, gradually becomes fluid, thereby dissolving the boundaries created by segmentation . . . What now comes to the fore is 'spontaneous arising' (*jinen shoki*), in which things inherently arise and open up the field of cosmic mutual interpenetration, and which is itself Nothing, without segmentation, and one with itself. This entire *Ekstase* is 'pure experience.'[141]

Heidegger is not, of course, the only writer of his time to yearn for linguistic expression that is truly poetic and, as such, able to transcend reasoning. Each of the other writers I am referring to has a personal view of the kind of expression that may escape the bonds of ordinary language and hint at something truly authentic. To show what a variety of ideals and literary practices can arise out of such a basic assumption, I follow Heidegger's view with a short description of three others.

The first of the three is the writer Antonin Artaud. I ask, though I will not attempt to answer, how Heidegger reacted (or might react) to him. Artaud is always trying and failing to find what he is searching for. He feels that his failure to catch his own thought is a sign of his imbecility and loss of himself. He gives his failure a more general basis, the conviction that language has grown limited and sterile because it relies too much on logic. In reaction, he tries to create a new 'theater of cruelty', whose language will break down the barriers of experience between persons and make spectators suffer as deeply as himself when either sane, semisane, or insane, and terrify the spectators free of their rationality.

Artaud's ideal is to return to the human condition in which soul is no different from body, and to the linguistic condition in which sound is not yet separated from sense. He prescribes that this "speech before words" should include 'hieroglyphs', by which he means writings that coordinate phonetic with visual, pictorial, and plastic elements. And he wants "the overlapping of images and movements" to culminate—by "the collision of objects, silences, shouts, and rhythms"—in a truly physical language with signs as its roots. Words will then become physical signs that "will be construed in an incantational, magical sense—for their shape and their sensuous emanations."[142] His writing reproduces his existence by pushing language to a frequently stammering, gibbering, broken, enraged eloquence that reflects his conviction that his supreme work of art is his lifetime of suffering.

I wonder, too, how Heidegger reacted (or might react) to Samuel Beckett—so unlike Hölderlin—who tries in a sense to escape from the rhetoric of ordinary language and remain in a direct, isolated present. His fragments and figments talk to one another very economically, try to penetrate to the essential self, but find only detours and get enmeshed in attempts to talk their way beyond language. Beckett's spare writing is meant to evade "the fatal leaning towards expressiveness"; and he longs to express himself by means of impassivity and muteness. He longs for the "real silence" that will give him "the right to be done with speech, done with hearing." All the while, his progress toward muteness is made in words that can only contradict the attempt and emphasize that it is empty because even words reduced to a minimum do not escape themselves. "I'm in words, made of words, nothing else," he says, and goes on, "yes, something else, something quite different, a wordless think in an empty place a hard shut dry cold black place, where nothing stirs, nothing speaks"—a 'place' like the emptiness in which a famous Rigvedic hymn located the first stirrings of the creative process.[143]

I wonder, too, how Heidegger really felt about the poetry of Paul Celan, whose parents were shot by the SS, and whose desperate desire to communicate was made so difficult by his instability and by the ineffectiveness of language itself to convey the horror of the Nazis' deeds. Like Hölderlin and Artaud, though for very different reasons, Celan's sanity was precarious—the impression he made on others was that of "a dark and isolated presence." In the end, he drowned himself in the Seine.

Celan often expresses his distrust of language itself. In the prose of *Conversation in the Mountains*, we read that he meets his cousin, and either he or the cousin remarks that he has come there perhaps because he has to talk either to himself or to him, the other person, because he has to talk with mouth and tongue and not only with his stick. He talks to stone, he says, and then asks to whom the stone talks. The answer, which carries a suggestion of Nietzsche or Heidegger, is given in the following simple, obscure words:

> He doesn't talk, he speaks, and he who speaks, cousin, talks to no one, he speaks because no one hears him and No One and then he, he says, not his mouth or his tongue, he says, and not only he: Do you hear?[144]

Though he knew a number of languages, Celan, who was close to his German-speaking mother, felt he could express his own truth only in his mother tongue, German. But the German in which he wrote his poetry is a language that has to pass, he says, "through its own unresponsiveness, pass through its own fearful muting, pass through the thousand deaths of death-bringing speech." The result has been described as a German written like a foreign language, one in which language mutates as words are broken down and reconstructed—nouns, for example, become verbs and acquire adverbial endings. Sometimes the sound becomes the equivalent of an "asthmatic rattle." This language of Celan grows dissonant and compressed enough to lie, it has been said, in "the nomansland between speech and silence."[145]

Compared with Hölderlin, who inspired him, Celan's success as a poet can still be questioned. There can be no question, however, about the obscurity with which he tries to represent a terror beyond rational description. I have asked, without knowing how to answer, how Heidegger really felt about Celan, who seems to have both loved and loathed him. In the poem *Left Back for Me*, Celan writes enigmatically of the "cross-beamed One" whose riddle he must unravel as the hempen-clothed cross-beamed One knits the stocking of mystery. The cross-beamed One is said to represent Heidegger, who often wore a peasant-style stocking cap, and whose philosophical knitting of mystery "is meshed with the plaiting of the hangman's noose."[146]

As he wrote in a letter, Heidegger was eager to get to know Celan. Soon thereafter, in July of 1967, they held a meeting in Heidegger's hut in Todtnauberg. The meeting disappointed Celan, we know.[147] Events had created a distance between the two evidently far greater than that between Heidegger and the reverent Japanese who had conversed with him on true speech and silence.

Derrida Seeks the Ineffable in Différance *with the Help of Nietzsche, Freud, Valéry, and Artaud, Subverts Language, Denies Metaphysical Intent, and Talks Voids and Emptiness*

Derrida acknowledges his descent from Heidegger but shows none of his romantic enthusiasm for the truth that shines forth in poetic language. Although he agrees with Heidegger that our fall into metaphysics began with Parmenides and Plato, he accuses even Heidegger of the primal sin of belief in metaphysical illumination by means of the true *logos* and the true, spoken word.[148] The unnameable that Derrida searches for is by no means "an ineffable Being which no name could approach." Sternly, thinking no doubt of Heidegger, he makes it clear that

> there will be no unique name, even if it were the name of Being. And we must think this without *nostalgia*, that is, outside of the myth of a purely maternal or paternal language, a lost native country of thought. On the contrary, we must *affirm* this, in the sense in which Nietzsche puts affirmation into play, in a certain laughter and a certain step of the dance.[149]

Proud though he is of his individuality, Derrida does not hesitate to name Nietzsche as a predecessor. He applauds Nietzsche's systematic distrust of the fixed in language, logic, and metaphysics; and, like Nietzsche, he wants to interpret interpretation itself.[150] Nietzsche, he says, recognizes the *trace*, the *différance*, that inherently elusive something that is both different from and deferred by the conceptual sameness that philosophical language requires. In deferring the trace, philosophy distances itself from the source of its own life, for it lives *in* and on the vital trace it is unable to capture between the artificial poles that constitute philosophical thought.

Derrida explains that Nietzsche's themes are linked to the symptoms by which one sees how the *trace* or *différance* is evaded in our language. Nietzsche reveals his insight by incessantly deciphering rather than merely uncovering the truth.

> Thus, *différance* is the name we might give to the 'active', moving discord of different forces, and of differences of forces, that Nietzsche sets up against the entire system of metaphysical grammar, wherever this system governs culture, philosophy, and science.[151]

Derrida also has an active interest in Freud, who, he says, undertook the "immense labor of deconstruction" of the metaphysical concepts that are "condensed and sedimented" within characteristic precautions.[152] In Derrida's words:

The unconscious is not, as we know, a hidden, virtual, or potential self-presence. It differs from, and defers itself; which doubtless means that it is woven of differences, and also that it sends out delegates, representatives, proxies; but without any chance that the giver of proxies might 'exist', might be present, be 'itself' somewhere, and with even less chance that it might become conscious.[153]

Derrida is attracted to Valéry no less than to Nietzsche and Freud. Like them, Derrida is a searcher for the nuances of experience that vanish as they appear, nuances that for all their presence-in-absence are vital to existence and to the ability to create. Paradoxical as it may sound, they can be searched for best—detached from the immediacy of speech—in texts and protocols.

Derrida shares Valéry's profound interest in the ways in which thinking, a subtle, half-vanishing internal process, is externalized in speech and the speaker, doubling and redoubling on his tracks, becomes in a sense a series of responses or echoes. It is as if in expressing himself the single person became also double or more; and as if his intimacy harbored an essential quality of nonintimacy, so that in showing and becoming himself he necessarily becomes strange to himself. In one of his many variations on his astonishment at this doubling, Valéry writes:

Between what I say and what I hear myself say, no exteriority, no alterity, not even that of a mirror, seems to interpose itself . . . The voice, it appears, therefore can accomplish the circular return of the origin to itself.[154]

According to Derrida, Valéry succeeds more than any philosopher, more even than Hegel or Husserl, in exploring the phenomenon of speaking within oneself and, in doing so, hearing oneself speak and rejoining or reappropriating the always elusive source from which the movement began. The source

is born of this very eluding, like a situated mirage, a site in a directionless field. It is nothing before being sought, only an effect produced by the structure of the movement. The source is therefore not the origin, it is neither at the departure or the arrival.[155]

Derrida offers a number of excerpts from Valéry's *Notebooks* in evidence. In one of them, Valéry writes to himself:

. . . no 'me' without 'you.' To each his Other, which is his Same. Or the *I is two*—by definition. If there is *voice*, there is ear. Internally there is voice, there is no sight of who is speaking. And who will describe, will define the *difference between the same sentence which is said* and *not pronounced*, and the *same sentence sounding in the air*. This identity and this difference are one of the essential secrets of the nature of the mind. . . . Within it lies the mystery of time, i.e. the existence of that which is not. Potential and unactual.[156]

Valéry asks about internal speech, and Derrida asks with him, "Who speaks, who listens? It is not exactly the same . . . The existence of the speech from self to self is the sign of a *cut*." If I speak to myself, Valéry muses, it appears that there is a difference between speaker and listener; and if I say something to myself, I influence myself and change what I will say to myself; and so each same but different *I* influences the other; and in emitting something toward myself, something like a foreign fact, I fecundate myself. I am made of two moments and—as if—of the delay between them.[157]

Artaud is still another writer for whom Derrida has genuine fellow-feeling. What Artaud teaches us, he says, is our unity prior to our dissociation. For Artaud's howls promise us art prior both to madness and to the work of art, the kind of existence that leads nowhere else but gives only itself in speech that is a body and a theater not enslaved by any ur-text or ur-speech. More than anyone before him, Artaud resists clinical or critical exegeses

by virtue of that part of his adventure . . . which is the very protest *itself* against exemplification *itself*. The critic and the doctor are without resource when confronted by an existence that refuses to signify, or by an art without works, a language without a trace . . . Artaud attempted to destroy a history, the history of the dualist metaphysics . . . the duality of the body and the soul which supports, secretly of course, the duality of speech and existence, of the text and the body, etc.[158]

Derrida asks if by such Artaudian transformation of writing into flesh we might destroy our necessary doubleness and our discourse might be magically reborn in an unchanging, perfect self-presence. As always, Derrida puts on his armor of qualifications; but he says of Artaud, as he says of himself, that he "keeps himself at the limit." This is the limit at which—like the great god Shiva—one simultaneously destroys and constructs, making use of the most profound motifs of Western metaphysics while affirming the necessary law of difference. Derrida wants his destructive discourses, like hostile children living at home, "to inhabit the structures they demolish, and within them . . . shelter an indestructible desire for full presence, for nondifference: simultaneously life and death."[159]

❦

So far, I have spoken less of Derrida himself than of his interest in certain predecessors. His own explicit view is that we are imprisoned in words, which by their fixity and their static concordances and oppositions do violence to life. The result, to him, has been a long shift to inauthentic being, which contrasts everything that is considered to be present, objective, intelligible, and true, with everything that is absent, subjective, sensed, and false. The users of at least the Western languages have been Platonized to the degree that they think and express themselves in signs that have lost their natural relationship to what they signify. The very medium by which we think and express ourselves imprisons us in its artificial dualisms and hard-and-fast concepts.[160]

Despite his admiration for Nietzsche's view of language, Derrida's attempt to subvert it is conceived differently. He says that his attack is less direct but more intimate. It is foredoomed to failure, he acknowledges, because it is conducted in the same language it intends to subvert. Yet Derrida believes that he is able at certain moments of subversion to glimpse the 'non-existent' *trace* or *différance* that in its 'inexistence' hints at what language misses. What it misses, he says, is the imagination, which is the kind of freedom that cannot ever be made explicit: Imagination is only an image to help one grasp something other than itself and therefore suggests that what is represented lacks something, which must be added; and therefore the image, which clarifies what is represented, so to speak announces its own dispossession, inexistence, or death.

The *trace* or *différance* is incapable of ever becoming present or manifesting itself because it is just that which is neither conceptual nor sensible, neither voiced nor written, but is located between them, before (so to speak) they are separate.[161] To say this is to exceed or transgress logic by means of language. Because we use language even to transgress logic, we resort to a code so irreducibly metaphysical that every gesture of transgression encloses us within logic again. "Transgression," says Derrida, "implies that the limit is always at work"; and the limit is at work when the "thought-that-means-nothing" is "given precisely as the thought for which there is no sure opposition between outside and inside."[162]

What exactly can such a statement mean? Derrida answers that when he puts meaning at risk, he enters into the play of *différance* and so prevents words and concepts from exercising their usual domination. He asks the question, "What is meaning to say?" and answers that the question "attempts to keep itself at the point of the exhaustion of meaning."[163]

It is inevitable that there should be a certain likeness between Heidegger, Derrida, and negative theology (soon to be described), in which the higher the reality, the more negatively it must be described, so that the superlative, unlimited reality must be described in negations alone. Derrida concedes that he has something in common with negative theologians; but he objects that, unlike himself, even the most negative of negative theologians are always trying to get beyond finite categories and disengage a 'superessentiality' or God that is denied the predicate of existence only to be granted an ineffable mode of being.[164]

But though he distances himself from negative theology, Derrida knows that his denial will probably be unpersuasive.[165] Surely the notion of *différance* is difficult and, as Derrida repeatedly insists, the attempt to use language to describe what it simultaneously is and is not, or is not and cannot be, is always playing with, verging on, and crossing over into self-contradiction. For Derrida's *différance* "is neither a word nor a concept" and has no name at all, "not even the name of essence or of Being, not even that of '*différance*', which is not a name, which is not a pure nominal unity, and unceasingly dislocates itself in a chain of differing and deferring substitutions"; and it is certainly not an ineffable, unnameable Being such as is called God.[166] Surrounding the word *thought* with quotation marks he considers significant, Derrida says, "In a certain way, 'thought' means nothing."[167]

Derrida's belief that language is unable to state what is most deep and creative recalls the nameless, invisible, silent, void, nonexistent tao encountered in 'Lao Tzu'. And his conscious use of reason to subvert reason and his complaints at the definiteness and conceptual polarity of language recall Chuang Tzu as well as the Zen monks resolutely at war with reason's distinctions.[168] There is also Zen wildness in Derrida if we interpret his later writings as a flight from all theorizing, ironic or not, in favor of "wild and private lucubrations" that undercut any attempt to say or solve the impossible. "Derrida has avoided Heideggerian nostalgia in the same way that Proust avoided sentimental nostalgia—by incessantly recontextualizing whatever memory brings back" and in this way extending the bounds of human possibility.[169]

Most of all, it appears to me, Derrida's negation and emphasis on the inexpressible make *différance* and 'thought' resemble Nagarjuna's *emptiness* and echo Nagarjuna's conviction that a name or word, being empty, is neither real nor unreal. This is because Nagarjunian emptiness or neither-reality-nor-unreality holds even of the concept of *emptiness*. Like everything else, emptiness is empty and no different from whatever is not empty. Since this is so, illusion (nonemptiness) and truth (emptiness) are not really different (or the same), and "the extreme limit of *nirvana* is also the extreme limit of the course of phenomenal existence (*samsara*)."[170]

This is all difficult, no less difficult than *différance*. Hear a contemporary scholar trying, with Tibetan help, to make clear that Nagarjunian emptiness "is not a *thing*, certainly not an inherently existing thing, in its own right." Emptiness is not

> some sort of really existing, Ultimate Reality or Essence, perhaps like the Brahman of Hinduism or the Godhead of other religions. Emptiness is thus not . . . the Ultimate Truth in the sense that it is an ultimately existing or inherently existing entity. If the object of analysis were to be emptiness itself then emptiness would also be found to lack inherent existence . . . Thus we come to emptiness of emptiness.[171]

Of course, Derrida and Nagarjuna do not think alike, and, of course, *différance* is not the same as *emptiness*; but the quality of thought that characterizes both concepts, denies them their conceptuality, and attempts to illuminate them by alternating positive and negative descriptions as if the descriptions neutralized one another and allowed the describer to walk on the dimensionless limit between them—all this makes *différance* and *nothingness* distant fraternal twins, both born of the union of mother Indetermination and father Precise Differentiation. I suspect that a conscientious attempt to say exactly how the two are different and the same would be very tiresome and would run into the difficulty that what cannot be named or described or can be described only by means of self-contradiction is a vague object for contrast and comparison and tempts one—tempts me—to take refuge in the excuse of the literal ineffability of ineffables.

Chapter 4

Reasons behind Reasons for Ineffability

So far, we have been concerned with the ways in which language has been exalted and devalued and reality found possible and impossible to describe in words. In presenting these ways, I have been concerned more with exposition than evaluation, but the time has come to alter the balance. From now on, the discussion will become more evaluative and, necessarily, more subjective.

I should begin by explaining why I do not intend to repay the philosophers much in their own coin. I mean, among the rest, that Bhartrihari will not be questioned as if he were engaged in a current philosophical debate, nor will the Neoplatonists be questioned more than briefly in their own philosophical terms. In spite of our distance in time from Bhartrihari and the Neoplatonists, my refusal to engage them on their own terms should not be regarded as self-evident—not self-evident because they were philosophically, I am convinced, on a level of sophistication much the same as our own; arguing with them should not be philosophically beneath us.

Having said this, I must immediately qualify and add that there is no doubt that modern science displays far more rigorous standards of empirical evidence and theory construction than those conceived by ancient Indian and Greek, even Hellenistic, philosophers.* Yet although our science intersects with philosophy in vague border areas, it does not bear obvious witness to the truth of any one philosophy. The aim of the Logical Positivists to create a seamless union of physics and philosophy

---

* This despite the Indians' algebra and scientific classification and the Greeks' Euclidean geometry, proof of the earth's sphericity, ingenious mechanisms, knowledge of the heart's valves, and declarations of allegiance to unbiased research. On Greek science, see the nuanced conclusions in G.E.R. Lloyd, *The Revolutions of Wisdom*, pp. 330–36. For India, see H.J.J. Winter's introductory "Science."

135

was extraordinarily premature and, by commission and omission, deflected philosophy from too much that thoughtful persons demand of it—having a "horror of meaning," they remained, in the end, without it.[1] History has decided that contemporary philosophy is not to be mistaken for contemporary science; and because philosophy as such is unable to create exact theories of a kind that can be refuted, corrected, or (temporarily) sustained in the light of empirical evidence, the relation of philosophy to evidence is much the same as it has always been—it makes sporadic use of the evidence but, with rare exceptions, does not explore it seriously.

No doubt we have statistical theories the Indian and Hellenistic philosophers lacked; we probably but not surely have different attitudes toward authoritative texts; we in the West do not believe in karma and the cycle of rebirths, but we often accept divine reward and punishment and survival after death. How, then, should we judge if we or they are philosophically superior? Surely not, in justice, by our own conviction that we are right. But if we judge the level of philosophy by the formal criteria of evidence it adopts and the careful detail in which its arguments are stated, it is not clear that we are in general superior. Those who think the proposed criteria show that our contemporary philosophers excel, do so, I suspect, because they have not studied the texts that show them to be wrong.[2]

My refusal to engage in the philosophical debate as such is therefore not based on a feeling that philosophical reasoning has become decisively keener. As is inevitable, it is based on the change in atmosphere—a matter of a changed civilization—but, above all, on the empirical evidence now at our disposal. Bhartrihari has been needed here because he is the most effective philosophical exalter of language of his metaphysical kind; and Plotinus and Proclus are needed because their realities are concepts—Platonic Ideas un-Platonically endowed with life—and because they are the most faithfully logical of the builders of the metaphysical hierarchies that will soon engage our attention. But to undertake to oppose or accept Bhartrihari or Plotinus, especially in a version that modern descendants might favor, should be done either at fitting length or hardly at all. I say "fitting length" because of the length of the history of philosophy, or, if one prefers to bypass history itself, because of the great variety of detailed arguments to deal with. And I say "hardly at all" because I feel obliged at least to indicate where I think the hierarchical reasoning of such philosophers is unpersuasive. The little I do say is enough to show the line of argument I favor, which any practiced philosopher is able to develop. But to argue seriously, to try to influence professional opinion, by the standards of careful (even ancient) philosophy would require long, close, and elaborate reasoning. Such reasoning would be interesting in itself, I hope, but experience shows that it would stand no chance of being decisive. The Indians of the different schools elaborated their arguments at subtle length for hundreds of years; and, in any case, I am not capable of arguing for long like one of them, nor do I really want to. As for the Neoplatonists, I would be taking part in a continuing argument that began with Plato himself, if not earlier, and with the possible exception of the darkest of the Dark Ages, has never abated for a single philosophical generation; and it gives no sign of ever ending. By the twentieth century it should be evident that to keep this argument going unempirically is to engage in a series of intellectual games that are games because played as if empirical evidence were irrelevant, but not games because the rules, changed to fit the particular player, are not really fixed, so that no one wins except by the unstated, probably unknown rules of the sociology of knowledge.

For these reasons, I have decided, as the title of this chapter shows, to devote proportionately little of my own argument to reasons of the kind given by the philosophers themselves, and, instead, to emphasize reasons such as many of them would consider irrelevant because unequivalent, that is, indiscriminately philosophical, sociological, anthropological, and, most often, psychological. It is with such 'irrelevant' reasons that I hope to account for the persistent use and frequent persuasiveness of the metaphysical arguments I report.[3]

After all, if the philosophers' kind of reasoning—philosophical reasoning per se—has not proved coercive after so long, their reasons, which conflict, cannot have been used and elaborated solely because of their rightness (self-evident rightness, they have often contended). Even if the conclusions of some philosopher were to turn out to be right in a general way, this, as everyone knows, would prove next to nothing about the correctness of the reasoning that led to it. The ancient Greeks, Indians, and Moslems (the antiphilosophical *Mutakallimun*) who developed the atomic theory were imaginative, resourceful thinkers. In the absence of the Greeks, the modern atomic theory would no doubt have taken longer to develop; but the sheer inadequacy of the philosophical arguments alone has become blatant, and such history teaches that when empirical evidence from any side seems applicable, disciplinary purity notwithstanding, it should not be dismissed out of hand as irrelevant.

All the same, should the love of philosophy cause anyone to prefer what ensues to be philosophy rather than nameless reasoning—if the history or quality of reasoning associated with philosophy appears significant enough—there are easy terminological tactics that might prove helpful. A pragmatists' principle could be adopted that, outside of mathematics, no philosophical argument should be undertaken in the absence of a corresponding effort to relate it to empirical evidence, especially as gathered and analyzed in other well-established disciplines. Philosophers would then begin with the assumption that the intellectual effort expended in the other disciplines was relevant until proved otherwise; and it would be only just for the other disciplines to return the compliment by consulting philosophers more often.[4] Then, no philosopher would think professionally about the nature of consciousness, perception, free will, or ineffability without knowing something of neuropsychology; no philosopher would take up ethics without consulting psychiatry, criminology and, maybe, ethology and genetics; and the philosopher of religion would need psychology, sociology, and anthropology—history, too, would help.

Thinking under such an obligation would require the collaboration of the different disciplines; and philosophy would require a strenuous more-than-philosophical effort. Even now, it might help terminologically to think of ugly-sounding hybrids such as sociophilosophy, psychophilosophy, and anthropophilosophy. These hybrids would not give final solutions to the problems that arise here, but would illuminate them in a light that empirical research could strengthen.

Summary of the Reasons behind the Reasons

I turn first to exalters of words such as Bhartrihari, whose position is based on the hierarchical argument, according to which the universe, the metaphysical hierarchy formed by 'words', expresses the absolute principle that itself cannot be put into words. I explain the relative persuasiveness of this and like types of hierarchical argument by means of four principles, to which I assign the names, *the principle of affinity, the principle of authority, the principle of hierarchy,* and *the principle of intimacy.*

1. According to the first principle, that of affinity, only things of the same metaphysical kind can affect or be directly relevant to one another. On this principle, material, that is, physical things are unable to account for mental, abstract, or spiritual ones. As it appears here, the hierarchical argument requires that the principle of affinity hold true.

2. The principle of authority—the social form of the principle of hierarchy—is central to the many conflicts between those who attack and those who support submission to author-

ity. Not infrequently, Buddhism has appeared to lean toward the one side, while Confucianism has always leaned toward the other—not necessarily toward authority as such, but toward *legitimate* authority. The principle of authority is allied with belief in omniscience and infallibility, neither of them by nature understandable.

3. The principle of hierarchy is developed in its most rigorously logical forms by the Neoplatonists, of whom I cite Plotinus and Proclus. The Neoplatonists claim to show that it is self-contradictory to deny that all that exists depends upon the absolute One. The One, they argue with logic and passion, is an absolute unity and, as such, beyond description.

4. The principle of hierarchy has influenced modern thinkers even outside of philosophy and theology. One example—which affects the relation of the 'language' of mathematics to usual, verbal language—is the hierarchy of mathematical inifinites invented or (if one prefers) discovered by Georg Cantor. Another, related example is the incompleteness theorem of the logician Kurt Gödel. To both Cantor and Gödel, hierarchy implies an ineffable 'height' or ineffable relationship.

5. The widely accepted 'big bang' cosmology raises an intellectual problem analogous to that of the Word of Bhartrihari or the absolute One of the Neoplatonists. The beginning of the cosmologists suggests the possibility that, taken without qualification, the absolute beginning is beyond our categories of thought.

6. A minimal conclusion is that hierarchical thinking of all fundamental kinds tends to favor the belief in an ineffable beginning related in ways we cannot easily understand to whatever follows from it.

7. The last principle, of intimacy, is used to give a psychological explanation why the essence of words has been regarded in mystical doctrine as itself ineffable. The extreme of such intimacy, whether Indian, Greek, Moslem, or other, is the ineffable state of union with the ineffable reality. Erotic analogies are usual in the mysticism of intimacy, as are states felt to be of superlative power or joy—all of them ineffable, say those who experience them.

8. Finally, the ideal of the metaphysical hierarchy, Bhartriharian and Neoplatonic, creates striking philosophical structures on foundations that reveal themselves to be shaky.

The Affinity Needed for Metaphysical Hierarchies Requires that Only Things of the Same Metaphysical Type Can Influence One Another

Like the other principles, the principle of affinity is old and ramified. It is related to a number of metaphysical doctrines, notably to realism in the medieval sense and to theories of causality, so the discussion here can be no more than the token of an adequate one.

I use the term *affinity* to distinguish everything that belongs together because it is essentially the same. For example, every pure example of the same chemical has the same formula as every other and cannot (insofar as pure) be distinguished from any other, and is in this sense identical. Or, to choose another kind of example, everybody who reads and understands the present sentence should ideally understand it (insofar as it is clear) in the same way and share in the same meaning, so that if one asks, "Considering all the readers of the sentence, present and future, how many instances of the sentence are there in all their minds?" the answer is, ideally, "Only one." Anyone who stresses affinity in this sense believes in universals and may easily slip into some form of Platonism, which itself slips easily into a position more or less like Bhartrihari's.

To show how a contemporary can take a Platonistic, near-Bhartriharian position, I quote the distinguished mathematician Paul Halmos:

> I see mathematics, the part of human knowledge that I call mathematics, as one thing—one great, glorious thing. Whether it is differential topology, or functional analysis, or homological algebra, it is all one thing. They all have to do with each other, and even though a differential topologist may not know any functional analysis, every little bit he hears, every rumor that comes to him about that other subject, sounds like something else that he does know. They are intimately connected, and they are all facets of the same thing. That interconnection, that architecture, is secure truth and is beauty. That's what mathematics is to me.[5]

The examples I have just given—of a pure chemical, a sentence understood identically, and mathematics as a whole—were chosen almost at random from among indefinitely many others. The term *belonging to-*

gether obviously refers to classification, which changes according to the needs of the classifier. If we insist on strict identity, the only sure candidates are numbers or other abstract symbols that belong to a purely abstract system. All occurrences of the same number in the same number system are defined as identical; but as soon as the rules of the number system are changed, or as soon as the numbers are applied to anything but other numbers in the same system, their identity comes into question and someone has to decide, by uncertain criteria, if they belong together as identical or not. As soon as one abandons identity for the looser criterion of similarity, there is a problem of how and to what purpose the similarity is measured. Biologists who try to classify living things into species are endlessly involved in decisions that appear quite simple to naive viewers.[6]

It is useful to remember these complications as we take up the sense of *affinity* most relevant to the present discussion: the capacity of one thing to affect another. From a contemporary standpoint, this capacity is defined by the various sciences, and to describe it in detail would be to describe their content, beginning with physics and chemistry and ending with the social sciences. Here, the meaning of *affinity* must be narrowed to fit the kind of argument native to Gorgias, Aristotle, and Descartes, not to speak of Bhartrihari.

Gorgias, it will be remembered, argues that each sense is the unique medium for what it alone can convey, and cannot convey what any other sense does; and that speech or thought, with its unique medium of words, is unable to convey external reality because, unlike the senses, it cannot *be* (be the same as) external things. In this argument, Gorgias proves his skeptical point by making a dogmatic separation of sense from sense and of all senses from thought; but we know of the rare persons who can hear colors and see and taste sounds; know that for all of us, there is an affinity of rhythm and intensity among the perceptions of the different senses; that what we see affects what we hear and vice versa; and that the testimony of sight can allow a previously blind person to identify by vision a shape previously known by touch alone.

However, if we stay on the level of the everyday experience of most of us, it is true enough that each sense testifies to a unique aspect of experience, and that perception as a whole strikes us as distinctly different from thought as a whole. We also are aware of the inability of those born blind to understand the primary experience of color.

On the basis of such observations and the Gorgias-like arguments that depend on them, and on the basis, as well, of the traditional separation of body and soul, Descartes contends that material things are space-filling or geometrical and therefore essentially different from ideas, so that the two kinds of existence, having no interface, cannot affect one another. He knows, no less than we do, that emotions affect the body, that fear makes the heart beat faster and sadness drains blood from the face. His response is to assign the emotions to the body-machine and leave to the mind or soul, which is dimensionless, the activities of under-standing and willing. It is true that Descartes goes on to concede that the contact between material things and ideas, though forbidden by logic, does in fact take place in a central organ of the brain; and he feels constrained to ascribe this logically incomprehensible contact to the in-comprehensible power of God.

Like Descartes, though to a contrary end—opposition to the idea of a separate, ghostly soul tenanting the body—the philosopher Gilbert Ryle believes that we can learn to think clearly only if we do not confuse our categories:

> During the three centuries of the epoch of natural science the logical categories in terms of which the concepts of mental powers and operations have been co-ordinated have been wrongly chosen . . . The logical type or category to which a concept belongs is the set of ways in which it is logically legitimate to operate with it . . . Philosophy is the replacement of category-habits by category-disciplines.[7]

There is no reason to believe that Bhartrihari or Descartes or, for that matter, Plato or Aristotle would have disagreed. Aristotle is the cru-cial philosopher here because he takes the trouble to develop the rea-sons for believing that the act of thinking is identical with its object. He begins from a usual Greek conception of vision: Whatever one sees is literally imprinted by light or by an airborne form of the object on the inward part of the eye, rather as writing is imprinted by a stylus on a tablet coated with wax. The imprinted picture is then supposed to be observed by the conscious soul.

In other words, the Greeks conceive vision to be a kind of touch-ing. The form that enters the eye or is grasped by it—the details are described in different obscure ways—is identical in place and structure with the impression it makes, so it is pointless to distinguish between form and impression. In Aristotle's opinion, when anything is seen, it is because a change in the air causes a change in the watery, equally transparent substance of the eye, which takes on the qualities—the shape and color—of the object, so that the eye becomes that very object.[8]

On the Aristotelian view that the perceiver and the perceived be-come literally identical, when an object emits a sound and someone hears it, the emission of the sound and the hearing are one and the same event. The characteristics that define the sound are what he calls its intelligible form, which, he believes, lodges in and is grasped by the person's thinking soul. The intelligible form is therefore *in* the soul, where thought attends to the features of the object that are essential to knowing just what it is.[9]

Aristotle's notion of vision as a kind of touching is still plausible—we say that vision depends on the photons that strike the retina. But instead of his watery impression of an airborne form, we speak of retinal nerve endings specialized for different colors, orientations, and intensities of light, and leading by electrochemical transmission to complex cells specialized for different directions of movement and different forms, the result projected in some complex way onto the visual cortex, where the testimony of both eyes is joined and reversed. I have not tried to summarize the process of vision in this last sentence, but only to suggest that we know far more about vision than Aristotle did. Yet despite all our new knowledge and our new, noninvasive methods for imaging the brain, we know little about the synthesis of perceptions in the central nervous system, and I am not sure that we grasp the nature of the final conscious perception—Aristotle's intelligible form—much better than Aristotle did; and we have not lost his habit of substituting verbal formulas for the understanding we lack.

Whatever the distance between Aristotle and ourselves, we can understand why the old argument took the path it did. Given the doctrine of intelligible form and of identity between knower and known, it is reasonable to think of understanding—in which one grasps and becomes identical with the essence of what is understood—as the activity that accounts for the existence of the world. This is the view of understanding held by the Bhartrihari, Plato, the Neoplatonists, and Hegel.

The Principle of Authority, Widespread and Powerful, Is Supported by Belief in Omniscience, Infallibility, and Ineffability

I go on to the principle of authority, the form that the hierarchic principle takes in social life. The gradation of authority is characteristic of many species of animals—among them birds (in stable flocks), seals, wild dogs, monkeys, apes, and human beings—and extends up to the various species of heavenly beings, who appear to be as conforming and rebellious as the others.

The hierarchical tendency always falls into conflict with an antihierarchical one, and the conflict may be displayed in metaphysics and cosmology no less than in social organization. Among the Greek cosmologies, atomism is analogous to the antihierarchical because each atom is an equal, indestructible constituent of the universe and the laws of the universe are no more than the sum total of the movements of the individual atoms. Is it a mere coincidence that the early atomists, Epicurus and Lucretius, did their best to liberate human beings from fear of the gods and of death?

Among the ancient Indians, Buddha stands out for his refusal to submit to hierarchical authority. Born in a community governed by a council of leading householders, he taught in the name of experience rather than ancient authority or heavenly decree, and he was ready to hold a reasoned discussion of anything he propounded. In his last sermon, preached on the verge of his death, he insisted that his disciples disregard their reticence and raise any question that still troubled them. Ask, he said to them, and do not afterwards complain that you could not ask your teacher face-to-face.

Caste does not seem to have been very important in Buddha's time and place, and even though sacred Hindu texts said that the hierarchy of castes had been fixed in the creation of the universe, he set no condition of birth for entry into the Buddhist community. His interest was in moral intentions, not purity of origin. Maybe it is not a coincidence that he resembles Epicurus and Lucretius in wanting to break things down into their smallest constituents and show that the soul, the metaphysical ego, is only an illusion that should give way to the knowledge that, having no ego, it is foolish, not to say painful, for humans to be egotistical, and that having no essential cohesion, it causes them no suffering to die and separate into their constituents.

Confucius differed from Buddha not only in his attitude to life and death, but also to authority. He taught his students as much by discernment as authority. Humble in his ceremonious way, he was ready to accept anyone, however poor, and to discuss the views of his students, to whose differences in personality he was sensitive, with quiet candor. However, in contrast to Buddha, he believed, as I have said, in the principle of hierarchy, the absence of which, he was sure, bred anarchic selfishness. He spoke, he insisted, in the name of authoritative ancient teachers and the truth that humans must live by the rules, implicit in nature itself and revealed, at the basic human level, in the relation of father to son and brother to brother.

Mostly, the world has agreed with Confucius on the importance of hierarchy. Societies everywhere have taught belief in a source of tradition the perfection of which shields it from the possibility of doubt and even explanation. The Confucian philosopher Hsün Tzu (3d century B.C.) held that man is born evil, meaning, with a predominating potentiality for evil, and must be transformed by education, ritual, and reward and punishment (*Hsün Tzu*, bk. 23). Hsün Tzu's Legalist students held as negative a view of human nature and advocated the severest, most devious methods of maintaining authority. So did the Indian school of the Science of Administration (*arthashastra*). The Legalists and Arthashastrans were not loved by conventional moralists, but they reflected social reality and had an influence that, though hard to measure, seems omnipresent in their cultures.[10]

Belief in authority takes the form of belief in inspiration, in omnipotence, and in divine origin of the texts considered sacred. I know of no tribal culture that did not believe in authoritative omens or dreams. The native inhabitants of North America sought inspiration actively and painfully. Wherever else shamanism was practiced, authoritative messages were brought from far off, from the distant sky perhaps. In this sense, the Chinese and Japanese, too, were shamanistic, for they thought that a god or spirit could transmit a message by way of a human messenger, such as a Taoist adept in the throes of trance.

In India, it was believed that a god could descend and take human form for the purpose of restoring virtue. The *Bhagavadgita* tells of the god Krishna, who, having taken the form of a human charioteer, preaches the saving, not uncomplicated truth. Among the Indian philosopher-theologians, there were those who contended that they themselves were incarnations of a god. Madhva (A.D. 1199–1278) thought himself an incarnation of the god Vayu and demoted his rival Shankara to the level of the incarnation of a little-known demon. And Vallabha (1479–1531), the advocate of pure monism and unlimited love of god, took himself to be an incarnation of the god Agni.

In Judaism and Islam, the doctrine of revelation and prophecy was a theological crux. Muhammad himself got his inspiration not by God's direct speech, the Quran says, but "behind a veil" or by a messenger (Quran 42.50), traditionally the angel Gabriel. Tradition says that on the Night of Power (so named in Quran 97), the Quran was sent down to the lowest of the seven heavens, from where Gabriel revealed it to Muhammad, part by part, as the occasion demanded. Sometimes Gabriel spoke out of a brightness surrounding Muhammad, sometimes by the disquieting sound of a bell, and sometimes only by his influence on Muhammad's mind.

This direct inspiration of the founder of a religion represents a theological challenge once the religion has taken root; and Jewish, Islamic, and Christian theologians have had to contend with the threat that a new prophet or mystic might arise and, on the strength of his inspired insight, claim the right to challenge tradition and the authorities who uphold it. The Jewish sages of the Talmudic period debated whether or not heavenly voices or prophets should continue to be granted authority. One answer was, "We pay no heed to heavenly voices," and another, "A prophet is not permitted from now on to introduce anything new."[11] In Islam, there was a clear and present danger to tradition in the mystics who began, as they reported, to converse with God. Al-Hallaj was beheaded in the year 922 for the claim ascribed to him that he had been unqualifiedly united with God (the execution may also have been motivated by his unorthodox populism).[12] For Christianity, the danger can be illustrated by Montanus (2d century A.D.), who would say in exaltation (maybe thinking of himself as a passive instrument), "I am the Lord God Almighty, who have descended in a man."[13]

Omniscience and its sequel, infallibility, come natural to all religions. The theoretical defense of omniscience was most developed, as far as I know, in India, where almost all the schools of thought—even those that denied the existence of a universal Creator and Governor—believed in supernormal perception and omniscience. Both forms of knowledge were said to divest everything of its illusory or accidental features, transcend the limitations of time, space, and cause, and grasp all the truth all at once. Only the Indian skeptics or materialists responded sarcastically to such claims. The 'school' of Mimamsa, which depended almost solely upon the injunctions of holy texts, gave many reasons why supernormal perception was impossible; by its philosophically expressed doubts, the school gave philosophical substance to the debate over the issue.

Let me cite an argument and counterargument from this Indian debate. The Mimamsa claimed that even if, for the sake of argument, one concedes the ability to perceive everything far and near, hidden and subtle, past, present, and future, omniscience is impossible because it is self-contradictory. Why so? Because to grasp everything in a single superlative cognition is to grasp contradictory qualities such as cold and heat simultaneously; but, being contradictory, they can be grasped only separately. Furthermore, if we assume that yogis grasp the truth of everything by successive acts of cognition, it would take an infinite length of time to grasp all the infinite number of things in the world.

This argument did not, of course, persuade those who were persuaded in advance that it must be false. One counterargument is that actual experience shows that contradictory qualities, such as yellow and blue, do in fact coexist in a single perception. Also, cold and heat can in fact be felt simultaneously by a person with his upper body in the sunlight and lower body in cold water. Hence it should at least be possible for yogis to see all the objects in the world—not excluding contradictory-seeming ones—in a single intuition.[14]

By definition, omniscience is a superlative ability, yet it was assumed by some that it has degrees of perfection and that only God, whose knowledge of everything is natural, eternal, indestructible, and uninterrupted, is capable of its highest degree.[15] Omniscience was a particularly useful ability in India, where the absolute truth was often supposed to have become known, without the intervention of any god, to particular sages, such as those responsible for the tradition of the school of (Raja) Yoga. Another example is Mahavira—the twenty-fourth and last of a line of omniscient 'victors' all possessing the same truth—whose enlightenment was the direct source of the doctrine of the Jains.[16] Like early Buddhist scriptures in relation to Buddha, Jain scriptures insist that Mahavira, a title meaning *Great Hero,* was a human being who found his own way without the help of any guru. In time, Mahavira came to earn the praise of his followers as one who explores "all beings, whether they moved or not, on high, below, and on earth, as well as the eternal and transient things. . . . Omniscient, wandering about without a home, crossing the flood, wise, and of an unlimited perception, without an equal, he shines forth like the sun, and he illuminates the darkness like a brilliant fire."[17]

To their believers, it was Buddha and Mahavira rather than a god who revealed the truth. Like them, the Upanishadic sages we have discussed depended on intuition. Shankara, the exponent of these sages, regarded the traditionally sacred texts as holy, but depended more seriously on inner realization. To the Mimamsa, the texts needed no warrant beyond themselves.

Elsewhere, it was usually a god who was regarded as the ultimate source of the truth that was recorded in a scripture—the thirtieth chapter of the Egyptian Book of the Dead, the Torah of the Jews, the New Testament of the Christians, the Quran of the Muslims, the Gathas or 'songs' of the Zoroastrians, and so on. There is more than enough evidence for the simple, almost self-evident point I want to make, which is that rulers and ruled alike, anxious over the stability of their societies, inherit or, if necessary, invent sources of authority presumed to be beyond criticism.

As wary of freedom as any Legalist or advocate of Arthashastra, Plato speaks out against atheism in the *Republic* and, in more detail, in the *Laws,* which advocates punishment for anyone who refuses to acknowledge that the world is ruled by a wise and just god. In Plato's opinion, the heretics who endanger human society are either forthright fools or clever but "beast-like" sophists (*Laws* 908). The fools, he proposes, are to be imprisoned and reeducated in a "sound-mind center" (*sophronisterion*) for five to seven years, and executed if they prove to be unreformed or if they relapse. The clever, vicious ones are to be imprisoned for life, in isolation from all free men (Laws 908–9).[18]

The reeducation Plato proposes for disbelievers must be education in his own theology. But God or no, just as Bhartrihari needs the Word beyond words as the absolute source of authority, so Plato needs his absolute, the Good or the One, or some equivalent principle of understanding and being that is beyond understanding and, strange as it may sound, perhaps beyond being itself. It seems that an ultimate that sounds too familiar may threaten the principle of authority and need to be replaced by another that inspires the respect due its unnegotiable distance and limitless authority.

Neoplatonism Creates a Logical Proof of the Metaphysical Hierarchy and Argues the Ineffability of Metaphysical Source

To say this is already to move on from the principle of authority to the more general one of hierarchy, which has directly intellectual substance and arouses questions that the human mind seems to find difficult to cope with. Hierarchy, which takes different forms, is one of several basic ways of ordering things. One form is the hierarchy in which the first element—for example, the foundation of a house—is the essential and therefore dominant basis. Another form is the hierarchy dominated by the power or intention of whoever or whatever stands at its apex. Such is the intention of the person who wants a house built and heads the entire hierarchy of people who work at building it: the architect, who has helpers of his own; perhaps a building engineer, who also has helpers; and a contractor, who has suppliers, subcontractors, and workers, all with assistants of their own.

A hierarchy can also be considered two-directional. To give a simple physical example, the roof of a house shields the other floors and the foundation, which it protects from the rain that might weaken it, and so the foundation is the most necessary element in one sense and the roof in another. Rather similarly, although the laws of nature are often thought of as constituting a hierarchy, a change in the characteristics of something literally as small as possible—a quark or a virtual particle—might require a fundamental change in the most sweeping laws of nature; so the highest laws are the most necessary elements in one sense and the constituents supposed to be ruled by the laws the most necessary in another. In such instances of interdependence it becomes unreasonable to assume that anything, whether general or particular, big or small, or theoretically deep or shallow, is more fundamental than anything else.

The hierarchies that most concern us are assumed to be ruled, like an ideal absolute monarchy, by what is metaphysically highest in them. This highest something is assumed to exist necessarily, regardless of the existence of anything else. Ruling over the hierarchy of existence, the highest something accounts for the existence of everything and is affected by nothing except, in a strange sense, itself. Its position at the top of the hierarchy lends it such distance from humans and their ordinary ways of thinking that even the words I have just used—*affected by itself*—are taken to be nothing more than a desperate attempt at a metaphor for the indescribable.

The hierarchies therefore have a single basic direction, that of the power of existence passing 'down' from the absolute unity (if such it is conceived to be) to the variety of things successively 'below' it. In Neoplatonism, which describes the world as such a hierarchy, there is also a returning movement, because beings are attracted back to their source. According to a favorite image of Plotinus, the going out resembles an expanding circle, its center a pure, unextended point the simplicity of which is reflected in its circumference.

Bhartrihari's hierarchy has been described and justified here approximately as he justified it. The justification of the analogous hierarchy of the Neoplatonists was worked out by them in eventually great detail. The justification depends on both positive and negative arguments, the negative designed to show that anyone who chooses another position contradicts himself. Because the justification is both concentrated and long, it cannot be summarized here; but something of its flavor can be transmitted.[19] First a warning: The justification is not at all persuasive unless one adopts the position that concepts or universals, although they have no physical body and occupy no space or time, have a real existence. I should add that the Neoplatonists believe in the real existence of concepts in the sense of Plato's Forms or Ideas. They take these to have objective existence and to constitute the framework of the world's existence. To some of the Neoplatonists (Proclus, for instance) the structure of the world, that is, the structure of its being, is clearly logical, so that the world—echoed in the order of logically connected words—is for the most part intelligible and should be appreciated as intelligibility in itself. Even so, language, as I will emphasize, has the inevitable defect that it splits the true oneness of existence into fragments.[20]

I have been reasoning in the Neoplatonic style, which non-Neoplatonists are likely to reject. The Neoplatonists were preoccupied with oneness and ready, in their way, to worship it. To understand their attitude toward *one*, we have to go further and show why they thought they could prove that *one* as a universal is metaphysically prior to anything else.[21]

To the Neoplatonists, if you try to think of a world in which the quality of oneness or unity is absent, you see that it is the *one*—the nature of which is to be fundamentally and indivisibly single—that clarifies the world by making it possible to distinguish between one thing and another. Every distinguishable thing is a *one* for itself, its oneness being (or accounting for) its unity and identity. This is because nothing can exist unless it is, so to speak, held together by being one rather than many. And so, if unity or oneness did not exist and was not basic, nothing would exist, not even manyness, plurality, or multiplicity, which is made up of ones, unities.

If, on the contrary, not *one* but multiplicity were basic, each of the ones or units this multiplicity contained would itself contain a multiplicity and make up a multiplicity of multiplicities; and if, to go on consistently, each unit of each of this multiplicity of multiplicities contained a further multiplicity, the result would be that an infinite (uncountably large) number would contain an infinite number of infinities, each of which would contain an infinite number of infinities, and so on, ad infinitum. Then we would arrive at the following paradox: Although infinity, being large beyond the possibility of counting, is the greatest quantity that can be or be thought of, it would contain within itself an infinity of other infinite numbers and so be infinitely smaller in quantity than the infinity of infinities it contained.

Consider some further consequences: If not *one* but plurality were the basic reality, numbers could not exist. The reason is that all other numbers depend on *one*, the single unit, the principle from which they are made by successive addition. If plurality were the basically real, it would be impossible to think about or know anything because every instance of knowledge is one of the identity of knower and known; and without unity, no identity would be possible and all beings would be unknowable.

Therefore, *one* is the basic reality, which is 'participated in' by every being; and this *one* of every being must be something purely one, with no admixture of anything more or different. If it were essentially both *one* and not-*one*, its unity would have to be imported into it from another *one*, which would require the existence of another *one*, and so on ad infinitum. If such were the case, there would be no self-sufficient source of unity.[22]

We have in effect established not only that the One (now capitalized to mark its absoluteness) is the basic reality, but also that plurality depends on unity and not vice versa. "Not being two," the One "is not limited in relation to itself or to anything else" (Plotinus, *Enneads* 5.5.11). Anything other than the One needs the One in order to be one, but the One does not need itself. But

> a thing which is multiple needs its full number of parts, and each of its parts, since it exists with the others and not independently, is in need of the others; so a thing of this kind shows itself to be defective as a whole and in each individual part.

In theological terminology, the One is transcendent and yet immanent in whatever is plural; and the One is the source of everything else:

> It is because there is nothing in it that all things come from it: in order that being may exist, the One is not being, but the generator of being . . . The One, perfect because it seeks nothing, has nothing, and needs nothing, overflows, as it were, and its superabundance makes something other than itself.(5.2)

The next step taken by the Neoplatonists is to show that the One is identical with the Good. To show this, they need only to point out that everything strives to maintain its own being, whether by its physical resistance to destruction or by other means. Therefore *good* is defined as remaining one. "Goodness, then, is unification, and unification goodness; the Good is one, and the One is primal good."[23]

Granted the supreme status of the One, which is the Good, the Neoplatonists proceed to work out the derivation or, rather, emanation of the world, beginning with Nous, the Intellect, which Plotinus regards as the horizon, the limit and definition, of the true, intelligible universe, the border at which it meets the Good beyond it.[24] In their derivation of the world from the One, the Neoplatonists parallel the cosmogony of Bhartrihari and, almost no less, the contemporary scientific cosmogonies I will soon mention. I will not summarize the Neoplatonists' now very implausible derivation, which can be followed in the text of Plotinus himself, and more systematically and at greater length in Proclus (as well as in the mercifully shorter summaries of the historians of Neoplatonism).

To anyone who accepts a few old philosophical assumptions, it should not be difficult to follow the main lines of this Neoplatonic reasoning. But the assumptions themselves are surely questionable. One of their major difficulties becomes evident in the very first of the derivations or emanations by means of which, the Neoplatonists think, the world is created. This first emanation is of the Intellect or Nous, which thinks and knows all Ideas simultaneously.[25] The Neoplatonists use the notion of the Intellect to explain how from the absolutely unitary One there is a time-less emanation of an obviously plural and often disorderly seeming world, a world that not only proceeds from the One but is also in a timeless 'process' of return to the One, its source—an eternal 'procession' out of the One, into (apparent, illusory) variety, and back in 'reversion' to its unity.[26]

To the Neoplatonists, this apparent world in apparent procession from and reversion to the One is essentially beautiful because even the diminished presence of the One is beautiful. Therefore, says Plotinus, to the sensitive person the world is the sounds of all voices in a universal melody. Loving sounds as he does, Plotinus uses the metaphor of sound to explain the essential nature of the world and the relation of the human soul to it. He prefers the metaphor of the sound of a voice to that of a sight because sound does not divide experience into parts but remains everywhere the same in the air, while sight, a pluralizing instrument, breaks things up and differentiates them. Yet although Plotinus makes use of the voice-metaphor, he at least once denies that in the fully real, intelligible world there can be any words or speech.[27]

A contemporary scholar says that metaphysics of Plotinus is not at all expressed in "the stammering utterance of a mystic" but is an intelli-gent, always-renewed struggle, using all the stylistic resources of the Greek language.

> Plotinus is convinced that the majesty of the world which transcends
> our senses, and still more the goodness of the One, can never be
> expressed in words: but if anyone ever could find adequate words
> for that world, Plotinus has succeeded in doing so.[28]

The case of the Neoplatonists is far more detailed than I have shown; but, as I have said and as the reader may well have felt, their attempts to prove it, although intellectually impressive, rest on assump-tions that make it vulnerable. All the same, given what has been said in their behalf, it becomes easy to see why they hold that the One is inher-ently indescribable. Their argument is that words necessarily describe a world of differences and limitations, in which thought is possible only if the thinker is split from the object of his thought. As they see it, when a person thinks of something other than himself and becomes identified with this other, the person is more nearly split into two than when think-ing of himself alone. Even thinking of himself alone, he "becomes a pair . . . while remaining one" (*Enneads* 5.6.1). In contrast, the One or Good does not think at all, because thinking is generated by desire and is a movement toward some good; but the Good does not think or need to think "for the Good is not other than itself" (5.6.5).

To the Neoplatonists it is therefore evident that language cannot be applied to the One or Good. The One is "beyond being" and nothing can be predicated of it, not even existence, for predication implies the distinction between subject and object and between what is and is not predicated. The consequence is that every description we give of the One is inaccurate and must be understood as though modified by the words *as if* (6.8.13). Negation, however, is less inaccurate than the use of positive words:

> It is more proper to reveal the incomprehensible and indefinable cause which is the One through negations; for assertions slice up reality, whereas negations tend to simplify them from distinction and definition in the direction of being uncircumscribed and from being set apart by their proper boundaries in the direction of being unbounded . . . It is only possible by these means to reveal the power of the One, which is incomprehensible and ungraspable and unknowable by particular intellects.[29]

As I have intimated, such Neoplatonic views were echoed and reechoed in later Jewish, Christian, and Islamic thought. In Europe they become standard theology, the lesson being (in the Socratic words of Nicholas of Cusa) that the more a person "knows that he is unknowing, the more learned he will be."[30]

The Mathematician Cantor and the Logician Gödel Encounter the Hierarchical Principle

The widespread influence of Neoplatonic theology and its parallel with Bhartrihari show that such ideas can be plausible at different times and places. Although it is easy to quarrel with the assumptions and logic used to erect Neoplatonic or Bhartriharian intellectual structures, it is more interesting to show that something central to them remains a temptation of thought no less effective now than it was in their times. To show this, I make a shift as dramatic as my earlier one from Chuang Tzu to Kierkegaard—this time from the Neoplatonists to Georg Cantor (1845–1920), whose view of the infinite changed the nature of mathematics.[31]

Cantor defied two conventions of thought. The first was that infinity could never be more than potential, and the second, vital for Neoplatonic argument, that the infinite was an absolute, not merely arithmetical, maximum. When Cantor proved that one infinite could be larger than another, he raised the prospect of a whole hierarchy of infinities, a prospect that led him to think of the culmination of the hierarchy in the set of all sets, and to choose the absolutely infinite succession of transfinite numbers as the fitting symbol for the Absolute or God.[32]

Cantor's solution of old difficulties led to a new one. His reasoning showed that, because of a conceptual difficulty, the absolute infinite number could not be understood. As Cantor himself made clear, every set gives rise to a larger set. This holds true even of the set of all sets, and so, using his famous 'diagonal argument', Cantor showed that the set of all its subsets has a higher number (a higher cardinality) than does the set of all sets itself. He had no doubt about the absolute meaning of the words "*all* sets"; but given that the set of all sets had to contain a set larger than itself, it was both a 'largest set' and not a 'largest set'. It therefore became clear that the Neoplatonists had been right in raising and rejecting a similar possibility because—as Cantor accepted—it turned out to be (or seem to be) possible to reach the self-contradictory notion of an absolute infinite that contained more than itself.[33] Remember the difficulty that Chuang Tzu raised: If we think of everything as one, when we say that it is one, we add the saying to whatever we thought to be one and so have two things—the unity and the statement about it; and the process continues until "even an expert calculator cannot get to the end of it."[34]

Cantor's conclusion was double. He concluded that one ought to stop thinking logically or mathematically of the set of all sets as having been completed because the assumption that all its elements had been unified into a whole, completed object had led to a contradiction. By concluding that at least one infinite set could never be regarded as completed, he surrendered in part to the traditional, Aristotelian view of infinites as in fact uncompletable. But he also concluded that this extraordinary set, which he called the "inconsistent" or "absolute" infinite set, could be accepted as real even though it was not understandable as a unity of all its elements. In the words of a commentator:

> Although he does not seem to have consciously or immediately recognized the inconsistencies of set theory, he always emphasized the impossibility of a largest cardinal number, which he originally interpreted as meaning that the set of all cardinal numbers was an *incomprehensible* one.[35]

Cantor had long been sympathetic with the Neoplatonic position. To him, any consistent idea was a possible one and, for the very reason of its possibility, necessarily existed in the mind of God. He was therefore sure that transfinite, like finite, numbers existed there as eternal ideas, all of them equally "at the disposal of the intentions of the Creator and His absolutely immeasurable Will."[36] This belief fortified Cantor against his critics, and he came to think that transfinite numbers led to the one "true infinity." His final conclusion was to go beyond mathematics. In mathematics, he said, the hierarchy of transfinites cannot be contained in any absolute but has to remain open—just as there can be no largest finite number, there can be no largest transfinite one. In metaphysics, however, the hierarchy he envisaged culminates in an absolute maximum beyond human understanding or description.[37] According to Cantor, in this case, metaphysics, conducted in words, shows a superior ability to express the true existence of a culminating object of thought. It may be thought ironical that some contemporary logicians find the idea of the set of all sets to be still useful in their discipline.

Perhaps the most famous logical discovery of the twentieth century is the so-called *incompleteness* theorem, which shows that consistent systems rich enough to contain elementary arithmetic always contain sentences that cannot be proved to be either true or false. The discoverer of this theorem, Kurt Gödel, has been called the greatest logician of the century.

To Gödel, the world is divided basically into objects and concepts. Objects include mathematical objects, which can be identified with sets; and sets, he thinks, are related to concepts because "every set is the extension of some concept."[38] Although Gödel is obscure at this point, in making sets extensions of concepts he goes some distance toward justifying Bhartrihari's inclusion of all forms of thought within language. In Gödel's eyes, the function of concepts is to unify experience, somewhat as Kant's categories do, except that Gödel takes concepts to have objective existence.[39]

From about 1925—in opposition to the dominant philosophies of mathematics of his time—Gödel, like Cantor, was an unwavering mathematical realist, that is, a 'Platonist'. To him, mathematical objects had as real and independent an existence as physical objects. In his conversations with Hao Wang, he argued, with nuances, that mathematical objects such as sets have an objective existence and that we "have something like a perception . . . of objects of set theory."[40] His view was that in the same way as we explain sense perceptions by assuming underlying physical objects and laws, we explain mathematical statements (and make a satisfactory system of mathematics possible) by assuming that they refer to underlying mathematical objects and axioms. Therefore, mathematical intuition can give us genuine mathematical knowledge. We are told that Gödel was strongly motivated by this realist philosophy of mathematics, which he credited "with much of the reason for his success in being led to the 'right' results and methods."[41]

Gödel wanted to create a richer logic as a theory of pure concepts. His desire was perhaps part of the more embracing ambition to create a whole axiomatic metaphysics bearing some resemblance, so he said, to the monadology of Leibniz.[42] But his main accomplishment was to prove that there could be no closed formal hierarchy of thought, no definition of arithmetic truth in arithmetic itself (as Tarski shows in his extension of Gödel's work), no decision procedure for the whole of mathematics, no strongest formal system, but only a kind of endless regress in which one system can always be extended by another.

The discovery of the necessary incompleteness of formal systems did not weaken Gödel's lifelong interest in theology or religious metaphysics, which he hoped would provide science and religion with a rational foundation.[43] Sadly, like Cantor, he was the sort of thinker whose depth and radicalism went with a life always in psychological danger. The very ambitious Cantor, who was more than once convinced that God had inspired him, underwent severe manic-depressive attacks; and the quite real antagonisms from which he suffered were augmented by even more embittering imaginary ones.[44] Gödel's psychological difficulties were evident in his extreme meticulousness and his dread of controversy. Unlike Plato, Descartes, and Husserl, he said, he wanted but failed to get the sudden illumination that could show him the world in a new light.[45] At one time he was close to suicide. After his death, his brother said of him that he had been unstable from childhood on, had spent time in a sanitarium, and that he had suffered from later "mental crises."[46] Gödel died of starvation caused by the fear that his food had been poisoned.

Apparently there was much that Cantor and Gödel did not and probably could not know about themselves. It is not surprising that they both found limitations in language, the one as a believer in mathematical and, even more, 'true' infinity, and the other as an investigator of completeness. Gödel is reported to have made the sad, astonishing remark, "The more I think about language, the more it amazes me that people ever understand one another."[47]

Having approached the end of our consideration of the principle of hierarchy, we can make a small collection of the inexpressibles we have inherited from Bhartrihari, Plotinus and Proclus, Cantor, and possibly Gödel. This collection includes the Word and the One, each of which contains in itself, in an indescribable unity, all the variety that issues from it. The Word and the One cannot be said to know themselves because this would require a split between the subject and the object of the act of knowing; and yet the Word and the One cannot be said not to know themselves. We can describe neither their unity nor their equivalent of what we know as knowledge; but the names *Word* and *One* are better than none, and the use of negation may help us to grasp what we know we cannot describe.

We see that Bhartrihari and the Neoplatonists are right in the sense that their logical defense of their doctrines puts intellectual pressure on us to accept a paradoxical reality. But can logic teach that it is ruled by a higher illogic or more-than-logic? As long as Cantor accepted the set of all sets, he intimated that the answer to the question was *yes*; and though he gave up the set of all sets, he held on stubbornly to the metaphysical infinite, which is fundamentally Neoplatonic.

Gödel takes a different, more austere line. By proving that mathematics cannot be exhausted by a single formal language, he shows us that there can always be 'stronger' languages, which form an inexhaustible or, to be cautious, unsurveyable totality. Using Gödel's techniques, Tarski shows that no consistent language can contain the notion of truth appropriate to that very language—we can always talk or think about languages by resorting to 'higher' languages, which form an inexhaustible hierarchy; but the requirement of consistency of a formal language makes that language incapable of speaking of the whole hierarchy in which it is found. To see the hierarchy for what it is, we have to enlist the help of an outside, natural language.[48]

The very informality of a natural language makes its paradoxes harmless and often bracing—we express our ambivalence with their help, enlist them for metaphors, make them into oxymoronic poetry, and use them as spurs to thought. And ways can sometimes be found to state them nonparadoxically and restore a more comfortable relationship with formal logic. And in a natural language, we can discuss the possibility that there is something in the mathematical infinite that resists a completely satisfactory formalization.[49] The product of a long evolution, natural language has an inbred resourcefulness: As compared with a formal language, a natural language, with its variety of contexts and expedients, including its rhythms and accentuations, may in a way be able to see itself as if it were partly outside of itself—a sight Valéry enjoys and Derrida tries to capture in the conviction that he will fail. A natural language allows us to think in one sense about what we cannot think in another, and it exploits the coexistence of clear perception with cloudy perception. With one eye closed, a person can see one side of his nose, and see it very clearly; but with both eyes open, he can make out his whole nose, though only vaguely. Clear and unclear vision work best when they are regarded not as competitive but supplementary, as clear fragments along with a vague but very useful whole.

In saying this, I may or may not be disagreeing with Ludwig Wittgenstein's belief that we cannot use words to express the supposed semantic links between language and reality. We know that he was convinced that we cannot get below, within, or above our language. As he put it:

> What is expressible through language I call thought. Then it can be translated from this language into *another*. I want to say: all thought must then take place in symbols. But if one says, "How am I supposed to know what he means, all I can see are merely his symbols," then I say, "How is *he* supposed to know what he means, all that he has are merely his symbols . . . A language can be explained only by means of language, wherefore *the language* cannot be explained.[50]

Interpreters quarrel over exactly what Wittgenstein meant in such statements, but in my own mind they are related to the impossibility of exhausting the process of explanation: Something always remains implicit and unsaid and, at least in this sense, unsayable.[51] Also, if we reason by relying on explicit logical principles, we are likely to justify them in the end by reiterating them stubbornly, by using them circularly, or by regressing with them into an infinite retreat. If, however, we rely in principle on no more than our psychobiological competence, we may see the proliferating forms of logic as the ways in which we try to imitate and extend abilities that we as humans in fact have even though we find it impossible to state or formalize them in a fully satisfactory way.

I deliberately refrain from spelling out what I mean by "fully satisfactory," but it is clear that our perception and thought are still much more adaptable than their computer equivalents. We surely will find out more about the functioning of our nervous systems, and will use and no doubt improve this knowledge in constructing computers and computer-run mechanisms; but at present, we most often cannot clearly say what we do and do not know, and so we think according to principles or intersections of principles that are still ineffable. The deepest conceptual structures—or, as I prefer, conceptual-emotive structures—of our thinking are largely hidden from us; and because we cannot bring them to clear consciousness or imitate them in symbols, they are beyond our ability to express in any way but intuition and action. Yet there is a natural continuum between what we can and cannot see clearly, and those who specify exactly what we can never know have often been proved to have drawn the line too sharply. Maybe, then, our condition is almost musical.[52]

A Diversion: Contemporary Cosmologists Encounter the Problem of the Hierarchy and Its Absolute Beginning

I end my account of the principle of hierarchy with a discussion of the effort of physicist-astronomers to describe the beginning of the universe.[53] The immediately following pages are a diversion in the sense that they are not directly on philosophy or religion. But the intellectual relationship between the old and the new cosmogonies is too obvious to avoid, especially because the new ones raise the same, not purely scientific issue of the beginning.

The physicists' very beginning is most often left unexplained. This modesty is reasonable because we have had no experience of such a beginning and know of no laws to explain it. All the same, cosmologists are too bold to suffer limits gladly. I am not technically equipped to discuss their competing proposals; but it is certain that in order to make them, that is, create their models, they have to make drastic simplifications in the world as we know it and drastic assumptions about what is beyond our ability to observe. A good example is the mathematical technique designed to get rid of the microstructural details that complicate the theorizing and are therefore regarded as 'noise'. This technique of 'coarse-graining' makes it possible to erase the troublesome details, or, in other words, to make the 'grain' of what one is concerned with coarser or larger and, in this way, more uniform.[54]

We have to keep in mind that the urge to theorize on the origin of the cosmos has to deal as best it can with information far too incomplete and models inevitably too simple to trace cosmic evolution in detail. This will remain true irrespective of probes into space, new telescopes, and an increasingly sophisticated understanding. With this qualification in mind, we can go on to the cosmologists' beginning. Although analogous to a beginning in the ordinary sense, it does not allow us to ask "What happened before?" because it is a beginning in time as well as space. This intellectual tactic, built into the theory itself, is the same as that used in medieval theology in response to the question "What happened before God created the universe?" If one does not accept the tactic, one cannot accept the theory.[55]

Some cosmologists speak of a beginning by accident. That is, they propose a 'quantum cosmology' according to which the universe, by analogy with 'virtual' particles, originates as a fluctuation of 'nothing' or 'vacuum' (vacuum in the physicists' sense of space empty of matter but having 'energy fluctuations'). An emergence of this kind from 'nothing', which does not violate any known law of conservation, gives a 'reason' for the emergence of the universe. It also has the advantage that its initial inhomogeneity helps to explain the inhomogeneities of the universe as we know it.[56]

I will return to quantum cosmology. For the moment, I go on with the still dominant conception: If we presuppose the cosmologist's beginning, the calculations describing what happens can start from an infinitesimal moment later. In the very beginning, if the theory in question allows the time zero, there is no space and time but only a 'singularity'. This is because at this incredible minimum, the force of gravity compresses matter and energy infinitely, space-time becomes infinitely 'curved', and the universe is shrunk to an extensionless point.[57]

When, according to this (big bang) theory, of which there are different versions, the universe began, so to speak, or was already, so to speak, in its beginning being, its temperature and density were infinite and everything was uniform, as structureless as possible. How structureless? There are no laws to appeal to and, as I have just said, even time, in the physicists' sense, did not 'yet' exist. Maybe then—infinitesimally 'after'?—in accord with a currently attractive kind of speculation, everything was nothing other than identical space-time 'strings' having eleven (or other fitting number of) mathematical dimensions, only the three familiar ones of which expanded and became our space. Already or extremely soon (when physics applied and time 'began') everything was hot, dense, and simple. Matter consisted of a minimal number of kinds of dissociated subatomic particles—say: (very speculatively) only preons or (less speculatively) only quarks and gluons, particles not known to have any size at all (meaning that matter in and by itself is empty, without volume, just as some Indians speculated).[58] Possibly all of the four great forces we know—electromagnetism, the two nuclear forces, and even gravity—were united in a single field of force. If all four were united, as physicists conjecture and hope, it should be possible to capture in a single equation what might be called the nature of nature.[59]

Something basic in this picture is reminiscent of the primal Word and the One, because for Bhartrihari, Plotinus, and the modern cosmologists everything that could possibly be or become was potentially there in the very beginning, concentrated in an infinitesimal not-yet space and time that were just beginning to become what we know them as, and nothing or almost nothing—the qualification turns out to be invaluable—was distinguished from anything else. For all the world like a philosopher or theologian, a cosmologist asks what he calls the 'uniqueness' question: "Why do the particular particles that we see exist?" The cosmologist may answer this question and others like it with a prefatory demurrer, "The important thing to understand about such questions is that they do not have to have answers. In fact they do not even have to be questions. The issue may have changed completely long before we get to such tiny distances."[60]

A difficulty arises for cosmology like the difficulty for both the Word and the One: How did this unity and uniformity become the varied universe in which we exist? In the older model of the 'big bang' theory, the universe develops too quickly for radiation to become as uniform as it is, so the universe is assumed to have been quite homogeneous or symmetrical to begin with.[61] Given the initial symmetry, however, further questions arise: Why did the symmetry break 'spontaneously' into dissymmetry?[62] And why did antimatter, which was theoretically paired exactly with matter, disappear from our vicinity? And how did galaxies form, and why are they distributed, as now appears, as if on the outside of enormous bubbles of space?[63] This last observation is based on a large-scale survey of the clustering of galaxies. The area and depth surveyed—for obvious practical reasons, limited—may well be critical to the answer given because, with galaxies too, what appears lumpy at one scale or distance can appear smooth at a greater one. It turns out that the sharply defined big structures, the lumps, of the one survey have, at the time I write these words, become the tentative smoothness of another, which is peering more deeply into space and time. But who knows what scale of surveying can be really definitive? I imagine that a theorist would prefer the cosmos to be homogeneous because the relevant mathematics is much easier to manage.

Not only are there the inhomogeneities (concentrations of galaxies) to explain, but there is also the remaining homogeneity. I mean that if, as assumed, the universe began quite homogeneous, it did not remain so for long, and the inhomogeneities that developed close to its beginning would have affected the cosmic background radiation and made it less even than it is.[64]

To make their cosmogony plausible, its creators had to assume so much about initial conditions, a quantum theory rival says, that finding the present universe in this model would be 'as unlikely as finding a pencil balanced on its point after an earthquake.'[65] The most successful answer to the cosmologists' problems has been the so-called inflationary theory. According to this theory, at an extremely brief time after the big bang, the universe expanded with extreme, explosive speed for an extremely tiny fraction (10^{-30}) of a second, after which it returned to a slower rate of expansion. During this tiny fraction of a second, each near-infinitesimal and therefore near-homogeneous part of this universe expanded enormously, the expansion smoothing out the signs (the variability) of the brief initial state that had preceded, so that space-time became even in every direction.

This is how the once-born universe underwent a second, far more explosive birth. To explain the transition from relatively slow to explosive growth and then back again to relatively slow, use is made of a theoretical symmetry-destroying field named after the physicist Peter Higgs. I mention this to show how far the physicists are ready to venture into purely theoretical construction. Their Higgs fields are assumed to permeate every point in space, interact with other quantum fields, and make possible the sharp, so-called phase transitions. While ordinary gravity would tend to hold particles together and keep the expansion relatively slow, force enough for the explosive acceleration was derived from a Higgs-field state of (never-observed) false vacuum (space itself with an energy density) that released enough energy to reverse the effect of ordinary gravity and cause the universe, still less than a foot in diameter, to expand explosively; and then, critical point by critical point, its unified force broke apart into its four constituent forces and many kinds of particles. The inherently random fluctuations of the Higgs fields resulted in the inhomogeneities that, stretched to astronomical size, became those of the universe (observable fraction of the universe) we now inhabit.[66] Or perhaps the inhomogeneities were not random fluctuations but, as a new theory would have it, were 'textures' resulting from a phase transition like that which causes the imperfections of the crystals of ice that are formed when water freezes.

All this must be as satisfying to the ingenious physicists who invented it, in formidable detail, as it is technically unintelligible to nonphysicists such as myself. Naturally, the inflationary theory exists in different varieties, none of which is free from problems or has direct observational support.

Despite all the growing resources of science, the physicists' answer, taken in a very broad sense, has an interesting resemblance to that of Bhartrihari or Plotinus: Development comes in a series of conjectured breaks (phase transitions and inflations) in the unimaginable, inexpressible, uniformly concentrated nothing-everything that evolves into our scattered, lumpy, noisy, heterogenous world. How can all this have happened, and why? We may or may not be able to know, but when we consider it, we are no more reduced to silence than Bhartrihari was. He had his scriptures and science of grammar to guide him, and we have our imaginations and science of physics. No wonder one of the physicists insists that his theorizing friends must retain some modesty in order to retain their seriousness:

> My personal suspicion is that nature is much more imaginative than we are. If we theorists approach her study with the proper respect, if we recognize that we are parasites who must live on the hard world of our experimental friends, then our field will remain healthy and prosper. But if we allow ourselves to be beguiled by the siren call of the 'ultimate' unification at distances so small that our experimental friends cannot help us, then we are in trouble, because we will lose that crucial process of pruning of irrelevant ideas which distinguishes physics from so many other less interesting human activities.[67]

Although the big bang theory is so widely accepted, its assumptions may not be impregnable. The theory rests on the view that the universe is expanding, as proved by the reddening of an object as it recedes—the greater the shift of light toward the red end of the spectrum, the greater the distance of the object being observed. But every once in a while, a quixotic physicist questions this truth. One recent proposal accounts for the reddening by the shrinking of the objects viewed; another accounts for it by the passage of light through a medium in which it is randomly scattered.[68]

A second basic assumption of the theory is that gravity has dominated the formation of the universe. However, a still quixotic-sounding scientist has argued that not gravity but electromagnetism has been dominant. If so, we should have to accept a plasma (kind of ionized gas) cosmology, in accord with a universe that "has been and remains a veritable sea of charged particles interlaced with complex magnetic fields and electric currents." By one such cosmology, the universe we observe condensed out of plasma in progressively smaller steps—there was no expansion or beginning, and there will be no end in time or of time.[69]

In such a universe I feel philosophically more comfortable, and the hierarchical problem, at least in its paradoxical or paradoxical-seeming form, vanishes. I find the image of the growth of the universe from 'nothing' intellectually disquieting and uncomfortably bound to a time that begins and perhaps ends. The cosmologist James Peebles, who maintains a certain skepticism about the cosmological enterprise, says, "to have a theory of the universe as a whole sounds to me more like a metatheory than physics as I know it."[70] And Steven Weinberg, the physicist and cosmologist, makes it clear that he would prefer the old-fashioned, unchanging universe that he cannot now have:

> I find it more comfortable to think about infinite time as well as infinite space, no boundary in time any more than a boundary in space, with *everything* being explained by physics without any arbitrary historical elements entering it.[71]

In contrast, the Russian Andrei Linde—an evangelist of inflation and the incommunicado universes resulting from it—confesses that he would prefer the kind of universe he finds in Indian philosophy, by which he means "an eternal, oscillating universe, which at each cycle of its evolution forgets what occurred before."[72]

The Principle of Hierarchy Involves the Idea and Ideal of Extraordinary, Radical Intimacy

Intimacy is the last of the principles with which I hope to explain why the essence of words or concepts is regarded as beyond expression in words. In order to show the relevance of the explanation, I will begin with representative descriptions of the ineffable state of unity. As a rule, they suggest intimacy. Sometimes, however, they dwell only on power or bliss. Both emphases occur in the Upanishads, on power where it is said the person who has found and awakened his Self "is the All-maker; for he is the Maker of Everything. Heaven is his; or rather, he *is* Heaven outright!" [73] Another, less power-oriented Upanishad says of the Absolute that love is his head, joy his right side, joyousness his left side, and bliss his trunk.[74]

An often-recurring description is of merger and the loss of individual identity. In a famous Upanishad, the separate self is described as merging with the great Self, a limitless mass of knowledge, which pervades and is everything, as inseparable from everything and as imperceptible apart from everything as salt is from the water in which it is dissolved. As the sea is the locality of all sea water, the skin of all touching, the nostrils of all smells, the tongue of all tastes, the eyes of all sights, so the earth is the sole locality of all sciences, the hands the sole locality of all deeds, the feet of all journeys, the genital organ of all delights, the anus of all evacuations, and Speech the sole locality of all Vedas—just as, by an unstated analogy, the Self is the sole locality of all things.[75] The one who knows quits his individuality and disappears into the divine Person as rivers flow and "disappear into the ocean."[76]

In a hymn, Shankara, the best known of all Indian philosopher-theologians, writes of the great joy of the vanishing of mind and world, of the this and not-this, of the going away of the world, of disembodiment, immutability, and I-aloneness. Twoness has vanished for him, banished forever by the knowing of oneness.[77]

Often, as in the previous reference to the Upanishads, the experience of merger is described in words implying great joy, and the desire for this joy can inspire intense longing. Plotinus writes of his desire to be mingled, to lose his boundaries, to experience beauty, and to be spiritually intoxicated.[78] He says of the Good:

> If anyone sees it, what passion will he feel, what longing in his desire to be united with it, what a shock of delight! . . . He who has seen it glories in its beauty and is full of wonder and delight, enduring a shock which causes no hurt, longing with true passion and piercing longing; he laughs at all other beauties and despises what he thought beautiful before . . . (*Enneads* 1.6.7)

As we see, the desire for merger can have sexual overtones, and, in fact, it is often explicitly sexual. In an Upanishadic passage, a sexual simile is used to describe emotion so engulfing that all distinctions vanish. This occurs in deep dreamless sleep:

> Just as a man who is embraced by a beloved woman knows nothing outer and inner, even so this bodily Self, when it is embraced by the Self consisting-of-intelligence, knows neither outer nor inner . . . In this state father is no father, mother no mother, worlds no worlds, god no gods, Vedas no Vedas, sacrifices no sacrifices . . . He is unaffected by good, unaffected by evil; for then he has transcended all sorrow of the heart . . . Though seeing, he sees no object of sight . . . there is not, then, any second thing, other and separate from him, which he might see.[79]

Plotinus, although personally ascetic, did not hesitate to use sexual metaphors: The soul prepares itself for union with the Good by making itself as beautiful as possible and merges with it so that there are no longer two but one, so that no distinction can be made between them. "Lovers and their beloveds here below imitate this in their will to be united." In their union, the soul no longer perceives the body within which it is and speaks of nothing else, because everything else would be a distraction. It has met what it has been seeking.

> In its happiness it is not cheated in thinking that it is happy; and it does not say it is happy when the body tickles it, but when it has become that which it was before, when it is fortunate . . . If all the other things about it perished, it would even be pleased, that it might be alone with this: so great a degree of happiness has it reached. (*Enneads* 6.7.34)

Love is the dominant image among the Moslem mystics, the Sufis, the Christian mystics of Spain, and, perhaps most remarkably, the devotional sects of India. The Sufi metaphor and, often, human reality was that of the love of a man for a man. Rather as in Plato's *Symposium*, "gazing at beardless boys" is the earthly glimpse of absolute beauty.[80]

According to a seventeenth-century justification of Sufi erotic imagery, a beloved's mole in a poem refers to the point of real unity between the human and the divine, the down on the beloved's cheek refers to the manifestation of reality in spiritual forms, and so on.[81]

The great Sufi poet Rumi (A.D. 1207–1273) loves and dedicates poems to his ideal Sufi, Shams al-Din, his passageway to the universal Intelligence.[82] Rumi writes that love is a boundless ocean in which the heavens are only a flake of foam, and that if not for love, the world would be frozen. Contrasting love and logic, he says that, as initiates know, there is no need to prove that "from Satan logic, but from Adam love."[83] Making equal though heterosexual use of the metaphor of love, St. John of the Cross (A.D. 1542–91) writes in his mystical poem *Black Night* of "night drawing side to side the loved and the lover—she that the lover loves, lost in the lover!"[84]

Among the devotional sects of India, the best known in the West are the worshippers of Krishna.[85] One of their great figures is the Krishna-intoxicated Chaitanya (A.D. 1486–1533), who gave new life to religion in the Bengal of his time. His followers took him to be the god Krishna himself in human form or, alternatively, the incarnation in a single person of Krishna, god of love, and Radha, his deified beloved.

Chaitanya was an Indian type of the religiously mad ecstatic.[86] He would act the sacred story of Krishna and Radha as if he were actually reliving Radha's love for the god:

> He had strange physical symptoms of his intense love—his body would become distorted, stretched, and compressed, sweat and blood oozing from his pores and saliva foaming at the mouth . . . His love was not a peaceful state, but a continuous fluctuation between divine and human personalities, between love and loneliness. He would mistake his environment for Krishna's Vrindavana, sing and dance, and then faint . . . Sometimes he would state his great love for Krishna and at other times he would deny that love, saying that his crying was deceitful and that he is a madman whom nobody believes.[87]

In Krishna worship, the male devotee, such as Chaitanya, plays the role of a particular kind of woman, that of the 'other' woman, who, regardless of her marriage, cannot check her passion. The devotee becomes a metaphorical woman because it is usual in India to assume that intense emotion and submissive surrender are characteristic of women in particular.[88] The overriding of conventions in the Krishna legend, especially those of marriage, caused theological trouble and inspired a neat theological solution: The married women who had intercourse with Krishna were really metaphysical forces intrinsic to Krishna, who contains everything within himself, so that no sins were committed.

Regardless of the emotion involved, theological justifications were socially and intellectually necessary, and with them came the usual metaphysical hierarchy, headed this time not by the undifferentiated Brahman but by Krishna—Krishna regarded as infinite consciousness with an infinite number of traits. Theological acumen succeeded in making this ideal greater than its theological rival, the undifferentiated Brahman. To make the Krishna-superlative superior to the Brahman-superlative, Krishna was given as one of his infinite qualities the extraordinary quality of being qualityless. As a question-saving theological grace, the relation between Krishna, reality-in-itself, and the lesser realities was declared beyond human understanding.[89]

There is no doubt that the love between Krishna and the women herders (gopis), who are represented by his devotees, is fully sexual and, by ordinary human standards, illicit. In Indian tradition, the three basic types of women are the wife, the courtesan, and the 'other', married woman. The romantic imagination of India, like that of the European troubadours, required the truest love to be adulterous, no doubt because in a traditionally chaste society the greatest dangers and tensions were those inspired by adulterous hopes and acts. Yet, as must be emphasized, the true devotee—the gopi by devotion—is a kind of sexual ascetic who is either unmarried or is allowed to have intercourse with his wife only for the purpose of childbearing.[90]

According to the testimony of the temple dancers of Orissa, who reenact the traditional love of the (married) gopis for Krishna, the Krishna-fantasy is that of a prolonged erotic tension that does not reach the stage of orgasm. For this there are a number of reasons. One of them is the persistent Indian belief that when the man ejaculates, he grows weaker and ages more quickly. Orgasm is also thought inadvisable because erotic tension vanishes with it, while ejaculation causes pregnancy and birth, both states all too human, utilitarian, and enmeshed in the cycle of life and death. So the devotee aims to experience the sweet sensuousness of love without the lust (kama) that joins husband and wife and results in the birth of children.

As an adult, sexual lover, Krishna continues to remain "unfallen," for he is "the one whose seed does not fall." And so Krishna and his women continue to exist in the perfect eternal tension of love in and for itself. His worshippers by erotic tension feel something of the exaltingly intense sweetness that they hope salvation will complete.[91]

A similar ideal is exemplified by the boundless love-as-such of Krishna's foster mother for Krishna the adorable child. This mother-child ideal can be quite as potent as the Krishna-lover one. It is particularly stressed in the sect ('transmission' to the Indians) that follows the teachings of Vallabha, the contemporary of Chaitanya.[92] In a Vallabhite temple, Krishna appears also in the image of a child, which is awakened and fed, as often and as carefully as a living child would be, is wrapped in blankets when presumed cold, and is serenaded to sleep at night. The child-Krishna image arouses the conscious, ritually and theatrically enhanced emotions that a parent feels towards a small child. Taught by these emotions, the devotee's empathy with the image may grow until it is perceived as alive; and this now living Krishna may answer, sadly or happily, to one's changing moods.[93]

In such a familial atmosphere of devotion, food—prepared with a mother's ritual intentness and eaten in an atmosphere that pleases the senses—becomes the instrument, real and symbolic, of selfless love. To the Vallabhites, such love arouses the grace that nourishes the souls of the devotees and the human-divine relationship in which they partake.[94]

Although there is no need here to aim at anything like a complete survey, I should like to continue with two more descriptions, this time as evidence of Greco-Roman attitudes toward mystical union. Both descriptions are given by Plotinus. In the first, which is of duality maintained in the midst of unity, Plotinus says of the intelligible world that everything in it, to its innermost part, is color and beauty. Those whose souls are entirely penetrated by beauty are not simply spectators:

> For there is no longer one thing outside which is looking at it, but the keen sighted has what is seen within, although having it he for the most part does not know that he has it, and looks at it as if it were outside because he looks at it as if it was something seen, and because he wants to look at it. (*Enneads* 5.8.10)

The second Plotinian description is that of the seeker who, "making no more separation, is one and all altogether with that god silently present, and is with him as much as he wants to be and can be." Plotinus adds, significantly, that if the seeker returns to his separateness, while he is pure, he stays close to the god in anticipation that the god will turn to him again:

> In this turning he has the advantage that to begin with he sees himself, while he is different from the god; then he hastens inward and has everything, and leaves perception behind in his fear of being different, and is one in that higher world; and if he wants to see by being different, he puts himself outside. (5.8.11)

A description or two that stress pure negation, and we are done with this series of examples. The most famous in the Upanishads are the repeated words that say that the Self is "not, not," for the Self cannot be grasped in any way.[95] In Plotinus, negation is regarded as a superior way of trying to describe what cannot really be described:

> We do indeed say something about it, but we certainly do not speak it, and we have neither knowledge nor thought of it . . . For we say what it is not, but we do not say what it is: so that we speak about it from what comes after it. But we are not prevented from having it, even if we do not speak it. (5.3.14)

In summary, the descriptions or reactions we have surveyed tell of superlative states of power, joy, and merger with the essence of things; or, in other approximations or metaphors, of the vanishing of everything and of immutability, longing, passion, loss of identity in sexual union, prolonged erotic tension, self-contemplation when penetrated by beauty, and becoming one and two and one again. Sometimes the state is said to be so utterly unique that it cannot be described or thought, though it can in some sense be experienced.

In theology and philosophy all this gets explained somehow and set into firm classifications, usually hierarchies of stages or states each superior to its predecessor, until the absolute is reached. For example, in yoga (Patanjali's Yoga), the mind climbs through stage after stage. Along the way, one is said to acquire powers, belief in which has been widespread in India. These powers include the ability to remember previous lives, to know other persons' minds, to know outer space and the extraordinary worlds in it, to enter other persons' bodies, to become as small as an atom, to touch the moon, to dive into the earth, to make the elements appear and disappear, and to make all things do as one wishes.[96] No wonder the yogi, though advised, for his own good, not to make use of these powers, might be tempted!

According to yoga—the parallel to which we have met in Buddhist meditation—the mind climbs the hierarchy of states up to the conscious 'trance' (of absorption, *samprajnata samadhi*), after which it reaches the highest stage, the supraconscious 'trance' (of absorption, *asamprajnata samadhi*). Some Hindu theologian-philosophers divide conscious 'trance' into two, some into six, and some into eight ascending types; and some divide even the highest type into two.[97]

All these descriptions, reactions, explanations, and classifications must have made a natural impression in their exact social context, by which I mean their exact human and religious neighborhood. In the context of Western thought now, they make a curious and, I should say, unnatural impression. This is in part the result of the unfamiliarity of the thought, but also of its prescientific nature. It is true that the Westerners and others who share scientific attitudes are often superstitious as well as scientific, are often religious, and are often superstitious, scientific, and religious at once, a state that betrays a normally human incoherence. Furthermore, some of those who share scientific attitudes have had an abiding interest in the extrasensory or have believed in the insight-giving powers of drugs. And those with scientific attitudes are just as apt as the others to undergo truly or apparently revelatory experiences. But the superstition, religiosity, and revelatory experience have not prevented the development of a skepticism new in the theoretical and practical rigor with which it separates the well-founded empirically from the ill-founded. This skepticism, born of the ruthlessness of science, accepts only evidence of a kind that would satisfy a rigorous historian or scientist dealing, it must be added, with his own special field.

One more general reaction: The experiences I have reported are claimed to be inexpressible, but this claim is not congruous with the language in which it is put. Oddly, instead of being confined to statements of helplessness, the mystics are inspired to use vivid similes and metaphors, and the poets among them, some of whom are great, now and then reach the heights of expressiveness of which words are capable. These mystics do not show the pessimism of someone who realizes that the words needed do not exist or, like the words in Zasetsky's shattered mind, do not connect with their meaning. These mystics are, in fact, exuberantly verbal and optimistic enough about words to believe that the eloquence of their complaints against them conveys how badly the words fall short of the quality and, above all, the intensity of the experience they report—the intensity of the complaints conveys the intensity's loss. However, the complaint leads to a misunderstanding because, as has been said earlier, anything not known to speaker and hearer can be very difficult to convey; and I do not feel that the gap between words and experience, which is, in description, always indefinitely great, is greater in the presumed experience of the absolute than in the experience of anything else unshared. The words in which I describe a fluid, multiform dream freeze its fluidity, like a stroboscopic photograph of anything moving, and make the multiform immutably single. The persuasive description given by a great writer is a verbal invention, a literary confabulation, because memory cannot hold or words transmit just what happens at any place and time except the here and now of the writing at the moment it occurs, the inventive present. That there is a problem of ineffability, I concede; but I cannot see that it is in principle different from the ineffability that accompanies the experiences of ordinary life.

As for the theologians' formal hierarchies and definitions of successive types of experience, if transposed into contemporary research, they might give rise to the regretful, "We have succeeded in making a beautifully detailed classification of what we do not really understand." But it can be argued, for both the theological past and the scientific present, that if the hierarchies and definitions and their practical uses are really as described, they constitute just what we usually mean by understanding, at least in a post-Humean, scientific age, when we aim less often at essences than at correlations. A great deal of science, from chemistry, geology, biology, and medicine to the social sciences, is made up of systematic classification based on good, though never perfect, empirical evidence and related in a roughly but incompletely circular way to theoretical principles. So even if the hierarchical classifications and the techniques taught by the Indian theologians are not convincing philosophically, they may prove to be important to the psychology of exceptional states of mind and, with luck, to psychotherapy.

Although Tempting, the Philosophers' Ineffable Source Is Questionable

In saying this, I have neglected the philosophers' argument that the source of all experience, the top of the metaphysical hierarchy, *must* be beyond the possibility of expression. I comment on their argument by way of two leading questions, the first on the imperfect understanding supposed to result from the subject-object split in human consciousness, and the second on the proof for the existence of the ineffable, creative unity.

First, then, I ask: Why is it assumed by the hierarchy builders (as by mystics in general) that the split between the subject and object of consciousness is a metaphysical flaw that makes true knowledge impossible? After all, knowledge in the sense we normally use requires a self-conscious knower who depends—to simplify greatly—on organs of perception, a nervous system, and experience. These comprise the necessary conditions for knowing, and any full account of perceptual and other knowledge takes account of them. Was there anything apart from abstract reasoning that could have persuaded the hierarchy builders that knowledge, in any sense, could forego the conditions that appear necessary for it? Maybe, in company with the less intellectual mystics, they remembered the states of empathy that make mutual understanding more accurate, or the states of exaltation in which the self is merged in its surroundings, or the states of apparent egolessness of anyone sunk in activity or in the reaction of many individuals sharing the same experience.

All these states, which are essential to everyone, can play an overwhelming role in the lives of persons especially sensitive to them. Our psychological boundaries fluctuate, sometimes diminishing or enlarging us, isolating or conjoining. This is metaphorical language for changes we all undergo in what we can think of as our emotional inclusiveness and emotional shape. As I say this, I feel dissatisfaction with the word *emotional* but find no better one. It is true that emotion or mood has a unity that may suggest superlative consciousness. Emotional states need no distinct, separable objects of thought: we often feel happy or unhappy without any cause we are aware of—though we are mostly aware that it is *we* who are in the state. But this absence of distinction gives no good reason to regard an emotional state as a superlative one. On the contrary, from an evolutionary standpoint, emotions and moods are primitive.

My agreement with the hierarchy builders on changes in emotional and intellectual inclusiveness does not mean that I agree on the possibility of abolishing the subject-object distinction. The builders extrapolate from variations in the sense of separateness to an impossible extreme of closeness. To do this for the superlative One, they have to abolish the body, the three-dimensionality of which sets a limit to how close we can come physically to anyone or anything. In abolishing the body, they abolish the distance between eye and object that makes vision possible, so they have to hypothesize a superlative vision without eyes or distance; but all we know by means of (non-metaphorical) vision is related to eyes and impossible without them. Do the hierarchy builders mean something like the associative, half-abstract understanding of vision developed by the blind? Or the diagrams and equations of geometrical optics as they are found in the consciousness of the physicist? The Bhartriharians and Neoplatonists answer these questions, but not, for most of us, very plausibly. As students of philosophy will recognize, the questions are characteristic of the attempt, so pronounced in medieval thought, to understand God. I will not continue with the questions, except to say that there is no difficulty in understanding the reasons for the hierarchy builders' extrapolation from experience; but they extrapolate so far that they abolish the very possibility of the knowledge whose superlative they revere. Or, because the nonexistence of something not merely abstract cannot be proved, they make the distance between superlative and merely human knowledge so great that the connection is lost and the superlative becomes incomprehensible—as, in fact, they like to emphasize.

The idea that the subject-object distinction can be abolished is associated with that of the identity of knower and known. As I have said, the synthesis of our perceptual knowledge in the brain is not well understood; but if we represent the subject-object identity by means of Aristotle's theory, the identity depends on his clearly obsolete understanding of perception. In modern terms, what we take in and interpret perceptually is structural information. The identity or, better, resemblance in question is one of information, not essence or substance.

My second, crucial question, is the following: Is it possible to prove or disprove the existence of the ineffable unity, source of everything? The answer is *no*, it cannot be either proved or disproved. In explaining this answer, I want to rule out intuition or mystical experience for the while and take into account only philosophical arguments. We know how important mystical experience is to the conviction that the ineffable unity really exists. But this evidence is not transferrable to anyone else, and because of its importance and special nature, I leave its consideration to the last chapter. Here, I go on to the possible objective proofs.

It was the Neoplatonists, above all, who thought they had proved the existence of the ineffable source by logic alone. In a way, their failure is a pity, because if all phenomena were perfect expressions of any logic we understood, we could deduce (as Leibniz hoped) all beings, relationships, and fates. The existence of anything at all would be proved by its deduction, and its nonexistence by the logical contradiction that would arise from the assumption that it existed.

I have already observed that the Neoplatonic argument, although worked out with a sense of logical rigor akin to that of Euclidean geometry, is not really compelling. Despite the philosophers and mathematicians who regard mathematics, and perhaps all valid abstractions, as having a kind of existence, there is a void between existence in the sense of an abstraction and existence in the physical or metaphysical sense. Cantor, it will be remembered, had to give up the conception of the set of all sets; but this renunciation of an idea impossible in mathematics because of its self-contradiction did not prevent him from accepting the more-than-logical reality of the Neoplatonists. The gap between logic or mathematics, on the one side, and physical reality, on the other, is demonstrated by the nature of the mathematical models constructed for physics, astronomy, and other fields of science. All these models have possible alternatives, the choice between which is often dictated by the simplicity of their use, and they are discarded and replaced at the scientific convenience of their inventors. No such model can be known in advance to fit the relevant phenomena perfectly, and so I see no great risk in saying that the models always fail at some point because the phenomena are less regular and more complex than they are.

For this reason, the discussion will center on proof of existence or nonexistence by means of the union of theoretical reason and empirical evidence. To begin with evidence of the simplest kind: To prove the existence or nonexistence of anything visible, one need only look for it; but if there are enough hiding places, or if the space or time to be searched is extensive enough, the failure to find what one is looking for proves nothing either positive or negative. Biologists keep looking for missing evolutionary links, historians for the data they need, and astronomers for evidence of civilization on other planets; the failure to find what they are looking for never proves that it does not exist. For the sake of the more complicated kinds of argument, I give three examples: the platypus, the electron, and the singularity.

The platypus belongs among the examples because it suffered the ignominy of having its existence denied. When English biologists first saw its dried skin, sent from Australia in 1798, it was so opposed to the established biological classification that it was assumed to be a fake stitched together from a duck's beak and the body parts of a mammal. The platypus seems anomalous because it lays eggs and has a ducklike beak, a bird- and reptile-like reproductive tract, a rather reptilian skeleton, and fur. When live platypuses arrived in England, they had to be acknowledged as genuine, but they continued to be a reproach to the logic of classification and were not accepted as mammals until found to have mammary glands, the defining organs for the biological class.[98]

In the case of the platypus, a moderately sized furry animal over-bore the systematized wisdom of biological experience and was proved to exist or, in view of the earlier doubts, not not to exist. The well-known case of the electron gives an altogether more subtle example of the difficulty in establishing existence. A bird-reptile-mammal contradicted experience, but a particle-wave contradicted logic as well. We see this in the intellectual struggles of such physicists as Niels Bohr and Werner Heisenberg. At first, Bohr pictured the atom in the form of a miniature planetary system, a microcosm to match the macrocosm of astronomy.[99] But while valid experimental procedures showed that electrons were, as Bohr supposed, tiny particles, other, equally valid procedures showed them to be continuously expanding waves; and each conception, that of particles and that of waves, was represented in a satisfactory theory. Habit has dulled our appreciation of how strange it at first seemed that indivisible particles shot through a screen with two slits arranged themselves on the other side in the pattern of waves. As Heisenberg recalled, when he and Bohr struggled with such paradoxes—how can one electron pass through two slits at once?—they felt despair.[100]

Heisenberg came to the conclusion that the submicroscopic world was not like anything visible. To represent it he abandoned what had been known of physical reality in favor of the unimaginable, strictly abstract grasp given by mathematical formalism.[101] For him, pictures or words were no longer adequate. The wave-particle duality was absorbed into quantum mechanics, which formulated the intrinsic uncertainty of nature in the small.

Bohr responded otherwise, with his principle of complementarity, which renounces a unified view of reality in favor of different but complementary views. Instead of an impossible reconciliation between a particle-image and a wave-image, or between classical, deterministic causality and the new indeterminacy, he accepted the different possibilities like messages in different languages, on the grounds that the wholeness of nature could not be expressed in consistent language all at once.

To understand Bohr, it is helpful to know that he was interested in William James, from whom he may have got the term *complementary*. James had used it to name the condition in which one's conscious and subconscious minds act at cross-purposes—he was thinking of hysteria; we might think of amnesia or split-brain experiments. In this condition, said James, a person's total consciousness is split and complementary, each consciousness sharing the objects of knowledge with the other but remaining ignorant of what the other knows.[102] James also dwelt on the paradoxical difficulty, which fascinated Bohr, too, of self-observation: When one tries to catch oneself in the middle of a thought and, by the act of catching it, terminates the thought, "like . . . trying to turn up the light quickly enough to see how the darkness looks."[103] To Bohr, such a difficulty was a reminder of how futile it is in forming ideas to try to separate subject from object—as futile as trying in physics to separate the observer from the observed and from the context of observation; or, to put it more narrowly, to separate the behavior of atomic objects from their interaction with the instruments that define the condition under which the atomic phenomena appear. The way one measures influences the results of the measurement.[104]

Bohr evidently preferred to emphasize rather than dilute the conflict of conceptions. He liked to repeat that the difference between trivial and profound truths is that the opposites of the trivial ones are clearly absurd but those of the profound ones are themselves profound truths.[105] It was no mere accident of biography that Bohr was interested in Kierkegaard, to whom paradox is a collision arising from the attempt to understand the ultimately inexpressible, unintelligible truth. Like Kierkegaard, he believed in the subjective quality of the search for insight.[106] For both, the discovery of truth depends on the readiness to use

paradox, and on the acknowledgment that we cannot really smooth away
the gaps in understanding that the paradox displays.

The closest, most spectacular analogue to the hierarchy builder's
source of everything is the singularity, which we have met as the
cosmologist's source of the whole universe. The question at issue is if
theory and observation are enough to prove the existence of this singularity. The short answer is no, not in the unqualified sense to which I am
referring.

To explain: The existence of this singularity is extrapolated from
the theorems of general relativity, which specify that wherever the concentration of matter is great enough, space-time becomes infinitely curved
and there is an end to each geodesic line—the shortest line between two
points on the curved surface, the path followed by a particle under the
influence of gravity. A particle on a geodesic that comes to the end of the
path, comes to the end of its space and time and (by the theory) stops
existing. The collection of all the ends of all the paths is the edge of
space-time, where existence ends for all particles.[107]

Strictly speaking, if one is cautious and prefers to think in terms of
the comprehensible universe, one speaks only of density and curvature
that *tend* to infinity, of particles that tend to come to the ends of geode-
sics, and of the universe tending to zero. But this caution is a matter of
philosophical taste, and for the present discussion, the bolder way of
speaking is more interesting. Boldly, at the singularity itself, if the word
itself may be used of it, nothing is predictable, anything (if anything can
be spoken of) can happen, because all the laws of nature, which have
space and time as their essential background or content, become meaningless. The singularity is at no place and no time. It is pointless to ask
when it occurred—though we know when cosmic evolution was already
in progress—or how long it lasted, because we know of no process
within it by which it could theoretically be timed. So the singularity is a
hypothesized terminal nothing, surely nothing we can experience, probe,
or know, although we know what leads to it and why it is needed, and
we give it a name, as Buddhists say nirvana is nothing or empty but not
exactly nothing, and as they give it a name and know something even in
words about knowing about it. The cosmologist can answer that such
remarks are extravagant because he is using a conceptual model—with
its limiting rules and its schematic endpoints to timelike and spacelike
lines—that has no claim to unqualified truth.[108] He is right; but, all the
same, cosmologists talk as if their models are close to physical reality.
And, to balance the cosmologist's protest, theologians and philosophers

repeat that all they say about absolutes is too conceptually biased and verbally imperfect to give more than a hint of the truth.

Can the singularity be improved into something less incomprehensible? Would it help if relativity theory, which rules our conception of the space-time universe, were successfully united with quantum theory, which rules our conception of particles? The union is especially tempting for the sake of the singularity, which, being dimensionless, cannot be interpreted by the laws of relativity, but is right in size, or sizelessness, for quantum mechanics. But to merge with relativity, quantum theory must arrive at what it still lacks, a complete, manageable explanation of gravity. Nevertheless, it is clear that to treat the singularity like a quantum would remove the incomprehensibility (the lawlessness) that characterizes it in relativity theory. Instead of being an arbitrary given, it would appear, like other quanta, out of the 'nothing' I have mentioned earlier. And because quanta have an indefinite size and location (a 'fuzziness' related to the uncertainty principle), it should be possible to get rid of the notion of the boundary of the universe, and with it, the dimensionlessness and infinite density of the beginning. Quantum theory seems to make possible a universal beginning of a nature systematized and verified for quanta and allowing theoretical calculations about the whole universe as accurate as those for quanta.[109] But such an application of the theory would also extend to the universe at large the philosophical challenges and discomforts of quantum theory, which I excuse myself from discussing here.

Hopes for progress abound, and so do unresolved problems. The physicist Chris Isham, who specializes in quantum gravity, says:

> It must be admitted that, at both the epistemological and ontological levels, our current understanding of space and time leaves much to be desired . . . Should we follow one ancient Greek line of thought and view space and time as an *a priori* container of 'things'? Or should we reverse the ontological order and, following Leibniz, regard 'things' as the primary concept, and relegate space and time to a secondary role of expressing relations between these 'things'? Twentieth century physics has oscillated (at times uncomfortably) between these positions and under the impact of quantum gravity studies, these oscillations threaten to become unstable![110]

To the problem under discussion, of the proof for the existence of the singularity, my answer must obviously be that even observation combined with theory are not enough to establish its existence in fact. I do not mean to imply the unrestrained doubt of the skeptic who would extend this verdict to everything else in science. *To prove* is taken in a moderate sense—I have no doubts about the existence of the platypus.

But the singularity goes immoderately beyond ordinary time-and-space-bound science. The theory of general relativity, from which the the singularity is deduced, is a great human achievement; but it would be a theory without precedent if it were true without limit.

This brings us back to the Bhartriharian and Neoplatonic origin, the reason for the examples given above. The cosmology discussed, like the modern theory of biological evolution, is based on the often revised pursuit of the truth by the intertwining of the empirical and logical, which achieves an existential force denied to Bhartrihari's and Plotinus's thought. Great as were their merits, the two were unable to lend their beliefs more than the force of a subjectively chosen concatenation of abstractions. They were encouraged, I suppose, by the model of a single consciousness ruling over a complex body and its purposeful activities, and by the assumption that consciousness is immaterial and immortal. Possibly their theories of evolution were influenced by the model of the seed from which a whole plant grows, or the act of impregnation that results in a living being—Bhartrihari marvels at the varicolored beauty of the peacock that comes out of a drab egg. But in these instances, we now know, the impression of initial simplicity is misleading; the genetic material by which heredity is transmitted is itself complex.

The Neoplatonists, especially Proclus, were led astray by the logic, worked out for geometry, of definitions, postulates, axioms, and propositions. Proclus, who wrote a commentary on the first book of Euclid's *Elements,* understood the Euclidean method metaphysically. To him, mathematics, "though beginning with reminders from the outside world, ends with the ideas that it has within; it is awakened to activity by lower realities, but its destination is the higher being of forms."[111] Given this view, it was all too easy for him to believe that the structure of reality could be revealed, without qualification or resort to empirical evidence, by sheer reasoning.

Having criticized the hierarchy builders, I add that each of the structures they built has its eloquence, its intricate cognitive rhythms, its hints of intimacy and glory, and its traditional associations, which together lend them depth of a sort lacking in the conceptual models of the cosmologists.

Whatever accounts for the Bhartriharian and Neoplatonic hierarchies, the point here is that there is no convincing evidence for their existence in fact. They prove to be built on unnecessary assumptions and to proceed by means of insufficient arguments to implausible conclusions, which might, just possibly, be true.

Chapter 5

In Judgment
of Ineffability

This is judgment chapter, so I begin it with a judgment: There is no compelling nonpersonal reason for believing that a superlative first cause can be grasped, weakly or strongly, by direct experience. The word *nonpersonal* is a severe qualification: it is meant to acknowledge that everyone has ineradicable private convictions respect for which is equivalent to respect for the person who holds them. But even with this qualification, my judgment would not please many of the thinkers to whom I have been referring. Remember, all of the exalters and many of the devaluers of words have believed in a superlative first cause that can at least be approached. Nagarjuna, Nagarjunians, and Zen Buddhists tend to deny this, but only in ambiguously affirming it as well. A militantly secular philosopher such as Nietzsche substitutes the superlative experience of human creation for that of closeness to the superlative first cause. All of this yearning, sacred and secular, raises the whole problem of the yearning for superlatives, which the philosophers' ideal of rationality has never eliminated from their discipline. Is an enormous ideal in the sky worth more than a small one in the hand?

The problem can be put in this way: A superlative first cause has been very widely accepted in philosophy and religion; but to the extent that this acceptance comes at the end of an abstract line of reasoning, it remains arguable. To me it seems that it is easier to deny than affirm it philosophically; but even if I am exaggerating, the history of philosophy demonstrates, as I have said, that the proofs for the existence of such a cause are not philosophically coercive. As for the ecstatic (or 'enstatic') or superlative experience that so many persons have reported, there is no impersonal (logical or factual) reason to accept it as decisive evidence for the existence or 'non existence' of whatever superlative has been presumed to be its cause or 'cause'. A psychological or medical explanation, even if incomplete or doubtful, may be more plausible, sometimes

179

even to the person who has undergone the experience. Of course, one may become the disciple of someone whose superlative experiences one accepts on faith, but faith is not an impersonal argument.

If there never has been any logical or factual evidence that could compel a well-disposed but reasonably skeptical person to accept some experience as that of a true superlative cause, why has there been so prevalent a belief in the cause and the experience supposed to reveal its existence? The belief had philosophically powerful opponents in ancient India, China, and Greece, not to speak of later Europe; but they were unable to dissuade the many others, often persons of penetrating intellect or great creative power, who found it more than plausible.

Let me to try to explain by mingling empirical, psychological reasons with other, philosophical ones. I begin with a psychoanalytic explanation that is doubly reductive—it reduces the many possible reasons to one reason, which, even if correct, further reduces all mystical experience to its lowest, most primitive common denominator. This is like explaining a gourmet meal by its nutritive value alone, or a sport as no more than a kind of exercise. I therefore want to take a moment to justify the use of reductive explanations.

The justification has two parts. The first is that all simply rational use of language is reductive, particularly if it takes the form of a rational explanation. The second is that the most highly reductive explanations may be the most useful. The first part of the justification can be brief: This book has shown in many ways how language falls short of representing our experience exactly. A description depends on what is easy to notice, remember, and put into words; and ease in putting it into words depends on what is being described, on one's verbal ability in relation to it, and on one's partner in conversation; and the words reduce the uniqueness of the experience to the level of generality that makes it possible to communicate by their means. But although they are reductive, descriptions are less so than explanations, the point of which is to distinguish what is important from what is not, a distinction made for a special purpose or in the light of the special interest of the explainer. For an explanation to explain, to make things intelligible, it has to put its object into the framework of common experience and subject it to logic by which it is reduced to something as much like others of its kind as possible, which is to say that it is reduced by having its uniqueness explained away. This is Nietzsche's complaint against science.

Now for the possible superiority of reductive over nonreductive explanations: The nonreductive make it their object to take into account the higher, more complex, more individual characteristics of whatever is to be explained. How is this done? One usual precaution is to refuse to interpret anything on a higher cultural level by means of a discipline dealing with a culturally lower one. On the scale beginning with physics and going up, successively, to biology, the human sciences (psychology, anthropology, sociology), philosophy, and religion, it is clear that the last two—which dispute their relative levels—are the highest in the sense that they come later in evolutionary development than the others, which form their basis, and are the most distinctively human. It follows that to be nonreductive, the explanation of a philosophical or religious phenomenon has to be philosophical or religious. Whether it is reductive to use philosophy to explain religion or religion philosophy is a matter for dispute between partisans of either side.

Another way to avoid reductiveness is to describe the object of explanation in all its significant details and reject explanations too general to account for the details. A natural way do this is to make use of several disciplines for the same purpose, all of them (perhaps geography, archeology, history, paleography, linguistics) chosen for their relevance to the object and their ability, when joined, to explain all its significant details.

Unfortunately, nonreductive explanations have their dangers. They begin on the assumption that the fuller they are, the closer in spirit and significant detail, the better; but they show in practice that the striving for fullness tends to reduce their intellectual usefulness. An explanation close in spirit and significant detail to what it explains limits itself to a narrow context and is useful only in immediate relation to it. And an explanation that accepts a great deal of, for instance, a religious faith without putting its principles into question (without making it possible to explain them away) can be satisfactory only to those who share the faith.

Other attempts to avoid reductiveness run into other difficulties. To give a philosophical or religious explanation of, respectively, a philosophical or religious problem keeps things on the same intellectual level but, being one-dimensional, is shallow, renouncing possibilities in the same way as the explanation of a quarrel in terms used by the quarrelers themselves misses causes (historical, social, psychological) that the quarrelers are unaware of or do not care to reveal. Explanations shallow in this way tend to turn the explainer into a participant and make it impossible to explain the activity as such by going outside it, or to reach the basis avoided as irrelevant because it is on a different disciplinary plane. You may quarrel with someone because (you say) he is mean, because (the psychologist says) he reminds you of someone you hate, because (the doctor says) you are in a feverish, irritable state, because (the philosopher says) both of you use words loosely, or because (the anthropologist says) there is a mismatching of symbolic systems. Such possibilities may well be testable, and though testing them in a convincing way is difficult, if you stop quarreling when the fever passes and resume it only when you again become feverish, the doctor is probably right. To limit the possibilities to the level of the quarrel alone (I said, he said, everybody would be insulted by, he doesn't care that, he shouted) would be to put a severe limit on the possibility of reaching a useful explanation. To make clear the usefulness of reduction, I should add that explanation on a different level (psychological, medical, anthropological) may not explain why you had this particular quarrel but explain very well what in general makes you quarrel, or quarrel about this particular subject or with this particular person. Such an explanation is both reductive and useful.

Another often unhelpful attempt to avoid reduction takes the opposite course. Instead of confining the explanation to the level of its object, it draws on several disciplines in order to approach the empirical reality more closely. But if such an explanation is given by an individual, it is rarely well-informed—have I myself avoided this weakness?—and if given by a team of experts, loses coherence. A good biography of a scientist, artist, writer, or philosopher, its scope limited by the experience of its protagonist, has a thicker, more lifelike texture than comparable histories. But when the subject to be explained is itself as complex as a culture or religion, or as a social or personal phenomenon that recurs at different times and places—mysticism is an example—a highly reductive explanation may be more useful because complicated explanations are less sharply clear, harder to devise tests for, and harder to qualify in the light of reason or experience. How can you cut cleanly with a knife that has many differently shaped blades set close together in the same handle? Imagine how hard it is to begin to understand a religion by trying to assimilate everything about it—its history, social and economic causes, religious environment, leaders, scriptures, ritual, theology, philosophy, and so on. The result can be a mass of data without form or intellectual use, or a feeling that so much has been explained that nothing is clear, because the need for explanation is best satisfied by reasons as simple as reasonably possible, by something essential, even if not sufficient, that we can play with intellectually as one element of thought among others.

Even an explanation restricted to one person and to, say, psychology can confuse if it lacks a simplifying emphasis. Let me give Nietzsche as an instance. When young, he wanted and was expected to follow the family tradition and become a pastor. He therefore took up the study of theology; but at the age of twenty-one, he announced to his tearful mother that he was giving it up and would no longer even attend church services. The most obvious reason for the weakening of his faith was his intellectual development, which was pushing him in the direction of the skepticism that characterized him later as a philosopher—an already nascent doubt had led him to study the sources of the New Testament. Having grown more objective, he understood that he believed in Jesus, as, in other circumstances, he would have believed in Muhammed, because he had been born to the Christian faith. David Strauss's *Life of Jesus Critically Examined* persuaded him that belief in Jesus might have to be given up, and he reacted by saying that to lose Jesus would be to lose God. Soon afterwards, his reading led him to Democritus, the English philosophers, Kant, and Darwin. Most fateful of all, he happened on a secondhand copy of Schopenhauer, in whom, he wrote, "I saw a mirror in which I beheld world, life, and my own nature in terrible grandeur. Here I saw the completely indifferent sun's eye of art, here I saw sickness and health, exile and refuge, hell and heaven."[1]

Such reasons can be taken to be philosophical and, as such, objective; but their appearance in a biographical context makes them less reductive because the otherwise objective reasons are colored by the accidental or subjective ones that made them more acceptable to Nietzsche at the time. The subjective reasons (the conscious and unconscious motives) included his readiness to assert his independence by opposing his mother's will. Another strong subjective influence was his heritage of abandonment and pain—the abandonment caused by the early death of his father, which he never stopped mourning, and the pain by his long, blinding headaches, which made him fear that he had inherited his father's brain disease. It was, above all, this fear, so I suspect, that led Nietzsche to identify Christianity—to him, his father was Christianity—with weakness and death. His father's piano improvisations, which he remembered with love, were echoed in his own eloquent improvisations and his love of music. Schopenhauer was a revelation to him because he fitted his psychological needs so well: the conviction that life was essentially suffering, that Christianity was only an allegory (a much lesser one than Buddhism), and that music had the power to reveal and save.

How is it possible to weigh and coordinate all these different factors: family tradition of piety, a father's early death, fear of inherited disease, inherited love of music, university studies, sharp intellect, and influence of friends, of Strauss, and of Schopenhauer—positive and negative emotion, personal influences, intellectual development, and musical, philological, and philosophical ambitions—all in the crucible of the mind that we divide simplistically into conscious and unconscious? I can answer only that if one is interested in understanding Nietzsche's thought in the revealing, nonreductive context of his life, one has to consider each factor in and by itself, and then do one's most clear-minded best,

which is, at once, subjective and objective, by which I mean that the
subjectivity, which is inevitable, merges with the objective information
that both stimulates and limits it. This implies not only the careful study
of Nietzsche's philosophy in his life and times, but also some knowledge
of the relevant psychology and, perhaps, medicine.

I return to psychoanalysis and its highly reductive explanation of
mystical experience. As a philosophical and religious phenomenon, mysticism is enormously complicated. Yet running through all this complication, there are similar intellectual defenses, and within the complication
there is a similar experiential core; defenses and core together justify us
in applying the same name, even if inexactly, to so many varying forms.
The intellectual defenses, which I have leveled down somewhat
reductively, have already been repeated here. Now, for the sake of clarity, I want to venture a simple hypothesis to account for the emotional
core. Because it is so simple, the hypothesis is easy to understand, easy
(in theory, not practice) to test, and easy to reject or modify. As will be
seen, I accept it; but having expounded it favorably, I would like to
qualify it—sometimes, maybe, to the point of near-abandonment—as the
empirical evidence suggests. But my fuller, less reductive explanation, in
which I try to bring out whatever the reductive one conceals, is difficult
to summarize because my judgment is not merely factual and philosophical but also emotional and aesthetic, and emotions and aesthetic perceptions summarize poorly. Still, put in brief, my position is as follows:

1. Ineffability has many possible sources and is of many kinds.
   Experiences are never shared exactly alike and often not
   shared at all, the result being that ineffability, weak and
   strong, is very common. When shared, experiences called
   ineffable are not fully so because words are enough to
   convey at least some of their nature.

2. Ineffability is relative to one's knowledge, specialized vocabulary, and linguistic ability. What strikes one person
   dumb, calls up the other's eloquence; what to one person
   is an inexpressible wilderness is to the other an easily described homeland.

3. An unquestionable, unanalyzable, or ineffable superlative
   may be needed to complete a postulated hierarchy of any
   kind, whether in science, politics, art, religion, or philosophy. When the principle of intelligibility is itself unintelligible, intelligibility becomes impenetrably numinous, the
   invisible god of vision, as bereft of purpose as Lao Tzu and
   Spinoza made out nature to be.

4. The term *ineffable* is used to protect certain cherished experiences from being explained or, rather, explained away. So used, the term is a declaration that one judges other things in the light of these cherished experiences, and not the opposite. The ineffable is then the experiential criterion that one refuses to judge in terms that one feels are alien to it and contradict its finality.

5. Despite this attitude, much of the preference of religious and philosophical thinkers for the ineffable can be given an ordinary psychological explanation, which is that it depends on experience of the sort that Freud called *oceanic*. This experience is extremely hard to put into words because it is at its most powerful when we are still in a prelinguistic state. Although it is universal, its nature and effects take forms that accord with the differences in the intimate life of different societies.

6. By joining sense with sound and evoking the quality of music, poets go beyond limits that ordinary speech imposes. Nonsense poetry crosses the gap between speech and music by reducing the cognitive intelligibility of speech and increasing its intelligibility as music.

7. Superlative, ineffable experience is the goal yearned for most by those with an especial hunger for completeness—the total, mystical connectedness expressed in philosophy and theology, in acts of charity or devotion, and in the arts. Wallace Stevens, Valéry, Whitman, Wagner, and Mahler are given as examples of poets and musicians with such a goal.

8. Superlatives aside, the unresolved and unresolvable debate between the exalters and devaluers of language may reflect their respectively satisfying or unsatisfying communication with others in early childhood. The effect of this communication may also account for the different values assigned by different persons to verbal as compared with nonverbal communication.

9. On a sympathetic view, religious beliefs, including those related to mystical experience, are psychologically deep, aesthetically complex, life-preserving fictions; but the sympathy expressed in such a view may erode the desire to know the truth as free of fiction as possible.

10. The ideal of the ineffable self-conscious unity is a reflection of one's conscious relation to oneself, to the unique intimacy in plurality in which one thinks of and experiences oneself.

11. No one discipline or group of disciplines, and no one artistic, scientific, religious, or philosophical position can be adequate to all of human experience or trusted to judge it in a final sense.

12. Everything conceivable can at least be hinted at in words; but the inevitable residue of what we want to and cannot accomplish with them is the degree of ineffability that we can never escape, and perhaps do not want to escape. The experience itself of ineffability, not to speak of the argument over it, is one of the many gifts of speech. A little ineffability is not at all a bad thing to have. But when it gets to be a lot, the ineffability is of another, deeper, probably darker color.

There Are Distinctly Different Explanations and Assessments of the Nature of Ineffability

I have asked why those who are convinced of the particular ineffability of superlative experience continue to use so many words to speak of what they say they are unable to speak. One contemporary answer is that the claim of ineffability is not what, on its face, it appears to be. First, it is contended, nothing can be either expressible or inexpressible except in relation to a particular language or, more broadly, symbol system. Apart from synesthesia or its surviving latent approximations, one cannot represent sound by color or color by sound. But what could it mean, it is asked, to be ineffable in any and all languages, especially when the claim is made by someone who speaks only one or a few languages.[2]

This view of ineffability holds true, it seems to me, to the extent that different vocabularies, languages, or symbol systems are particularly adapted to some area of experience, which they express more easily and exactly. It is for this reason that specialists in a given field perceive its subject matter—in aspects important to them—better than nonspecialists do, and are able to speak of it in greater analytical detail. In much the same way, the aboriginal San of South Africa were better than Westerners in reading the tracks and explaining the behavior of the animals they had learned to observe closely. In certain philosophies, as great an effort is made to develop a vocabulary for what, according to them, is impossible to catch conceptually as for what is easy to catch.

If it is granted that ineffability is relative to what a certain kind of person is able to see or misses, then maybe those who use the term *ineffable* mean it to signify that, granted their view of the limits of experience, this is how the ineffable should be defined. To give an example, we need only recall that Lao Tzu begins by saying that the way, the tao , that can be spoken of is not the constant way, and the name that can be named is not the constant name. This statement is perhaps no more than a rule prescribing that anything that can be spoken of or named is not that which is being referred to. When you refer to the constant way or constant name, the rule says, in order to be faithful to the way you *should* view experience, it is legitimate to refer to it in only the barest way, as if no more than pointing it out or discriminating it from lesser ways or names. For the constant way or name, you are not allowed to use any descriptive words, so that the tao in question is kept bare, undescribed, opaque, mysterious—kept so by direct fiat. The words used concerning this tao are needed to establish the rules that prescribe infallibility.[3] Perhaps in a sense like that used by Schopenhauer and the early Wittgenstein, the term tao—like Kant's term *noumenon*—marks the boundaries of one's language and therefore of one's speakable world. The use of such a bounding term may then express the sense of awe at what one feels lies outside the speakable world, or express the incredibility of the fact—felt by Leibniz, Heidegger, and Wittgenstein—that the world exists at all.

To continue this line of thought, it may be added that the paradoxicality said to make superlative experience impossible to put into words is not the paradoxical nature of the experience itself. Experiences may be most unusual, but, strictly speaking, only logic is paradoxical, so that when Proclus or Nagarjuna construes logic in a way designed to express his view of the universe, the effect is to teach neophytes what to take as mysterious and what to identify as ineffable.[4] In summary:

> The mystic's identification of his experience requires a commitment to a certain kind of explanation or, what comes to the same thing, the exclusion of a particular kind of explanation. He must identify his experience under a certain description, and that description must preclude naturalistic explanation. The assumption that the experience cannot be exhaustively accounted for in naturalistic terms is included in the criteria for identifying an experience as mystical. Not surprisingly, then, it turns out that mystical experiences elude natural explanation.[5]

According to this line of thought, anyone—poet, philosopher, or theologian—who labels an experience *ineffable* means that its value is uniquely high and fears that if concepts are applied it, it will be denatured and seem other than it really is. We know that a description or analysis of the experience can miss it. In the fear of missing the essential, shared by practitioners of all the arts, there persists the opinion that words, being external to experience, mislead everyone except the individual who knows the experience directly and needs no explanation.

So, often, "the more highly we prize some experience, the more we shun applying concepts to it."[6] Therefore the language we do use in relation to the valued experience is poetic and paradoxical, meant less to explain than to point, less to solicit logical analysis than to indicate the undesirability of logic. By the usual Buddhist view, we can use the proper words and logic in careful, graduated conjunction with meditative experience, to get beyond logic and words—because words are to be used not only for their conceptual content, but for their ability, like shouts, blows, insults, and humor, to break the smooth surface of illusion by disabusing, shocking, and prodding. The Zen Buddhists take this shocking and prodding function of language to its extreme. The blatant illogic of Zen koans is a warning to check our logic at the door because here, at the paradox-revealed limits of the conceptual world, logic kills the experience we should be searching for with stubborn persistence.[7]

Finally, when we call highly valued experiences *ineffable*, we mean to praise them, just as we use the word *beautiful* to praise things that please us most by their appearance.[8] *Ineffable* is often the most effective superlative we can use. Using it can also express our frustration at the failure to describe what we should most like, by describing it, to share. It is this feeling of frustration that appears to have stimulated the most eloquent mystics to express themselves as well as they in fact have done.[9]

When I come to judge the assessments of ineffability I have just reviewed, I hesitate. Not so much because I disagree with them—they fit in easily with my own bias—but because they appear to me inadequate. They are inadequate at least in the sense that many of the language-exalters and language-denigrators we have come to know would reject them as missing the main point. Yes, the Zen Buddhists would acknowledge that they used words like blunt instruments, to beat logic on the head, just as they used literal sticks to beat attentiveness and possibly illumination into neophytes. And yes, Lao Tzu, if he ever existed and if he stooped to use our logic, might agree that he was stipulating that tao in the superlative sense was unnameable and indescribable—but not *merely* stipulating, because he believed in the real and not merely stipulative existence of the great tao . And Chuang Tzu, who debated his views with his logician-friend, meant precisely to deny that words, with their *this* and *that, yes* and *no, good* and *bad, beautiful* and *ugly,* could be accurate to any experience they pretended to convey. He knew, I suppose, only varieties of Chinese; and although he had a sharp understanding of fundamentals of logic, he might be puzzled by talk of other symbolic systems. But there would be no difficulty in applying his view to all languages and symbolic systems because it was the fixity of language and its polarized concepts to which he objected. Even the notion of a coherent language system with a fixed limit would seem absurd to him because the limit itself would appear too fixed, polar, and judgmental.

And what of Bhartrihari or Plotinus and Proclus, with their view of the universe as a hierarchy of meanings or Ideas culminating in and issuing from an indescribable reality, impossible by the standards of ordinary experience or logic but made necessary—like Cantor's short lived set of all sets and the cosmologists' singular state—by the structure of the universe as they thought it out to be? Their ineffable superlative was, to them, a structural necessity.

And what of Nagarjuna, whose undermining of concepts would extend to the concepts of those who would minimize 'emptiness' by considering it merely prescriptive? His opponents were less well informed scientifically than we are but no less clever philosophically, and I doubt that we can hit on an argument that they did not in principle raise and that he or his successors did not refute. I do not mean that I agree with him; but though I think his Indian heritage led him to argue in terms of categories we may think outmoded or dogmatic, his reasoning could be transformed without essential loss into some contemporary radical relativism which, however spurned by other philosophers, could defend itself against the analyses I have reported. Such analyses would themselves be much too explicitly logical for Nagarjuna to accept.

And what of Schopenhauer, Nietzsche, Wittgenstein, Heidegger, and maybe Derrida? I strongly suspect that, like other creative philosophers, they would not submit to evaluations made in any spirit but their own. Again, what I mean to say is not that they were right but that they could temper their swords sharp enough to duel with the sharpest of their critics, so that simply philosophical evaluations of their philosophies are not by themselves persuasive enough to anyone who can enter imaginatively into these philosophies and extend them.

We have come on still another instance of the combating of one set of philosophical preferences by means of another set. My own preference is to go beyond such preferences and look for empirical evidence by which to help to judge between the positions taken. I feel that all of the positions are inadequate in the sense that they are one sided, largely because they rest on preferences that reflect personality and experience more than the abstract reasoning they profess.

Superlative Experience Can Be Given Partial but Plausible Psychological Explanations

My own, not particularly original suggestion is that we should for the moment forget terminological refinements and philosophical arguments and reread—as philosophers may not—the old, affecting descriptions of the bliss of unity, the loss of smallness, fear, mortality, and other human imperfections, in the light of ordinary human psychology. After all, the experiences described as ineffable resemble ordinary, equally ineffable ones, and their higher levels of intensity and their local terminology may not make them more resistant to psychological understanding.

As a self-evident intellectual experiment, why not use the psychology of sex to explain why sexual analogies so often appear in mystical texts? And why not try to see if the negative philosophical descriptions are related to familiar psychological defenses, such as the narcissistic devaluation of everyone and everything regarded as irrelevant to oneself? Or why not ask about the very usual defense that stimulates the identification of oneself with something overwhelmingly powerful? Positive or negative, the descriptions may suggest a depressive turning of world or self into something unreal and the effort to turn this unreality into a shield against the self diminution it reflects. Or the descriptions may suggest a manic or manic-depressive temperament.

I go back then, for a time in the context of psychological explanation, to the superlative states we have repeatedly encountered, states of power, joy, merger with the essence of things, vanishing of all distinctions, immutability, longing, passion, loss of identity in sexual union, prolonged erotic tension, contemplation of self as penetrated by beauty, and transformation into the true one, the apparent two, and the true one again. There is so tremendous a reality in which to be consumed!

Speaking psychologically, superlative states or beings are fantasies of the sort that appear in myths and legends, which everyone enjoys for what they are. However, at their subjectively convincing extreme these fantasies suggest states of even mania or paranoia. It is usual and, within limits, normal that fantasies like these characterize wholehearted identification with anything or anyone thought great—a great artist, leader, or prophet; or a revered language, tradition, nation, religion, or god. Such an identification and the feeling of perfection and power that go with it have been called narcissistic and considered (by the psychoanalyst Kohut) to be the adult's translation of the child's feeling of identity with an idealized parent, whose greatness the child takes over and exults in.

The feeling of merger with the essence of things or of oneness with something totally protective appears to go back to the early relation between child and mother and the experience for which Freud borrowed the name *oceanic*. This name has been applied by J. Moussaieff Masson (a Sanskrit scholar who, before he repented completely of therapy, became an orthodox and then rebellious psychoanalyst) to the superlative experiences of Indian religious literature.[10] In the adult, says Freud, seriously and humorously at once, it is this overwhelming experience that causes a man in love, against all the evidence of his senses, to declare that he and his beloved are one, and to be prepared to behave as if this were a fact.[11]

The intense early closeness of child and mother has been called *symbiosis*. According to a risky though not implausible hypothesis, after various developmental adventures, the symbiosis gives way to the clear differentiation of child and mother. Another reading of the infant's experience begins not with a natural symbiosis but with a strong, instinctive attachment, the nature of which is influenced by the intensive, largely wordless dialogue between mother and infant. To this dialogue I shall later attribute much of the difference between those who do and do not feel that they can express themselves and be understood.

Just what happens subjectively in early infancy is impossible to make out because it is unreasonable to assume that an infant's feelings and thoughts can be compared easily with those of an adult. Infants are not simply human beings still too stupid to talk and too uncoordinated to walk; and most adults are not just large, strong, children who have learned how to walk, talk, and think. Although research often exhibits unexpected resourcefulness, it is improbable that any of the theories of child development is exactly right, or, if right, can be proved to be so.

One great difficulty in verifying the theories is the fact, as has been stressed, that the child forgets everything experienced in early life. That is, the child consciously forgets, because it is obvious that what it learns at first remains the basis for what it learns afterwards. The forgetting, though universal for the earliest time, is less than complete, and the forgotten experience, we have assumed, is 'remembered' in characteristic responses and in character itself. For there is evidence enough that the closeness or distance of young children to their parents has a deep influence on their adult emotions and on the way they regard themselves and others. A good mother and father are sources of self-assurance throughout the whole of life, and poor ones, of weakness and ambivalence.

Some degree of ambivalence is inevitable because every child undergoes the double pull—the pull back to the protective parent and the pull away, toward independence. There is a never-ending tension between the I that wants to diffuse itself back into the warm strength of mother and father and the I that asserts itself against them; and an endless tension between these *I*s and the *I* that has almost really separated itself.

How can one make a clear separation between the little child half asleep and warm in his mother's protective arms and the mother that holds him (I say *him* because I turn immediately to Plotinus and Krishna)? The selves of child and mother in this state diffuse into one another almost as their heat diffuses in both directions. The child who separates himself in order to become a more distinguishable member of the duo, knows that it is possible to run back and become one again—remember Plotinus's words. He returns because, for some fleeting reason, he simply wants to, or because he longs to be reunited, or because a sudden threat, real or imaginary, arouses his need for protection. And then, lying in mother's arms, warm and erotically aroused, the child sees himself mirrored in mother's smile, soft words, and caresses.

Lying there, the child is, if lucky, a still wordless Plotinus; and when, in later life, there are words to use, the child continues to feel that they are not enough because they neither *are* nor bring about the state of warm, joyous unity, and because the experience—which comes before speech and vanishes from explicit memory—does not go easily into words, which standardize adult experience and make it speakable.

And the child lying there is Krishna, too, because he can remain in prolonged erotic tension while enfolded in his mother's arms and lovingly fondled by her; and the warm tension, the fondling, which repeats itself in endless variations, and stimulates, teases with anticipation, and then satisfies without ever being all discharged, seems to be able to go on forever. The child Krishna is his mother's lover and king, and she his endless primal consort, not really quite himself and yet really as much within as outside him, possessing and surely being possessed, essentially just as will happen, by the god's prerogative, when he grows up to become an adult lover.

Here, in the case of Krishna, our descriptive language seems explicit enough; but explicitness is not the same as adequacy. Everything individual is hard or impossible to put exactly into words; so why is it surprising that, whether as Plotinus, Krishna, or simply ourselves, we cannot get the enveloping experience of a prelinguistic animal exactly into words? I qualify with *exactly* because something does go into words, of the sort I have used; but they are fairly distant and not warm or diffuse enough; and they are the medium of an adult, linguistic animal who lives in keeping with verbalized generalities. Words penetrate us and become our conventional substance, though their forms dissolve in unremembered memories and experiences too strong for verbal bonds.

Poets and Musicians Give Especially Clear Examples of the Desire for Complete Experience and Inclusive, Superlative Connectedness

We have already learned that music and poetry convey experience in some ways more completely than speech. Poetry has often been understood as the union of music with language, and as such a union, to resist prosaic explanation. This resistance poses a challenge I will exemplify by the attempt of Marshall Edelson, a psychoanalyst, to grasp the total sense of Wallace Stevens's poem *The Snow Man*. Edelson tries to show that the syntactic order of the poems's language resembles both the order of the poet's act of meditation and the order of the reality he meditates on. As the analyst reads the poem, he has a feeling of listening to some elusive, subsurface music, of timbres too deep for expression in words. But sharing his profession's passion for understanding, he strains to analyze this music in detail, and as he does so, he follows the analyst's precept according to which he should remain conscious of what is going on in himself at the same time. He discovers that his act of interpretation

> arises from a subtle interaction between anticipations and retrospections. Anticipations are aroused by linguistic events—phonemes, words, phrases—which occur as the surface form unfolds through time. To a larger extent than he supposes, on the basis of his linguistic competence, his knowledge of the rules of phonology, syntax, semantic, and rhetoric, the psychoanalyst imaginatively creates in his mind at each moment what is to follow. In each moment of a present language event, the psychoanalyst is both remembering a past language event and anticipating a future language event. In music also, at each moment the listener is both remembering a past event and anticipating a future event.[13]

Paul Valéry gives a detailed explanation of the music of poetry, especially his own. To further this music, he hopes that the role of poetic words will be changed—in reciting the poem, the reader will find its accents and sonorities in himself and recreate its music of meaning.[14]

Valéry recalls that Mallarmé would leave concerts filled with sub-lime jealousy and would try desperately to find the means to recover for poetry what music had taken from it. Valéry himself wants to explore the possibilities of music as a spiritual experience, an emotional liberation, an intensification of hidden feelings—unreligiously religious feelings—in community with every other hearer.

Characteristically, Valéry is unwilling to surrender his intellectual control, so rather than abandon himself to the effects of music, he (like the psychoanalyst) observes himself responding to it and comments on what he feels. He says that the unconscious, although essential to the poetry, gives birth to incoherent, formless material, which only the con-scious, self-critical mind can transform into art. "Restriction," he says, "has been inventive at least as often as a superabundance of freedom."[15] Pursuing the analogy with music, he considers organizing passages of poetry, like those of a musical composition, in an andante, largo, presto, scherzo, and the like. To help himself achieve music with poetry, he puts down groups of words the sounds or contrasts of which suggested one another. Sometimes he turns to etymology for old meanings, or shifts to synonyms or derived words; and sometimes he groups words by allitera-tion, rhyme, or homonomy. And he writes words to form transitions between passages, uses images to relieve his language of excessive ab-straction, and experiments to see how different rhymes change the effect of similar ideas. As Valéry puts it, the poet has to search in this way, and discover or invent what he cannot simply conceive, because "the great-ness of poets is that they grasp with their words what they only glimpse with their minds."[16]

Voicing a theme that we have heard in the analysis of Wallace Stevens's poem, Valéry says that the melody of a poem is its continuity, the expectation, as in music, that certain sounds lead to certain others, these others, which are the resolution of the sounds that precede them, leading on to the next resolution and creating an irresistible though episodic and variously interrupted movement. In poetry, it is melody that resists interruption and can eventually help the listener to grasp the shape of the whole. Melody in this sense refers to the poem's theme and the images around which the poem develops; as the melody unfolds, it prompts the reader to think of the poem's individual direction.[17]

To make the musical characteristics of poetry more evident and precise, Valéry would like a special kind of notation. Although, he ob-serves, the strictly musical resources of poetry are limited, the ideal re-mains the clear marking of "the enchainment of sounds" and the musical continuity of the poem. This recognizable whole is "a sort of verbal body that has the solidity, and also the ambiguity, of an object. Experience shows that a poem that is too simple (e.g., abstract) is *insufficient*. It is not even a poem." A true poem-object can stand out naturally, though, on reflection, mysteriously, like a crystal, flower, or seashell "from the disorder of perceptible things."[18]

Valéry often plays with the idea of allowing sound itself to take over the composing of his poetry, but his dominant ideal remains the poem in which sound and sense are indivisible. In one of his images, the balance between sound and sense is "an equilibrium by counterbalance like that of a tightrope walker." In another image, "the effect of a fine verse is like a pendulum. It puts 'the soul' in a state of oscillation between its form and its meaning." Therefore, "a comprehensible but 'beautiful' line of poetry is *beautiful by what is incomprehensible in it*." Seen in this way, poetry "aims to *express* by means of language precisely that which language is powerless to express."[19]

Always, to Valéry, the voice must be called to mind. "The qualities that can be enunciated in a human voice are those that must be studied and communicated in poetry. And the 'magnetism' of the voice must be transposed into a mysterious and ultra-fine alliance of ideas and words." This voice is individual. "The poet searches for the verse that suits his *voice*."[20]

❧

Despite the romantic—and to me, cogent—flavor of Valéry's aesthetics, much of what he says is applicable to a kind of poetry of which he was hardly thinking. I am referring to nonsense poetry, which often finds itself, it has been said, in a boundary dispute with 'what is normally taken to 'make sense'.[21] This dispute concerns the sensible translation that can possibly be wrung out of the nonsense, but also concerns the suspicion that what we take to be sensible makes no real sense at all because, as Wallace Stevens comments, it is "life's nonsense" that "pierces us with strange relation." In a time of bewilderment or depression, every attempt to get at the meaning of things is likely to end in the conviction that they are gibberish. Faith too can be gibberish then, and so can the poem that tries to penetrate beyond the impenetrable surface to the possible meaning beyond it. "The poem goes from the poet's gibberish to/The gibberish of the vulgate and back again./Does it move to and from or is it of both/At once?"[22]

Nonsense poetry—the simpler kind delighted in by children—returns us to the stage when, as infants, we babbled and the meaning of our babbling was what it could convey to anyone who sensed the mood of its sounds and rhythms, its pleasure in euphony for itself and for what it suggested, and its freedom from the bonds of utilitarian logic. Children celebrate what freedom they retain by glorying in nonsense, and we adults celebrate the children we remain by taking part in the same pleasure, however shamefacedly.

Its purpose to avoid making sense can make nonsense especially revealing. Lewis Carroll tells that when he wrote *The Hunting of the Snark* he didn't mean anything but nonsense; but he adds (like Valéry and to the same effect), "Words mean more than we mean to express."[23] His *The Hunting of the Snark* is a parodic equivalent of any quest to reach an unknown object or solve an insoluble problem; and its nonsensicality fits our nature, our efforts, and our quixotic tilting at we-know-not-whats: The snark *is* caught, and turns out to be a frightening, enigmatic boojum the finding of which causes the finder, the unfortunate Baker, to meet the fate that he dreads, which is to softly and suddenly vanish away, never to be met with again.[24]

The linguistic freedom that poets have claimed in the past and, even more, in the twentieth century has been nourished by the nonsense poets' freeing of words from their burden of conventional meaning. James Joyce's *Ulysses* and *Finnegan's Wake*, with their elaborate puns, portmanteau words, and other linguistic tricks and traps, would hardly have been possible in the absence of the precedent of nonsense poetry.

To the psychologist, nonsense poetry has the quality of the fantasy or dream that reveals by making clear what it conceals. Dada and surrealism are filled with such revealing nonsense, even the prose of which is made poetic by its topsy-turvy logic, strange associations, strange syntax, strange vocabulary, and gibberish, pulled like iron filings to the magnetic hungers of self-love, self-doubt, self-hate, sex, violence, pain, gluttony, and infinite paradisal ambition. In order to be nonsensical, parodic, rebellious, and transcendental, one has to use the sense-creating medium of language in sense-defying ways; and sense defying language uses all the qualities of language that are parallel to those of music—except that remnants of 'meaningful' words enter into the musicality and create vague ripples of verbal meaning.

For those who are interested in the whole elusive truth, I add that nonsense syllables are more likely to be processed together with words, in the left side of the brain, and not—in the tested syllables, 'such as *pa* and *ka*—in the right, more obviously musical side.[25]

The yearning to undergo full experience and to return to primoridal superlative states prompts me to recall the synesthesia not of neurology but of imaginative experience and, I should say, of the hunger for completeness. An example or two will help make clear what I mean. First, remember Valéry's ambition to unite the two apparent opposites, music and abstract thought, and create a verbal body as solid and ambiguous as an object. He wants to succeed in creating what Heidegger calls the "poetry that thinks" and attributes to Hölderlin.[26] In creating poetry that thinks, the poet joins imagined appearances with real desires and with pliant abstractions, and runs together the most different modalities of perception and the most different species of thought.

As used by the poet, words and modalities merge while remaining separate, like the fluid colors that touch and blend here and there but never simply merge, or like the leaves "falling like notes from a piano."[27] Only in such a fluid world can it have happened, as in a poem by Wallace Stevens, that

> The lake was full of artificial things,
> Like a page of music, like an upper air,
> Like a momentary color, in which swans
> Were seraphs, were saints, were changing essences.
> The west wind was the music, the force
> To which the swans curveted, a will to change,
> A will to make iris frettings on the blank.[28]

What Valéry, Heidegger, and Stevens value is the old ideal of total connectedness. Ordinary words give too little of this; poetry and music give much more. Poetry and music because they are able to give a heightened feeling of connection of the sort that "corresponds to our lived sense of being continuous selves in a continuous world." For "our impulse seems to be to flood the channels of passing time with a sense of the relationships that constitute us, so that they can there "acquire a sense of tangible presence."[29]

Walt Whitman is an example of the prodigious desire for connection and for flooding of the channels. He unites love for the most humble and deformed with love for nature; and unites this love with love for women and men, especially men who are athletic and "negligent"; and with the self-love of autoerotic experience and dream; and with an expansively loving identification with the universe in as much additive detail as he can muster.[30] He even has a fantasy of swallowing the world, incorporating "gneiss and coal and long-threaded moss and fruits and grains and esculent roots."31

In the preface to the 1855 edition of *Leaves of Grass*, Whitman's inclusive ambitions are expressed in these words (the interpolated dots are all his):

The greatest poet does not only dazzle his rays over character and scenes and passions. . . . he exhibits the pinnacles that no man can tell what they are for or what is beyond. . . . he glows a moment on the extremest verge. He is most wonderful in his last half-hidden smile or frown . . . by that flash of the moment of parting the one that sees it shall be encouraged or terrified for many years. The greatest poet does not moralize or make applications of morals . . . he knows the soul. The soul has that measureless pride which consists in never acknowledging any lessons but its own. But it has sympathy as measureless as its price and the one balances the other and neither can stretch too far while it stretches in company with the other. The inmost secrets of art sleep with the twain. The greatest poet has lain close beneath both and they are vital in his style and thoughts.[32]

It is apparent that in poets such as Whitman, as in many composers, the appetite for connectedness is one for whole imaginative worlds whose life is breathed into them by the language or music in which they are created. Poets and composers of this kind remind me of a Tantric adept who—like a Schopenhauer able to lift the veil of illusion and experience himself as the metaphysical will—ceremonially retracts himself into the creative source of the cosmos. To retract himself so, the adept reverses the process of creation, one element after another, and dissolves himself into the source. Dissolved, he can begin to recreate self and cosmos. He now enjoys complete bliss and joins egos with the goddess who is reality. Limb by limb, the adept becomes identical with her. Then, this time against Schopenhauerian principles, the adept conceives the cosmos into being again, in the form of his all-embracing mansion that is contained within himself; for the goddess, Reality, is now in his heart and he and she are identical.[33]

Such a Tantric dissolver and recreator of the universe, who contains everything that appears external to him, reminds me of Mahler because of the boundless desire he exhibits to be everything, create everything, connect with everything. The Tantric adept, unless a very stubborn individualist, is himself subordinate to his guru and his punctilious tradition, while the Western artist, the Whitman or Mahler, is the stubborn individualist—although he needs the help of patrons whom he obviously cannot himself create any more than the Tantrist can escape the obligation to serve, mediate on, and worship the guru.

When Nietzsche still loved Wagner—his love was by then already troubled—he wrote of him that his art always conducted him along a twofold path,

from a world as an audible spectacle into a world as a visible spectacle enigmatically related to it, and the reverse; he is continually compelled—and the beholder is compelled with him—to translate visible movement back into the soul and primordial life, and conversely to see the most deeply concealed inner activity as visible phenomenon and to clothe it with the appearance of a body.[34]

We no doubt hear Schopenhauer in these words, hear Nietzsche himself, and hear Wagner, with whom Nietzsche was then intimate. We also hear the Tantrist's cosmic ambition. It is said that the older Wagner, influenced by Schopenhauer, came to regard the music of his operas as more important than the words—what took place on the stage were, he said, "deeds of music made visible."[35] But for an ambition as embracing as his, a synthesis of the musical, erotic, poetic, dramatic, mythic-religio-philosophical (Schopenhauerian, old Germanic, Christian, Buddhist), no expressive medium could be sacrificed, certainly not that of words.

Mahler, too, allied music with poetry and conceived cosmic dramas. Sunset was not only itself but also a symbol of the end of life and of evil overpowering the light, as his orchestra had to suggest. To him, everything suggested everything:

> To realize his ghostly vision—the dread of disaster, the dream of earthly bliss—Mahler constantly experimented with the inclusion of new instruments to satisfy his need for special sounds: The somber tenor horn in his introduction to the Seventh Symphony, the delicate cowbells in the Sixth Symphony, the guitar and mandolin in the *Nachtmusik 2* of the Seventh Symphony. Vaster vistas for the musical eye were also sought by the use of offstage orchestra.[36]

For his music, Mahler used, that is, needed, both the classic and the romantic composers; and he needed military marches, bird cries, scenery, and much else. Despite his ambivalence on the matter, he also needed programs for himself, and, of course, words to be sung—altogether, everything that had or had not been put into music before. In his three last compositions, *Das Lied von der Erde,* the Ninth Symphony, and the Tenth Symphony, there was a collision between his avidity for life and his fear of death. After studying Mahler's Ninth Symphony, Alban Berg said:

> The first movement is the most heavenly thing Mahler ever wrote; it is the expression of an exceptional fondness for this earth, the longing to live in peace on it, to enjoy nature in its depths—before death comes. For he comes irresistibly. The entire movement is permeated by premonitions of death . . . most potently, of course, in the colossal passage where this premonition becomes certainty, where in the midst of greatest strength, of almost painful joy of life, Death itself is announced with greatest force.[37]

In his last as in his earlier compositions, Mahler runs through very many moods, of the kinds that words can and cannot describe. Perhaps he tries both to say his farewells and to assimilate death, as he has tried to assimilate everything else, and make it part of himself, who is the cosmos he lives in but also creates.

Generalizations on Word-Devaluers and Exalters

Before I continue with my judgments, I should like to advance the discussion by classifying the various devaluers of words, to whom I have devoted less attention than to the exalters. Then I will ask the protagonists—devaluers and exalters alike—a rhetorical question. The remarks that follow will lead into a psychological explanation of why exalters and devaluers both require an ineffable source but make opposite evaluations of language, which, according to the one view, reflects the ineffable source, but, according to the other, creates an illusory veil over it.

1. There are the devaluers—such as Gorgias and Nagarjuna—who say that language is meaningless by the very standards professed by the philosophers who prize it.

2. There are the devaluers—such as Nagarjuna, Dignaga, Nietzsche, and, in a sense, Kant—who say that language teaches us nothing about reality in itself because it imposes its own arbitrary forms on experience.

3. There are also those—such as Kierkegaard, Nietzsche, and the Zen Buddhists (influenced by Nagarjuna)—who say that language is by nature superficial and can stimulate deeper penetration only by means of its technical failure in self contradiction.

4. There is at least one philosopher, Chuang Tzu, who belongs to all the three groups mentioned, in a perhaps inconsistent way consistent with his defence of inconsistency and naturalness.

All these language-devaluers appear to me to be faced, in different degrees, by a variant of the difficulty that has already been raised a number of times: They argue their negative positions in ordinary language, which they must regard as to some degree accurate or at least helpful. Furthermore, they usually admit that while language has no access whatsoever to the ultimate reality—'emptiness', 'tao', 'noumenon', 'truth'—it does have practical usefulness and is to be distinguished from illusion and error in the usual sense. But as I have asked, how can they account for this usefulness if language is not at least partially in keeping with the noumenon? This is no more than a commonsense kind of objection, but I find it to be powerful.

Let me put the objection in the form of the sort of metaphor we have met with a number of times. Suppose that the truth you are searching for is high up in a tree and can be reached only with the help of a ladder, which you get rid of as soon as the truth is in your hands. Has the ladder helped because it truly got you up to the truth or for some other, unexpressed reason that makes it right to discard it once the aim, the truth, has been reached? What better evidence is there of the truth of the way to the truth than helpfulness of this ladder kind? Is the true way to the truth not itself also true? On what more persuasive ground than the ability to attain the truth can the truthfulness of the ladder or anything else be based? My question and my implied answer have a pragmatic air, but why should this disqualify them?

The thinkers we have considered have been divided, too neatly, into two basic groups, the one of exalters and the other of devaluers of words or concepts. The first group, of exalters, tries painstakingly to rid words of everything adventitious, in order to reach the pure force of their conceptuality. The exalters' aim is to get experientially beyond words to their source. The second group, of devaluers, uses painstaking techniques painfully pursued to exclude concepts from true consciousness, or to weaken the hold of concepts, with the same aim of getting experientially beyond them. (Nietzsche neither quite fits nor quite evades this description.)

The first group of thinkers tries to purify and concentrate consciousness, which they regard as identical with selfhood. The Buddhist members of the second group try the opposite tactic: to break up consciousness into its constituents and destroy the delusion of selfhood and get experientially beyond it, or to deny the reality even of the constituents of consciousness in order to arrive at emptiness. Yet the stages described by the Buddhists—stages in which consciousness rises beyond conceptualization—belong to the same kind of yogic purification as adopted by the Indian exalters of words. Historically speaking, it is not clear what methods of going up the experiential ladder these Buddhists could have arrived at if they had not had their Hindu opponents to borrow from (and also often teach).

For the most part, the positions of the two groups, those I have called exalters and those I have called devaluers, appear to be in polar opposition. But both make compromises, by means of which the concept-exalters see ordinary concepts as illusory, while the concept devaluers distinguish between complete illusion and the illusory but pragmatically useful concepts necessary for everyday life.

My suspicion is that the experiential results of both positions are not very different, and the superiority of the one or the other cannot really be proved—the testimony of the few serious persons who have gone from one position to the other is not at all conclusive. In practice, the most conscientious pursuit of such ends was undertaken by monks in individual seclusion or in monasteries. The testimony given by monks suggests that there is a good deal of personal variation within the same religious position, by which I mean the position that depends upon the same authoritative texts and techniques of liberation. And both of the polar extremes rest upon a doctrine of the indescribable, often as the superlative of a hierarchical order.

One may, of course, accept the arguments of one or another side. Although the arguments became elaborate, neither the positive ones of the world-exalting side—ending in a faith vaguely specified by negations—nor the negative ones of the word-devaluing side—also ending in a faith so specified—are coercive. The evidence for this conclusion lies in the persistent inability of either side to convince the other and, more immediately, in the detectible weaknesses of the arguments used. As a result, it was recognized on both sides that arguments had to be accompanied and finally displaced by experience, which alone could be entirely convincing.

The disputants were therefore offering not only competing arguments but competing teachers and ways of life. Yet experience, too, is a judge whose verdicts can be ambiguous. What can be proved by the agreement between those persuaded by a certain guru and scripture (its text sometimes discovered or intuited by him)? The agreement can easily be attributed to psychological and sociological causes like those that persuade the disciples of other gurus and scriptures. The fact that certain exercises in concentration lead to certain states of mind does not necessarily validate the metaphysical claims, in any case many and varied, by which they are explained. And while gurus talk high-flown metaphysics, neurologists talk brain chemicals with increasing plausibility. Exercises that cause a kind of sensory deprivation can lead to a feeling of exaltation; but that is not proof enough that one has come closer to reality-in-itself or whatever exalted state one may choose to call or avoid calling what one is aiming at. When investigated, normal perception proves to be extremely complex—still well beyond technological imitation—and extraordinarily sensitive to the changes it reports and often, for good practical reasons, conceals. What is proved by subjecting our perceptual mechanisms to such unusual conditions that they give reports that fit certain metaphysical preconceptions, which themselves may have been derived from psychological states severe enough to lead to perceptual changes of a sort a disbeliever is tempted to call malfunctions?

The Exaltation and Devaluation of Words May Both Reflect the Communicative Temper of Early Childhood

I think it is possible to explain at least some of the difference between the two attitudes—word-exaltation and word-devaluation—by returning to early life, this time with emphasis on the ways in which a very young child learns to feel the feelings of other people, or, more exactly, learns how feelings and feeling-tinged perceptions are interchanged and teach one sensitized person to respond to another. It is important for us to understand the nature of this at first quite wordless dialogue and to see how it is prolonged, changed, and to some extent negated in the simply linguistic dialogue that begins later.[38]

Communicative confidence and suspicion begin in this long, fateful dialogue. Modern Western philosophers have spent a good deal of effort in thinking about solipsism; but what, to my mind, can be really troubling is not the difficulty in proving abstractly that solipsism is false, but the loneliness and misunderstanding that many people really face, to the point that they feel themselves a world apart and feel sometimes that they are not quite real, or that the others and the world the others inhabit is not quite real. This tendency to solipsism in fact, like the relative immunity to such solipsism, is likely to have its origin in the complex emotional and linguistic dialogue to which I am referring.

Think once again—for almost the last time—of an infant and a mother, or an infant and any other person who comes into close and frequent contact with it. How, at first, do the two persons learn to communicate when the one is still unable to speak and for a while even to point? How does a mother learn to know what the child feels and wants, and how does the child learn to know the mother?

To understand the answer we have to begin with the ability of child and mother to mirror and empathize with one another, to feel as the other feels, to feel so closely with one another as to be each almost situated within the other, to know the other rather accurately almost in the same way as one knows oneself. Lacking a more basic explanation, we have to begin by assuming that the ability is native to every human from the start.

If we watch the child and mother, as investigators have watched them with great care, we see an increasingly effective interchange of movements, facial expressions, and sounds. The mother uses words, which the child cannot at all recognize as such. Their interchange has a notable parallelism: movement is answered with movement, facial expression with facial expression, and sound with sound, in each case with a comparable quality and degree of intensity; and if movement, facial expression, or sound is answered in another modality—sound, for example, by facial expression—then the parallelism is preserved by the quality and intensity of the response. That is, the hand of one person moves in emotional and rhythmic response to that of the other, the head of the one moves in similar response to the head of the other, and the voice of the one accompanies the hand or head of the other as it moves. In each instance, rhythm and duration match rhythm and duration, quality matches quality—in the ways that one modality can suggest or match the other, as the amplitude, vigor, and timing of a gesture match those of a sound, and vice versa.[39]

This process, by which one persons's state is matched by the state of the other, reminds me of the dialogue in an opera by Mozart, in which the responses are also by gesture and music, and therefore fuller than it could be if the two were exchanging only words. The sharing of states between mothers and children is distinguished by such names as *interaffectivity* , *interintentionality,* and *empathy*—interaffectivity for the sharing of feelings, interintentionality for the sharing of intentions, and empathy for the shared interaction of cognitive and muscular or emotional responses.[40] Whatever the descriptive word used, the result is that each of the two persons learns to 'be with' the other.

All this holds true to the extent that there is genuine closeness and, with it, genuine sharing. But if experience is not successfully shared toward the beginning of life, the child learns to feel that its inward states are unshareable and, by virtue of this feeling, may actually make them unshareable. The early success or failure of the sharing helps determine how well one can be attuned to the inward life of another person and how accurately and with what sense of conviction one can translate externals—tones, gestures, and facial expressions—into what is felt internally.[41]

As the child learns to speak, the sense of mutuality is furthered and complicated, and in some ways probably injured. Speaking gives the child the ability to express much that could not be expressed at all before, or expressed only much more vaguely. But words, for all the emotion they may convey by the manner or vocal quality of their expression, grow so powerful that they interfere with the earlier kinds of interchange. This is because words allow the speaker to remain a word's length away from direct experience and emotional participation. On the one hand, the abstract, representative quality of words helps children to imagine, to represent, and to gain distance from themselves; but on the other hand, it helps them to misrepresent and evade; and the earlier, nonverbal kind of sharing of experience grows less dominant in their lives and is at times at cross-purposes with the new, verbal mode of expression.[42] Although he could not resist exaggerating, what Nietzsche said of words was surely perceptive.

This point deserves to be elaborated. Language brings closeness and brings distance. Speaking children become more human, make more effective contact with persons outside of the family, and discover more easily that they are part of a larger human community. But the structure of language is different from that of the emotions, and it expresses feelings and even perceptions in a standard, standardizing way because these are so difficult to put exactly into words.[43] The word that allows a child to express always variable perceptions as a single, uniform abstraction tends to split him into a partly hidden, clumsily expressed 'existential' self and an easily externalized and shareable verbal self. And then a hidden, private, 'true' self is created that contrasts with and often contradicts the external, public, spoken 'self.'[44]

Again, language cuts off and joins:

> Language forces a space between interpersonal experience as lived and represented. And it is exactly across this space that the connections and associations that constitute neurotic behavior may form. But also with language infants for the first time can share their personal experience of the world with others, including being with others in intimacy, isolation, loneliness, fear, awe, and love.[45]

The Point Is Humanized with Kafka's Help

All through the present chapter, I have been implying that the metaphysical explanations for the doctrines of ineffability are less enlightening than nonmetaphysical ones. I add, to be fair, that it is very difficult to try to think things out metaphysically without encountering the feeling that we are in a world we can never fully understand, a feeling like that of the questioner in a brief ironic and unsettling story by Kafka:

> It was very early in the morning, the streets clean and deserted, I was on my way to the station. As I compared the tower clock with

my watch I realized that it was much later than I had thought and that I had to hurry; the shock of this discovery made me feel uncertain of the way, I wasn't very well acquainted with the town as yet; fortunately, there was a policeman at hand, I ran to him and breathlessly asked him the way. He smiled and said: "You are asking me the way?" "Yes," I said, "since I can't find it myself." "Give it up! Give it up!" said he, and turned with a sudden jerk, like someone who wants to be alone with his laughter.[46]

This Kafkesque feeling of being lost in a world in which every destination has become obscure has its intellectual counterpart in our unsettling ignorance of so much that we should like to know, in our inability to sum up the endless variety of contexts into a single thinkable one, and in our frustrating sense of a universe too old, big, and numerous to be captured in the philosophical questions that return and return and breed dilemmas only sharpened by our attempts to solve them.

Anyone who is much troubled by such thoughts experiences a feeling of helplessness or loneliness—which is as likely to be the cause as the effect of the troubling thoughts. Not surprisingly, the antidote that may be discovered is a form of emotional safety that doubt cannot touch or analysis diminish. Hence the frequent relationship between safety and ineffability; because if the safety one needs is not beyond the reach of words, it is not beyond the doubts that words can express and is therefore not deep or protective enough. But the relationship with words may be approving if the safety one needs is found less in the devaluation of words than in an enveloping intimacy, personal or communal. And the relationship may be even excellent if, like those with creative occupations, one discovers how to merge instead of separating awareness, action, and self-expression. In merging them, one learns to use one's ability in a given medium in order to achieve self-transcendence, the sinking of one's self in something other and larger.[47] The relationship in fact is excellent if one's medium is language, because then, regardless of what one says about words, one's competence and hope are invested in their success.

To create something is helpful. But I add the almost unspoken condition that I do not mean to substitute rhetoric of any kind for our often inescapably difficult lives, and I do not the feel the temptation to migrate seriously toward any psychological utopia.

The Point Is Complicated with Anthropological and Psychological Hypotheses

The taking of an empirically tested psychological point of view is not, in itself, empirically decisive. This is true not only because of the variety of psychological points of view that can be taken, but also because psychology intersects with other social sciences, each of which imposes a different perspective. Think of what I have said about religious devotion to Krishna. Think, first, how it might look if transposed into the concepts of the sociology of religion or symbolic anthropology. For them, to see how the cult depends on the natural relationship of mother and child or illicit lover and woman is only to begin to understand. The sociologist (of a certain type) would go on and ask: How exactly have these natural relationships achieved their social power and symbolic depth; and why have they achieved it in just their particular social or symbolic forms; and why and how are these forms peculiar to each of the different kinds of Krishna worship? The symbolic anthropologist would be interested in reading the symbolic code as a kind of language spoken in symbolic objects and actions.

To adopt a sociological or anthropological attitude and give developed answers to these questions would take us too far beyond the bounds of this book and of my competence. However, I will give examples of the attitude of the anthropologists, who take ritual to be "a culturally constructed system of symbolic communication" designed to shape and intensify experience.[48]

Seen in this light, the devotees of Krishna make use of profound emotions in order to humanize themselves more deeply, neutralize their pains and fears more effectively, and consolidate their communities more closely. The emotions they use—mother love and adult sexual love— create strong reciprocal ties. These ties are augmented by poems, paintings, flower arrangements, food, music, and ceremonies, each of these with its own sensory effects, each simultaneously material and metaphorical, each created, prepared, or performed by members of a special subtradition, and each exerting a synergistic effect on all the others.

In a tradition of this sensory opulence so soaked in implicit meanings, emotions are named, organized, and explained so that members of the religious tradition know what they are expected, even obliged, to experience; and what they know is specific to the community and tradition—Chaitanyaite, Vallabhite, or other—by which the devotees' emotions "are culturally constructed and symbolically mediated." This construction can be so highly socialized that in a Chaitanyaite community "it is believed that the collective religious experience itself is the living body of Krishna, superior not only to his iconic representation but even the god himself."[49] Speaking of the Chaitanyaites, an anthropologist says, "Perhaps in no other religious system have human emotional potentials been so considered, categorized, and sacralized."[50]

The position of the anthropologists I have been summarizing limits the tendency to generalize because it assumes that each symbolic system is highly specific to its tradition and, perhaps, its time and place. Every traditional kind of symbolic depth, they seem to feel, is so grossly and subtly different from every other that it is very difficult for an outsider to enter, and probably futile for the outsider to criticize.

The position of psychologists, by whom I mean, in this instance, psychoanalysts, is quite different. First, they begin with a different stock of experiences and presuppositions. Secondly, whereas the anthropologist tries not to disturb the community under study—a strong disturbance would counteract the purpose of studying it—the psychoanalyst's whole purpose is to intervene, knowingly and carefully, in order to lessen suffering, not of the community, of course, but of the individual. In other words, the contemporary anthropologist wants to share in the understanding of others in order to analyze and appreciate their cultural symbol-systems; the analyst, now as before, wants to share in the experience of others in order to mitigate individual pain. It is a case of the translator-connoisseur as against the physician. However, because analytic training has assumed a relatively uniform human nature, the analyst may discover, as the anthropologist knows to begin with, that human nature has different cultural patterns.

I have been putting the difference abstractly. But contrast the attitude of the anthropologists with that of the Indian psychoanalyst Sudhir Kakar, who is primarily concerned, he says, with fantasies of intimacy. In his informal account, he draws not only on his experience as an analyst, but also on Indian myths, folktales, novels, and films.

Kakar points out that among some Hindu communities sexual taboos are still very strong, especially for upper caste women. He thinks that these taboos play a part in impoverishing and souring sexual experience. In spite of the importance of bearing sons, he explains, traditional rules set severe limits on the time available for marital intercourse; and the sexual indifference and hostility found in the upper castes are no less prevalent in the lower ones. "The general disapproval of the erotic aspect of married life continues to inform contemporary attitudes."[51]

This disapproval fits in with the Indian kind of preoccupation with sex. Indian men still accept the old belief that the emission of semen is weakening and, if excessive, will shorten their lives. Sexual restraint is therefore assumed to improve men's health and lengthen their lives. In orthodox Hinduism, celibacy is a prerequisite for anyone who aspires to a religious vocation; and, by traditional medical-mystical teachings, the man who resists temptation even in thought and learns to direct his semen upward, refines the semen and gains spiritual realization. Indian mythology records many instances of holy men who by their sexual restraint attained nearly godly powers, which were instantly abolished by the temptation that caused even a drop of semen to be emitted.

Although seminal restraint is close to holiness and to the superlative experience that holiness promotes, opposite ideals have also been cultivated in India. These are evident in the art surrounding the worship of Krishna. The opposites activate one another: The alchemy of restraint is opposed by the alchemy of abandon; and, not infrequently, the two are joined in an alchemy of abandon as elaborately solicited as it is severely restrained.

Given such a background, Indians (we are told) are fascinated by Freud. To Jung, whose doctrine appears on its face to be well adapted to Indian beliefs, they are, on the contrary, indifferent.[52] The reason is that so much of Indian religion is consciously based on sublimation in the direct, Freudian sense.

In infancy and early childhood, an Indian, especially a boy, is treated with great indulgence. The father may be distant; but the mother is always there, and the little boy is touched, fondled, embraced, cuddled, fed, protected, and indulged by her and by the other women around him. Rather than punish a child, the mother will distract it with something pleasing; but the child becomes very sensitive to the mother and when her mood is bad, acts in a way that will improve it. The child's sensitivity is reflected in the grown person's openness to nonverbal clues and emotional states, not to speak of susceptibility to praise and shame.[53]

The birth of a new child drives the older one from the mother's bed and arms, and adds to the internalized image of the good, indulgent mother that of the evil, denying one; and when the child approaches the age of four, its yoke of obedience becomes far heavier. Yet the tie to the mother remains strong and sensual enough for the grown man—now also displaced in his mother's affections by the father whose continuation he knows himself to be—to feel close in emotional, imaginative ways to a woman, which is almost to say, close to *being* a woman. To put it in the analyst's language, "One is struck by the fluidity of the patients' cross-sexual and generational identifications. In the Indian patient, the fantasy of taking on the sexual attributes of both the parents seems to have a relatively easier access to awareness."[54]

After the man marries, socially speaking in order to continue the family line, the pleasure of sexual intercourse is devalued and easily becomes a source of anxiety or guilt. The wife is apt to be regarded as prone to infidelity, and as demanding what the man can supply only at too great a cost to his health and spiritual well-being. Rather like the young Krishna of mythology, the Krishna kind of lover in Indian films is aggressive in drawing women's attention to himself and teases and startles them, and the more they dislike his attentions, the more they excite him, because "love is fun only when the woman is angry."[55] His most satisfying conquests are of an innocent adolescent, and his sexual importunities must be powerful enough to transform her initially androgynous coolness into masochistic, feminine surrender. But even though she surrenders to her dark lord, she is not, in the myth, the potential wife—someone who threatens to displace the mother—but only the woman as the force of servile, clinging passion. A woman's seductions are too like the unclearly remembered but extremely powerful ones of the mother; and this seductive woman is felt to be as apt to betray as the betraying, evil mother; and so for the sake of the tie to the mother, new seductions must be resisted. In a full, honorable sense, the man can love only the (good) mother. Somehow, to retain the tie with the mother, he must—now or later—deprive the other woman of her full sexuality or, recognizing her as dangerous, desexualize himself.[56]

So far, the views of the Indian analyst Kakar. What we have seen until now, as in the discussion of Krishna, is the closeness of the erotic to the ascetic, the possibility of identification either with the mother or with the woman who is the adoring object of Krishna's phallic potency, or with the union itself of woman and man, Radha and Krishna. There is also the deeply learned sensitivity to mood and to the wordless communication it entails. At least for the Indian devotee of Krishna, the search for intimacy with a consumingly spiritual and endlessly gratifying reality turns out to mirror his intimate experience with his mother—protector, gratifier, and implicit lover—or with the dreamed innocent who confirms his virility without robbing him of his pure, powerful innocence.

Longing for intense closeness, the best years of which are not consciously remembered, longing as much for social approval as for self-approval, and schooled by a tradition the direct sources of which he finds in his intimate experience, the traditional and sometimes the untraditional Indian easily comes to regard his spiritual advancement as the most important goal of his life. For the sake of this goal, he may pray, worship, meditate, and attach himself to a spiritual mentor. Maybe because of his early, deeply ingrained symbiotic relationships, which give him his ability to neutralize and cross the boundaries of his physical self, it is easy for the Indian to experience himself as actually, bodily or spiritually, affected by what others consider to be no more than mythical or symbolic.[57]

Such descriptions persuade me that to understand the nature of transcendent ineffable experience, it is essential to consider the effects of a person's longing for complete closeness, that is, the longing to merge with the source of love and protection, which is with love and protection in themselves. One longs to merge or share one's self, or to lose one's individual self in merger with a greater one: one's self strives by nature to become the reciprocal (one-many) whole it feels itself to be. In this spirit, one issues from one's self, emits one's desire, and draws in perfection from its source. It is in this spirit that the disciple gazes fixedly at his guru in order to assimilate him—and assimilate the other disciples who assimilate him. So, too, by perfecting his devotion, the devotee assimilates and becomes Krishna or Radha-Krishna—as well as the whole community of devotees who become him or her-and-him. In every case, one becomes one's self by again becoming the great, singularly plural self of one's infancy.[58]

The Preference for Secular, Often Psychological Explanations Is Indecisive and Apt to Leave an Aura of Ineffability

The sort of claims I have been making—which a psychiatrist, psychoanalyst, or clinical psychologist is likely to find acceptable, a philosopher evasive, and a theologian belittling—seem to me worth exploring further. It is not possible for philosophy to give up the problems I have been addressing, but it is so often inconclusive, as I have said, that light cast from any other direction should be welcome to philosophers; and if psychology, too, can rarely if ever be conclusive, its light shows what otherwise remains unseen or seen with merely casual eyes, which lack the educated sharpness taught by a discipline in relation to its own subject matter. In the final analysis, however, I think that the psychological hypotheses I have used are too limited even when they turn out to be empirically useful. I mean not only that empirical hypotheses are all fallible and the psychological ones among them often especially fallible, but that the very claim that a limited discipline of any kind can offer a really final explanation of any kind strikes me as wrong. We see this indirectly in the various attempts, resembling those of the symbolic anthropologists, to make psychology or psychoanalysis more adequate to religious experience and claims.[59] Such attempts require us to give up the view of Freud himself that religion is nothing but an illusion, with a psychopathological basis.

By now it is not unusual for psychoanalysts to emphasize the human need for religious attitudes. The Freudian view is that the fantasies that dominate childhood should yield to a mature objectivity in the adult. The response to this view may be that it presumes that the separation between subjective and objective can be neat and decisive. But—continues the response—the separation is, in fact, impossible and the attempt to make it perhaps damaging. When we get to the border of the unknown and the ideal, it is argued, we have no choice except to run the

objective and subjective together. A child is able to achieve a coherent
self, transformed from its earlier indeterminate, uncontrolled existence,
by virtue of the parents it has taken into itself; and, in the same pattern,
the grown-up achieves coherence by virtue of God, whose unifying nature consolidates the personal world together with the person at its center. The beginning of the sense of God is the infantile sense of closeness
to the protector, to the protector's warmth, touch, voice, habits, and
benign authority. This infantile closeness is no longer enough for an
adult, but it becomes the core of the necessary sense of God. God, we
may then say, is one of the necessary fictions by which we live:

> The fictive creations of our minds . . . have as much regulatory po-
> tential in our psychic function as people around us in the
> flesh . . . Human life is impoverished when these immaterial charac-
> ters made out of innumerable experiences vanish under the repres-
> sion of a psychic realism that does violence to the ceaseless creativ-
> ity of the human mind. In this sense, at least, religion is not an
> illusion.[60]

But what exactly does it mean to say that, taken as "fictive creations
of our minds," the "immaterial characters" of religion are not illusory?
The psychoanalytic investigator who said this is apparently no literalist.
But how literally must the believers themselves take their myths and
immaterial characters in order to do themselves no psychic violence?
Dogmas give official answers to what must and must not be literally
believed, but it remains unclear to what extent an established dogma
determines the private beliefs of the individuals who in practice accept it.
My suspicion is that here, too, there are great individual variations, more
easily revealed, of course, where the penalties for expressing them are
weak. Many people, I assume, would find it difficult, unpleasant, and
unnecessary to distinguish between three different ways of valuing their
myths: as parablelike encouragement to adopt a certain religious point of
view; as symbolic expression of the truth that theologians know how to
put more abstractly; and as the simple, literal truth—itself perhaps regarded as a secondary, merely empirical kind of truth.

Psychological research into such questions is too intimate to be
easy. Psychologists who explore religious experience are obliged to be
aware of and discount their own biases, and to be aware, as well, of the
social context of the life they are exploring. But their discipline forbids
them to begin by accepting religious beliefs at their face value, and a
psychological explanation may therefore diminish or conflict with religious claims, especially when they are literal. Yet the psychologist's discovery of how religious attitudes are embedded in the most intimate

human relations, beginning in infancy, in no way discredits religious experience. Artistic, scientific, and philosophical attitudes are embedded in these relations no less deeply than is religion.[61]

What, then, is at stake? To answer, I want to distinguish between the attitudes of the psychologist who professes allegiance to science and the mystic who professes allegiance to a different, intuitively known truth, which may be understood as either antagonistic to science or as superior to it. The distinction is not that science changes and religion is fixed, because religious doctrines, mystical ones among them, undergo a constant process of revision. Even the doctrine most carefully fixed in scriptures must be reinterpreted when transmitted to other persons and generations. However, to make the comparison of psychology (with a scientific ideal) and religion closer and more difficult, for the moment I take into consideration only doctrines that are conscious corrections of past ones and—what is rarer—allow the possibility of future correction.

In keeping with the theme of this book, the only constant required in such self-correcting religions is that they have an ineffable ideal known, to whatever supposed degree, by ineffable experience. The ideal itself may be sanctioned by tradition or by faith in the leaders who profess it. As for the experience, it may be undergone by ordinary believers, but must have been undergone at least by their teacher or by their teacher's ultimate teachers, in which case ordinary believers accept the reality of the experience on faith. But what is the criterion of this experience? Maybe its authoritative description, which makes it possible to distinguish it from less significant experiences. In Zen, the Master decides. The experience overrides doubts (which sometimes return); but what connects it with the doctrine that establishes and interprets whatever it is that is not doubted? Training, surely, and philosophy, which formulates, justifies, and defends against rival methods and doctrines.

All this can be construed to resemble the process by which science is taught and verified. It particularly resembles clinical psychology and, even more, psychoanalysis, which has often been accused of being a religion. In mysticism as in psychoanalysis, the criterion is the doctrine's persuasiveness, verified by the well-being given in some sense by experience—the mystical experience or the experience of effective psychoanalytic insight. But however well or ill the ideal is pursued, the scientific ideal—accepted, I assume, by psychology and psychoanalysis—is significantly different, and the difference is that the overwhelming power of the experience or the sense of well-being or security that follow are not enough in themselves because, instead of explaining, they must themselves be explained. I must acknowledge that this difference is far from absolute: there is always a partly circular relationship between theory and experience, each being used both to justify the other and to correct the perception of the other. But difference there is, and it is rooted in a different sense of what constitutes truth and how it is to be reached, verified, modified, and fitted into a framework of experience judged with the greatest commitment to objectivity of which human beings are capable. A psychology that abandons the ideal of objectivity as science, in its often uncertain way, has established it, is—to that extent only—the same as religion. I put the difference starkly, although the history of science, too, is a tangled web, and the distinction more difficult to express exactly than it may seem at first; or impossible to express exactly because science is not at all uniform and fades off, without a clear borderline, into its opposites.

Yet when the defense of possibly life-giving fictions goes so far as to threaten the distinction between the objective (what is more or less objectively verifiable) and the fictional (what is imagined because needed or desired), the scientist's mercilessly consuming search for truth is attentuated—though granted the deflections of individual scientists, it is more realistic to see the search as merciless only in its collaborative force. The philosophic affirmers such as Bhartrihari and Plotinus assimilate the search for objective truth into the search for the perfection that accounts for and, so far as humans go, surpasses it. But the others, the deniers, deny incredibly much in order to be able to deny the search as well, and then, after declaring subjectivity and objectivity indistinguishable, to submerge themselves in primal experience: Lao Tzu, Chuang Tzu, Nagarjuna, the Zen masters, Schopenhauer, Nietzsche, Heidegger. Ambivalence, paradox, humor, pain, yearning, deconstruction—all are enlisted for the denial. Logic, too, is enlisted, as when Nagarjuna uses both the law of contradiction and the technique of binegation to break down the border between logical, conventional truth and neither-logical-nor-alogical emptiness; and conceptual analysis is used—along with the meditative identification of the object of one's thought with nothingness—in order to reverse and still the voice of abstract and objective thought.

So while our final aspirations are not discredited by the depth to which they are rooted in our origins, when we clothe them in fictions and make nonfictional demands in their name, we endanger the aspiration to know the truth as free of fiction as possible. And yet, as I have been saying, the truth is that there is no discipline—whatever its hostility or its receptiveness to fiction—that is adequate to the truth as a whole; for all disciplines are such by virtue of the limitation of their respective points of view. This holds, I should say, even of disciplines as embracing as philosophy and theology—I use the word *theology* to emphasize that a discipline must be technically developed and not merely amorphous. Hence the effect on us of powerful art, of Wagner, Kafka, Joyce, Artaud, or Marquez, and hence the effect of such antiphilosophical philosophers as Kierkegaard, Nietzsche, and the later Heidegger.

I see that in the process of making whatever final judgments I can, I am intruding myself more and more openly into the argument, and I think that I ought to make my philosophical attitude explicit. Although I am politically and intellectually very unlike George Santayana, I share a trait with him that is both a philosophical bias and an imaginative openness: like him, I am irredeemably secular, but also like him, I have the greatest interest in the life of the imagination, and sometimes the greatest admiration for the imaginative and intellectual structures built on what I regard as transparently dogmatic, even intellectually absurd, foundations.

Such interest, admiration, and rejection extend to all the great philosophical systems I am acquainted with. Much that is admirable or useful—much that, without these systems, we should never see so clearly—can be salvaged from every one of them; but as systems meant to capture the whole truth and the truth alone, even if only by way of negation, they are invariably unconvincing and often deeply absurd—impressive castles of sand, exhilarating in their architecture and the sagacity that glitters on their walls here and there, but as sadly fragile to criticism as they are to time.

My conclusion is that both philosophy and religion are inevitable because we or our immediate neighbors need them, but that they both are always intellectually inadequate. Their intellectual inadequacy is not diminished by the emotional help they give or the social cohesion they maintain. They are what we have, but what we have is not enough.

The Ideal of an Absolute, Ineffable Unity Reflects the Intimate Unity of the Self

I return to the exalters and devaluers and their ideals. The exalters and many of the devaluers conceive an origin that appears logically inconceivable because it is an absolute unity that, all the same, embraces the variety of the world that we humans perceive and inhabit. Weak analogies for such a unity are available. The number *one* breaks into an infinity of fractions; but the unqualified metaphysical existence of numbers is not self-evident, they do not enjoy biological existence, they have no consciousness, and they do not pay homage to the *one* from which they proceed. To the nonmathematical, a seed or an egg, as I have mentioned, is a more impressive analogy, a small, tight unity out of which a loose, large, noisy, adventurous plurality can develop. The child grows within the mother and for a while after birth is nourished by her body, her warmth, her milk perhaps, her care, and her empathy. Although inadequate, these analogies have a richness we have far from exhausted in the study of genetics and embryology.

Something like this richness is hoped for and retrospectively imagined in family life. In the West, similar hope and imagination have nourished the romantics' dream of the love in which the completeness of the partners' unity is enhanced by the tension that overcomes their separateness. Such a unity in plurality is the recurrent dream of the musician, actor, dancer, acrobat, or lion tamer whose performance engages the audience so deeply that it breathes and moves in the unison that lasts a little beyond the end of the performance, that invigorates performer and audience alike with the depth of its mutuality, and that sometimes earns the performer—who is grateful for the life-giving attention of the audience—the grateful near-worship of its members. Something like this unity is found in the repeated experience of the person who sinks deeply into work, whether of body or thought (or meditation), and who is led by this work to others who engage in it, lose themselves in it, or profit from it. Such loss of self makes the self grow: the writer or scientist lost in work imagines the self enlarged by the closeness of all the others who lose themselves in this way or at least share in the work or its results.

These are all forms of actual or hoped-for closeness with others. But there is a more intimate form of closeness that plays a primary role in creating the ideal of intimacy. This is one's intimacy with oneself, in which one's constituents or fragments go variously in and out of consciousness and show that they belong together and apart. Remember Valéry's preoccupation, especially in his daily encounters with his notebooks and his self made of selves. As we see in the notebooks, Valéry experiences the internal *I*, his mind that speaks and by its speech recognizes itself as one among many objects, but that also recognizes itself as the source that is the space in which this object that is no object finds itself . Let me express Valéry's reaction in his own words:

> There is nothing more astonishing than this 'interior' speech, which is heard without any noise and is articulated without movement. Like a closed circuit. Everything comes to be explained and thrashed out in this circle similar to the snake biting its tail. Sometimes the ring is broken and emits the internal speech.[62]

As Valéry points out, this circle, whole and broken, though very familiar, is an interiority without real parallel in the rest of our experience. The circle of our consciousness is, as he says, a very full plurality. There are the momentary shifts in experience and indefinite possibilities of association. There are the memories and fragments of memory that return in response to anything of any sort like them, and especially emotions, because our memories ride on and are ridden by moods and emotions, with which they are as indissolubly united as are pictures with the pigments in which they are painted. Thoughts, perceptions, and sensations come and go, in and out of concordance with one another. Pains, hopes, imaginations, ambitions, appetites strong and weak; and the body shifts, attention wanders, sleep overwhelms, dreams and dreams of dreams appear. And all this inward experience is divided between *the witness*—as the Indian philosophers call it or him—and the object of the witnessing, and between these two and whatever is too wandering or vague to be considered either the subject or the object of consciousness. Plotinus, we may remember, finds a similar experience in his closeness to the Good.

Can all this be *you* or *I*, a single extraordinary though fluctuating and fragile unity of consciousness in full communion with what enters it from without—the world out there—or from within, the equally rich and unknown inner world that we know consciously only by its expected and unexpected entries and exits? Surely from this extraordinary and extraordinarily full and varied unity comes the notion of a great, perfect, perfectly conscious, richly divided, fully unified consciousness that is not only a world in itself but is the world itself, assuming the forms that consciousness assumes, and furnished with the infinite depth and enormous gratification of what it contains but in a sense creates within itself and so, by illusion, outside itself.

Aristotle had technical reasons for conceiving his god as thought thinking itself, but I doubt if he could have conceived this philosophers' ideal if he had not experienced its analogue—he was an extraordinarily thinking man thinking extraordinary thoughts.

Without the unique inwardness that each of us subjectively *is*, there would be no experience that, by analogy, would lead to the conception of Brahman, of Word, or of the One that is the Good; or that would lead to Nietzsche's inner conversations and his impatience with the externality of outward speech; or that would lead to Heidegger's clumsy romance with the eruption of emotive, poetic speech out of the nowhere that we might suppose to be his unconscious; or that would lead to Gadamer's romantically imagined dissolution of all great strangeness in the inwardness of truly inward reaching conversation; or that would lead to Derrida's search for the miracle of inward plenitude escaping through the cracks between the grimly domineering oppositions of concepts; or that would lead—if one stretches the idea of origin—to the conception of true infinites within other true infinites and to the set of all sets.

The experience of the rich inwardness of oneself is related outwardly to what we call *holism*. But holism, though it can play a constructive role in science, has often competed to its disadvantage with reductive analysis. The worlds that the learned build out of their analyses and accumulations of facts are creviced everywhere; too much necessarily escapes them—as it also escapes every form of holism. Something always escapes both analysis and synthesis, just as it escapes enumeration and escapes our conception of escaping.

The Truth!

How does one combine what we learn to grasp intellectually—science, philosophy, theology, or any intellectual enterprise to which we can set a name—with lyricism, or with humor, and, as well, with the title above, the shadow of a joke? How is the egocentricity of the individual's consciousness situated in relation to a world filled with other equally egocentric nodes, each with a demand for the understanding and empathy that only an infinitely selfless, totally altruistic bodhisattva could give? What can it mean to be an infinitely selfless ex-human being?

The truth is that we are made to be partial in every way. In the light of our past and present, the near-objectivity of the exact sciences appears very difficult, almost freakish; and every way of looking at the world, even the comprehensive, so-to-speak synesthetic ways of the richer, more hospitable philosophies and theologies, and even the structured emotivity of the arts, cannot and, I suppose, should not encompass everything we might hope them to. Tales of the kind we tell ourselves for our cosmic comfort's sake have grown in time to be profoundly deep, profoundly local expressions of our human condition. To compare them, too parochially, with a few recent Western novelists, these religious tales have grown to be more filled with moral indignation, droll eccentrics, theatrical denouements, and touching lads and ladies than Dickens; more pessimistically humorous and objectively compassionate than Chekhov; more carefully verbose in reliving the fictions of love and the ambiguities of sex than Proust; more religiously tragic, self-contentious, psychologically probing, and ethically passionate than Dostoyevski; more epically panoramic and loving, intuitive, and hating than Tolstoy; more starkly, realistically, comically nightmarish than Kafka; more interpenetratingly kaleidoscopic, pun-charged, disgrammatical, and zanily freighted with every-thing and everything else than Joyce—always more, to the extent that these and all other writers are single individuals whose wisdom is bounded by the brevity of their lives and the necessary narrowness of an individual's perspective. For the shortest (though long enough) merely literary proof of what I have said, consult the Mahabharata or Ramayana—together with their literary prolongations and commentaries. But I mean to go beyond such literary evidence and include religious traditions, among which I have chosen to explain only some that pertain to Krishna. And yet the tales for comfort, though enriched so extraordinarily far beyond an individual's span of life and imagination, are still limited by their nature as tales for comfort.

We know we are capable of small fractions of truth, and tale tellers or not, are always discovering who and what we are as we talk with others and with ourselves in any of the various human modes of expres-sion, including plain words. Deaf, we hear something all the same, and blind, we see something even with our blind eyes. And everything we discover and say truly, increases our knowledge and, in doing so, reveals new perspectives of ignorance, which allow us to discover and say again.

Such is the light in which I have learned to see ineffability. To stress the inadequacy of language, which is such an extraordinarily liberating invention, seems to me a sour way of showing gratitude to this power that allows us to experience so much of our rich inwardness, and that gives us so much of our ability to imagine what we do not experience immediately, and so much of our power to investigate and create. I'd much rather worship a god of speech than a god of silence. Speech, for all the complaints made of it, shows itself to be as flexible and as able to assume shapes as water. Not only does it take the shape of our indeter-minate and ambivalent desires, but—unlike formal logic—it is able to declare it own limits and, by the declaration itself, to hint what these limits are and where they end. After all, what does a declaration of ineffability declare? That there is an inchoate union between one's own ultimate worth and something half-else that continues and justifies this worth. This self–else is speakably sacred but not speakably questionable. So by ineffability we mean that everything conceivable can at least be hinted at in speech, but that this hint should not be expanded too explic-itly or spoken of in any way that invites depreciation. That we are able to say all this in a few formulaic words is a tribute to the subtlety that language confers on us.

Yet there is always the residue: what has not been said, what one has forgotten or cannot remember, what one has not conceived or con-ceived clearly, and what escapes because it is too delicate or quick. For

such reasons, we should speak not of ineffability but of the many ineffabilities—neurological, synesthetic, musical, logical, philosophical, and religious, personal, familial, and tribal, childish and adult, normal, abnormal, and outright pathological—that make our speech less regular and
more human. These ineffabilities are the demons (and maybe angels) of
incompleteness and incompletability. They are also our rest, after and
between speech, in silence, which derives its possible eloquence from
the speech that surrounds it. The gaps themselves of speech translate our
intermittancy into still another of its complex perfections.

We've come a long way together. I can't have finished what I want
to say, but for the while, I've said what I could.

Notes

Chapter 1. Psychological Prelude

1. Robinson, *Emily Dickinson*, p. 91 (Emily Dickinson, poem no. 811).

2. Johnson, *The Body in the Mind*, pp. 31, 126.

3. Friedman, "The Modification of Word Meaning by Nonverbal Cues."

4. Argyle, *Bodily Communication*, pp. 118–19, 107–8.

5. Ibid., pp. 108–10, chap. 10.

6. Ibid., pp. 145–47.

7. Ostwald, "Acoustic Methods in Psychiatry," p. 83.

8. Friedman, "The Modification of Word Meaning by Nonverbal Cues," pp. 61, 65.

9. Dascal, *Pragmatics*, pp. 89–90; Grice, *Studies in the Way of Words*; Levelt, *Speaking*, chap. 2.

10. Jackendoff, *Consciousness and the Computational Mind*, pp. 319–23. Shanon, "Why Do We (Sometimes) Think in Words?" p. 5. Shanon and Atlan, "Von Foerster's Theorem on Connectedness and Organisation," pp. 79–80.

11. Levelt, *Speaking*, pp. 22, 413.

12. Shanon, "Why Do We (Sometimes) Think in Words?"

13. Jackendoff, *Consciousness and the Computational Mind*, p. 321.

14. Singer, "Sampling Ongoing Consciousness," p. 328. Shanon and Atlan, "Von Ferster's Theorem on Connectedness and Organisation."

15. Scharfstein, *The Philosophers*, pp. 62–64.

16.   Einstein, *Ideas and Opinions*, pp. 25–26.

17.   Jansons, "A Personal View of Dyslexia," pp. 502–3.

18.   Ibid., pp. 504–5.

19.   Wittgenstein, *Zettel*, sections 328, 450.

20.   D. L. Hull, *Science as a Process*, p. 7.

21.   Chafe, "Some Reasons for Hesitating." p. 79; Argyle, *Bodily Communication*, p. 106.

22.   Leroi-Gourhan, *Les racines du monde*, p. 323; as quoted in Clifford, *The Predicament of Culture*, p. 124.

23.   Scollon, "The Machine Stops," pp. 24–25; Tannen, "Silence: Anything But"; Saunders, "Silence and Noise as Emotional Management Styles," pp. 180–81.

24.   Scollon, "The Machine Stops," p. 25; Saville-Troike, "The Place of Silence," pp. 12–13.

25.   NWoye, "Eloquent Silence Among the Igbo of Nigeria."

26.   Roland, *In Search of Self in India and Japan*, p. 82.

27.   Kafka, *The Complete Stories*, p. 431.

28.   Merleau-Ponty, *The Visible and the Invisible*, pp. 129, 179; as quoted in Dauenhauer, *Silence*, p. 115. See also Merleau-Ponty, *La prose du monde*.

29.   See Goodstein and Reinecker, "Factors Affecting Self-Disclosure"; Resnick and Amerikaner, "Self-Disclosure"; and Woods, ed., *Self-Disclosure*.

30.   Hill and Stull, "Gender and Self-Disclosure," p. 94.

31.   Hill and Stull, "Gender and Self-Disclosure," p. 82; Resnick and Amerikaner, *Encyclopedia of Clinical Assessment*, pp. 445–49.

32.   Berg, "Responsiveness and Self-Disclosure," pp. 124–26; Resnick and Amerikaner, "Self-Disclosure," pp. 445–49.

33.   Stokes, "The Relation of Loneliness and Self-Disclosure," pp. 177–79, 194–97; Carpenter, "The Relationship between Psychopathology and Self-Disclosure," pp. 223–24.

34.   Resnick and Amerikaner, "Self-Disclosure," p. 449.

35.   Stokes, "The Relation of Loneliness and Self-Disclosure," p. 179. Coates and Winston, "The Dilemma of Distress Disclosure," p. 230.

36.   Coates and Winston, "The Dilemma of Distress Disclosure," pp. 237–38, 249.

37. Hill and Stull, "Gender and Self-Disclosure," p. 83, 95.

38. Fitzpatrick, "Marriage and Self-Disclosure," pp. 150–52.

39. Nicholi, "The Therapist-Patient Relationship."

40. Ibid.

41. Spence, "Language in Psychotherapy"; Edelson, *Language and Interpretation in Psychoanalysis*, p. 23; Schafer, *The Analytic Attitude*; R. Chessik, *The Technique and Practice of Listening in Intensive Psychotherapy*.

42. Enelow, "The Silent Patient," pp. 153, 155–56.

43. Coltart, " 'Slouching towards Bethlehem,' " p. 195.

44. Ibid., p. 198.

45. Modell, "Affects and Their Non-Communication," pp. 259, 260, 261, 262, 265.

46. Kurtz, "On Silence."

47. Tsuang, Faraone, and Day, "Schizophrenic Disorders," esp. p. 263.

48. Rosenberg and Abbeduto, "Adult Schizophrenic Language."

49. Rosenbaum and Sonne, *The Language of Psychosis*, pp. 97, 11–12 (quoted).

50. For psychosis and philosophy see Scharfstein, *The Philosophers*, esp. pp. 262–79.

51. Loewald, *Sublimation*.

52. Schachtel, "On Memory and Childhood Amnesia," p. 192.

53. Ibid., pp. 197–98.

54. Parkin, *Memory and Amnesia*, pp. 169–71.

55. Salaman, "A Collection of Memories," pp. 54, 55.

56. Ibid., pp. 55–56, 59.

57. Ibid., p. 63.

58. Luborsky, "Recurrent Momentary Forgetting," p. 233.

59. Luria, *The Mind of a Mnemonist*, pp. 7–12.

60. Ibid., pp. 76, 85.

61. Ibid., pp. 64, 66.

62. Ibid., pp. 114–15, 120, 136, 157.

63. Rosenfeld, *The Invention of Memory,* pp. 163–66, 201–9; Parkin, *Memory and Amnesia,* pp. 40–41.

64. Rosenfeld, *The Invention of Memory,* p. 165; from Gloor et al., "The Role of the Limbic System," p. 140. Rosenfeld, *The Invention of Memory,* from S. Freud, "Inhibitions, Symptoms and Anxiety," *Standard Edition,* vol. 20, p. 120; and "Notes upon a Case of Obsessional Neurosis," *Standard Edition,* vol. 10, p. 196.

65. Parkin, *Memory and Amnesia,* pp. 48–49.

66. Evans, "Posthypnotic Amnesia."

67. Kolb, "Recovery of Memory and Repressed Fantasy," pp. 270–71.

68. Parkin, *Memory and Amnesia,* pp. 155–56.

69. Weiskrantz, "Some Contributions of Neuropsychology of Vision and Memory," p. 185; Schacter, McAndrews, and Moscovitch, "Acess to Consciousness," pp. 244–47.

70. Hirst and Gazzaniga, "Present and Future of Memory Research"; Springer and Deutsch, *Left Brain, Right Brain,* pp. 168–70; Weiskrantz, "Some Contributions of Neuropsychology of Vision and Memory"; Spelke, "The Origins of Physical Knowledge"; Schacter, McAndrews, and Moscovitch, "Access to Consciousness."

71. Gazzaniga, "The Dynamics of Cerebral Specialization," pp. 446–47. See also Gazzaniga and Smylie, "What Does Language Do for a Right Hemisphere?" pp. 200ff.

72. Gazzaniga and Smylie, "What Does Language Do for a Right Hemisphere?" pp. 207–8; Gazzaniga, "The Dynamics of Cerebral Specialization," pp. 446–47; Kertesz, "Cognitive Functions in Severe Aphasia," p. 491.

73. Bisiach, "Language without Thought," p. 481.

74. Editor's note in Weiskrantz, *Thought without Language,* p. 487.

75. Chary, "Aphasia in a Multilingual Society," pp. 194–96.

76. Lieberman, *Uniquely Human,* p. 85.

77. Goshen-Gottstein, *Recalled to Life,* p. 17.

78. Lieberman, *Uniquely Human,* pp. 27–28.

79. Young, "Functional Organization of Visual Recognition," pp. 94, 97. See also Mesulam, "Neural Substrates of Behavior"; Parkin, *Memory and Amnesia,*" p. 75; Blumstein, "Neurolinguistics."

80. Luria, *The Man with a Shattered World,* pp. 11–13.

81. Ibid., pp. 101–2, 105.

82. Hirst and Gazzaniga, "Present and Future of Memory Research," pp. 204–5; Parkin, *Memory and Amnesia,* pp. 88–100.

83. B. Shanon, "Remarks on the Modularity of Mind."

84. Mandler, "Problems and Direction in the Study of Consciousness," pp. 10–13.

85. Rosenthal, "The Wolf at the Door," p. 36.

86. Maurer and Maurer, *The World of the Newborn,* pp. 65–67.

87. Ibid., p. 197.

88. Ibid.

89. Cytowic, "Tasting Colors, Smelling Sounds." For details, the author refers to his forthcoming *Synesthesia: A Union of the Senses,* the publication details of which I do not know.

90. Snyder, *Drugs and the Brain,* pp. 180, 181. See also Cytowic, "Tasting Colors, Smelling Sounds," p. 36; Critchley, "Ecstatic and Synaesthetic Experiences during Musical Perception," p. 223.

91. Snyder, *Drugs and the Brain,* pp. 201–5.

92. Luria, *The Mind of a Mnemonist,* p. 27; Merriam, *The Anthropology of Music,* p. 87; Gregory, "Blindness, Recovery from."

93. Luria, *The Mind of a Mnemonist,* pp. 22–23.

94. Critchley, "Ecstatic and Synaesthetic Experiences during Musical Perception," p. 224.

95. Luria, *The Mind of a Mnemonist,* in order of pp. used, 25–26, 24, 25, 80–81, 77.

96. Critchley, "Ecstatic and Synaesthetic Experiences during Musical Perception," p. 221; Cytowic, "Tasting Colors, Smelling Sounds," p. 33.

97. Merriam, *The Anthropology of Music,* p. 93.

98. Baudelaire, *Oeuvres complètes,* notes pp. 839–47.

99. Poling, *Kandinsky's Teaching at the Bauhaus,* p. 48.

100. Griffiths, *Oliver Messiaen,* p. 203; Massin, *Messiaen,* p. 43.

101. Messiaen, *Recherches et expériences spirituelles,* p. 10, as quoted in Godwin, *Harmonies of Heaven and Earth,* p. 69.

102. On Amusia see Sidits, Marin, Benton, Critchley.

103. Treffert, *Extraordinary People,* pp. xxv–xxviii. See also Shuter-Dyson, "Musical Ability."

104. Ibid., p. 189.

105. Ibid., p. 190.

106. Ibid., pp. 32, 258–59.

107. Ibid., pp. 29–30, 161–63, 197–210, 221–23.

108. Springer and Deutsch, *Left Brain, Right Brain,* 171; Gardner, *Art, Mind, and Brain,* p. 329.

109. Sidits, "Music, Pitch Perception, and the Mechanisms of Cortical Hearing," pp. 93, 100–105, 107, 110. Gardner, *Art, Mind, and Brain,* pp. 329–30; Gardner, *Frames of Mind,* pp. 117–18.

110. Gardner, *Art, Mind, and Brain,* pp. 229–30; Gardner, *Frames of Mind,* p. 119; Marin, "Neurological Aspects of Musical Perception and Performance," pp. 465–69; Springer and Deutsch, *Left Brain, Right Brain,* pp. 170–71; Treffert, *Extraordinary People,* p. 234.

111. Stravinsky, *Poetics of Music,* p. 27.

112. Kundera, *The Art of the Novel,* pp. 97–88.

113. For deafness see: Bellugi; Evans and Falk; Kyle and Woll; Lane; Mindel and Vernon; Padden and Humphries; Rymer; Sacks.

114. Padden and Humphries, *Deaf in America,* p. 22. For the preceding part of the paragraph see Evans and Falk, *Learning to be Deaf,* p. 183; Padden and Humphries, *Deaf in America,* pp. 16–17.

115. Lane, *When the Mind Hears.*

116. Wilson, *Diderot* (referring to Diderot's "Letter on the Blind"), p. 122.

117. "Letter on the Blind," in Crocker, *Diderot's Selected Writings,* p. 18.

118. "Letter on the Blind," in Wilson, *Diderot,* p. 98; "Lettre sur les aveugles," in Diderot, *Oeuvres philosophiques,* pp. 89, 97–98.

119. Evans and Falk, *Learning to Be Deaf,* pp. xvii–xviii, 52.

120. Evans and Falk, *Learning to Be Deaf,* pp. 52, 83 (quoted); Sacks, *Seeing Voices,* pp. 41, 67.

121. Evans and Falk, *Learning to Be Deaf,* p. 50.

122. Ibid., p. 47.

123. Keller, *The Story of My Life*, pp. 14, 20–21 (quoted), 187 (quoted), 184.

124. Sacks, *Seeing Voices*, p. 56.

125. Evans and Falk, *Learning to Be Deaf*, p. 1; Kyle and Woll, *Sign Language*, p. 265.

126. Kyle and Woll, *Sign Language;* Evans and Falk, *Learning to Be Deaf*, p. 4; Bellugi, "The Acquisition of a Spatial Language," pp. 158–59; Padden and Humphries, *Deaf in America*, p. 7; and see Sacks, *Seeing Voices*, p. 88.

127. Kyle and Woll, *Sign Language*, pp. 28–29, 86–87.

128. Quigley and King, "The Language Development of Deaf Children and Youth," pp. 448–51; Kyle and Woll, *Sign Language*, pp. 202–205; Keller, *The Story of My Life*, p. 169.

129. Kyle and Woll, *Sign Language*, pp. 68–81; Sacks, *Seeing Voices*, p. 97.

130. Sacks, *Seeing Voices*, pp. 88–89, 100–101.

131. Padden and Humphries, *Deaf in America*, p. 106.

132. Ibid., p. 84.

133. Evans and Falk, *Learning to Be Deaf*, pp. 147, 150.

134. Sacks, *Hearing Voices*, pp. 97–99.

135. Padden and Humphries, *Deaf in America*, p. 99.

136. Ibid., pp. 93–96.

137. Sacks, *Hearing Voices*, pp. 7–8, note.

138. Bibliography: Fraiberg; Gregory, "Blindness, Recovery from"; Landau and Gleitman; Weiskrantz, "Some Contributions."

139. Fraiberg, "Parallel and Divergent Patterns," pp. 281, 288, 296.

140. Critchley, "Ecstatic and Synaesthetic Experiences during Musical Perception," p. 226.

141. Landau and Gleitman, *Language and Experience*, pp. viii, 20, 15.

142. Keller, *The Story of My Life*, p. 164.

143. "Letter to the Blind," in Crocker, *Diderot's Selected Writings*, p. 15.

144. J. M. Hull, *Touching the Rock*, p. 23.

145. Diderot, "Lettres sur les aveugles," in *Oeuvres*, p. 111.

146. Landau and Gleitman, *Language and Experience*, pp. 88–90.

147. Ibid., pp. 95–96.

148. Ibid., pp. 170, 172.

149. *The New Yorker,* December 19, 1988, pp. 66–67.

150. Landau and Gleitman, *Language and Experience*, pp. 172, 165.

151. Ibid., pp. 96–97.

152. J. M. Hull, *Touching the Rock*, pp. 25–27.

153. Weiskrantz, "Some Contributions of Neuropsychology," pp. 186–92.

154. J. M. Hull, *Touching the Rock*, pp. 217–18.

155. Sacks, *Seeing Voices*, p. 5.

Chapter 2. The Exaltation of Words

1. Eimas, "The Perception of Speech in Early Infancy."

2. Vygotsky, *Thought and Language*, p. 82; citing W. Stern, *Psychologie der fruehen Kindheit*, Leipzig, 1914, p. 108.

3. Stern, *The Interpersonal World of the Infant*, pp. 163–65, 170ff.

4. Coward and Raja, "Introduction to the Philosophy of the Grammarians," pp. 38–38.

5. For the epic see Pritchard, *Ancient Near Eastern Texts*, pp. 60–72, 501–503; Dalley, *Myths from Mesopotamia;* Jacobsen, *Treasures of Darkness.*

6. Dalley, *Myths from Mesopotamia*, pp. 235–37.

7. Ibid., p. 238.

8. Oppenheim, *Ancient Mesopotamia*, pp. 201–6.

9. Dalley, *Myths from Mesopotamia*, pp. 233–34.

10. Ibid., p. 250.

11. Ibid., p. 255.

12. Kramer, *The Sumerians*, pp. 115–16; Wolkenstein and Kramer, *Inanna*, pp. 147–48; Kramer and Maier, *Myths of Enki, The Crafty God*, pp. 38–56.

13. Jacobsen, *The Harps that Once*, pp. 151–57.

14. Kramer and Maier, *Myths of Enki, The Crafty God,* pp. 38–56.

15. Jacoben, *Treasures of Darkness,* pp. 135–43; she has so many functions that he equates her with infinite variety.

16. S. Langdom "Works (Sumerian and Babylonian)," and G. Foucart, "Names (Egyptian)," in J. Hastings, ed., *Encyclopaedia of Religion and Ethics. Theology of Memphis,* in Pritchard, *Ancient Near Eastern Texts,* p. 46. See also Staal, "Oriental Ideas on the Origin of Language," p. 6.

17. Ibid., pp. 1–6.

18. Jeremiah 23.29, Isaiah 55.11. See Boman, *Hebrew Thought Compared with Greek.*

19. Guthrie, *A History of Greek Philosophy,* vol. 5, pp. 25–31; Crombie, *An Examination of Plato's Doctrines,* vol. 2, pp. 376–78, 475–86.

20. C. Hansen, "Chinese Classical Ethics," pp. 69–73.

21. Confucius, *Confucian Analects,* trans. Legge.

22. From the works of Hsün Tzu (born ca. 310 B.C. and surviving to his late nineties or even a hundred), *pian* 22. The translation is from Elwin, "Was There a Transcendental Breakthrough in China," p. 348. For a different translation see Dubs, *The Works of Hsüntze,* p. 282.

23. Hall and Ames, *Thinking through Confucius,* p. 255.

24. Quoted in Fung, *A History of Chinese Philosophy,* vol. 2, pp. 85–86. See Bao, "Language and World View in Ancient China."

25. Creel, *Shen Pu-hai.* See also Dubs, *The Works of Hsüntze,* bk. 22, "On the Rectification of Names"; Hall and Ames, *Thinking through Confucius,* pp. 268–75; Harbsmeier, "Marginalia Sino-logica," esp. p. 141ff.; Schwartz, *The World of Thought in Ancient China,* pp. 91–93, 311–14, 337–39; Staal "Oriental Ideas on the Origin of Language," pp. 6–9.

26. Calame-Griaule, *Ethnologie et langage,* pp. 25, 33, 59, 69. The criticism of the Griaule school I am in particular referring to is that made by the Dutch anthropologist Walter van Beek. At the time I write this, his book on his research among the Dogon is about to appear.

27. Ibid., p. 24.

28. Ibid., pp. 26–27, 31, 94.

29. Ibid., pp. 363, 81, 102.

30. Sullivan, *Ichanchu's Drum,* pp. 253–55.

31. Ibid., pp. 267–68.

32. Ibid., pp. 268, 277.

33. Ibid., p. 277.

34. Ibid., pp. 285–87.

35. Bierhorst, *The Sacred Path*.

36. Witherspoon, *Language and Art in the Navajo Universe*, p. 76.

37. Ibid., p. 22.

38. Ibid., pp. 29–30, 35.

39. Ibid., p. 36.

40. Ibid., p. 31.

41. Ibid., pp. 31–32.

42. Ibid., p. 334.

43. Ibid., p. 60.

44. Arapura and Raja, "Speculative Elements in Vedic Literature," pp. 102–4; "La Parole," trans. Renou, *Hymns spéculatifs du Véda*, pp. 123–24; Edgerton, *The Beginnings of Indian Philosophy*, pp. 71–72; O'Flaherty, *The Rig Veda*, pp. 52–64.

45. Arapura and Raju, "Philosophical Elements in Vedic Literature," p. 102; Edgerton, *The Beginnings of Indian Philosophy*, pp. 58–59; O'Flaherty, *The Rig Veda*, pp. 61–62; Renou, *Les hymns spéculatifs du Véda*, pp. 71–73; Renou, "Les pouvoirs de la parole dans le Rigvéda," pp. 22–23; Staal, "Rigveda 10.71 on the Origin of Language."

46. Renou, "Les pouvoirs de la parole dans le Rigvéda"; see review by Thieme. Gonda, *The Vision of the Vedic Poets*.

47. Buitenen, "Aksara"; Padoux, *Recherches sur la symbolique*, chap. 1; Ruegg, "La spéculation linguistique dans le Veda," in *Contributions à l'histoire de la philosophie linguistique Indienne*, chap. 1.

48. Gonda, *The Vision of Vedic Poets*.

49. Hume, *The Thirteen Principal Upanishads*, pp. 87–88.

50. On Mantras in general, see Alper, *Mantra*.

51. Staal, "Vedic Mantras," pp. 71–82; Wheelock, "Mantra in Vedic and Tantric Ritual," pp. 117ff.

52. Staal, "Vedic Mantras," p. 95.

53. *Mandukya Upanishad*, in Hume, *The Thirteen Principal Upanishads*, pp. 391–92. See Deussen, *The Philosophy of the Upanishads*, pp. 390–91.

54. Hoens, "Transmission and Fundamental Constituents of the Practice," pp. 94, 101–102; from Padoux, *Recherches sur la symbolique*, pp. 51, 297.

55. Muller-Ortega, *The Triadic Heart of Siva*, p. 172. See Alper, "The Cosmos as Siva's Language-Game."

56. Scholem, *On the Kabbalah and Its Symbolism*, p. 36. See Idel, *Kabbalah*, pp. 97–103.

57. Idel, *Language, Torah, and Hermeneutics in Abraham Abulafia*, pp. 23–24.

58. Ibid., pp. 11–13, 1–2, 6, xv, 122–24. See also the "Introduction" in Alper, *Mantra*.

59. Coward, *Sphota Theory of Language*, pp. 34–42.

60. Matilal, *The Word and the World*, Part 1; Staal, "Oriental Ideas on the Origin of Language."

61. Matilal, *The Word and the World*, pp. 7–8. Staal, "Sanskrit Philosophy of Language," pp. 502–6, and "Oriental Ideas on the Origin of Language," pp. 9–11.

62. On Indian philosophy of language in general see: Arapura, Biardeau, Coward, Coward and Raja, Matilal, Ruegg ("Contributions"), Sastri, and Solomon. Matilal's *The Word and the World* is a lucid general introduction with a good many pages on Bhartrihari. Iyer's *Bhartrihari* is full and exact; his book *The Vakyapadia: Some Problems* is unfinished. In the beginning, I had only Biardeau's translation to work with. I often retranslated it, with some changes, into English. The result was then sometimes modified in the light of Iyer's translation or displaced by it. Pillai's translation, too, was useful. Aklujkar gives a fifty-page paraphrase.

63. Iyer, *The Vakyapadiya of Bhartrihari with the Vritti*, pp. xii–xv.

64. Iyer, *Bhartrihari*, pp. 153–54.

65. Ibid., pp. 153, 179.

66. Ibid., pp. 143–44; and Staal, "Sanskrit Philosophy of Language," pp. 509–14. The Neo-Vedantist philosopher Shankara was also opposed to the *sphota* doctrine. See Chakrabarti, "Sentence-Holism, Context-Principle and Connected-Designation *Anvitabhidhana*," where the Mimamsa and Nyaya positions are compared with the sentence-holism of Bhartrihari, Quine, and others. For the

word-sentence controversy in Indian thought, see Coward and Raja, "Introduction to the Philosophy of the Grammarians," pp. 63–97; and Matilal, *The Word and the World,* pp. 106–19.

67. Matilal, *The Word and the World,* pp. 8–10, 55–61; Staal, "Sanskrit Philosophy of Grammar," p. 508.

68. Iyer, *Bhartrihari,* p. 62.

69. Ibid., pp. 192–93. See also Herzberger, *Bhartrihari and the Buddhists,* chap. 2.

70. Iyer, *Bhartrihari,* p. 86.

71. Ibid., pp. 84–87.

72. Chomsky, *Language and the Problems of Knowledge,* pp. 93, 98.

73. Ibid.

74. Iyer, *Bhartrihari,* pp. 89–92.

75. Matilal, *The Word and the World,* p. 134.

76. Iyer, *Bhartrihari,* p. 100.

77. Herzberger, *Bhartrihari and the Buddhists,* p. 100; Ruegg, *Contributions à l'histoire de la philosophie linguistique Indienne,* p. 67.

78. Sastri, *The Philosophy of Word and Meaning,* p. 21.

79. Coward and Raja, "Introduction to the Philosophy of the Grammarians," pp. 44–50.

80. Ibid., pp. 138–46.

81. Distinctions are distinctions. The final state is bliss according to one commentator, but absolute consciousness according to another. See Sastri, *The Philosophy of Word and Meaning,* pp. 9–12.

82. Ibid., pp. 38–44.

83. Iyer, *The Vakyapadiya of Bhartrihari,* chap. 3. pt. 2.

84. Ibid., pp. 108–12; Sastri, *The Philosophy of Word and Meaning,* pp. 13–21, 26–44.

85. Sastri, *The Philosophy of Word and Meaning,* pp. 27–28; Herzberger, *Bhartrihari and the Buddhists.*

86. See earlier references and Iyer, *Bhartrihari,* p. 134; Sastri, *Philosophy of Word and Meaning,* pp. 1–25.

87.   Robins, *A Short History of Linguistics*, p. 175.

88.   Aarsleff, *From Locke to Saussure*, p. 306. See also Chakrabarti, "Sentence-Holism, Context-Principle and Connectedness-Designation."

89.   Frege, *Foundations of Arithmetic*, p. x; see also Frege, *Kleine Schriften*, ed. I. Angeli, p. 236—both quoted in Sluga, *Gottlob Frege*, p. 94. As Sluga notes on p. 133, Michael Dummett holds that about 1890 Frege abandoned the doctrine that words have meaning only in the context of a proposition. Sluga nevertheless thinks Frege is unlikely to have abandoned the doctrine (pp. 97, 134). Matilal, *The Word and the World*, pp. 115, 119, compares Frege's opposition to 'epistemological atomism' to that of Prabhakara (ca. A.D. 670), the dominanat figure in one of the two schools of Mimamsa.

90.   Robins, *A Short History of Linguistics*, p. 139 (quoted); Luria, *Language and Cognition*, p. 116.

91.   Quine, *Theories and Things*, pp. 69–70.

92.   Ruegg, *Contributions à l'histoire de la philosophie linguistique Indienne*, pp. 60–63.

93.   Konopacki, *The Descent into Words*, pp. 78–79.

94.   Ibid., pp. 98, 103 (quoted), 55 (quoted).

95.   Rosen, *The Limits of Analysis*, p. 232.

96.   Gadamer, *Truth and Method*, p. 268.

97.   Ibid., p. 268.

98.   Ibid., p. 362.

99.   Ibid., p. 363.

100.   Ibid., pp. 352, 363 (quoted), 364–65.

101.   Ibid., pp. 386 (quoted), 408 (quoted).

102.   Ibid., pp. 410, 411.

103.   Ibid., pp. 415–16.

104.   See his note on p. 118 of W. Dilthey, *Grundriss der allgemeinen Geschichte der Philosophie*. I owe this information to Prof. Frits Staal.

105.   See Iyer, *The Vakyapadia of Bhartrihari Chapter 1*, pp. 119–19 (*Vakyapadiya* 1.130–131); and Iyer, *The Vakyapaidia: Some Problems*, pp. 48–49.

106.   Gadamer, *Truth and Method*, pp. 124, 379–83 (382 quoted), 393, 395, 439 (quoted), 459.

107. Ibid., p. 431.

Chapter 3. The Devaluation of Words

1. Sextus Empiricus, *Against the Schoolmasters* 7.65, reporting on Gorgias, *On the Nonexistent or On Nature*, in Sprague, *The Older Sophists*, pp. 42–46; *Sextus Empiricus*, vol. 1, pp. 41–45; Kerford, *The Sophistic Movement*, pp. 78–84, 93–100.

2. *Sextus Empiricus*, vol. 1, pp. 217–83; vol. 2, pp. 307–11; vol. 4, pp. 25–153. Brunschwig, "Proof Defined."

3. Jayatilleke, *Early Buddhist Theory of Knowledge*, pp. 310–32.

4. Ibid., pp. 362–63, 366. Matilal, *Logical and Ethical Issues of Religious Belief*, pp. 105–109.

5. Matilal, *Logical and Ethical Issues of Religious Belief*, pp. 95–107; Matilal, *Epistemology, Logic, and Grammar in Indian Philosophical Analysis*, pp. 34–46.

6. Herzberger, *Bhartrihari and the Buddhists*, esp. chap. 3.

7. In general see Fenner, Hayes, Huntington, Lindtner, Lopez, Nagao, Ruegg, Tuck, and Williams.

8. Lindtner, *Nagarjuniana*, p. 153. See pp. 121–27 for Lindtner's answer to doubts on the authenticity of this text.

9. Lindtner, "Atisa's Introduction to the Two Truths, and Its Sources," pp. 186, 187.

10. Ruegg, "Does the Madhyamika Have a Philosophical Thesis?" Siderits, "Nagarjuna as Anti-Realist."

11. Horn, *A Natural History of Negation*, pp. 60–75.

12. Nagao, *The Foundational Standpoint of Madhyamika Philosophy*, p. 152, note 8.

13. Ibid., p. 142.

14. R. M. Gimello, doctoral dissertation, quoted in Huntington, The *Emptiness of Emptiness*, p. 31.

15. Nagao, *The Foundational Standpoint of Madhyamika Philosophy*, p. 67.

16. Lobsang, "What is Non-Existent and What is Remanent in Sunyata," p. 90.

17. Hayes, *Dignaga and the Interpretation of Signs,* p. 108.

18. Siderits, "The Madhyamika Critique of Epistemology, II." On the obvious tendency of Western scholars to interpret Nagarjuna in keeping with whatever philosophy is in favor at the time, see Tuck, *Comparative Philosophy and the Philosophy of Scholarship* and, for a later example, P. Williams, "On the Interpretation of Madhyamaka Thought," a review of Huntington and Wangchen, *The Emptiness of Emptiness.* Oetke, "Remarks on the Interpretation of Nagarjuna's Philosophy," p. 322, hopes that in the future "scholars will attach more importance to transparency in establishing interpretational hypotheses in order that their basis, their explanatory scope and their limitations can be clearly discerned."

19. King, *Theravada Meditation,* pp. 16, 90, 108–9.

20. Buddhaghosa, *The Path of Purification,* pp. 127–28 (4.14–16).

21. Ibid., pp. 129–31 (4.31–33).

22. Ibid., p. 150 (4.98).

23. Ibid., p. 163 (4.146).

24. Ibid., pp. 165 (4.152), 165–69 (4.153–75).

25. E.g., *Middle Length Sayings,* vol. 1, pp. 151–53, 260–61; Buddhaghosa, *The Path of Purification,* pp. 354–71 (chap. 10). See also King, *Theravada Meditation,* chap. 3; Griffiths, *On Being Mindless,* chap. 1.

26. King, *Theravada Meditation,* chap. 6.

27. Gomez, "Purifying Gold," p. 99.

28. Ibid., p. 108.

29. Ibid., pp. 84, 104.

30. Klein, *Knowledge and Liberation,* pp. 16–17.

31. Klein, *Knowledge and Liberation,* pp. 16 (quoted), 17 (quoted).

32. In addition to the sources I will note below, I have used: Ahern, Ch'en Ky-ying, Graham, Harbsmeier, Rump, Schen, Schwartz.

33. Lau, *Tao Te Ching,* pp. 133–41. For a reconstruction of the origins of the legend, see Graham, "The Origins of the Legend of Lao Tan" in his *Studies in Chinese Philosophy and Philosophical Literature.* The quoted translation is from p. 122; but the occupation assigned to Lao Tzu of *shou-ts'ang shih* means, more simply, *keeper of archives* or *archivist.* The historian Ssu-ma Ch'ien, who gives this information, elsewhere says that the meaning is *keeper (curator) of books.*

34. Lau, *Tao Te Ching*, p. 3.

35. Ibid., p. 267. See also Henricks, *Lao Tzu: Te-Tao Ching*, who translates (p. 188) "As for the Way, the Way that can be spoken of is not the constant Way; / As for names, the name that can be named is not the constant name."

36. Ibid., bk. 1, chaps. 52, 4, 62, 28, 32, 35.

37. Chan *The Way of Lao Tzu*, pp. 6–7.

38. Lau, *Tao Te Ching*, p. 37 (chap. 25).

39. Ibid., pp. 21–23 (chap. 15).

40. Ibid., p. 191 (chap. 14). See also Chan, The Way of Lao Tzu, pp. 7–8.

41. Liao, *The Complete Works of Han Fei Tzu*, pp. 192–193.

42. Ibid., pp. 193, 95; Chan, *The Way of Lao Tzu*, p. 8.

43. Lao, *Tao Te Ching*, pp. 69–70 (chap. 48), 5 (chap. 2).

44. Roth, "Who Compiled the *Chuang Tzu*"; and Graham, "Reflections and Replies," pp. 279–83.

45. Graham, trans., Chuang Tzu: *The Seven Inner Chapters*, p. 53 (Chuang Tzu, ch. 2).

46. Hansen, "A Tao of Tao in Chuang-tzu," pp. 44, 37, 45; Graham, *Chuang Tzu*, p. 52.

47. Hansen, "A Tao of Tao in Chuang-tzu," pp. 46–47; Graham, *Chuang Tzu*, pp. 52–53.

48. Graham, trans., *Chuang Tzu*, pp. 53, 54–55, 60; Legge, *The Texts of Taoism*, pp. 195–96.

49. Hansen, "A Tao of Tao in Chuang-tzu," p. 49; Graham, *Chuang Tzu*, p. 56.

50. Graham, trans., *Chuang Tzu*, p. 57. See Legge, *The Texts of Taoism*, pp. 55–57.

51. Watson, *The Complete Works of Chuang Tzu*, p. 46. See Graham, *Chuang Tzu*, p. 58; Legge, *The Texts of Taoism*, p. 192.

52. Dumoulin, *Zen Buddhism*, vol. 1, chap. 7.

53. Ibid., pp. 172–73.

54. Izutsu, "Sense and Nonsense in Zen Buddhism," pp. 195–96, 214.

55. Dumoulin, *Zen Enlightenment*, pp. 139, 142–47.

56. Ibid., pp. 144–46, 150–51 (quoted).

57. Watson, "Zen Poetry," p. 115.

58. Lynn, "The Sudden and the Gradual in Chinese Poetry Criticism," pp. 386, 393.

59. Ibid., p. 411.

60. Watson, "Zen Poetry," pp. 113–14.

61. Ibid., p. 118.

62. Kierkegaard, *The Journals of Søren Kierkegaard*, entries 562–63 (from the description by Israel Levin, Kierkegaard's secretary).

63. Ibid., entry 42 (March 1836).

64. Ibid., entry 155 (September 4, 1837).

65. Ibid., entry 42 (March 1836). Quotation as translated in Malantschuk, *Kierkegaard's Thought*, p. 38.

66. *Søren Kierkegaard's Journals and Papers*, vol. 6, entry 6883. See also *The Journals of Søren Kierkegaard*, entry 42.

67. *The Journals of Søren Kierkegaard*, entry 130 (1837).

68. Kierkegaard, *Journal, Extraits*, 1854–1855, pp. 244–46 (1854).

69. Kierkegaard, *Philosophical Fragments*, p. 29.

70. Ibid., p. 39.

71. Ibid., pp. 40 (quoted), 44 (quoted).

72. Ibid., p. 41.

73. Ibid., pp. 47, 50, 53 (quoted).

74. This summary is influenced by the presentation in Magee, *The Philosophy of Schopenhauer*, pp. 137–39.

75. Schopenhauer, *On the Fourfold Root of the Principle of Sufficient Reason*, pp. 146–47; Schopenhauer, *The World as Will and Representation*, vol. 1, sec. 10 (p. 55).

76. Schopenhauer, *The World as Will and Representation*, vol. 2, chap. 7 (pp. 74, 75, 77).

77. Ibid., vol. 1, p. 196.

78. Ibid., pp. 197–98.

79.   Wheeler, *German Aesthetic and Literary Criticism*, p. 110.

80.   Schelling, *The Philosophy of Art*, xxiv (quoted from Schelling's *System of Transcendental Idealism*).

81.   Chissel, *Schumann*, p. 80; Cardinal, *German Romantics in Context*, pp. 43–44.

82.   Schopenhauer, *The World as Will and Representation*, vol. 1, sec. 52, p. 250. See also Budd, *Music and the Emotions*, p. 86–96.

83.   Schopenhauer, *The World as Will and Representation*, vol. 1, p. 261. See also Budd, *Music and the Emotions*, p. 92.

84.   Ibid., p. 264.

85.   Ibid., chap. 39, p. 448.

86.   E.g., *The Birth of Tragedy*, sec. 66, as translated in Nietzsche, *Basic Writings of Nietzsche*, pp. 101–3.

87.   *The Birth of Tragedy*, secs. 24, 25, in Nietzsche, *Basic Writings*, pp. 139–43 (141 quoted).

88.   Nietzsche, *The Will to Power*, sec. 853, p. 452. See also Schacht, *Nietzsche*, chap. 8.

89.   Nietzsche, *The Will to Power*, sec. 801, p. 428; *Götzendämmerung*, ("Sprüche und Pfeile," 33), p. 58.

90.   Letter to Mathilde Wesendoncke, December 1, 1858; in Wagner, *Selected Letters of Richard Wagner*, pp. 497–98. See also letter to her of December 1, 1858.

91.   Dahlhaus, *Schönberg and the New Music*, p. 85; Gartenberg, *Mahler*, pp. 9, 41; Plantinga, *Romantic Music*, p. 453.

92.   Dahlhaus, *Schoenberg and the New Music*, pp. 81, 82, 87, 95, 83.

93.   Nietzsche, "On Truth and Lies in a Nonmoral Sense," in Brezeale, *Philosophy and Truth*, p. 83.

94.   Ibid.

95.   Ibid., pp. 86–88, 97 "Introduction" p. xxxix. See also Nietzsche, *The Birth of Tragedy*, sec. 15.

96.   Nietzsche, *Human All Too Human*, sec. 11 (p. 16).

97.   Lampert, *Nietzsche's Teaching*, pp. 186–244; Shapiro, *Nietzschean Narratives*, pp. 71–96.

98. Ibid., p. 296.

99. Ibid., p. 297, 298.

100. Nietzsche, *Zarathustra*, p. 329.

101. Ibid., p. 332.

102. Ibid., pp. 336 (quoted), 343 (quoted).

103. Ibid., pp. 408, 409.

104. Nietzsche, *The Will to Power*, secs. 516, 517 (pp. 279–80); sec. 481 (p. 267); sec. 481 (p. 267); sec. 477 (p. 263) (quoted).

105. Halbfass, *India and Europe*, pp. 105–20.

106. Nietzsche, *The Will to Power*, sec. 154 (pp. 95–96); sec. 580 (p. 312). See Mistry, *Nietzsche and Buddhism*, esp. pp. 12–18, and Halbfass, *India and Europe*, pp. 124–28.

107. McGuiness, *Wittgenstein*, pp. 39, 253.

108. Wittgenstein, *Culture and Value*, p. 36e. Weiner, *The Ill-Will against Time*, p. 2.

109. This applies to the sections of the Tractatus numbered 5.61 to 5.641, and 6.362 to 7. See Hacker, *Insight and Illusion*, pp. 87–100; Weiner, *The Ill-Will against Time, passim*.

110. Wittgenstein, *Notebooks 1914–16*, p. 80.

111. Weiner, *The Ill-Will against Time*, pp. 79–110.

112. Ibid., pp. 61–67.

113. Engelmann, *Letters from Ludwig Wittgenstein*, pp. 82–84.

114. Wittgenstein, *Culture and Value*, p. 70e (1948).

115. Schopenhauer, *Parerga and Paralipomena*, p. 49.

116. Schopenhauer, *The World as Will and Representation*, vol. 2, chap. 7 (p. 80).

117. Pillai, *The Vakyapadia* 2.38e (p. 45).

118. *The Middle Length Sayings* (*Mahajhma-Nikaya*), 1.134–35 (p. 173).

119. Chang, *Original Teachings of Ch'an Buddhism*, p. 41.

120. Schopenhauer, *The World as Will and Representation*, vol. 1, p. 5.

121. Ibid., vol. 2, p. 287.

122. Weiner, *The Ill-Will against Time*, pp. 118–19.

123. Ibid., pp. 120–25.

124. Engelmann, *Letters from Ludwig Wittgenstein*, p. 7.

125. Wittgenstein, *Culture and Value*, p. 10e.

126. Pears, *The False Prison*, vol. 2, pp. 266–67.

127. Wittgenstein, *Culture and Value*, p. 792. For his change of view see Wittgenstein, *Philosophical Investigations*, p. 217; Budd, *Wittgenstein's Philosophy of Psychology*, pp. 143–44.

128. Mehta, *The Philosophy of Martin Heidegger*, pp. 144–47, 245–48; Pöggeler, *Martin Heidegger's Path of Thinking*, pp. 162–63; Seidel, *Martin Heidegger and the Pre-Socratics*, pp. 30–46.

129. Heidegger, *Poetry, Language, Thought*, pp. 72, 189 (quoted).

130. Heidegger, *On the Way to Language*, p. 59.

131. Derrida, Of Spirit, pp. 70–72; Pöggeler, *Martin Heidegger's Path of Thinking*, p. 226; Seidel, *Martin Heidegger and the Pre-Socratics*, pp. 131–32.

132. Parkes, "Thoughts on the Way," pp. 105–106.

133. Chang, *Original Teachings of Ch'an Buddhism*, p. 97.

134. Hsiao, Heidegger and Our Translation of the *Tao Te Ching*," pp. 93, 97–98.

135. Ott, *Martin Heidegger*, p. 322, 326. Pöggeler, "West-East Dialogue," pp. 51–52, speaks of a breakdown in December 1945, during denazification proceedings, as a result of which Heidegger "had to be taken to a sanatorium for three weeks." On Gebsattel see Speigelberg, *Phenomenology in Psychology and Psychiatry*, pp. 249–59.

136. Heidegger's lecture of 1949, "Insight into That Which Is," as summarized in Pöggeler, "West-East Dialogue," pp. 61–61. Compare Lao Tzu, chap. 11. Heidegger, "On the Way to Language," p. 92 (quoted); for comment see Bruns, *Heidegger's Estrangements*, pp. 140–42.

137. Yuasa, "The Encounter of Modern Japanese Philosophy with Heidegger."

138. Pöggeler, "West-East Dialogue," pp. 50, 57–58; Heidegger, *On the Way to Language*, p. 199. For a brief commentary on the lecture, see Parkes, "Afterwards—Language."

139. Heidegger, *On the Way to Language*, p. 13.

140. Ibid., pp. 51–53.

141. Kotoh, "Language and Silence," p. 206.

142. Derrida, *Writing and Difference*, pp. 241, 191 (quoted). Artaud, *Le théâtre et son double*. See also Esslin, *Artaud*.

143. Wolosky, "Samuel Beckett's Figural Evasions," pp. 180 (quoting *U* (sic!), p. 390), 181 (quoting *U*, p. 393), 183 (quoting *U*, p. 183).

144. Celan, *Last Poems*, 210.

145. K. Washburn, "Introduction" to Celan, *Last Poems*, viii, ix, xxi, xxviii.

146. K. Washburn, "Introduction" to Celan, *Last Poems*, pp. xxx, xxxi. For an unfavorable assessment of Celan's poetry see Seymour-Smith, *Guide to Modern World Literature*, pp. 660–61, 665–67.

147. Ott, *Martin Heidegger*, pp. 341–42; Pöggeler, "West-East Dialogue," p. 75.

148. Derrida, *Positions*, p. 11; Habermas, *The Philosophical Discourse of Modernity*, pp. 162, 183–84.

149. Derrida, *Margins of Philosophy*, p. 27.

150. Ibid., p. 301.

151. Ibid., pp. 305, 17–18.

152. Derrida, *Writing and Difference*, p. 198.

153. Derrida, *Margins of Philosophy*, pp. 20–21.

154. Quoted in Derrida, *Margins of Philosophy*, p. 127.

155. Ibid., p. 287.

156. Ibid., p. 288, from Valéry, *Cahiers* 22, p. 304, 1939; Valéry's italics.

157. Ibid., pp. 189 (from Valéry, *Cahiers* 7, p. 615, 1920), 290.

158. Derrida, *Writing and Difference*, pp. 174–75.

159. Ibid., p. 194.

160. Ibid.

161. Derrida, *Margins of Philosophy*, p. 8.

162. Derrida, *Positions*, p. 12.

163. Ibid., p. 14.

164. Derrida, *Margins of Philosophy*, p. 6.

165. Bruns, *Heidegger's Estrangements*, pp. 208–211, note 5 (citing Derrida, *Psyché: Inventions de l'autre*, Paris, 1987, pp. 535–95).

166. Derrida, *Margins of Philosophy*, pp. 7, 26.

167. Derrida, *Positions*, p. 49.

168. See Cheng, "A Taoist Interpretation of 'Differance' in Derrida"; Chien, " 'Theft's Way': A Comparative Study of Chuang Tzu's Tao and Derridean Trace"; Odin, "Derrida and the Decentered Universe of Chan/Zen Buddhism"; and Magliola, "Differentialism in Chinese *Ch'an* and French Deconstruction."

169. Rorty, "From Ironist Theory to Private Allusions: Derrida," p. 137.

170. Streng, *Emptiness*, pp. 142–44.

171. Williams, *Mahayana Philosophy*, pp. 62–63.

Chapter 4. Reasons behind Reasons for Ineffability

1.   Coffa, *The Semantic Tradition from Kant to Carnap*, p. 3.

2.   Anyone seriously skeptical of my evaluation is invited to test it by sampling the following literature: Potter, ed., *The Tradition of Nyay-Vaisesika up to Gangesa* (for an introductory discussion of the instruments of valid judgment *[pramana]*, see pp. 154–78); Chatterjee, *The Nyaya Theory of Knowledge*; Matilal, *Perception*; and Solomon, *Indian Dialectics*.

3.   For an untechnical but fairly elaborate defense of the introduction of psychological considerations into philosophy, see Scharfstein, *The Philosophers*.

4.   There of course have been more than a few attempts to cross the boundaries. Yet in the recent *Investigating Psychology: Sciences of the Mind after Wittgenstein*, edited by John Hyman, a number of articles make no reference or almost no reference to any work by psychologists.

5.   Albers and Alexanderson, *Mathematical People*, pp. 126–27.

6.   For a discussion of similarity and difference, especially in relation to context and the similarities and differences between cultures, see Scharfstein, *The Dilemma of Context*. The problem of biological classification is dealt with knowledgeably in D. L. Hull, *The Metaphysics of Evolution*.

7.   Ryle, *The Concept of Mind*, p. 8.

8.   Lindberg, *Theories of Vision from Al-Kindi to Kepler*, pp. 1–9.

9.   Sorabji, *Time, Creation and the Continuum*, pp. 145–46, drawing on Aristotle's *De Anima* and *De Memoria*.

10.   For Hsün Tzu and the Leglists, see Hsiao, *A History of Chinese Political Thought*, chaps. 3, 6, 7. The most careful study of Hsün Tzu is Knoblock, *Xunzi—*

only two of the three planned volumes have been issued so far. For the *Arthashastra,* as for Indian political thought in general, see Ghoshal, *A History of Indian Political Ideas,* chaps. 5–7.

11. Urbach, *The Sages,* vol. 1, p. 118. See also pp. 301–302.

12. Baldick, *Mystical Islam,* pp. 46–49.

13. See Pelikan, *The Emergence of the Catholic Tradition,* pp. 97–108 (p. 102 quoted).

14. Sinha, *Indian Psychology,* vol. 1, ch. 17, esp. pp. 363–65.

15. Ibid., pp. 367–71.

16. Jaini, *The Jaina Path of Purification,* chap. 1.

17. Jacobi, *The Jaina Sutras,* pp. 187–88 (*Sutrakritanga* 6.6).

18. See the careful account in Saunders, *Plato's Penal Code,* pp. 301–318.

19. For translations I have used Armstrong for Plotinus's *Enneads,* Dodds for Proclus's *Elements of Theology,* Saffrey and Westrinck for Proclus's *Platonic Theology* (*Théologie platonicienne*), and Morrow and Dillon for *Proclus Commentary on Plato's* Parmenides. Expositions of Neoplatonism used are those of Bussanich, Charles-Saget, and Lloyd.

20. Wallis, *Neoplatonism,* pp. 18, 54, 123; O'Meara, *Pythagoras Revived,* p. 167; Lloyd, *The Anatomy of Neoplatonism,* pp. 68–70; and especially Charles-Saget, *L'Architecture du divin,* p. 100, 303, 310, 317.

21. Proclus, *Elements of Theology,* pp. 3–7; Proclus, *Théologie platonicienne,* bk. 2, chap. 1.

22. Proclus, *Elements of Theology,* p. 5.

23. Proclus, *Elements of Theology,* p. 17.

24. Bussanich, *The One and Its Relation to Intellect in Plotinus,* p. 141.

25. Lloyd, "Plotinus on the Genesis," p. 179.

26. See Bussanich.

27. Bussanich, *The One and Its Relation to Intellect in Plotinus,* pp. 97–98, citing *Enneads* (3.2.17; 5.1.12; 6.4.12; 4.3.18).

28. Ibid., p. 5, citing H.-R. Schwyzer.

29. *Proclus Commentary on Plato's* Parmenides, trans. Morrow and Dillon, p. 427.

30. Hopkins, *Nicholas of Cusa on Learned Ignorance*, p. 51; from Nicholas of Cusa, *Learned Ignorance* 1.1.

31. In general: A. W. Moore, *The Infinite*.

32. Dauben, *Georg Cantor*, p. 245.

33. For a clear, simple exposition of the difficulty see Moore, *The Infinite*, pp. 147–51.

34. Graham, trans., *Chuang Tzu*, p. 56 (Chuang Tzu, ch. 2).

35. Dauben, *Georg Cantor*, p. 243.

36. Ibid., p. 123.

37. Ibid., pp. 122–128, 228–29, 241–47.

38. Wang, *Reflections on Kurt Gödel*, pp. 193–94.

39. Ibid., pp. 191, 128; Gödel, "Russell's Mathematical Logic," in Benaceraff and Putnam, eds., *Philosophy of Mathematics*, p. 456.

40. Wang, *Reflections on Kurt Gödel*, p. 188. See also "Gödel's Life and Works," in Gödel, *Collected Works*. For a clear overview see A.W. Moore, *The Infinite*.

41. Gödel, *Collected Works*, pp. 30–32 (32 quoted).

42. Ibid., pp. 192, 196.

43. Ibid., pp. 164–65, 192.

44. Dauben, *Georg Cantor*, pp. 271–99.

45. Wang, *Reflections on Kurt Gödel*, p. 196.

46. R. Gödel, "History of the Gödel Family," p. 27.

47. Wang, *Recollections of Kurt Gödel*, p. 106.

48. Title lecture in Putnam, *Realism with a Human Face*. In comparing languages with transfinites, Langendoen and Postal, *The Vastness of Natural Languages*, pp. vi–viii, maintain that the collection of sentences comprising a natural language has a magnitude beyond that of transfinites and strictly parallel to that of the collection of all sets, which itself has no fixed magnitude at all. Matilal, *The Word and the World*, pp. 144–47, compares the contemporary principle of expressibility or effability (whatever can be thought or meant can be said) with Bhartrihari's even more radical view that cognition and speech are in essence identical.

49. A. W. Moore, *The Infinite*, chap. 14.

50. Hintikka and Hintikka, *Investigating Wittgenstein*, p. 19. The quotation, from a manuscript, comes from Wittgenstein's early middle period.

51. See Dascal, *Pragmatics and the Philosophy of Mind*, p. 89.

52. For similar views see Jackendoff, *Consciousness and the Computational Mind*, pp. 321–25.

53. For general introductions, see Barrow, *The World within the World;* Horgan, "Universal Truths"; Overbye, *Lonely Hearts of the Cosmos;* and Lightman and Brawer, *Origins,* especially its clear beginning chapter, "Introduction to Modern Cosmology."

54. Bruce and Wallace, "Critical Point Phenomena."

55. Grünbaum, "The Pseudo-Problem of Creation in Physical Cosmology," pp. 389–93.

56. Guth and Steinhardt, "The Inflationary Universe," pp. 52–53; Grünbaum, "The Pseudo-Problem of Creation in Physical Cosmology," pp. 391–92; Munitz, *Cosmic Understanding,* pp. 129–36. On quantum cosmology in general, see Barrow, *Theories of Everything;* Overbye, *Lonely Hearts of the Cosmos,* chap. 20; Hawking, "The Edge of Spacetime"; and Halliwell, "Quantum Cosmology and the Creation of the Universe."

57. Davies, *The Cosmic Blueprint,* p. 128; Grünbaum, "The Pseudo-Problem of Creation in Physical Cosmology," pp. 390–93; Hawking, "The Edge of Spacetime," pp. 65–66, 68–69.

58. There is a clear, simple, and still up-to-date account in Lederman and Schramm, *From Quarks to the Cosmos,* pp. 159–87. For the successive states of nuclear matter under different degrees of extreme pressure and temperature, see Gutbrod and Stöcker, "The Nuclear Equation of State."

59. Davies, *The Cosmic Blueprint,* p. 125.

60. Georgi, "Grand Unified Theories," p. 144.

61. Guth and Steinhardt, "The Inflationary Universe," p. 35.

62. George, "A Flaw in the Universal Mirror"; Georgi, "Grand Unified Theories," pp. 145.

63. Lederman and Schramm, *From Quarks to the Cosmos,* pp. 174–78; Vilenkin, "Cosmic Strings"; Lightman and Brawer, *Origins,* p. 27.

64. Gulkis et al., *The Cosmic Background Radiation,* pp. 8–9. See also Joseph Silk, in Lightman and Brawer, *Origins,* p. 197, who is made uneasy (in 1988) by "possible distortions in the microwave background."

65.   Halliwell, "Quantum Cosmology and the Creation of the Universe, p. 29.

66.   Guth and Steinhardt, "The Inflationary Universe," p. 41–44, 45–53; Rees, "Origin of the Universe," pp. 21–23. On the speculative nature of the 'inflationary' cosmology, see Penrose, *The Emperor's New Mind*, p. 347, note 12. For clear, simple accounts see Barrow, *The World within the World*, pp. 217–26; the first, introductory chapter of Lightman and Brawer, *Origins*, pp. 41–46 and the interviews with Guth and Linde; and Overbye, *Lonely Hearts of the Cosmos*, chaps. 12–14.

67.   Georgi, "Effective Quantum Field Theories," p. 564. See also Schramm and Steigman, "Particle Accelerators Test Cosmological Theory."

68.   Peratt, "Not with a Big Bang," pp. 31–31; *Scientific American*, January 1990, pp. 12–13.

69.   Peratt, "Not with a Big Bang"; Horgan, "Universal Truths," p. 83.

70.   Lightman and Brawer, *Origins*, p. 216.

71.   Lightman and Brawer, *Origins*, p. 465.

72.   Ibid., p. 490.

73.   Edgerton, *The Beginnings of Indian Philosophy*, p. 163 (*Brihadaranyaka Upanishad* 4.4.17).

74.   Deussen, *The Philosophy of the Upanisads*, p. 144 (*Taittirya Upanishad.* 2); Deussen, The System of the Vedanta, pp. 164–67.

75.   Edgerton, *The Beginnings of Indian Philosophy*, pp. 167–68 (*Brihadaranyaka Upanishad* 2.4.12, repeated 4.5.12–13).

76.   Deussen, *The Philosophy of the Upanishads*, p. 352; Hume, *The Thirteen Principal Upanishads*, p. 376 (*Mundaka Upanishad* 3.2.8).

77.   Siegel, *Fires of Water, Waters of Peace*, pp. 94–95.

78.   Sorabji, *Time, Creation and the Continuum*, pp. 159–60.

79.   Edgerton, *The Beginnings of Indian Philosophy*. p. 157 (*Brihadaranyaka Upanishad* 4.3.21–123).

80.   Baldick, *Mystical Islam*, p. 20.

81.   Arberry, *Sufism*, pp. 113–15.

82.   Ibid., pp. 90–91.

83.   Nicholson, *Rumi*, pp. 121, 165.

84. Nims, *The Poems of St. John of the Cross*, p. 19.

85. For general background on the *bhakti* (devotional) movements in 'medieval' and later India see Farquhar, *An Outline of the Religious Literature of India*, chap. 6, especially on the Chaitanyas and Vallabhas; Gonda, *Medieval Religious Literature in Sanskrit*, chap. 3; and Goswamy, "The Cult."

86. McDaniel, *The Madness of the Saints*, p. 7; Dasgupta, *A History of Indian Philosophy*, pp. 389–90.

87. McDaniel, *The Madness of the Saints*, pp. 35–36.

88. Hawley and Juergenmeyer, *Songs of the Saints of India*, p. 119.

89. Dasgupta, *A History of Indian Philosophy*, pp. 390–93.

90. McDaniel, *The Madness of the Saints*, p. 274.

91. Marglin, "Types of Sexual Union and Their Implicit Meanings," pp. 305–7. See also the summary in Kakar and Ross, *Tales of Love, Sex, and Danger*, p. 89; and see Hein, "Comments: Radha and Erotic Community," pp. 119–20.

92. See Farquhar, *An Outline of the Religious Literature of India* and Goswamy, "The Cult." For the doctrine, in the form of Vallabha's theological commentary on the story of Krishna's love (as embodied in the *Bhagavata Purana*), see Redington, *Vallabhacarya on the Love Games of Krsna* [sic].

93. Toomey, "Krishna's Consuming Passions," pp. 167–69; and Bennett, "In Nanda Bab's House," p. 183.

94. Ibid.

95. Edgerton, *The Beginnings of Indian Philosophy*, pp. 150, 165 (*Briadaranyaka Upanishad* 3.9.28, 4.4.27).

96. Masson, *The Oceanic Feeling*.

97. Sinha, *Indian Psychology*, vol. 1, pp. 347–54.

98. D. Macdonald, ed., *The Encylcopaedia of Mammals*, pp. 822–24.

99. A. I. Miller, *Imagery in Scientific Thought*, pp. 129, 250.

100. Ibid., p. 251.

101. Ibid., pp. 127–29, 295–96.

102. James, *The Principles of Psychology*, vol. 1, p. 206; as quoted in Holton, "The Roots of Complementarity," pp. 125–26.

103. Quoted in Holton, "The Roots of Complementarity," p. 124.

104. Ibid., p. 103.

105. Ibid., pp. 132–33, on the testimony of Bohr's son, Hans.

106. Ibid., pp. 128–32.

107. Barrow, *The World within the World,* pp. 228–29, 308–10; Barrow, *Theories of Everything,* pp. 56–61; Misner, Thorne, and Wheeler, *Gravitation,* pp. 769–70, 813–14, 934–40; Munitz, *Cosmic Understanding,* pp. 82–115.

108. Munitz, *Cosmic Understanding,* pp. 167–180.

109. Barrow, *Theories of Everything,* pp. 66–70; Hawking, "The Edge of Spacetime," pp. 67–69; Isham, "Quantum Gravity" (more technical); Overbye, *Lonely Hearts of the Cosmos,* pp. 124, 367–81 (storylike but convincing); and Halliwell, "Quantum Cosmology and the Creation of the Universe" (particularly clear).

110. Isham, "Quantum Gravity," p. 72.

111. Proclus, *A Commentary on the First Book of Euclid's Elements,* p. 16.

Chapter 5. In Judgment of Ineffability

1.   Letter to Gersdorff, August 4, 1869, as quoted in Scharfstein, *The Philosophers,* p. 12.

2.   Proudfoot, *Religious Experience,* p. 126.

3.   Ibid., pp. 126–29.

4.   Ibid., pp. 134–36.

5.   Ibid., p. 137.

6.   Gale, "Mysticism and Philosophy," pp. 116.

7.   Gimello, "Mysticism in Its Contexts," pp. 71–72, 78–79.

8.   Smart, "Understanding Religious Experience," p. 120.

9.   Moore, "Mystical Experience, Mystical Doctrine, Mystical Technique," p. 102.

10.   Freud, *Civilization and Its Discontents,* pp. 1–10. Masson, *The Oceanic Feeling,* pp. 35–50.

11.   Freud, *Civilization and Its Discontents,* p. 3.

12.   On the early life of children, see Bowlby; Eagle; Kahn; Mahler, Pine, and Bergman; and Stern. For the translation of children's memories and yearnings into various stories and traditional ideals see Kakar and Ross.

13. Edelson, *Language and Interpretation in Psychoanalysis,* pp. 126, 168–71, 139–40 (quoted).

14. Stimpson, *Paul Valéry and Music,* pp. 11–13.

15. Ibid., pp. 25, 47, 45, 48; Whiting, *Paul Valéry,* pp. 48, 51; Valéry, *Aesthetics,* p. 54 (quoted).

16. Stimpson, *Paul Valéry and Music,* pp. 112–17; Valéry, Poems, p. 401.

17. Stimpson, *Paul Valéry and Music,* pp. 136–39, 203.

18. Whiting, *Paul Valéry,* p. 55 (from Valéry, *Cahiers* II, 1074); Valéry, *Aesthetics,* p. 71.

19. Valéry, *Poems,* pp. 421, 423, 429.

20. Ibid., pp. 418, 400. For parallelisms between portry and music, see Kramer, *Music and Poetry.*

21. Haughton, "Introduction," *The Chatto Book of Nonsense Poetry,* p. 2. See also Steiner, *After Babel,* pp. 187ff.

22. Stevens, "Notes Toward a Supreme Fiction," in *Transport to Summer,* pp. 120, 135.

23. Haughton, "Introduction," *The Chatto Book of Nonsense Poetry,* p. 17.

24. Giuliano, "A Time for Humor."

25. Springer and Deutsch, *Left Brain, Right Brain,* p. 78; Sidits, "Music, Pitch Perception, and the Mechanisms of Cortical Hearing," p. 107.

26. Heidegger, *Poetry, Language, Thought,* pp. 12, 95.

27. Stevens, "Contrary Theses (II)," in *Collected Poems.*

28. Stevens, "It Must Change," in *Collected Poems,* p. 397.

29. Kramer, *Music and Poetry,* p. 241.

30. Whitman's autoerotic dreams appear in his "Song of Myself," section 28. For commentary see Miller, *Walt Whitman's "Song of Myself,"* pp. 100–101.

31. Whitman, "Song of Myself," line 670. Commentary in Miller, *Walt Whitman's "Song of Myself",* p. 107.

32. Whitman, *Complete Poetry and Collected Prose,* p. 13.

33. Gupta, "Tantric Sadhana: Puja," in Gupta, Hoens, and Goudriaan, *Hindu Tantrism,* pp. 136–37.

34. Nietzsche, *Untimely Meditations,* p. 223.

35. Wagner, "Über die Benennung 'Musikdrama,' " as quoted in Millington, *Wagner*, p. 233.

36. Gartenberg, *Mahler*, p. 228.

37. Ibid., p. 334.

38. Stern, *The Interpersonal World of the Infant*.

39. Ibid., chap. 7.

40. Ibid., pp. 139–46.

41. Ibid., pp. 151–58.

42. Ibid., pp. 162–63.

43. Ibid., pp. 175–81.

44. Ibid., p. 226.

45. Ibid., p. 181.

46. Kafka, *The Complete Stories*, p. 456.

47. Csikszentmihalyi and Csikszentmihalyi, *Optimal Experience*.

48. Bennett, "In Nanda Bab's House," p. 185.

49. Toomey, "Krishna's Consuming Passions," pp. 175, 171.

50. Brooks, "Hare Krishna, Radhe Shyam," p. 264.

51. Kakar, *Intimate Relations*, p. 19.

52. Ibid., p. 118. On the congeniality of Jung's doctrine, see D.M. Wulff, "Prolegomenon to a Psychology for the Goddess."

53. Roland, *In Search of Self in India and Japan*, p. 263.

54. Kakar, *Intimate Relations*, p. 130.

55. Ibid., p. 37.

56. Ibid., 144.

57. Roland, *In Search of Self in India and Japan*, pp. 253–54, 299–307.

58. Here I have drawn on Collins, "From Brahman to a Blade of Grass." Collins, who makes particular use of Kohut's concept of narcissism, draws interesting analogies between Indian mythology, traditional Indian ideas (e.g. *karma*), and the psychological development of the Indian self.

59.   See Roland, *In Search of Self in India and Japan*, chap. 9, "The Spiritual Self: Continuity and Counterpoint to the Familial Self"; Jones, *Contemporary Psychoanalysis and Religion;* and Loewald, *Sublimation.*

60.   Anne Marie Rizzuto, quoted in Jones, *Contemporary Psychoanalysis and Religion*, p. 44.

61.   Ochse, *Before the Gates of Excellence* gives an up-to-date account of the psychology of creativity. Music is dealt with in Feder, Karmel, and Pollock, eds., *Psychoanaltic Explorations in Music*. For philosophy and art see, respectively, Scharfstein, *The Philosophers,* and Scharfstein, *Of Birds, Beasts, and Other Artists.* For science, one might begin with Roe, *The Making of a Scientist.* D. L. Hull, *Science as Process* is a detailed and convincing case history of the effect of scientist's human relations on their work (and vice versa).

62.   Derrida, *Margins of Philosophy,* p. 287; quoting Valéry, Cahiers 24, p. 99, 1940.

Bibliography

AARONSON, D., AND R. E. Rieber, eds. *Psycholinguistic Research*. Hillsdale, N.J.: Lawrence Erlbaum, 1979.

AARSLEFF, H. *From Locke to Saussure*. Minneapolis: University of Minnesota Press, 1982.

ADAIR, R. K. "A Flaw in a Universal Mirror." *Scientific American* (February 1988).

ADAMS, R. M. "Kierkegaard's Arguments against Objective Reasoning in Religion." In *Contemporary Philosophy of Religion*, ed. S. M. Cahn and D. Shatz.

AHERN, D. M. "Ineffability in the *Lao Tzu*." *Journal of Chinese Philosophy* 4.4 (1977).

AKLUJKAR, A. "Bhartrihari: *Trikandi* or *Vakyapadia*." In *Encyclopedia of Indian Philosophies*, ed. H. G. Coward and K. K. Raja.

ALBERS, D. J., AND G. L. ALEXANDERSON. *Mathematical People*. Boston/Basel/Stuttgart: Birkhauser, 1985.

ALLINSON, R. E., ed. *Understanding the Chinese Mind*. Hong Kong/New York: Oxford University Press, 1989.

ALPER, H. A., ed. "The Cosmos as Siva's Language Game." In H. A. Alper, *Mantra*.

———. *Mantra*. Albany: State University of New York Press, 1989.

ARAPURA, J. G. "Some Perspectives on Indian Philosophy of Language." In *Revelation in Indian Thought*, ed. H. Coward and K. Sivaraman.

ARAPURA, J. G., AND K. K. RAJA. "Philosophical Elements in Vedic Literature." In *The Philosophy of the Grammarians*, ed. H. G. Coward and K. K. Raja.

ARBERRY, A. J. *Sufism*. New York: Macmillian, 1950.

ARGYLE, M. *Bodily Communication*. 2d ed. London: Methuen, 1988.

ARMSTRONG, A. H. *Plotinus*. London: Allen and Unwin, 1953.

ARTAUD, A. *Le théâtre et son double*. Paris: Gallimard, 1964.

BALDICK, J. *Mystical Islam*. London: Tauris, 1989.

BAMBROUGH, R. "Intuition and the Inexpressible." In S. T. Katz, ed., *Mysticism and Philosophical Analysis*.

BAO, ZHIMING. "Language and World View in Ancient China." *Philosophy East and West* 40.2 (1990).

BASHAM, A. L., ed. *A Cultural History of India*. London: Oxford University Press, 1975.

BARROW, J. D. *Theories of Everything*. Oxford: Oxford University Press, 1991.

———. *The World within the World*. New York: Oxford University Press, 1988.

BAUDELAIRE, C. *Oeuvres complètes*. Vol. 1. Paris: Gallimard, 1975.

BÉHAR. J., AND M. CARASSOU, eds. *Le Surréalisme*. Paris: Librairie Générale Française, 1984.

BELLUGI, W. "The Acquisition of a Spatial Language." In *The Development of Language and Language Researchers*, ed. F. S. Kessel.

BENACERAFF, P., AND H. PUTNAM, eds. *Philosophy of Mathematics*. 2d ed. Cambridge: Cambridge University Press, 1983.

BENNETT, P. "In Nanada Bab's House: The Devotional Experience in Pushti Marg Temples." In *The Social Construction of Emotion in India*, ed. O. M. Lynch.

BENTON, A. L. "The Amusias." In *Music and the Brain*, ed. M. Critchley and R. A. Henson.

BERG, J. H. "Responsiveness and Self-Disclosure." In *Self-Disclosure*, ed. V. J. Derlega and J. H. Berg.

———. *Self-Disclosure*. New York: Plenum Press, 1987.

BIARDEAU, M. *Théorie de la connaissance et philosophie de la parole dans le brahmanisme classique.* Paris: Mouton/Ecole Pratique des hautes Etudes, 1964.

————, trans. *Vakyapadiya Brahmakanda.* Paris: Boccard, 1964.

BIERHORST, J., trans. *The Sacred Path.* New York: William Morrow, 1933.

BISIACH, E. "Language without Thought." In *Thought without Language,* ed. L. Weiskrantz.

BLEICHER, J. *Contemporary Hemeneutics.* London: Routledge and Kegan Paul, 1980.

BLUMENTHAL, H. J., AND A. C. LLOYD, eds. *Soul and Structure of Being in Late Neoplatonism.* Liverpool: Liverpool University Press, 1982.

BLUMSTEIN, S. E. "Neurolinguistics: An Overview of Language-Brain Relations in Aphasia." In *Language,* ed. F. J. Newmeyer.

BOMAN, T. *Hebrew Thought Compared with Greek.* London: SCM Press, 1982.

BOULEZ, P. *Orientations.* Cambridge: Harvard University Press, 1986.

BOWLBY, J. *Separation.* New York: Basic Books, 1973.

BREAZEALE, D. *Philosophy and Truth: Selections from Nietzsche's Notebooks of the Early 1970s.* Atlantic Highlands, N.J.: Humanities Press, 1979.

BRIGGS, J., AND F. D. PEAT. *Turbulent Mirror.* New York: Harper and Row, 1989.

BROOKS, C. R. "Hare Krishna, Radhe Shyam: The Cross-Cultural Dynamics of Mystical Emotions in Brindaban." In *Divine Passions,* ed. O. M. Lynch.

BRUCE, A., AND WALLACE, D. "Critical Point Phenomena." In *The New Physics,* ed. P. Davies.

BRUNS, G. L. "Disappeared: Heidegger and the Emancipation of Language." In *Languages of the Unsayable,* ed. S. Budick and W. Iser.

————. *Heidegger's Estrangements.* New Haven: Yale University Press, 1989.

BRUNSCHWIG, J. "Proof Defined." In Schofield, M., M. Burnyeat, and J. Barnes. *Doubt and Dogmatism.* London: Oxford University Press, 1980.

————. *Wittgenstein's Philosophy of Psychology.* London: Routledge, 1989.

BUDD, M. *Music and the Emotions.* London: Routledge & Kegan Paul, 1985.

BUDDHAGHOSA. *The Path of Purification (Visudhimagga).* 4th ed. Trans. Bhikkhu Nanamoli. Kandi, Sri Lanka: Buddhist Publication Society, 1979.

BUDICK, S., AND W. ISER, eds. *Languages of the Unsayable: The Play of Negativity in Literature and Literary Theory.* New York: Columbia University Press, 1989.

BUITENEN, J. A. B. VAN. *"Aksara." Journal of the American Oriental Society* 79 (1959).

BUJIU, B. *Music in European Thought 1851–1912.* Cambridge: Cambridge University Press, 1988.

BUSSANICH, J. *The One and Its Relation to Intellect in Plotinus.* Brill: Leiden, 1988.

BUTTERWORTH, G., AND L. GROVER. "The Origins of Referential Communication in Human Infancy." In *Thought without Language,* ed. L. Weiskrantz.

CAHN, S. M., AND D. SHATZ, eds. *Contemporary Philosophy of Religion.* New York/Oxford: Oxford University Press, 1982.

CALAME-GRIAULE, G. *Ethnologie et langage.* Paris: Gallimard, 1965.

CARDINAL, R. *German Romantics in Context.* London: Studio Vista, 1975.

CARPENTER, B. N. "The Relationship between Psychopathology and Self-Disclosure." In *Self-Disclosure,* ed. V. J. Derlega and J. H. Berg.

CARR, I., D. FAIRWEATHER, AND B. PRIESTLY. *Jazz.* London: Paladin, Grafton Books (Collins), 1987.

CARRIER, D. "Interpreting Musical Performances." *The Monist* 66.2 (1983).

CELAN, P. *Last Poems.* Trans. K. Washburn and M. Guillemin. San Francisco: North Point Press, 1986.

CHAFE, W. "Some Reasons for Hesitating." In *Perspectives on Silence,* ed. D. Tannen and M. Saville-Troike.

CHAKRABARTI, A. "Sentence-Holism, Context-Principle and Connected-Designation *Anvitabhidhana*: Three Doctrines or One?" *Journal of Indian Philosophy* 17.1 (1989).

CHAN, W.-T. *The Way of Lao Tzu*. Indianapolis: Bobbs-Merrill, 1963.

CHANG, CHUNG-YUAN. *Original Teachings of Ch'an Buddhism*. New York: Pantheon, 1969.

CHARLES-SAGET, A. *L'Architecture du divin*. Paris: Les Belles Lettres, 1982.

CHARY, P. "Aphasia in a Multilingual Society." In *Language Processing in Bilinguals*, ed. J. Vaid.

CHATTERJEE, S. *The Nyaya Theory of Knowledge*. 2d ed. Calcutta: University of Calcutta, 1950.

CH'EN, KY-YING. *Lao Tzu: Text, Notes, and Comments*. San Francisco: Chinese Materials Center, 1977.

CHENG, CHUNG-YING. "A Taoist Interpretation of Differance in Derrida." *Journal of Chinese Philosophy* 17.1 (March 1990).

CHESSIK, R. *The Technique and Practice of Listening in Intensive Psychotherapy*. Northvale, N.J.: Jason Aronson.

CHIEN, CHI-HUI. "'Theft's Way': A Comparative Study of Chuang Tzu's Tao and Derridean Trace." *Journal of Chinese Philosophy* 17.1 (March 1990).

CHISSEL, J. *Schumann*. New ed., London: Dent, 1956.

CHOMSKY, N. *Language and the Problems of Knowledge*. Cambridge: MIT Press, 1988.

CHUANG TZU. See Graham, Legge, Watson.

CLIFFORD, J. *The Predicament of Culture*. Cambridge: Harvard University Press, 1988.

COATES, D., AND T. WINSTON. "The Dilemma of Distress Disclosure." In V. J. Derlega and J. H. Berg, *Self-Disclosure*.

COFFA, J. A. *The Semantic Tradition from Kant to Carnap*. Cambridge: Cambridge University Press, 1991.

COLLINS, A. "From Brahma to a Blade of Grass: Towards an Indian Self-Psychology." *Journal of Indian Philosophy* (June 1991).

COLTART, N. E. C. "'Slouching towards Bethlehem' . . . or Thinking the Unthinkable in Psychoanalysis." In *The British School of Psychoanalysis*, ed. G. Kohon.

CONDILLAC, E. B. DE. *An Essay on the Origins of Human Knowledge*. 1746. Trans. Gainsville, Fla.: Scholars' Facsimiles and Reprints, 1971.

————. *Oeuvres philosophique de Condillac.* Ed. G. le Roy. Vol. 1. Paris: Presses Universitaires, 1947.

CONFUCIUS. *Confucian Analects.* Trans. J. Legge. 1893. Reprint. New York: Dover, 1971.

COOKE, D. *The Language of Music.* Oxford: Oxford University Press, 1959.

COWARD, H. G. *Sphota Theory of Language.* Delhi: Motilal Banarsidass, 1980.

COWARD, H. G., AND K. K. RAJA. "Introduction to the Philosophy of the Grammarians." In *The Philosophy of the Grammarians*, ed. H. G. Coward and K. K. Raja.

————. eds. *The Philosophy of the Grammarians.* Vol. 5 of *Encyclopedia of Indian Philosophies.* Delhi: Motilal Banarsidass, 1990.

COWARD, H. G., AND K. Sivaraman, eds. *Revelation in Indian Thought.* Emeryville, Calif.: Dharma Publishing, 1977.

CREEL, H. G. *Shen Pu-hai.* Chicago: University of Chicago Press, 1974.

CRITCHLEY, M. "Ecstatic and Synaesthetic Experiences during Musical Perception." In *Music and the Brain*, ed. M. Critchley and R. A. Henson.

————. "Occupational Palsy in Musical Performers." In *Music and the Brain*, ed. M. Critchley and R. A. Henson.

CRITCHLEY, M., AND R. A. HENSON. *Music and the Brain.* Springfield, Ill.: Charles C. Thomas, 1977.

CROCKER, L. S., trans. *Diderot's Selected Writings.* New York: Macmillan, 1966.

CROMBIE, I. C. *An Examination of Plato's Doctrines.* Vol. 2. London: Routledge and Kegan Paul, 1963.

CRYSTAL, D. *The Cambridge Encyclopedia of Language.* Cambridge: Cambridge University Press, 1976.

CSIKSZENTMIHALYI, M. "The Flow Experience and Human Psychology." In *Optimal Experience*, M. Csikszentmihalyi and I. S. Csikszentmihalyi.

CSIKSZENTMIHALYI, M., AND CSIKSZENTHIHALYI, I. S. *Optimal Experience: Studies of Flow in Consciousness.* Cambridge: Cambridge University Press, 1988.

CYTOWIC, R. E. "Tasting Colors, Smelling Sounds." *The Sciences* (September/October 1988).

DAHLHAUS, C. *Aesthetics of Music.* Cambridge: Cambridge University Press, 1982.

———. *Nineteenth-Century Music.* Berkeley: University of California Press, 1989.

———. *Realism in Nineteenth-Century Music.* Cambridge: Cambridge University Press, 1985.

———. *Schoenberg and the New Music.* Cambridge: Cambridge University Press, 1987.

DALLEY, S., trans. *Myths from Mesopotamia.* Oxford: Oxford University Press, 1989.

DASCAL, M. *Pragmatics and the Philosophy of Mind.* Vol. 1. *Thought in Language.* Amsterdam/Philadelphia: John Benjamins, 1983.

DASGUPTA, S. *A History of Indian Philosophy.* Vol. 4. Cambridge: Cambridge University Press, 1949.

DAUBEN, D. *Georg Cantor.* Cambridge: Harvard University Press, 1979.

DAUENHAUER, B. P. *Silence.* Bloomington: Indiana University Press, 1980.

DAVIES, P. *The Cosmic Blueprint.* New York: Simon and Schuster, 1988.

———. ed. *The New Physics.* Cambridge: Cambridge University Press, 1989.

DEMIÉVILLE, P. *Entretiens de Lin-tsi.* Paris: Fayard, 1972.

———. "The Mirror of the Mind." In *Sudden and Gradual,* ed. P. N. Gregory.

DENZIN, N. K. *On Understanding Emotion.* San Francisco: Jossey-Bass, 1984.

DERLEGA, V. J., AND J. H. BERG, eds. *Self-Disclosure: Theory, Research, and Therapy.* New York: Plenum Press, 1987.

DERRIDA, J. *Margins of Philosophy.* 1972. Trans. Chicago: Chicago University Press, 1982.

———. "My Chances." In *Taking Chances,* ed. J. H. Smith and W. Kerrigan. Baltimore: Johns Hopkins University Press.

————. *Positions*. 1972. Trans. Chicago: University of Chicago Press, 1981.

————. *Of Spirit: Heidegger and the Question*. 1987. Trans. Chicago: University of Chicago Press, 1989.

————. *Writing and Difference*. 1967. Trans. Chicago: University of Chicago Press, 1978.

DEUSSEN, P. *The Philosophy of the Upanishads*. Reprint. New York: Dover, 1966.

————. *The System of the Vedanta*. Reprint. New York: Dover, 1973.

DEUTSCH, D., ed. *The Psychology of Music*. Orlando: Academic Press, 1982.

DIDEROT, D. *Oeuvres philosophiques*. Paris: Garnier, 1961.

————. *Rameau's Nephew* and *D'Alembert's Dream*. Trans. L. Tancock. Harmondsworth: Penguin, 1966.

DILTHEY, W. *Grundriss der allgemeinem Geschichte der Philosophie*. Ed. and supplemented by H.-G. Gadarmer. Frankfurt: Klostermann, 1949.

DUBS, H. H., trans. *The Works of Hsüntze*. London: Probsthain, 1928.

DUMOULIN, H. *Zen Buddhism: A History*. 2 vols. New York: Macmillan, 1988, 1990.

————. *Zen Enlightenment*. Tokyo: Weatherhill, 1979.

EAGLE, M. N. *Recent Developments in Psychoanalysis*. Cambridge: Harvard University Press, 1987.

EDELSON, M. *Language and Interpretation in Psychoanalysis*. Chicago: University of Chicago Press, 1975.

EDGERTON, F. *The Beginnings of Indian Philosophy*. Cambridge: Harvard University Press, 1965.

EIMAS, P. "The Perception of Speech in Early Infancy." *Scientific American* (January 1985).

EINSTEIN, A. *Ideas and Opinions*. New York: Crown Publishers, 1954.

ELLIS, E., AND G. BEATTIE, eds. *The Psychology of Language and Communication*. London: Weidenfeld and Nicolson, 1986.

ELWIN, M. "Was There a Transcendental Breakthrough in China?" In S. N. Eisenstadt, ed. *The Origins of Diversity of Axial Age Civilizations*. Albany: State University of New York Press, 1986.

ENELOW, A. E. "The Silent Patient." *Psychiatry* 23 (1960).

ENGELMANN, P. *Letters from Ludwig Wittgenstein, with a Memoir.* Oxford: Blackwell, 1967.

ESSLIN, M. *Artaud.* Glasgow: Fontana/Collins, 1976.

EVANS, A. D. AND FALK, W. W. *Learning to Be Deaf.* Berlin/Amsterdam: Mouton de Gruyter, 1986.

EVANS, F. J., "Posthypnotic Amnesia: Disassociation of Content and Context." In *Hypnosis and Memory,* ed. H. M. Pettinati.

FARQUHAR, J. N. *An Outline of the Religious Literature of India.* London: Oxford University Press, 1920.

FEDER, S., R. L. KARMEL, AND G. H. POLLOCK, eds. *Psychoanalytic Explorations in Music.* Madison, Conn: International Universities Press, 1990.

FENNER, P. *The Ontology of the Middle Way.* Dordrecht: Kluwer, 1990.

FODOR, J. AND E. LEPORE. *Holism.* Oxford: Blackwell, 1992.

FITZPATRICK, M. A. "Marriage and Self-Disclosure." In *Self-Disclosure,* ed. V. J. Derlega and J. H. Berg.

FORD, J. "What is Chaos that We Should Be Mindful of It?" In *The New Physics,* ed. P. Davies.

FOUCART, G. "Names (Egyptian)." Hastings, *Encyclopaedia of Religion and Ethics.*

FRAIBERG, S. "Parallel and Divergent Patterns in Blind and Sighted Infants." In *The Psychoanalytic Study of the Child,* vol. 23. London: The Hogarth Press, 1968.

FREEMAN, W. J. "The Physiology of Perception." *Scientific American* (February 1991).

FREUD. S. *Civilization and Its Discontents.* London: Hogarth Press, 1969.

————. *The Standard Edition of the Complete Psychological Works of Sigmund Freud.* 24 vols, ed. and trans. J. Strachey. London: Hogarth Press and Institute of Psychoanalysis, 1953–74.

FRIEDMAN, H. S. "The Modification of Word Meaning by Nonverbal Cues." In *Nonverbal Communication Today,* ed. M. R. Kay.

FUNG, YU-LAN. *History of Chinese Philosophy.* Vol. 2. Princeton: Princeton University Press, 1953.

GADAMER, G. *Truth and Method.* 1965. Trans. New York: Crossroad Publishing Co., 1984.

GALE, R. M., "Mysticism and Philosophy." In *Contemporary Philosophy of Religion*, ed. S. M. Cahn and D. Shatz.

GARDNER, H. *Art, Mind, and Brain.* New York: Basic Books, 1982.

———. *Frames of Mind.* New York: Basic Books, 1983.

GARTENBERG, E. *Mahler.* New York: Schirmer Books, 1978.

GAZZANIGA, M. S. "The Dynamics of Cerebral Specialization and Modular Interactions." In *Thought without Language*, ed. L. Weiskrantz.

———, ed. *Handbook of Cognitive Neuroscience.* New York: Plenum Press, 1984.

———, ed. *Perspectives in Memory Research.* Cambridge: MIT Press, 1988.

GAZZANIGA, M. S., AND SMYLIE, C. S. "What Does Language Do for a Right Hemisphere?" In *Handbook of Cognitive Neuroscience*, ed. M. S. Gazzaniga.

GEORGI, M. "Effective Quantum Field Theories." In *The New Physics*, ed. P. Davies.

———. "Grand Unified Theories." In *The New Physics*, ed. P. Davies.

GHOSHAL, U. N. *A History of Indian Political Ideas.* London: Oxford University Press, 1959.

GILHOOLY, K. J., M. T. G. KEANE, R. H. LOGIE, AND G. ERDOES, eds. *Lines of Thinking.* Volume 1. New York: Wiley.

GIMELLO, R. M. "Mysticism in Its Contexts." *Mysticism and Religious Traditions*, ed. S. T. Katz.

GIULIANO, E. "A Time for Humor: Lewis Carroll, Laughter and Despair, and *The Hunting of the Snark*." In *Lewis Carroll: A Celebration*, ed. E. Giuliano. New York: Clarkson Potter, 1982.

GLOOR ET AL. "The Role of the Limbic System in Experimental Phenomena of Temporal Lobe Epilepsy." *Annals of Neurology* 12 (1982).

GÖDEL, K. *Collected Works.* Ed. S. Feferman et al. Vol. 1. New York/London: Oxford University Press, 1986.

———. "Russell's Mathematical Logic." In *Philosophy of Mathematics*, 2d ed., ed. P. Benaceraff and H. Putnam. Cambridge: Cambridge University Press, 1983.

GÖDEL, R. "History of the Gödel Family." In P. Weingartner, P. and L. Schmatterer, eds. *Gödel Remembered*. Naples: Bibliopolis-Edizione di filosofia e scienze, 1987.

GODWIN, J. *Harmonies of Heaven and Earth*. London: Thames and Hudson, 1987.

GOMEZ, L. O. "Purifying Gold: The Metaphor of Effort and Intuition in Buddhist Thought and Practice." In *Sudden and Gradual*, ed. P. N. Gregory.

GONDA, J. *Medieval Religious Literature in Sanskrit*. Wiesbaden: Harrassowitz, 1977.

———. *The Vision of the Vedic Poets*. The Hague: Mouton, 1963.

GOODSTEIN, L. D., AND V. M. REINECKER. "Factors Affecting Self-Disclosure: A Review of the Literature." In *Progress in Experimental Personality Research*, ed. B. Maher and W. Maher.

GOSHEN-GOTTSTEIN, E. *Recalled to Life: The History of a Coma*. New Haven: Yale University Press, 1990.

GOSWAMY, K. "The Cult." In *Krishna the Divine Lover: Myth Legend through Indian Art*, ed. A. L. Dallapiccola. London/Boston: Serindia Publications/David Godine, 1982.

GOULD, J. L., AND GRANT, C. *The Honeybee*. New York: Scientific American Library, 1988.

GRAHAM, A. C. *Disputers of the Tao*. La Salle, Ill.: Open Court, 1989.

———. "Reflections and Replies." In *Chinese Texts and Philosophical Contexts*, ed. H. Rosemont.

———. *Studies in Chinese Philosophy and Philosophical Literature*. Albany: State University of New York Press, 1990.

———. "Taoist Spontaneity and the Dichotomy of 'Is' and 'Ought'." In *Experimental Essays in Chuang-tzu*, ed. V. H. Mair.

———, trans. *Chuang Tzu*. London: Allen and Unwin, 1981.

GREENE, D. M. *Greene's Biographical Encyclopedia of Composers*. London: Collins, 1985.

GREGORY, P. N., ed. *Sudden and Gradual: Tibetan Buddhist Epistemology in Support of Transformative Religious Experience*. Honolulu: University of Hawaii Press, 1987.

GREGORY, R. L. "Blindness, Recovery from." In *The Oxford Companion to the Mind,* ed. R. L. Gregory.

———. "Consciousness in Science and Philosophy." In *Consciousness in Contemporary Science,* ed. A. J. Marcel and E. Bisiach.

———, ed. *The Oxford Companion to the Mind.* Oxford University Press, 1987.

GRICE, P. *Studies in the Way of Words.* Cambridge: Harvard University Press, 1989.

GRIFFITHS, P. *Olivier Messaien and the Music of Time.* Ithaca: Cornell University Press, 1985.

GRIFFITHS, P. *On Being Mindless: Buddhist Meditation and the Mind-Body Problem.* La Salle, Ill.: Open Court, 1986.

GROHMANN, W. *Paul Klee.* New York: Abrams, 1954.

GRÜNBAUM, A. "The Pseudo-Problem of Creation in Physical Cosmology." *Philosophy of Science* 56 (1989).

GULIK, R. H. VAN. *Hsi K'ang and His Poetical Essay on the Lute.* New ed. Tokyo/Rutland, Vt.: Tuttle, 1969.

———. *The Lore of the Chinese Lute.* Tokyo: Sophia University, 1940.

GULKIS, S., P. M. LUBIN, S. S. MEYER, AND R. F. SILVERBERG. "The Cosmic-Background Explorer." *Scientific American* (special issue, *Exploring Space,* 1990).

GUPTA, S., D. J. HOENS, AND T. GOUDRIAAN. *Hindu Tantrism.* Leiden: Brill, 1979.

GUTBROD, H., AND H. STÖCKER. "The Nuclear Equation of State." *Scientific American* (November 1991).

GUTH, A., AND STEINHARDT. "The Inflationary Universe." In *The New Physics,* ed. P Davies.

GUTHRIE, W. K. C. *A History of Greek Philosophy.* Vol. 5. Cambridge: Cambridge University Press, 1978.

HABERMAS, J. *The Philosophical Discourse of Modernity.* Cambridge: MIT Press, 1987.

HACKER, P. M. S. *Insight and Illusion: Themes in the Philosophy of Wittgenstein.* Rev. ed. Oxford: Oxford University Press, 1986.

HALBFASS, E. *India and Europe: An Essay in Understanding.* Albany: State University of New York Press, 1988.

HALL, D. L., AND R. T. AMES. *Thinking through Confucius*. Albany: State University of New York Press, 1987.

HALLIWELL, J. I. "Quantum Cosmology and the Creation of the Universe." *Scientific American* (December 1991).

HAMMERSTEIN, R. "Music as a Divine Art." In *Dictionary of the History of Ideas*, ed. P. P. Wiener. New York: Scribners, 1973.

HANSEN, C. "Classical Chinese Ethics." In *A Companion to Ethics*, ed. P. Singer. Elaborated in Hansen's *A Daoist Theory of Chinese Thought*, to be published by Oxford University Press, New York.

———. "Language in the Heart-Mind." In *Understanding the Chinese Mind*, ed. A. Allinson, New York: Oxford University Press, 1989.

———. "Should the Ancient Masters Value Reason?" In *Chinese Texts and Philosophical Contexts*, ed. H. Rosemont.

———. "A Tao of Tao in Chuang-tzu." In *New Perspectives on Chuang-tzu.*, ed. V. Mair.

HANSLICK, E. *Hanslick's Musical Criticisms*. Reprint of *Music Criticisms 1846–99*. Baltimore: Penguin Books, 1963.

HARBSMEIER, C. "Marginalia Sino-logica." In *Understanding the Chinese Mind*, ed. R. E. Allinson.

HARGREAVES, D. J. *The Developmental Psychology of Music*. Cambridge: Cambridge University Press, 1986.

HARVEY, I. E. *Derrida and the Economy of Différance*. Bloomington: Indiana University Press, 1986.

HASTINGS, J., ed. *Encyclopaedia of Religion and Ethics*. New York: Scribners, 1928.

HAUGHTON, H., ed. *The Chatto Book of Nonsense Poetry*. London: Chatto and Windus, 1988.

HAWKING, S. "The Edge of Spacetime." In *The New Physics*, ed. P. Davies.

HAWLEY, J. S. AND JUERGENSMEYER, trans. *Songs of the Saints of India*. New York: Oxford University Press, 1988.

HAWLEY, J. S. AND WULFF, D. M. *Divine Consort: Radha and the Godesses of India*. Boston: Beacon Press, 1986.

HAYES, R. P. *Dignaga on Interpretation of Signs*. Dordrecht: Kluwer Academic Publishers, 1988.

HEIDEGGER, M. *On the Way to Language*. 1952. Trans. New York: Harper & Row.

———. *Poetry, Language, Thought*. 1950–60. Trans. New York: Harper and Row, 1971.

HEIN, N. "Comments: The Reversal and Rejection of *Bhakti*." In Hawley and Wulff, *The Divine Consort*.

HENRICKS, R. G., trans. *Lao-Tzu: Te-Tao Ching*. London: Bodley Head, 1990.

HERZBERGER, D. *Bhartrihari and the Buddhists*. Dordrecht: Reidel, 1986.

HILL, C. T. AND D. E. STULL. "Gender and Self-Disclosure." In *Self-Disclosure*, ed. V. J. Derlega and J. H. Berg.

HILMY, S. S. *The Later Wittgenstein*. Oxford: Blackwell, 1987.

HINTIKKA, M. B., AND S. HINTIKKA, *Investigating Wittgenstein*. Oxford: Blackwell, 1986.

HIRST, W., AND M. S. GAZZANIGA, "Present and Future of Memory Research and Its Applications." In *Perspectives in Memory Research*, ed. M. S. Gazzaniga.

HOENS, D. J. "Transmission and Fundamental Constituents of the Practice." In *Hindu Tantrism*, ed. S. Gupta, D. J. Hoens, and T. Goudriaan.

HOLLANDER, M. C. "Hysteria and Memory." In *Hypnosis and Memory*, ed. H. M. Pettinati.

HOLMES, J. *Conductors*. London: Gollancz, 1988.

HOLTON, G. "The Roots of Complementarity." In G. Holton, *Thematic Origins of Scientific Thought*. Rev. ed. Cambridge: Harvard University Press, 1988.

HOPKINS, J., trans. *Nicholas of Cusa on Learned Ignorance*. Minneapolis: Banning Press, 1981.

HORGAN, J. "Universal Truths." *Scientific American* (October 1990).

HORN, L. R. *A Natural History of Negation*. Chicago: University of Chicago Press, Chicago: 1989.

HOROWITZ, M. J., ed. *Psychodynamics and Cognition*. Chicago: University of Chicago Press, 1988.

Hoy, D. C. *The Critical Circle.* Berkeley: University of California Press, 1982.

Hsiao, Kung-chuan. *A History of Chinese Political Thought.* Princeton: Princeton University, Press, 1979.

Hsiao, P. Shih-yi. "Heidegger and Our Translation of the *Tao Te Ching.*" In *Heidegger and Asian Thought,* ed. G. Parkes.

Hull, D. L. *The Metaphysics of Evolution.* Albany: State University of New York Press, 1989.

———. *Science as a Process.* Chicago: University of Chicago Press, 1988.

Hull, J. M. *Touching the Rock: An Experience of Blindness.* New York: Pantheon, 1990.

Hume, R. E. *The Thirteen Principal Upanishads.* London: Oxford University Press, 1934.

Huntington, C. W., Jr. (with G. N. Wangchen). *The Emptiness of Emptiness.* Honolulu: University of Hawaii Press, 1989. See review by P. Williams, *Journal of Indian Philosophy* 19.2 (June 1991).

Hyman, J., ed. *Investigating Psychology: Sciences of the Mind after Wittgenstein.* London: Routledge, 1991.

Idel, M. *Kabbalah: New Perspectives.* New Haven: Yale University Press, 1988.

———. *Language, Torah, and Hermeneutics in Abraham Abulafia.* Albany: State University of New York Press, 1989.

Isham, C. "Quantum Gravity." In *The New Physics,* ed. P. Davies.

Iyer, K. A. S. *Bhartrihari.* Poona: Deccan College, 1969.

———. *The Vakyapadiya: Some Problems.* Poona: Bhandakar Oriental Research Institute, 1982.

———, trans. *The Vakyapadiya of Bhartrihari with the Vrtti.* Chapter 1. Poona: Deccan College, 1965.

———, trans. *The Vakyapadiya of Bhartrihari.* Chapter 3, Part 2. Delhi: Motilal Banarsidass, 1973.

Izutsu, Toshohiko. "Sense and Nonsense in Zen Buddhism." In *Man and Speech,* ed. A. Portmann and R. Ritsema. Leiden: Brill, 1973.

JACKENDOFF, R. *Consciousness and the Computational Mind.* Cambridge: MIT Press, 1987.

JACOBI, H. *JAINA SUTRAS.* Part 2. 1895. Reprint. Dover: New York, 1968.

JACOBSEN, T. *The Harps that Once . . . : Sumerian Poetry in Translation.* New Haven: Yale University Press, 1987.

————. *Treasures of Darkness: A History of Mesopotamian Religion.* New Haven: Yale University Press, 1976.

JAINI, P. S. *The Jaina Path of Purification.* Berkeley: University of California Press, 1979.

JAMES, W. *The Principles of Psychology.* 2 vols. 1890. Reprint. New York: Dover, 1950.

JANSONS, M. "A Personal View of Dyslexia and of Thought without Language." In *Thought without Language,* ed. L. Weiskrantz.

JAYATILLEKE, K. N. *Early Buddhist Theory of Knowledge.* London: Allen and Unwin, 1963.

JOHNSON, M. *The Body in the Mind.* Chicago: University of Chicago Press, 1987.

JOHNSON, R. S. *Messiaen.* Berkeley: University of California Press, 1975.

JONES, J. W. *Contemporary Psychoanalysis and Religion: Transference and Transcendence.* New Haven: Yale University Press, 1991.

JORDENS, J. T. F. "Medieval Hindu Devotionalism." In *A Cultural History of India,* ed. A. L. Basham.

KAFKA, F. *The Complete Stories.* Ed. N. N. Glatzer. New York: Schocken, Centennial ed., 1983.

KAGAN, A. *Paul Klee: Art and Music.* Ithaca: Cornell University Press, 1983.

KAHN, M. M. R. *Hidden Selves.* London: Hograth Press, 1983.

KAKAR, S. *Intimate Relations: Exploring Indian Sexuality.* New Delhi: Penguin, 1990.

KAKAR, S., AND ROSS, J. M. *Tales of Love, Sex, and Danger.* London: Unwin, 1987.

KATZ, N. *Buddhist Images of Human Perfection.* Delhi: Motilal Banarsidass, 1982.

KATZ, S. T. "The Conservative Character of Mysticism." In *Mysticism and Religious Traditions*, ed. S. T. Katz.

———. "Language, Epistemology, and Mysticism." In *Mysticism and Religious Experience*, ed. S. T. Katz.

———, ed. *Mysticism and Religious Experience*. New York: Oxford University Press, 1978.

———, ed. *Mysticism and Religious Tradition*. New York: Oxford University Press, 1983.

KAY, M. R., ed. *Nonverbal Communication Today*. Amsterdam: Mouton, 1982.

KELLER, H. *The Story of My Life*. 1902. Reprint. New York: Airmont, 1965.

KERFORD, G. B. *The Sophistic Movement*. Cambridge: Cambridge University Press, 1981.

KERMODE, F. "Endings, Continued." In *Languages of the Unsayable*, ed. S. Budick and W. Iser.

KESSEL, F. S., ed. *The Development of Language and Language Researchers*. Hillsdale, N.J.: Lawrence Erlbaum, 1988.

KERTESZ, A. "Cognitive Function in Severe Aphasia." In *Thought without Language*, ed. L. Weiskrantz.

KIERKEGAARD, S. *Journal, Extraits, 1854–1855*. Trans. K. Ferlov and J.-J. Gateau. Paris, 1961.

———. *The Journals of Søren Kierkegaard*. Trans. A. Dru. London: Oxford University Press, 1938.

———. *Philosophical Fragments*. Trans. H. V. Hong and E. Hong. Princeton: Princeton University Press, 1985.

———. *Søren Kierkegaard's Journals and Papers*. Vols. 5 and 6. Trans. H. V. Hong and E. H. Hong. Bloomington: Indiana University Press, 1978.

KING, W. L. *Theravada Meditation*. University Park: Pennsylvania State University Press, 1980.

KIVY, P. *The Corded Shell*. Princeton: Princeton University Press, 1980.

KLEIN, A. *Knowledge and Liberation*. Ithaca, N.Y.: Snow Lion Publications, 1986.

KNOBLOCK, J. *Xunzi: A Translation and Study of the Complete Works.* 2 vols. (to be completed in 3). Stanford University Press, 1988, 1990.

KOHON, G., ed. *The British School of Psychoanalysis.* London: Free Association Books, 1986.

KOHUT, H., AND S. LEVARIE. "On the Enjoyment of Listening to Music." In S. Feder, R. L. Karmel, and G. H. Pollock, *Psychoanalytic Explorations in Music.*

KOLB, L. S. "Recovery of Memory and Repressed Fantasy in Combat-Induced Post-Traumatic Stress Disorder of Vietnam Veterans." In *Hypnosis and Memory,* ed. H. M. Pettinati.

KONOPACKI, S. A. *The Descent into Words: Jacob Böhme's Transcendental Linguistics.* Ann Arbor: Karoma Publishers, 1979.

KOTOH, T. "Language and Silence: Self-Inquiry in Heidegger and Zen." In *Heidegger and Asian Thought,* ed. G. Parkes.

KOTRE, J., AND E. HALL. *Seasons of Life.* Boston: Little Brown, 1990.

KRAMER, L. *Music and Poetry: The Nineteenth Century and After.* Berkeley: University of California Press, 1984.

KRAMER, S. N. *The Sumerians.* Chicago: University of Chicago Press, 1963.

KRAMER, S. N., and J. Maier. *Myths of Enki, The Crafty God.* New York: Oxford University Press, 1989.

KUNDERA, M. *The Art of the Novel.* New York: Harper and Row, 1988.

KURTZ, S. A. "On Silence." *Psychoanalytic Review* 71 (1984).

KYLE, J. G., AND B. WOLL. *Sign Language: The Study of Deaf People and Their Language.* Cambridge: Cambridge University Press, 1985.

LAMPERT, L. *Nietzsche's Teaching.* New Haven: Yale University Press, 1986.

LANDAU, B., AND GLEITMAN, L. R. *Language and Experience: Evidence from the Blind Child.* Cambridge: Harvard University Press, 1985.

LANE, H. *When the Mind Hears.* London: Penguin Books, 1988.

LANGDON, S. "Words (Sumerian and Babylonian)." In Hastings, *Encyclopaedia of Religion and Ethics.*

LANGENDOEN, D. T., AND P. M. POSTAL. *The Vastness of Natural Languages.* Oxford: Blackwell, 1984.

LAU, D. C., trans. *Tao Te Ching.* Hong Kong: The Chinese University Press, 1982. (Much of this translation also in Penguin Books edition [1963].)

LEBRECHT, N. *Mahler Remembered.* London: Faber and Faber, 1987.

LEDERMAN, M., AND SCHRAMM, D. N. *From Quarks to the Cosmos.* New York: Scientific American Library, 1989.

LEGGE, J., trans. *The Texts of Taoism.* London: Oxford University Press, 1891.

LERDAHL, F., AND JACKENDOFF, R. *A Generative Theory of Music.* Cambridge: MIT Press, 1983.

LEROI-GOURHAN, A. *Les racines du monde.* Paris: Pierre Belford, 1982.

LEVELT, W. J. M. *Speaking.* Cambridge: MIT Press, 1989.

LIAO, W. K., trans. *The Complete Works of Han Fei Tzu.* Vol. 1. London: Probsthain, 1939.

LIEBERMAN, P. *Uniquely Human: The Evolution of Speech, Thought, and Selfless Behavior.* Cambridge: Harvard University Press, 1991.

LIGHTMAN, A., AND R. BRAWER, eds. *Origins: The Lives and Worlds of Modern Cosmologists.* Cambridge: Harvard University Press, 1990.

LIIVOJA-LORIUS, J. "The Bow." In *The Book of the Violin,* ed. D. Gill. Oxford: Phaidon, 1984.

LINDBERG, D. C. *Theories of Vision from Al-Kindi to Kepler.* Chicago: University of Chicago Press, 1976.

LINDTNER, CHR. "Atisa's Introduction to the Two Truths, and Its Sources." *Journal of Indian Philosophy* 9.2 (1981).

———. *Nagarjuniana.* Copenhagen: Akademsk Forlag, 1982.

LITOWITZ, B. W. "Language and the Young Deaf Child." In *They Grow in Silence,* ed. E. D. Mindel and M. Vernon.

LLOYD, A. C. *The Anatomy of Neoplatonism.* Oxford: Oxford University Press, 1990.

———. "Plotinus on the Genesis of Thought and Existence." In *Oxford Studies in Ancient Philosophy* 5 (1987).

———. "Procession and Division in Proclus." In *Soul and Structure of Being in Late Neoplatonism,* ed. H. J. Blumenthal, and A. C. Lloyd.

———. *The Revolutions of Wisdom.* Berkeley: University of California Press, 1987.

LOBSANG, DARGYAY. "What Is Non-Existent and What Is Remanent in Sunyata." *Journal of Indian Philosophy* 18.1 (March 1990).

LOEWALD, H. W. *Sublimation*. New Haven: Yale University Press, 1988.

LOPEZ, D. S. *Study of Svatantrika*. Ithaca, N.Y.: Snow Lion Publications, 1989.

LUBORSKY, L. "Recurrent Momentary Forgetting." In *Psychodynamics and Cognition*, ed. M. J. Horowitz.

LURIA, A. R. *Language and Cognition*. New York: Wiley, 1982.

————. *The Man with a Shattered World*. New York: Basic Books, 1972.

————. *The Mind of a Mnemonist*. New York: Basic Books, 1968.

LYNCH, O. M., ed. *The Social Construction of Emotion in India*. Berkeley: University of California Press, 1990.

LYNN, N. "The Sudden and the Gradual in Chinese Poetry Criticism." In *Sudden and Gradual*, ed. P. N. Gregory.

McDANIEL, J. *The Madness of the Saints: Ecstatic Religion in Bengal*. Chicago: University of Chicago Press, 1989.

MACDONALD, D., II ed. *The Encyclopaedia of Mammals: 2*. London: Allen and Unwin, 1984.

MACDONALD, M. Schoenberg. London: Dent, 1976.

McGUINESS, B. *Wittgenstein: A Life. Young Ludwig (1889–1921)*. London: Duckworth, 1988.

MAGEE, B. *The Philosophy of Schopenhauer*. Oxford: Oxford University Press, 1983.

MAGLIOLA, R. "Differentialism in Chinese *Ch'an* and French Deconstruction: Some Test-Cases from the Wu-Men-Kuan." *Journal of Chinese Philosophy* 17.1 (March 1990).

MAHER, B., AND MAHER, W., eds. *Progress in Experimental Personality Research*. New York: Academic Press, 1974.

MAHLER, M., S. F. PINE, AND A. BERGMAN. *The Psychological Birth of the Human Infant*. New York: Basic Books, 1975.

MAIR, V. H., ed. *Experimental Essays in Chuang-tzu*. Honolulu: University of Hawaii Press, 1983.

MALANTSCHUK, G, *Kierkegaard's Thought.* Princeton: Princeton University Press, 1971.

MANDLER, G. "Problems and Directions in the Study of Consciousness." In *Psychodynamics and Cognition,* ed. M. J. Horowitz.

MARCEL, A. J., AND E. BISIACH. *Consciousness in Contemporary Science.* Oxford: Oxford University Press, 1988.

MARGLIN, F. A. "Refashioning the Body: Transformative Emotion in Ritual Dance." In *The Social Construction of Emotion in India,* ed M. Lynch.

———. "Types of Sexual Union and Their Implicit Meanings." In *The Divine Consort,* ed. J. S. Hawley and D. M. Wulff. Berkeley: University of California Press, 1982.

MARIN, O. S. "Neurological Aspects of Music Perception and Performance." In *The Psychology of Music,* ed. D. Deutsch.

MARK, T. C. "Philosophy of Piano Playing." *Philosophy and Phenomenological Research* 41 (1980–81).

MASSIN, B. *Messiaen.* Aix-en-Provence: Alinea, 1989.

MASSON, J. M. *The Oceanic Feeling.* Dordrecht: Reidel, 1980.

MATILAL, B. K. *Epistemology, Logic, and Grammar in Indian Philosophical Analysis.* The Hague: Mouton, 1971.

———. *Logical and Ethical Issues of Religious Belief.* Calcutta: University of Calcutta, 1982.

———. *Logic, Language and Reality.* Delhi: Motilal Banarsidass, 1985.

———. *Perception.* Oxford: Oxford University Press, 1986.

———. *The Word and the World.* Delhi/Oxford: Oxford University Press, 1990.

MAURER, D., AND C. MAURER. *The World of the Newborn.* New York: Basic Books, 1988.

MEHTA, J. L. *The Philosophy of Martin Heidegger.* New York: Harper and Row, 1971.

MERLEAU-PONTY, M. *La prose du monde.* Paris: Gallimard, 1969.

———. *The Visible and the Invisible.* Evanston: Northwestern University Press, 1968.

MERRIAM, A. P. *The Anthropology of Music*. Evanston, Ill.: Northwestern University Press, 1964.

MESSIAEN, O. *Entretien avec Claude Samuel*. Recording with accompanying translation. Paris: Erato.

———. *Recherches et expériences spirituelles*. Paris: Leduc, 1977.

MESULAM, M.-M. "Neural Substrates of Behavior: The Effects of Brain Lesions upon Mental State." In *The New Harvard Guide to Psychiatry*, ed. A. M. Nicholi, Jr.

MEYER, L. *Music, the Arts, and Ideas*. Chicago: Chicago University Press, 1967.

MIDDLE LENGTH SAYINGS (Majjhima-Nikaya). Vol. 1. Trans. B. Horner. London: Pali Text Society, 1954.

MILLER, A. I. *Imagery in Scientific Thought*. Boston: Birkhäuser, 1984.

MILLER, E. H. *Walt Whitman's "Song of Myself."* Iowa City: University of Iowa Press, 1989.

MINDEL, E. D., AND M. VERNON, eds. *They Grow in Silence*. 2d ed. Boston: Little Brown, 1987.

MISNER, C. W., K. S. THORNE, AND J. A. WHEELER. *Gravitation*. San Francisco: Freeman, 1972.

MISTRY, F. *Nietzsche and Buddhism*. Berlin: de Gruyter, 1981.

MODELL, A. H. "Affects and Their Non-Communication." *The International Journal of Psycho-Analysis* 61 (1980).

MONTGOMERY, G. "The Mind in Motion." *Discover* (March 1989).

MOORE, A. W. *The Infinite*. London: Routledge: 1990.

MOORE, P. "Mystical Experience, Mystical Doctrine, Mystical Technique." In *Mysticism and Philosophical Analysis*, ed. S. T. Katz.

MULLER-ORTEGA, P. E. *The Triadic Heart of Siva*. Albany: State University of New York Press, 1989.

MUNITZ, M. K. *Cosmic Understanding*. Princeton: Princeton University Press, 1986.

NASS, M. L. "Some Considerations of a Psychoanalytic Interpretation of Music." In *Psychoanalytic Explorations in Music*, ed. S. Feder, R. L. Karmel, and G. H. Pollock.

NAGAO, G. *The Foundational Standpoint of Madhyamika Philosophy.* Albany: State University of New York Press, 1989.

NEISSER, U., ed. *Memory Observed: Remembering in Natural Contexts.* San Francisco: Freeman, 1982.

NEUBAUER, J. *The Emancipation of Music from Language.* New Haven: Yale University Press, 1986.

NEWMEYER, F. J., ed. *Language: Psychological and Biological Aspects.* Vol. 3 of *Linguistics: The Cambridge Survey.* Cambridge: Cambridge University Press, 1988.

NICHOLI, A. M., JR. "The Therapist-Patient Relationship." In *The New Harvard Guide to Psychiatry,* ed. M. M. Nicholi, Jr.

————, ed. *The New Harvard Guide to Psychiatry.* Cambridge: Harvard University Press, 1988

NICHOLSON, R. A. *Rumi.* London: Allen and Unwin, 1950.

NIETZCHE, F. *Basic Writings of Nietzsche.* Trans. W. Kaufmann. New York: Modern Library, 1968.

————. *Goetzendämmerung.* 1889. G. Colli and M. Montinari, eds. Berlin: de Gruyter, 1969.

————. *Human All Too Human.* Vol. 1-1878, 1886; vol. 2-1879, 1886. Trans. R. J. Hollingdale. Cambridge: Cambridge University Press, 1986.

————. *Untimely Meditations.* 1-1873; 2, 3-1874; 4-1876. Trans. R. J. Hollingdale. Cambridge: Cambridge University Press, 1983.

————. *The Will to Power.* Trans. W. Kaufmann and R. J. Hollingdale. London: Weidenfeld and Nicolson.

————. *Zarathustra.* 1883/1885, 1887. Trans. W. Kaufmann. In W. Kaufmann, *The Portable Nietzsche.* New York: Viking, 1954.

NIMS, J. F., trans. *The Poems of St. John of the Cross.* 3d ed. Chicago: University of Chicago Press, 1989.

NOY, P. "Form Creation in Art: An Ego Psychological Approach to Creativity." In *Psychoanalytic Explorations in Music,* ed. S. Feder, R. L. Karmel, and G. H. Pollock.

NWOYE, G. O. "Eloquent Silence Among the Igbo of Nigeria." In *Perspectives on Silence,* ed. D. Tannen and M. Saville-Troike.

OCHSE, R. *Before the Gates of Excellence: The Determinants of Creative Genius.* Cambridge: Cambridge University Press, 1990.

ODIN, S. "Derrida and the Decentered Universe of Chan/Zen Buddhism." *Journal of Chinese Philosophy* 17.1 (March 1990).

OETKE, C. "Remarks on the Interpretation of Nagarjuna's Philosophy." *Journal of Indian Philosophy* 19.3 (September 1991).

O'FLAHERTY, W. D., trans. *The Rig Veda.* Harmondsworth: Penguin Books, 1981.

O'MEARA, D. J. *Pythagoras Revived.* Oxford: Oxford University Press, 1989.

OPPENHEIM, A. L. *Ancient Mesopotamia.* Chicago: University of Chicago Press, 1964.

OSTWALD, P. F. "Acoustic Methods in Psychiatry." *Scientific American* (March 1965).

OTT, H. *Martin Heidegger: Unterwegs zu seiner Biographie.* Frankfurt: Campus Verlag, 1988.

OVERBYE, DEBBIS. *Lonely Hearts of the Cosmos.* London: Macmillan, 1991.

PADDEN, C., AND HUMPHRIES, R. *Deaf in America: Voices from a Culture.* Cambridge: Harvard University Press, 1988.

PADOUX, A. *Recherches sur la symbolique et l'énergie de la parole dans certains textes tantriques.* Paris: de Boccard, 1963.

PARKES, G. "Afterward—Language." In *Heidegger and Asian Thought,* ed. G. Parkes.

————. "Thoughts on the Way." In *Heidegger and Asian Thought,* ed. G. Parkes.

————, ed. *Heidegger and Asian Thought.* Honolulu: University of Hawaii Press, 1987.

PARKIN, A. J. *Memory and Amnesia.* Oxford: Blackwell, 1987.

PEARS, D. *The False Prison: A Study of the Development of Wittgenstein's Philosophy.* 2 vols. Oxford: Oxford University Press, 1987, 1988.

PELIKAN, J. *The Emergence of the Catholic Tradition (100–600).* Vol. 1, *The Christian Tradition.* Chicago: The University of Chicago Press, 1971.

PENROSE, R. *The Emperor's New Mind.* Oxford: Oxford University Press, 1989.

PERATT, A. L. "Not with a Big Bang." *The Sciences* (January/February 1990).

PERRY, C. W., J.-R. LAURENCE, J. D'EON, AND B. TALLANT. "Hypnotic Age Regression Techniques in Elicitation of Memories" In *Hypnosis and Memory*, ed. H. M. Pettinati.

PETTINATI, H. M., ed. *Hypnosis and Memory*. New York: Guilford Press, 1982.

PILLAI, K. R., trans. *The Vakyapadiya*. Cantos 1 and 2. Varanasi: Motilal Banarsidass, 1971.

PLANTINGA, L. *Romantic Music*. New York: Norton, 1984.

PLATO, *The Laws*. Trans. T. J. Saunders. Harmondsworth: Penguin Books, 1970.

PLOTINUS, ENNEADS. Trans. A. H. Armstrong. London: Allen and Unwin, 1953.

————. *Enneads*. Trans. A. H. Armstrong. 7 vols. Cambridge: Harvard University Press, 1966–88.

PÖGGELER, O. *Martin Heidegger's Path of Thinking*. Atlantic Highlands, N.J.: Humanities Press, 1987.

————. "West-East Dialogue: Heidegger and Lao-tzu." In *Heidegger and Asian Thought*, ed. G. Parkes.

POLING, C. V. *Kandinsky's Teaching at the Bauhaus*. New York: Rizzoli, 1986.

POTTER, K. H. *The Tradition of Nyaya-Vaiseska up to Gangesa*. Vol. 2 of *The Encyclopedia of Indian Philosophies*. Delhi/Princeton: Motilal Banarsidass/Princeton University Press, 1977.

PREMAK, D. "Minds with and without Language." In *Thought without Language*, ed. L. Weiskrantz.

PRITCHARD, J. B., ed. *Ancient Near Eastern Texts*. 3d ed. Princeton: Princeton University Press, 1969.

PROCLUS. *Elements of Theology*. Trans. E. R. Dodds. 2d ed. Oxford: Oxford University Press, 1963.

————. *Théologie platonicienne*. Trans. H. D. Saffrey and L. G. Westerink. Paris: Les Belles Lettres, 1968–81.

————. *A Commentary on the First Book of Euclid's Elements*. Trans. G. R. Morrow. Princeton: Princeton University Press, 1970.

————. *Proclus' Commentary on Plato's Parmenides*. Trans. G. R. Morrow and J. M. Dillon. Princeton: Princeton University Press, 1987.

PROUDFOOT, W. *Religious Experience*. Berkeley: University of California Press, 1985.

PUTNAM, H. *Realism with a Human Face*. Cambridge: Harvard University Press, 1990.

QUIGLEY, S. P., AND KING, S. M. "The Language Development of Deaf Children and Youth." In *Handbook of Applied Psycholinguistics*, ed. S. Rosenberg.

QUINE, W. V. *Theories and Things*. Cambridge: Harvard University Press, 1981.

REDINGTON, J. D. *Vallabhacarya on the Love Games of Krsna* [sic]. 2d ed. Delhi: Motilal Banarsidass, 1990.

REES, M. J. "Origin of the Universe." In *Origins*, ed. A. C. Fabian. Cambridge: Cambridge University Press, 1988.

RENOU, L. *Hymns spéculatifs du Véda*. Paris: Gallimard, 1956.

————. "Les pouvoirs de la parole dans le Rigvéda." In L. Renou, *Etudes védiques et paninéennes*, Vol. 1. Paris: de Boccard, 1955.

RESNICK, J. L., AND M. AMERIKANER. "Self-Disclosure." In *Encyclopedia of Clinical Assessment*, ed. R. H. Woods.

ROBINS, R. H. *A Short History of Linguistics*. London: Longmans, 1967.

ROBINSON, J. *Emily Dickinson*. London: Faber and Faber, 1986, p. 91 (poem no. 811).

ROE, A. *The Making of a Scientist*. New York: Dodd Mead, 1953.

ROLAND, A. *In Search of Self in India and Japan*. Princeton: Princeton University Press, 1988.

RORTY, R. "From Ironist Theory to Private Allusions: Derrida." In R. Rorty, *Contingency, Irony, and Solidarity*. Cambridge: Cambridge University Press, 1989.

ROSEMONT, H., JR., ed. *Chinese Texts and Philosophical Contexts*. La Salle, Ill.: Open Court, 1991.

ROSEN, S. *The Limits of Analysis*. New Haven: Yale University Press, 1985.

ROSENBAUM, B., AND SONNE, H. *The Language of Psychosis*. New York: New York University Press, 1986.

Rosenberg, S., ed. *Handbook of Applied Psycholinguistics.* Hillsdale, N.J.: Lawrence Erlbaum, 1982.

Rosenberg, S., and Abbeduto, L. "Adult Schizophrenic Language." In *The Psychology of Language and Communication*, ed. A. Ellis and G. Beattie.

Rosenfeld, I. *The Invention of Memory.* New York: Basic Books, 1988.

Rosenthal, E. "The Wolf at the Door." *Discover* (February 1989).

Roth, H. "Who Compiled the *Chuang Tzu?*" In *Chinese Texts and Philosophical Contexts*, ed. H. Rosemont.

Rousseau, J. *Essai sur l'origine des langues.* 1781. Ed. J. Starobinsky. Paris: Gallimard, 1990.

Ruegg, D. S. *Contributions à l'histoire de la philosophie linguistique Indienne.* Paris: de Boccard, 1963.

———. "Does the Madhyamika Have a Philosophical Thesis?" In *Buddhist Logic and Epistemology*, ed. B. Matilal and R. D. Evans. Dordrecht: Reidel, 1986.

———. *The Literature of the Madhyamika School of Philosophy in India.* Wiesbaden: Harrasowitz, 1981.

Rump., A., trans. (with W.-t. Chan). *Commentary on the* Lao Tzu *by Wang Pi.* Honolulu: University of Hawaii Press, 1979.

Rushton, J. *Classical Music.* London: Thames and Hudson, 1986.

Ryle, G. *The Concept of Mind.* London: Hutchinson, 1949.

Rymer, R. "Signs of Fluency." *The Sciences* (September/October 1988).

Sacks, O. *Seeing Voices.* Berkeley: University of California Press, 1989.

Salaman, E. "A Collection of Moments." In *Memory Observed*, ed. U. Neisser.

Sastri, D. *The Philosophy of Word and Meaning.* Calcutta: Calcutta Sanskrit College, 1959.

Saunders, G. R. "Silence and Noise as Emotional Management Styles: An Italian Case." In *Perspectives on Silence*, ed. D. Tannen and M. Saville-Troike.

Saunders, T. J. *Plato's Penal Code.* Oxford: Oxford University Press, 1991.

Saville-Troike, M. "The Place of Silence in an Integrated Theory of Communications." In *Perspectives on Silence*, ed. D. Tannen and M. Saville-Troike.

SCHACHT, R. *Nietzsche*. London: Routledge and Kegan Paul, 1983.

SCHACHTEL, E. G. "On Memory and Childhood Amnesia." In *Memory Observed*, ed. U. Neisser.

SCHACTER, D. L., M. P. McANDREWS, AND M. MOSCOVITCH. "Access to Consciousness: Dissociations between Explicit Knowledge in Neuropsychological Syndromes." In *Thought without Language*, ed. L. Weiskrantz.

SCHAFER, R. *The Analytic Attitude*. New York: Basic Books, 1983.

SCHAFFER, J. *New Sounds*. New York: Harper and Row, 1987.

SCHARFSTEIN, B.-A. *Of Birds, Beasts, and Other Artists: An Essay on the Universality of Art*. New York: New York University Press, 1988.

————. *The Dilemma of Context*. New York: New York University Press, 1989.

————. *The Philosophers*. New York: Oxford University Press, 1980.

SCHELLING, F. W. J. *The Philosophy of Art*. Trans. D. W. Stott. Minneapolis: University of Minnesota Press, 1989.

SCHEN, E. M. *The Tao Te Ching*. New York: Paragon House, 1989.

SCHOLEM, G. G. *On the Kabbalah and Its Symbolism* London: Routledge and Kegan Paul, 1965.

SCHOPENHAUER, A. *On the Fourfold Root of the Principle of Sufficient Reason*. Trans. E. F. J. Payne. La Salle, Ill.: Open Court, 1974.

————. *Parerga and Paralipomena*. Vol. 2. Trans. E. F. J. Payne. London: Oxford University Press, 1974.

————. *The World as Will and Representation*. 2 vols. Trans. E. F. Payne. Reprint. New York: Dover, 1966.

SCHRAMM, D. N., AND STEIGMAN, G. "Particle Accelerators Test in Cosmological Theory." *Scientific American* (June 1988).

SCHWARTZ, B. I. *The World of Thought in Ancient China*. Cambridge: Harvard University Press, 1985.

SCOLLON, N. "The Machine Stops: Silence in the Metaphor of Malfunction." In *Perspectives on Silence*, ed. D. Tannen and M. Saville-Troike.

SEBEOK, T. A., ed. *Linguistics in South Asia*. Vol. 5 of *Current Trends in Linguistics*. The Hague: Mouton, 1969.

SEIDEL, G. J. *Martin Heidegger and the Pre-Socratics*. Lincoln: University of Nebraska Press, 1964.

SENDEN, M. VON. *Space and Sight*. London: Methuen, 1960.

SEXTUS EMPIRICUS. *Sextus Empiricus*. Trans. R. G. Bury. 4 vols. Cambridge: Harvard University Press, 1933–49.

SEYMOUR-SMITH, M. *Guide to Modern World Literature*. Rev. ed. London: Macmillan, 1986.

SHANON, B. "Remarks on the Modularity of Mind." *British Journal of the Philosophy of Science* 39 (1988).

———. "Semantic Representation of Meaning: A Critique." *Psychological Bulletin*, no. 1 (1988).

———. "Why Do We (Sometimes) Think in Words?" In *Lines of Thinking;* ed. K. J. Gilhooly et al., vol. 1.

SHANON, B., AND H. ATLAN. "Von Foerster's Theorem on Connectedness and Organisation: Semantic Applications." *New Ideas in Psychology* 8.1 (1990).

SHAPIRO, G. *Nietzschean Narratives*. Bloomington: Indiana University Press, 1986.

SHUTER-DYSON, D. A. "Musical Ability." In *The Psychology of Music*, ed. D. Deutsch.

SIDERITS, M. "The Madhyamika Critique of Epistemology, II." *Journal of Indian Philosophy* 9.2 (1981).

———. "Nagarjuna as Anti-Realist." *Journal of Indian Philosophy* 16.4 (1988).

SIDITS, J. J. "Music, Pitch Perception, and the Mechanisms of Cortical Hearing." In *Handbook of Cognitive Neuroscience*, ed. M. S. Gazzaniga.

SIEGEL, L. *Fires of Water, Waters of Peace*. Honolulu: University of Hawaii Press, 1983.

SINGER, J. L. "Sampling Ongoing Consciousness and Emotional Experience." In *Psychodynamics and Cognition*, ed. M. J. Horowitz.

SINGER, P., ed. *A Companion to Ethics*. Oxford: Blackwell, 1991.

SINHA, J. *Indian Psychology*. 2 vols. Calcutta: Sinha Publishing House, 1958, 1961.

Sluga, H. *Gottlob Frege.* London: Routledge and Kegan Paul, 1980.

Smart, N. "The Purification of Consciousness and the Negative Path." In *Mysticism and Religious Traditions,* ed. S. T. Katz.

———. "Understanding Religious Experience." In *Mysticism and Philosophical Analysis,* ed. S. T. Katz.

Smith, J. A. *Schoenberg and His Circle.* New York: Schirmer Books, 1986.

Smith, W. J. *The Behavior of Communicating.* Cambridge: Harvard University Press, 1977.

Snyder, S. H. *Drugs and the Brain.* New York: Scientific American Books, 1986.

Solomon, E. A. *Avidya—A Problem of Truth and Reality.* Ahmedabad: Gujarat College, 1969.

———. *Indian Dialectics.* 2 vols. Ahmedabad: B. J. Institute of Learning and Research, 1976, 1978.

Sorabji, R. *Time, Creation and the Continuum.* London: Duckworth, 1983.

Spelke, E. S. "The Origins of Physical Knowledge." In *Thought without Language,* ed. L. Weiskrantz.

Spence, D. S. "Language in Psychotherapy." In *Psycholinguistic Research,* ed. D. Aaronson and R. W. Rieber.

Spender, N. "Music, Psychology of." In *The Oxford Companion the Mind,* ed. R. L. Gregory.

Spiegelberg, H. *Phenomenology in Psychology and Psychiatry.* Evanston: Northwestern University Press, 1972.

Sprague, R. K., ed. *The Older Sophists.* Columbia, S.C.: University of South Carolina Press, 1972.

Springer, S. P., and Deutsch, G. *Left Brain.* Rev. ed. New York: Freeman, 1985.

Staal, F. "Oriental Ideas on the Origin of Language." *Journal of the American Oriental Society* 99.1 (1979).

———. "Rigveda 10.71 on the Origin of Language." In *Revelation in Indian Thought,* ed. H. G. Coawrd and K. Sivaraman.

———. "Sanskrit Philosophy of Language." In *Linguistics in South Asia,* ed. T. A. Sebeok. "Vedic Mantras." In *Mantra,* ed. H. A. Alper.

STAROBINSKY, S. *Jean-Jacques Rousseau: La transparence et l'obstacle.* Paris: Gallimard, 1971.

STEINER, G. *After Babel.* London: Oxford University Press, 1975.

STERN, D. *Diary of a Baby.* New York: Basic Books, 1990.

―――. *The Interpersonal World of the Infant.* New York: Basic Books, 1985.

STEVENS, W. *Collected Poems.* London: Faber and Faber, 1955.

―――. *Transport to Summer.* New York: Knopf, 1951.

STEWART, I. *Does God Play Dice?* Oxford: Blackwell, 1989.

STIMPSON, B. *Paul Valéry and Music.* Cambridge: Cambridge University Press, 1984.

STOKES, J. P. "The Relation of Loneliness and Self-Disclosure." In *Self-Disclosure*, ed. V. J. Derlega and J. H. Berg.

STRATTON, J. S. AND D. M. WULFF, eds. *Divine Consort: Radha and the Goddesses of India.* Boston: Beacon Press, 1982.

STRAVINSKY, I. *Poetics of Music.* Cambridge: Harvard University Press, 1947.

STRENG, F. J. *Emptiness.* Nashville: Abingdon Press, 1967.

―――. "Language and Mystical Awareness." In *Mysticism and Philosophical Analysis*, ed. S. T. Katz.

SULLIVAN, L. E. *Icanchu's Drum: An Orientation to Meaning in South American Religions.* New York: Macmillian, 1988.

SUNDBERG, J. "Perception of Singing." In *The Psychology of Music*, ed. D. Deutsch.

TANNEN, D. "Silence: Anything But." In *Perspectives on Silence*, ed. D. Tannen and M. Saville-Troike.

TANNEN, D., AND M. SAVILLE-TROIKE, eds. *Perspectives on Silence.* Norwood, N.J.: Ablex, 1985.

TAYLOR, R. *Franz Liszt.* Grafton Books (Collins), 1986.

TETSUAKI, KOTOH. "Language and Silence: Self-Enquiry in Heidegger and Zen." In *Heidegger and Asian Thought*, ed. G. Parkes.

THIEME, P. Review of Renou, *Hymns spéculatifs du Véda. Journal of the American Oriental Society* 77.1 (January–March 1947).

TOOMEY, P. M. "Krishna's Consuming Passions." In *The Social Construction of Emotion in India*, ed. O. M. Lynch.

TREFFERT, D. A. *Extraordinary People*. New York: Bantam Press, 1989.

TSUANG, M. T., FARAONE, S. V., AND DAY, M. "Schizophrenic Disorders." In *The New Harvard Guide to Psychiatry*, ed. A. M. Nicholi, Jr.

TUCK, A. P. *Comparative Philosophy and the Philosophy of Scholarship: On the Western Interpretation of Nagarjuna*. New York: Oxford University Press, 1990.

URBACH, E. E. *The Sages*. 2 vols. Jerusalem: Magnes Press, 1975.

VAID, J., ed. *Language Processing in Bilinguals*. Hillside, N.J.: Lawrence Erlbaum, 1986.

VALÉRY, P. *Aesthetics*. New York: Pantheon, 1964.

———. *Cahiers*. 2 vols. Ed. J. Robinson. Paris, Gallimard, 1973, 1974.

———. *Poems*, vol. 2. Trans. D. Paul. Princeton: Princeton University Press, 1984.

VILENKIN, A. "Cosmic Strings." *Scientific American* (December 1987).

VYGOTSKY, L. S. *Thought and Language*. New ed. Cambridge: MIT Press, 1986.

WAGNER, R. *Selected Letters of Richard Wagner*. Ed. S. Spencer and B. Millington. London: Dent, 1987.

WANG, H. *Reflections on Kurt Gödel*. Cambridge: MIT Press, 1987.

WATSON, B. "Zen Poetry." In *Zen: Tradition and Transition*, ed. K. Kraft. London: Rider, 1988.

———, trans. *The Complete Works of Chuang Tzu*. New York: Columbia University Press, 1968.

WATSON, D. *Liszt*. London: Dent, 1989.

WEINER, D. A. *The Ill-Will against Time: Schopenhauer's Influence on Wittgenstein's Early Philosophy*. Ph.D. Diss., Yale University, 1989. Pub. in rev., abbrev. version as *Genius and Talent*. London/ Toronto: Associated University Presses, 1992.

WEISKRANTZ, L. "Some Contribution of Neuropsychology of Vision and Memory to the Problem of Consciousness." In *Consciousness in Contemporary Science*, ed A. J. Marcel and E. Bisiach.

———, ed. *Thought without Language*. Oxford: Oxford University Press, 1988.

WHEELER, K., ed. *German Aesthetics and Literary Criticism: The Romantic Ironists and Goethe*. Cambridge: Cambridge University Press, 1984.

WHEELOCK, W. T. "Mantra in Vedic and Tantric Ritual." In *Mantra*, ed. H. A. Alper.

WHITING, C. G. *Paul Valéry*. London: Athlone Press, 1978.

WHITMAN, W. *Complete Poetry and Collected Prose*. Ed. J. Kaplan. New York: The Library of America, 1982.

WILCOX, J. T. *Truth and Value in Nietzche*. Ann Arbor: University of Michigan Press, 1974.

WILLIAMS, P. *Mahayana Buddhism*. London: Routledge, 1989.

———. "On the Interpretation of Madhyamaka Thought." *Journal of Indian Thought* (June 1991).

WILSON, A. M. *Diderot*. New York: Oxford University Press, 1972.

WILZEK, F. "The Cosmic Assymmetry between Matter and Antimatter." *Scientific American* (December 1980).

WINSTON, T. "The Dilemma of Distress Disclosure." In *Self-Disclosure*, ed. V. Derlega and J. H. Bergs.

WINTER, H. J. J. "Science." In *A Cultural History of India*, ed. A. L. Basham.

WITHERSPOON, G. *Language and Art in the Navajo Universe*. Ann Arbor: University of Michigan Press, 1977.

WITTGENSTEIN, L. *Culture and Value*. Ed. C. H. von Wright. Oxford: Blackwell, 1980.

———. *Notebooks 1914–16*. Ed. G. H. von Wright and G. E. M. Anscombe. Oxford: Blackwell, 1961.

———. *Tractatus Logico-Philosophicus*. Trans. D. F. Pears and B. F. McGuiness. London: Routledge and Kegan Paul, 1961.

———. *Zettel*. Oxford: Blackwell, 1967.

WOLKENSTEIN, D., AND KRAMER, S. N. *Innana: Queen of Heaven and Earth*. New York: Harper and Row, 1983.

WOLOSKY, S. "Samuel Beckett's Figural Evasions." In *Languages of the Unsayable*, ed. S. Budick and W. Iser.

Woods, R. H., ed. *Encyclopedia of Clinical Assessment.* San Francisco: Jossey-Bass, 1980.

Wulff, D. M. "Prolegomenon to a Psychology for the Goddess." In *Divine Consort,* ed J. S. Hawley and D. M. Wulff.

Young, A. W. "Functional Organization of Visual Recognition." In *Thought without Language,* ed. L. Weiskrantz.

Yuasa, Y. "The Encounter of Modern Japanese Philosophy with Heidegger." In *Heidegger and Asian Thought,* ed. G. Parkes.

Yün-hua Jan. "A Comparative Study of 'No-thought' (Wu-Nien) in Some Indian and Buddhist Texts.' *Journal of Chinese Philosophy* 16 (1989).

Index of Names

CPSIA information can be obtained at www.ICGtesting.com
Printed in the USA
LVOW12s1745150414

381822LV00003B/648/A